# History of modern architecture

# History of modern architecture

Leonardo Benevolo

Volume one

The tradition of modern architecture

The M.I.T. Press
Cambridge, Massachusetts

First MIT Press Paperback Edition, 1977

First published in Italy in 1960
Storia dell'architettura moderna
© Giuseppe Laterza & Figli, 1960
Translated from the third revised
Italian edition, 1966
by H. J. Landry
This English translation first published
in Great Britain 1971: © Routledge & Kegan Paul, 1971

Second printing, 1978
Third printing, 1979
Fourth printing, 1980

Published in the United States of America by
the M.I.T. Press, Cambridge, Massachusetts 1971

ISBN 0 262 02081 5 (hardcover)
ISBN 0 262 52044 3 (paperback)

Library of Congress Catalog Card number: 77-157667

Printed in the United States of America

# Contents to volume one

# Contents to volume two

# Acknowledgements

When photographs have been taken from books or magazines, their source has been indicated in the captions. Original photographs, largely taken specially for this work, are the property either of the author, or of the following people and organizations:

A.C.I., Brussels; Aerofilms Ltd., London; Franco Albini, Milan; Fratelli Alinari, Florence; The Brazilian Embassy, Rome; The British Embassy, Rome; Photographic archives, Paris; Archivo Historico de la Ciudad, Barcelona; Artek, Kolmio; Vanni Barucci, Rome; Studio B.B.P.R., Milan; Berliner Bild-Bericht, Berlin; Biblioteca Germanica, Rome; Bibliothèque Nationale, Paris; Arnaldo Bruschi, Rome; Bulloz, Chicago; Foto A. Cartoni, Rome; Central Office of Information, London; Carlo Chiarini, Rome; C.P.L.I., Amsterdam; Curtisa, Bologna; David Publishing Co. Ltd., Tokyo; Dell & Wainwright, London; Direction Générale du Tourisme, Paris; Durand-Ruel, Paris; Hermann Ege, Krefeld; Bill Enddahl, Hedrich-Blessing, Chicago; Fairchild Aerial Surveys Inc., New York; Fotocielo, Roma; Fotogramma, Milan; Fototecnica Fortunati, Milano; Gabinetto Fotografico Nazionale, Rome; Galleria Nazionale d'Arte Moderna, Rome; Vittoria Ghio, Rome; Inge Goertz-Bauer, Düsseldorf; Philip Harben; Havas, Helsinki; Foto Insolera, Rome; Karl E. Jacobs, Berlin; S. C. Johnson & Son Inc., Racine, Wisconsin; Giovanni Klaus Koenig, Florence; K.L.M., Amsterdam; Romualdo Landriscina, Rome; Studio Lisa Ltd., London; London County Council; Lossen, Stuttgart; Paolo Marconi, Rome; Rollie McKenna, New York; Carlo Melograni, Rome; Sandro Mendini, Milan; Ministero della Difesa Aeronautica, Rome; Ministry of Health, London; Foto d'arte Montacchini-Amati, Parma; Eugenio Montuori, Rome; Leonardo Mosso, Turin; M.R.L., Paris; Museum of Finnish Architecture, Helsinki; National Buildings Record, London; Netherlands National Tourist Office, London; Aero-photo Nederland, Rotterdam; Manfredi Nicoletti, Rome; Giuseppe Nicolosi, Rome; Luigi Pellegrin, Rome; Photoflight Ltd., London; Agenzia fotografica Pierluigi, Rome; Pierre-Andre Pittet, Geneva; Paolo Portoghesi, Rome; Fernand Rausser, Bern; Luciano Rubino, Rome; Ryner, Société Editions de France, Marseilles; Science Museum, London; Secrétariat d'État à la Présidence du Conseil, Paris; Julius

Shulman, Los Angeles; Gordon Sommers, Beverly Hills; Atelje Sundhal, Stockholm; Photo Sylvestre, Lyon; Manfredo Tafuri, Rome; U.S.I.S., Rome; Gustav Velin, Turku; Victoria & Albert Museum, London; Lucien Viguier, Paris; Giuseppe Vindigni, Rome; O. Volckers, Munich; J. A. Vrijhof, Rotterdam; *The Yorkshire Post*, Leeds.

Some of the photographs have been very kindly supplied by the photographers themselves and the following bodies, to whom we should like to express our thanks:

The French Embassy, Rome; The British Embassy, Rome; The Brazilian Embassy, Rome; The Embassy of the Federal German Republic; Direction Générale du Tourisme, Paris; *Casabella*, Milan; Victor Gruen Associates, New York; Prestel Verlag, Munich; J. C. Pritchard, London; Paul Schneider-Esleben, Düsseldorf; J. M. Sostres Maluquer, Barcelona; *Urbanistica*, Turin.

# Preface

The task of a history of modern architecture is to present contemporary events within the framework of their immediate precursors; it must, therefore, go far enough into past history to make a complete understanding of the present possible and to set contemporary events in adequate historical perspective.

The first difficulties that arise concern the scope of the investigation: how far back into the past should one go? And since the concept of architecture has never been conclusively defined, but varies from age to age, it is not easy to say what facts should be covered by this research. Both these problems are relevant to the very basis of this work, and an immediate explanation should therefore be given of the means by which I have tried to solve them.

1 Until the second half of the eighteenth century it is easy to comprehend architectural developments as one single whole; forms and methods of design, the behaviour of designers, patrons and architects vary according to time and place, but they exist within the limits of a basically fixed and assured relationship between architecture and society; there were variations in the particular problems posed to the architect and in the answers he provided, but the nature of the service he rendered society and the task society unquestioningly delegated to him, had long been established.

So far, then, one can simply apply the usual methods of art history, with its emphasis on the study of formal values since these, correctly interpreted, summarize within themselves all external circumstances and relationships, so that their own fluctuations point to the variations of all the other factors.

After the middle of the eighteenth century, without the continuity of formal activity being in any way broken, indeed while architectural language seems to be acquiring a particular coherence, the relations between architect and society begin to change radically. One can continue to follow the old thread, tracing the history of the late eighteenth- and nineteenth-century architecture along the lines of earlier periods – as do most general books on the subject – using the mutations of the formal repertoire to distinguish artists, schools and periods; thus after the Baroque came the neo-classical, the neo-Gothic, eclecticism and so on. But at a certain point it becomes clear that the activity of which one is speaking covers only a small section of the cultural interests and production of the time, that its links with

society have slackened and that new problems, unconnected with the traditional ones,
have come into the foreground.

It is therefore necessary to extend the
field of observation and to take into account
many technical, social and economic factors
that have altered so rapidly since 1750, even
if their connection with architecture is not
immediately apparent.

New material and spiritual needs, new
ideas and modes of procedure arise both
within and beyond the traditional limits, and
finally they run together to form a new
architectural synthesis that is completely
different from the old one. In this way it is
possible to explain the birth of modern
architecture, which would otherwise seem
completely incomprehensible; if this history
were a history of forms only, one would have
to postulate a sudden break with tradition,
which might be considered possible for the
sake of argument but which would be
historically inadmissible.

The modern movement was deeply rooted
in the European cultural tradition and was
linked to the past by a gradual succession of
experiences. There was however a difference
in scope between the field from which the
modern movement emerged – which was
very broad, particularly at the beginning,
and embraced various activities which came
to fruition in different sectors of industrial
civilization – and the field in which the
heritage of the architectural movements of
the past came, progressively, to be contained.
While events developed with continuity
within the two fields, the movement from
one to the other obviously could not be continuous, but was achieved by repeated
breaks and at the expense of considerable
strife; because the modern movement was,
in another sense, a revolutionary experiment,
which implied a complete re-examination of
the cultural inheritance of the past.

We shall use the word 'architecture',
therefore, in its broadest possible sense. A
neat definition is this one given by William
Morris in 1881: 'Architecture embraces the
consideration of the whole external surroundings of the life of man; we cannot escape
from it if we would so long as we are part of
civilization, for it means a moulding and
altering to human needs of the very face of
the earth itself, except in the outermost
desert.'[1]

We shall not attempt to define this concept
theoretically, or to specify in abstract terms
which aspects must be considered and which
not, in this work of modification of the
human environment; the pattern of historical
development itself will indicate the breadth
of the field to be covered, today, by this
distinguished and traditional notion 'architecture', which is still developing before our
very eyes.

Logically speaking, this may seem a
vicious circle, since the object of the search
is not defined in advance and acquires
significance during the investigation itself;
but our method cannot be rigidly demon-
strative because we are not sufficiently
detached from the subject in question, and
imagine that our readers are not indifferent
and disinterested either, but involved – as
architects, contractors, clients or users of the
finished product – in the constantly changing
aspects of their own surroundings.

A history of modern architecture is
naturally centred on the present, and the
basic point of reference for this whole work
is the architecture of today, which immediately involves us in an operative choice,
before becoming the object of historical
investigation. This involvement limits the
certainty of judgment, but we doubt that it
can be eliminated by a simple effort at
abstraction; it is better to accept it openly
and to take it into account by tempering the
certainty of our critical judgments.

2  We have used the expression 'modern
movement' because it has assumed a reasonably precise meaning in modern phraseology.
Here too the most appropriate definition

is probably that of Morris: 'the art we are striving for is a good thing we can all share, which will elevate all; in good sooth, if all people do not soon share it there will soon be none to share.'[2] This points to the deep-rooted relationship between modern architecture and industrial civilization; just as industry has made it possible to produce tools and amenities in sufficient quantities to allow everyone to benefit from the same material opportunities, so the task of modern architecture is to transmit equally, to all men, certain cultural opportunities which were originally differentiated according to the social hierarchy; and it can, therefore, be described as 'a programme for the redistribution of artistic goods'[3] according to the needs of modern society.

No-one can yet say what the results of this will be because only recently have men begun to work towards it, and the definition is merely a temporary signpost pointing largely to the future.

These are sufficient generalizations for the moment. The term 'modern movement' may or may not be considered apt, and another term may eventually prove preferable, but it has become part of current usage and should be kept to, because it is not only a historical term but also a living policy, a rule of conduct; I shall try to define and clarify its meaning by historical description, but I do not think it wise to restrict it in advance by a theoretical formula.

What must be done, however, is to define the limits of its application with regard to the past. One may shelve the question: what is modern architecture? but one is still faced with another: when did it begin? I believe there are three different answers to this question, depending on what one means by 'begin':

*a* Modern architecture was born of the technical, social and cultural changes connected with the Industrial Revolution; if, therefore, one intends to discuss the single components which then came together into a single synthesis, one can say that modern architecture began with the effects of the Industrial Revolution on building and town-planning, i.e. between the end of the eighteenth century and the beginning of the nineteenth, and more particularly in the years immediately after Waterloo. At first these component factors appeared in different sectors of social life, and it is impossible to link them together if one remains within the culture of the time: it is only in considering what follows that one discovers the unity towards which they were moving.

*b* When the single elements had emerged with sufficient clarity, there arose the need for their mutual integration. When this need became a clearly formulated opinion and then a policy, modern architecture was born as a coherent line of thought and action. This really happened for the first time in England, with Morris. In fact one might say that modern architecture began with Morris's practical career or, to be yet more precise, with the founding of the firm Morris, Faulkner, Marshall and Co., in 1862.

*c* Once the aim has been specified, there is the problem of finding a method of putting it into practice, a method general enough to bring together the various individual efforts and to communicate results. This is the crucial point of the whole development and demands the greatest effort, because the problem was to bridge the gap between theory and practice and to undertake action in contact with reality, bearing in mind all its aspects. This step was achieved immediately before and after the First World War, and more precisely in 1919, when Gropius opened the Weimar school. Strictly speaking, this is the point at which one can begin to talk of the 'modern movement'.

It is important to bear in mind the continuity of the three phases but also of the disjunction between them, particularly between the second and third.

Immediately after the war people believed that a new system of universally valid forms could promptly be established, and refused to have any contact with the past as a matter of principle. Events revealed the untimeliness of this attempt and contemporary thought, still deeply affected by that failure, has embarked on an enormous analytical work of re-examination and evaluation of its theses, exploring possibilities which had been initially overlooked and scrutinizing the heritage of the past to distinguish between what is living and what is dead. This is why minor and preceding experiments are being studied with renewed interest.

This necessary re-assessment opens the way to the dangers of a new and facile eclecticism, which accepts all experiments as valid providing they strike the imagination. The history of architecture may encourage this danger by presenting the past impartially as a succession of works and tendencies all equally interesting.

This misleading impartiality may serve a provisional purpose in making up a rough inventory of the recent past, still little known and little documented, but in fact the moment has come to deepen historical discussion and to make a distinction, in the past, between fundamental and incidental experiments, between those that are now concluded and those that are still bearing fruit, so as to give some solid indication of direction to those who are working in the present.

I believe that there is a basic line of thought and action, which began with Owen and the Utopians of the first half of the nineteenth century, passed through Ruskin and Morris and the *avant-garde* European experiments between 1890 and 1914, was contributed to by American builders and by Wright, became generally acclaimed in the immediate post-war years through the work of Gropius and gave rise to a unified movement with the potential for developments far broader than those promised by its original premises.

It is impossible to gauge the exact impor-

tance of Gropius's achievement in 1919, but it was demonstrably fundamental as far as the present day situation is concerned. The experiments that logically precede it – those of Morris, Horta, Wagner, Hoffmann, Berlage, Loos, Perret, Sullivan, Wright – are interesting and important, since they made the modern movement possible, but they belong to another moment in history, they resolve problems that are different from our own. They can act as fine examples or useful exortations, but Gropius, Oud, Mies van der Rohe, Dudok, Aalto, Jacobsen and Tange have begun an experiment in which we are all involved and upon which our way of life depends.

The first part of this book aims to describe the component parts of modern architectural thought and to discover their origins in the various fields in which they arose, following their movement of convergence from 1760 to 1914. Discussion will necessarily be fragmentary and disjointed, and will touch upon many matters apparently unconnected with architecture in general but which contain the roots of some aspects of modern architecture. The unity of this discussion depends on what happens subsequently: therefore the events of this period will be presented from a somewhat Vasarian viewpoint and judged with regard to the formation of the modern movement.

As I have said before, I do not believe that one can dispense with this point of reference; though we no longer believe, as Vasari did, that we have reached the perfect style, the golden age, and we know that the success of the attempts currently under way is by no means a foregone conclusion, but we believe that the way taken by the modern movement is the only one to take, the only way to understand and to continue the cultural heritage of the past.

First of all I have attempted to describe the physical events which gave birth to the modern European city, from 1760 to 1890, retaining as far as possible the time sequence of the events dealt with (Section 1), then to trace within these events the line of thought which led to William Morris (Section 2), to repeat the process for the American city, explaining why certain experiments took place in America earlier than in Europe (Section 3) and lastly to describe European *avant-garde* movements between 1890 and 1914 (Section 4).

The second part, concerned with the modern movement, deals with a much smaller subject and is not divided into sections; I have tried to make it as coherent as possible and to emphasize the unity of the movement, by rejecting the usual system of separate biographies for the various architects.

There exist various monographs on each of the most important masters where the reader can find all the necessary biographical details and documentation but where historical perspective is almost always distorted because of the need to emphasize the continuity of the individual personality.

When one talks about modern architecture one must bear in mind the fact that it implies not only a new range of forms, but also a new way of thinking, whose consequences have not yet all been calculated. It is probable that our habits of thought and our terminology are more out of date than the object that is being talked of.

It seems advisable, therefore, not to force the subject-matter into current methodological frameworks, but rather to try and adapt the methodology to the subject-matter, to try and perceive, within the modern movement itself, the historiographic hints which it potentially contains. The risks inherent in this attempt seem to be compensated for by the fact that it probably gives one a more accurate grasp of the meaning of the events involved.

# Introduction
# Architecture and the industrial revolution

On 14 April 1791 the union of the building workers (*charpentiers*) – the men working on the sites of Sainte-Geneviève, the Place de la Concorde and the new bridges over the Seine – invited employers to agree to regulate wages on the basis of a minimum wage.[1]

One month before, a decree by the Constituent Assembly had suddenly abolished the traditional organization of the guilds which had regulated labour relations until that time. The workers, excluded from elections for the Constituent Assembly, were unmoved by the spirit of this ruling; they did not regret the disappearance of the old guilds, where they had been oppressed by their masters, but neither did they show any particular enthusiasm for the freedom of labour proclaimed by the liberal economists, as can be seen from the *cahiers* of the fourth estate presented in 1789; they were concerned for their immediate livelihood and believed that the new arrangement should produce an improvement in their standard of living, or at least leave them a margin to defend their own interests themselves. For this reason they turned directly to their employers, inviting them to negotiate.

The employers did not reply. So the union appealed to the Municipality of Paris to intervene in its favour. Bailly, the Mayor

of Paris, realized that there was an important matter of principle lurking beneath this dispute and preferred to reply publicly with a manifesto that was put in the Paris streets on 26 April and which solemnly reaffirmed the theoretical principles of the liberalism which had led up to the abolition of the guilds, and condemned the very existence of workers' associations let alone their demands:

'The law has abolished the guilds which held the monopolies of production. It cannot, therefore, authorize unions which, by replacing them, would set up a new sort of monopoly. For this reason, those who entered these workers' unions, or who encourage them, are plainly going against the law, are enemies of freedom and punishable as disturbers of the peace and of public order. [Therefore, the request to settle wages by law could not be entertained.] It is true that all citizens have equal rights, but they have not equal abilities, talents and means; it is, therefore, impossible that they should all hope to be able to earn the same amount. A union of workers, aiming to bring daily wages to a uniform amount, would plainly be going contrary to their interests'.[2]

On 30 April the employers in their turn

**1**   *J.L. David,* Oath of the Tennis Court *(1791)*

addressed a petition to the Municipality; they stated that workers' associations were contrary to the existing laws and that they aimed to impose their conditions by force; this conduct 'constitutes an outrage against the rights of man and the liberty of individuals' and is counter to the principles of the economy, 'since competition alone is enough to contain mutual interests within their natural limits'.[3]

This unrest among building workers spread to those in other trades, in Paris and elsewhere, while employers too began to aim at some sort of organization among themselves; many workers went on strike and on 22 May the problem was brought before the National Assembly. The employers claimed that the workers' associations were simply a new version of the old guilds; the workers firmly refused to accept this analogy, claiming that it was a completely new form of organization, indispensable in view of the changed

state of affairs and that their employers too were an organized body, and more easily so, in view of their smaller numbers.

'The National Assembly' – ran a workers' memorandum – 'by destroying all privileges and guilds, must have foreseen that this declaration would be of some use to the poorest class, which for so long has been the plaything of the despotism of its employers'.[4]

On 14 June the deputy Le Chapelier – a representative of the third estate – presented his outline of a law that accepted, basically, the requests of the employers, and reaffirmed the theoretical neutrality of the State with regard to labour relations. The problem raised was connected with the freedom of association, sanctioned in the declaration of the rights of man; but 'it must be forbidden to citizens belonging to a particular profession to gather together in the cause of their own so-called common interests' since the new state does not recognize the existence of these so-called interests; 'within the state, there exists only the particular interest of each individual, and the general interest'.[5] Personally, Le Chapelier was convinced that the workers' demands were reasonable; but the Assembly could not and must not intervene and support them with a law, because from here would come a basis for the rebirth of the old guild system and the momentary gains would be cancelled out by permanent damage.

The Le Chapelier law, passed on 17 June 1791, impartially prohibited 'both workers' aims to increase wages, and employers' coalitions to lower them';[6] it also forbade both parties the right to hold meetings, forbade administrative bodies to hear requests of this type and set up various punishments – though not harsh ones – for transgressors.

France's example was followed, a few years later, by England. In 1800 – here too after a disturbance among building workers – the Combination Act was issued, prohibiting all meetings of members of a common trade. In this way, during the crucial period of the industrial revolution, the attitude of the political power to labour relations was defined by means of a theoretically unexceptionable statement. But facts soon proved the untenability of this solution. In France the agricultural crisis, the devaluation of paper money and the hardships of war prevented the revolutionary government from maintaining its liberal attitude in economics, and soon forced it towards a system of rigid control; then came the Empire, which not only re-established trade associations compulsorily in 1813 but also went even further than the Monarchy in controls, to the point of setting up state industries. In England the general liberal tendency was maintained partially even during the Napoleonic wars, though the Combination Act immediately proved unsuitable for regulating the expanding British economy, and after being modified in practice, was abolished in 1824.

So after a generation the whole problem was open again, and had to be faced in a way that was very different from that arrived at by the French deputies of 1791: not by a declaration of principle but by the gradual building of a whole new organizational structure quite different from the original one and certainly no less complex.

The immediate causes for this development were, undoubtedly, class interests. The French bourgeoisie, having gained power with the help of the fourth estate, did not intend to share with them the advantages of this newly gained position. In England manual labourers were similarly excluded from public life.

But this was not the whole story. The legislators of 1791 and 1800 were inspired not only by self-interest but also by a theoretical vision which seemed, at the time, to be the only one possible; for the moment all the workers had to set against it were bitter complaints about their own conditions, or a backward-looking attachment to vanished institutions. Le Chapelier was an independent jurist moved by a theoretical stubbornness which did not prevent him from recognizing, in the very report with which he presented his law, that current wages were too low and needed to be raised. It is true that the workers' cause was defended in Marat's *Ami du Peuple*, but three months earlier the same paper had also protested against the abolition of the guilds, without producing reasons other than the most reactionary platitudes against industrial progress.[7]

There was an obvious imbalance between the solutions put forward and the problems to be solved. A real and difficult question would be treated in theoretical terms and resolved along these lines, leaving aside the most important difficulties; an eminently dynamic situation would be expressed in absolute terms, as though the theses upheld had the value of eternal and natural laws. Practical difficulties, furthermore, were pre-

**2, 3**   *Versailles, The Petit Trianon (A.J. Gabriel, 1762), and Marie Antoinette's village (R. Mique, 1783–6)*

sent and visible to everyone, so that disregard of them was to some degree deliberate, by a sort of convention accepted by all parties.

The terms of theoretical discourse were apparently quite clear, but ambiguous in this particular context. Words as used by politicians, employers and workers did not have the same meaning: 'freedom' for the first meant a programme derived from the philosophers of the Enlightenment, for the second a slackening of state controls on their activities, for the third the right to a reasonable standard of living. Yet all used the same conventional phrases and allowed discussion to take place in metaphorical terms, through habit or calculation.

Thus the formulation arrived at seemed conclusive and unimpeachable, but was in fact provisional and uncertain; instead of solving the problem, it gave rise to an endless series of new developments.

This phenomenon could be observed in many other fields. Theories proved ill-

suited to solving the practical difficulties of the processes they had helped to put into motion, and could remain consistent only by conventionally restricting their own fields.

Since the fortunes of architecture depended on the balance between theory and practice – and since the conditions of building workers were part and parcel of architecture after all, even though the thought of the time did not like to admit it – this subject must form the starting-point for our discussion.

At the risk of appearing to exaggerate, one might say that Le Chapelier's law was laid on the new problems of union organization like the neo-classical façades laid upon the new industrial buildings – and was equally irrelevant to their real needs.

In both cases the problem was regarded as solved by postulating the identity of certain theoretical models with practical reality. But what actually occurred was a process of revision of the whole of contemporary thought, from which current opinion on

**4** *The poor man's house, engraving by C.N. Ledoux,* L'Architecture considérée sous le rapport de l'art des moeurs et de la législation, *1806. 'This vast universe that amazes you is the poor man's house, the house of the rich man who has been despoiled. For his ceiling he has the vault of the sky and he is in communication with the assembly of the gods. The poor man asks for a house without any of the decorations used in the houses of the modern Pluto. Art must interpret his needs and submit them to proportion.'*

political economy and architecture emerged profoundly altered.

One cannot, therefore, begin to talk of architecture without considering the nature and limits of what was meant by architecture at that time. One must first consider briefly the general pattern of social and political changes, the views that contemporary thinkers formulated about these changes and the position within this pattern of the system of ideas and experiments transmitted by the architectural tradition of the past.

The industrial revolution is characterized by certain basic changes which occurred first in England, from the middle of the eighteenth century onwards and which were repeated, sooner or later, in the other countries of Europe: increase in population, increase in industrial production and the mechanization of productive systems.

In the middle of the eighteenth century England had about six and a half million inhabitants; in 1801, when the first census was taken, there were 8,892,000 and in 1831 about fourteen million inhabitants. This increase was not due to a rise in the birth-rate which was more or less constant throughout the period, between 37·7 and 36·6 per thousand – nor to an excess of immigration over emigration, but to a decisive lowering of the death-rate which fell from 35·8 (in the decade 1730–40) to 21·1 (in the decade 1811–21).[8] It has been established that the causes of this drop were mainly connected with hygiene: improved food, personal hygiene, public services and housing, progress in medicine and better organized hospitals.

The population increase was accompanied by an unheard of increase in production: during the seventy years between 1760 and 1830 the production of iron rose from 20,000 to 700,000 tons, that of coal from 4,300,000 to 115 million tons; the cotton industry, which in the mid-eighteenth century produced four million pounds, produced about 270 million in 1830. The increase was both quantitative and qualitative: there were more types of industry, more types of products and more processes for producing them.

The rise in population and the increase in industry influenced one another in a highly complex fashion.

Some of the improvements in hygiene were dependent on industry; for instance, better food was due to the progress made in food-growing and transport, while personal cleanliness was made possible by more soap and cheaper cotton underwear; housing was improved by the replacement of wood and thatch by more durable materials, and still more by the separation of home and work-place; more efficient sewers and water mains were made possible by the progress in hydraulic engineering, and so on. But the decisive causes were probably the advances made in medicine, which had their effects on even the non-industrialized European countries, where a rise in population was similarly produced.

At the same time the need to feed, clothe and house a rising population was certainly one of the incentives for the production of manufactured goods, though it could also produce a simple lowering of the standard of living, as it did at the beginning of the nineteenth century in Ireland and as is still the case in Asia (it should be noted that the rapid mechanization of English industry was due, in part, to the disparity between the labour that could be used in manufacturing and the demands of trade, that is, precisely to the fact that the population was not increasing as fast as the volume of industrial production; and that the late mechanization of French industry was connected, on the other hand, with the country's large population – twenty-seven million at the outbreak of the Revolution, almost three times that of England).

Industrialization was one of the possible answers to the population increase, and it was dependent on an ability to intervene actively in productive relations, in order to adapt them to the new needs.

Various particular circumstances, favourable to economic expansion, have been put forward to explain it: in England, the increase in agricultural incomes following the enclosures, the existence of vast sums of capital because of the unequal distribution of income, the low interest rate, the increasing labour force, the many technical inventions produced by the high standard of purely scientific research and the high degree of specialization, the large number of employers eager to make use of the simultaneous presence of inventions, skills and capital (a marked vertical mobility between the classes created the most profitable situation for the exploitation of natural talent), the relative freedom granted to nonconformist groups and religious dissenters who proved very active in industry, and the attitude of the State in imposing less rigid restrictions than usual on economic activities, both because it now had fewer strategic and financial worries and because of the influence of the liberal theories put forward by Adam Smith and noted by important politicians such as Pitt.

These facts probably had their roots in a single starting point, the current spirit of enterprise, the open-minded desire for new results and the belief that they could be obtained by calculation and hard thought.

Throughout history writers have been amazed at their contemporaries' rage for novelty, but during the second half of the eighteenth century this theme became very frequent indeed, almost unanimous; an English writer wrote: 'the age is running mad after innovation; all the business of the world is to be done in a new way; men are to be hanged in a new way; Tyburn itself is not safe from the fury of innovation',[9] and a German: 'the existing state of things seems to have become generally offensive and sometimes contemptible. It is a singular fact that everything old is now judged with disfavour. New impressions make their way into the bosom of our families and trouble their order; even our housewives can no longer endure old furniture'.[10]

However, this same spirit of enterprise was constantly involving the protagonists of the industrial revolution in risky decisions and inconsistent and contradictory actions and indeed causing them to make a constant series of mistakes which weighed on society on a scale proportionate with the new quantities at stake.

All historical descriptions of this period, since they have to attribute a different degree of importance to the general guiding principles of development and to chance incidents, tend to give an over-simplified idea of the phenomenon and to imply that things went more smoothly than in fact they did. But in reality the path of the industrial revolution was troubled by a continuous series of failures, momentary retrogressions, crises and suffering for large numbers of town-dwellers; contemporaries, according to whether they were struck by the positive or negative aspects of the state of affairs, have presented us with two contrasting pictures of the time, one rosy and optimistic, the other gloomy and pessimistic.

In 1859 Charles Dickens drew up this surprising judgment of the industrial revolution:

'It was the best of times, it was the worst of times, it was the age of wisdom, it was the age of foolishness, it was the epoch of belief, it was the epoch of incredulity, it was the season of light, it was the season of darkness, it was the Spring of hope, it was the winter of despair, we had everything before us, we had nothing before us, we were all going direct to Heaven, we were all going direct the other way . . .'.[11]

The main cause of the evils that struck the writer, and that still strike the historian, is the lack of co-ordination between scientific and technical progress in the various sectors, and the general organization of society; in particular, the lack of suitable administrative provisions for controlling the consequences of the economic changes.

The dominant political theories of the time were largely responsible for this failure in timing. The conservatives did not even realize that they were living in a time of rapid changes. For instance Edmund Burke, who published his *Reflections on the French Revolution* in 1790, was amazed at the events taking place in France, which he regarded as monstrous, and was concerned mainly that these changes should not spread to England to upset the *status quo*.

As Trevelyan says, 'the conservatives, with unconscious irony, were every day proclaiming their aversion to every sort of change. They did not manage to grasp that they themselves were living in the middle of a revolution far more profound than that which was drawing all their thoughts across the Channel, and they did not raise a finger to impede its fiery course'.[12]

The liberal followers of Smith and the radicals inspired by Malthus realized that they were living in an age of great change, and demanded the reform of existing society, but they saw this reform as the recognition of certain laws inherent in the movement of society, and as the removal of the traditional chains that prevented it.

In 1776 Adam Smith published his *Inquiry into the Nature and Causes of the Wealth of Nations.* Here he gave scientific and incontrovertible form to the liberal theory, and persuaded his contemporaries that the world of economics was ruled by objective and impersonal laws like the world of nature; the main foundation for these laws was not the demands of the State but the free activity of individuals, inspired by a sense of their own personal gain.

The *Essay on the Principle of Population* by Thomas Malthus, which appeared in 1798, was almost as important in determining the practical behaviour of the protagonists of the industrial revolution. Malthus was the first to relate the problems of economic development to that of population, and proved that only the poverty of a certain number would maintain the balance of the two factors, since the natural increase in population was greater than the increase in means of subsistence and found its limit only in hunger, which prevents further increase.

Both Smith and Malthus – and particularly the former – had reservations, and admitted that there were certain exceptions to their theories. But the public interpreted them with far less flexibility; many liberals thought that the State should not interfere in economic affairs and that the best way of serving the public interest was to leave everyone free to carry on their own business; many also believed that Malthus had proved the impossibility of abolishing poverty and the pointlessness of all philanthropic action on behalf of the poorer classes.

These ideas coincided with the interests of the rich, who wielded political power, and perhaps that is why they seemed so convincing to the governing classes; but a political explanation cannot fully account for their influence.

There was a universally held belief that the whole posed a problem no different from that of the sum of its component parts, and that one need only concern oneself with the single element – the single enterprise, the single invention, the single profit – for a balance to reassert itself automatically throughout the whole. Men believed that they were moving towards a 'natural' order of economics and society, which could be known *a priori* from the analysis of its elements, like Newton's physical world. The structures of traditional society – the political privileges of feudal origin, the corporate organization of the economy, the political limitations to freedom in business – appeared as artificial obstacles, which could be removed so that the world could move forward into the imagined natural order.

It has been noted that the theories of English liberalism more or less mirrored the state of the economy before 1760, when industrialization was just starting up and each element – men, capital, equipment etc. – was extremely mobile, while organizational demands were still relatively slight. Thus theory minimized the organizational aspects of the world that was emerging from the industrial revolution, and encouraged the destruction of old forms of society, suddenly and violently in France, very gradually in England; only later did it become clear that new and suitable forms of organization would have to replace the old.

In France the tone of social and economic theories was made even more abstract by the abolition of every form of spontaneous political life and by the social unrest which was shortly to make the French Revolution inevitable: de Tocqueville writes:

'The very position of these writers led them to relish general and abstract theories in the matter of government and to trust them blindly. In the almost unlimited detachment, in which they lived from practice, no experience tempered the ardour of their temper . . . and so they became much bolder in their novelties, more enamoured of general ideas and of systems, more contemptuous of ancient wisdom and more confident still in their individual reason, than is generally seen in authors who write speculative books on politics. [The Revolution, at least in its first phase] . . . was conducted precisely in the same spirit, that it caused so many abstract books to be written on government – the same attraction for general theories, complete systems of legislation and exact symmetry in the laws; the same contempt for existing facts; the same confidence in theory, the same taste for the original, the ingenious and the novel, in institutions; the same desire to rebuild at once the entire constitution according to the rules of logic and on a single plan, in place of trying to amend it in parts'.[13]

The same spirit of criticism and innovation affected architectural thinking, but found itself confronted with a unique tradition, linked from the Renaissance onwards with a demand for intellectual balance.

Together with painting and sculpture, architecture makes up the triad of the major arts; it and the other arts are conditioned by a system of rules, partly drawn from antiquity and partly selected from those common to most Renaissance artists, which were regarded as universal and unchanging, being based on the nature of things and on the experiences of antiquity, conceived of as a second nature.

This discipline may be interpreted in various ways, as a spontaneous or as a deliberate attitude; in either case, the limitations deriving from it had proved extremely fruitful.

The existence of certain general rules ensured unity of style, adaptability to all circumstances and communicability of results. Imitating ideal models, rather than real prototypes, the artists' spontaneity is only partly shackled, since he is free to imitate these models in many different ways; individual freedom is moved, so to speak, to a more restricted domain, where the various experiments might be more easily compared and evaluated; so that differences of interpretation among themselves acquired extraordinary importance because of the constant reference to a fixed term of comparison.

Thus throughout the past three centuries the classical repertoire had been used by all civilized countries and adapted to the most varied practical and aesthetic needs; the intentional universality of the canonical forms had been almost translated into reality through an almost infinite number of applications.

But the whole system of classical architecture was based on an initial conception, that of attributing an essential and super-historical character to a particular choice. The supposed natural and inimitable laws of architecture were expressed in certain constants, deduced roughly from Roman monuments, from Vitruvius or even from the works of modern masters; their universality was an attribute given by history, not inherent in their nature.

As long as it remained within the sphere of classical culture, this convention could never be stated directly; it was felt from time to time, as a limit or set-back to certain more basic experiments, and the tension deriving from it was one of the main forces that inspired architectural thinking, particularly in its last phases.

But the Enlightenment in the eighteenth century set itself the task of scrutinizing all traditional institutions in the light of reason. Turning to architectural thought, the *esprit de raison* seized upon and clarified something that had remained in obscurity since the fifteenth century, i.e. the exact importance of the formal rules of classicism, objectively analysing current stylistic elements and studying their historical sources, the architecture of the ancient world and the Renaissance. Thus it naturally found itself having to deny the previously asserted universality of these rules and to place them within a

**5** *G. B. Piranesi,* The Temples of Paestum, *1778*

correct historical perspective, upsetting the premises of classicism itself and putting an end, after more than three centuries, to the movement that had been based on them.

The new attitude made itself felt before the middle of the century with a change of tone in architectural production and a development in archaeological studies.

Two relevant examples are the change in architecture between the reigns of Louis XIV and Louis XV in France, and the change in the course of Roman Baroque in 1730 with Clement XII. The observance of the canonical precepts became stricter and the rational control over design more rigorous and systematic; Baroque fluidity was lessened in the interests of a growing tendency towards the analysis of every part of the building; often the architectural orders were disengaged from the inner shell of masonry and the frame of columns and cornices were given greater emphasis.

At the same time it was felt that old monuments should be known exactly, by means of accurate and direct examination and not through vague approximations. The wealth of archaeological remains, barely touched upon in the Renaissance despite humanistic enthusiasm, was now systematically investigated. This period saw the first excavations at Herculaneum (1711), the Palatine, Hadrian's villa at Tivoli (1734), Pompeii (1748); the first systematic collections of reliefs (and not only Roman ones) were published, and scholars began to try and gain a direct knowledge of Greek art (Gronovius 1720), Early Christian art (Boldetti 1720), Etruscan art (Gori 1734) and even prehistoric art, which aroused interest in Paris around 1730. Thus classical antiquity, which had hitherto been regarded as an age of gold, ideally set at the boundaries

**6** *G. B. Piranesi,* The Temples of Paestum, *1778*

of history, began to be known in its objective position in time.

The preservation of ancient objects ceased to be regarded as a mere private pastime and became a public problem. In 1732 the first public museum of antique sculpture opened on the Campidoglio in Rome; in 1739 the Vatican collections were made accessible to the public, as were the Luxembourg collections in Paris in 1750; in 1753 Sir Hans Sloane left his *objets d'art* to the nation; his house in Bloomsbury was opened to the public in 1759, constituting the first nucleus of the British Museum.

The contributions made during the first half of the century were utilized and rationally organized by Johann Joachim Winckelmann (1717–68) at the beginning of the second half.

Winckelmann went to Rome in 1755 and his main work, the *History of Ancient Art*,

appeared in 1764. For the first time he set out to study ancient art as it was, objectively, and not as it was seen by the fashions of the time, and for this he deserves to be known as the founder of art history; at the same time he set up ancient works as definite models to be imitated and became the theoretician of the new movement: neo-classicism.

Winckelmann put forward his aims as follows:

'Those who have hitherto written of beauty, from laziness rather than from lack of knowledge, have fed us with metaphysical ideas. They have imagined an infinity of beauties and have perceived them in Greek statues, but instead of showing them to us they have talked about them in the abstract . . . as though all the monuments had been destroyed or lost. Therefore, to treat of the art of design of the Greeks and to point out

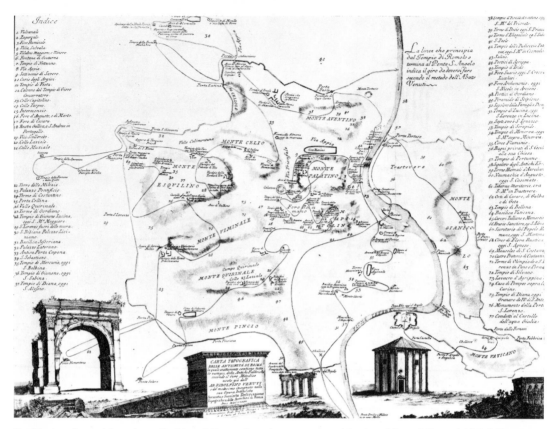

**7**  *Itinerary for a visit to the antiquities of Rome, from* Accurata e succinta descrizione delle antichità di Roma dell'abate Ridolfino Venuti, *Rome, 1824*

its excellence both for those who admire it and for artists themselves, it is necessary to come from the ideal to the sensible, from the general to the particular; and to do this not with vague and ill-defined discussions, but with a precise determination of those outlines and delineaments which produce those appearances that we call beautiful forms'.[14]

In 1763 he produced this surprising definition: 'The true feeling for beauty is like fluid gesso poured over the head of the Apollo [Belvedere], which touches and clothes it in its entirety'.[15] These words have the same spirit of open-mindedness and faith in one's own powers that was mentioned earlier about industrial inventions and

activities; at the same time they herald the formulation within whose bounds the artistic culture of the time was to be frozen.

In fact the classical rules, once their relevance to artistic practice had been recognized and experienced, were still retained as conventional models for contemporary artists. Thus outwardly nothing was changed since the same forms were being used, but beneath this a real cultural upheaval was taking place, because there was no longer any leeway between general rules and their concrete realization, and the supposed models could be known with absolute accuracy. Conformity with these models depended upon a simple abstract decision of the artist taken irrespective of any real conditioning need; from the moment

**8** *Eighteenth century, anonymous,* The Colosseum in an imaginary landscape *(Lemmermann Collection, Rome)*

that it was scientifically defined, classicism became an arbitrary convention and was transformed into neo-classicism.

But this new attitude soon spread beyond the limits of classical forms; the same treatment could be applied to all types and conventional forms from the past, the medieval, the exotic etc., producing the respective 'revivals': neo-Gothic, neo-Byzantine, neo-Arabian and so on. In its broadest form, Anglo-Saxon writers called this movement historicism, which is an apt enough term if one puts aside the meaning given to the word in the history of philosophy.

The theses of humanistic culture – unity of style and the freedom granted to artists within the bounds of this style itself – were now transformed into irreconcilable contradictions.

From one point of view the unity of style seemed definitively assured, since the objective knowledge of historical monuments made it possible to imitate a given style as

faithfully as was possible; but there were so many styles, all present simultaneously in the architect's mind, so that on the whole the repertoire of historicism was totally incoherent.

In one sense the margin of individual freedom was reduced to nought, yet in another it was increased a hundredfold. The criterion for the application of each style was historical fidelity; the artist could accept certain references, or refuse them, or manipulate them, but they came to him from outside himself and he had no margin of freedom (theoretically) to adapt them in his own way because he was not dealing with ideal models but with real examples that could actually be known by experience. On the other hand abstractly speaking the architect enjoyed boundless freedom because he could decide whether to use style A or style B.

Historicism may be considered as a sort of *reductio ad absurdum* of Renaissance culture, and it appeared as an epilogue, closing the

**9**  *Rome, Artificial ruin in Villa Borghese (A. Asprucci, c. 1790)*

three-centuries-old cycle of European classicism. But seen in relation to the economic and social changes and to technical developments, historicism also appears as an opening towards the future because its very abstract nature made it possible for the traditional means of expression to be adapted, as far as possible, to new needs, and for the new experiments (that were to lead to the modern movement) to mature in the meantime.

From the above discussion on artistic unity and freedom, it is plain that these old terms had assumed meanings different from the traditional ones and had become ambivalent, like the terms of the political discussions mentioned at the beginning. In both cases these were formal discussions that avoided real problems; but the repeated attempts to apply these formal solutions to reality taught men to delve deeper into reality itself, and did in fact lead towards basic solutions.

One immediate consequence of historicism was the division of the task of the architect into various different spheres of activity. The gulf between design and execution first opened in the Renaissance, when the designer took upon himself all the decisions and left to others only the practical realization of the building. But this did not prevent designers and executors from understanding one another because, once a stable stylistic unity had been reached, even if planning was not modelled on execution as had happened in the Middle Ages, execution could at least

**10**  Top, *Osterley Park, Middlesex (R. Adam, 1775)*

**11**  Middle, *Richmond, Virginia, the Capitol (T. Jefferson, 1785)*

**12**  Bottom, *Milan, Porta Ticinese (L. Cagnola, 1801)*

model itself on planning so that the same working agreement could be reached in another way.

But now there were a large number of styles, and in the first half of the nineteenth century they multiplied still further; so that the executors, unless they specialized in building houses only in a certain style, had to remain, so to speak, neutral amid the many different possibilities and restrict themselves to the mechanical task of translating certain designs into stone, wood, iron or brick, without any possibility of personal participation. The executive means best adapted to this situation was of course the machine, which at this time was being ever more widely used in industry and, to some degree, on building sites as well.

The machine was very demanding and tended implacably towards the least costly solutions; on the other hand the demands of style were restricted to the formal appearances of objects, so that the concept of style itself tended to be ever more restricted and was finally regarded as a mere decorative covering to be applied as occasion demanded to a generic supporting skeleton; the architect concerned himself with artistic matters and left the technical and constructional problems to the others. This was the origin of the rival and parallel fields of activity still represented today by the two figures of architect and engineer.

This fact too must be looked at from within and without, so to speak, in order to be correctly interpreted.

In comparison with the cultural unity of the past, this duality was a serious setback. Those who continued to be referred to as 'architects' rose above the fray, declared themselves pure artists and concerned them-

**13, 14**  *Munich, The Propylaea and Glyptothek*
(*L. Klenze, 1816–46*)

**15** *London, Chester Terrace (J. Nash, 1825)*

selves purely with formal problems, ignoring technical ones. Meanwhile philosophers, for instance Schelling, attributed an independent and often absurdly exaggerated value to this pure art. Technicians were in a rather better situation, and although they were regarded with a certain degree of disdain they never completely lost contact with reality, at least within the limited sphere of their own activity; but they were quick to be convinced that decisions about the final purposes of the work should be taken by others, and their activity became abstract in another way, in that it adapted itself readily to any situation and followed any lead.

Thus architecture as a whole was cut adrift from the important problems of its time: the artists, who should have been concerned with the aims of architectural production, concerned themselves with imaginary problems in prudent isolation; the engineers, concentrating on the means of realizing their creations, forgot the ultimate aim of the work and meekly allowed themselves to be used to any end whatsoever.

But now let us look at the other side of the picture. Their mutual isolation was the condition which made it possible for both parties to perform their immediate respective tasks, in accordance with the analytical methods of early industrial thought, and to ensure the continuity of experiment, beneficial to future progress; it allowed artists to peruse the whole traditional repertoire in their search for forms suited to the new distributive and constructional needs and thus gradually to rid themselves of the whole weight of tradition and the visual habits connected with it; it enabled the engineers to tackle the immediate consequences of the industrial revolution in building and to make progress in constructional theory and practice, thus working towards future experiments.

In practice, relations between artists and engineers, though conditioned by the antagonism we have already mentioned, were not completely severed. Since they were forced to work in the same field despite everything, they both adapted their respective methods and a sort of parallelism emerged between the two fields of activity – mainly, as I shall show, between the neoclassical repertoire and building practice – which made it possible for the two spheres to adjust themselves to one another when the right time came, so that the work of the one could be disengaged from that of the other.

This relationship was purely one of convenience, but it made it possible for those concerned to gain the experience needed, later, to re-establish a new cultural unity, which obviously could not consist of a pure and simple return to the pre-industrial situation, when the architect performed all tasks himself, but which had to take into account the specialization and division of labour which were now indispensable in the modern world.

Finally architecture, which is a matter of co-ordination and synthesis, was broken up into its various elements by the changes that took place in the second half of the eighteenth century. Several factors basic to the thought of the Enlightenment were operative in this transformation: the spirit of analytical investigation and the belief that there existed a type of natural organization of all the elements which could be deduced from the elements themselves; this last belief, coming into contact with an illustrious tradition, made possible the formal survival of the classical style, and concealed the basic transformations beneath the apparent continuity of its repertoire.

Thus that part of architectural culture that carried on the ancient tradition in the abstract, gradually lost touch with the realities of its time.

Meanwhile the elements of a new synthesis were coming into existence, a synthesis that was to occur when artists agreed to involve themselves wholeheartedly in the organization of a new society.

**16**  *J.L. David,* The Death of Marat *(1793)*

The episode recounted at the beginning is an excellent example of the nature of the organizational problem that faced industrial society.

Let us consider Le Chapelier's statement that, in the new State, 'there is no longer anything other than the particular interest of each individual and the general interest'. This concept is already in Rousseau, who attributed political power to the 'general will' of the community; the general will consists of what is common to the wills of the various individuals after differences caused by personal interest have been discounted. For the general will to become apparent, each citizen must judge for himself; then personal differences 'will be mutually destroyed, and the sum of the differences will be the general will'.

'But when factions, partial associations, are formed to the detriment of the whole society, the will of each of these associations becomes general with reference to its members, and particular with reference to the State; it may then be said that there are no longer as many voters as there are men, but only as many voters as there are associations. The differences become less numerous and yield a less general result. Lastly, when one of these associations becomes so great that it predominates over all the rest, you no longer have as a result the sum of small differences, but a single difference; there is then no longer a general will, and the opinion which prevails is only a particular opinion. It is important, then, in order to have a clear declaration of the general will, that there should be no partial associations in the State, and that every citizen should express his own opinions'.[16]

Rousseau's 'general will' is a theoretical concept; in practice, its place was immediately taken by the authoritarian state which, unimpeded by the existence of any partial society, became the sole judge of what should be understood by 'public' and 'private'. Thus democracy became tyranny without the apparent terms of the discussion needing to be changed, since the citizen 'shall be able to be forced to be free' as Rousseau says, in a phrase whose tragic irony we can so well appreciate today.

Thus Le Chapelier's formula contains implicitly the two guiding principles of the French Revolution: the two souls, as Salvatorelli says,[17] which were so shortly to enter into conflict and to condition all modern political thought: the need for personal freedom and the vindication of the authority of the State.

A similar process of polarization of the social structure had been taking place in France for some time under the *ancien régime*: as de Tocqueville says, 'the central power . . . had already managed to destroy all intermediate powers, and nothing existed between it and the private individual except for an immense empty space'.[18]

For the moment this space was occupied by the clash of two abstract principles, that of freedom and that of authority, and as happened in theoretical debate they tended to overlap unexpectedly since there was no intermediate structure to prevent them.

But modern thought was not content with this alternative and obstinately tried to integrate freedom and authority in a way that might transform them from abstract and contradictory notions into practical and complementary realities. The problem was gradually to fill de Tocqueville's 'empty space' with new institutions that would take into account the changed economic and technical conditions, to apply the same spirit of unprejudiced enquiry – that had produced so many successes in single undertakings – to the problems of co-ordination and balance between these enterprises themselves, to learn to make the various choices appropriately in time and scale, so as to combine a maximum of freedom with a minimum of control.

In the political field this attempt was known as democracy, as planning; the hopes of bettering the world that was being transformed by the industrial revolution were committed to this possibility, which was now coming into existence, continually exposed to the dangers of being frozen into a series of authoritarian decisions or of withering away amid the multiplicity of new enterprises. Modern architecture was born at the moment when constructional activity was drawn into the sphere of this attempt.

In the following chapters we shall follow the difficult and fragmented progress of architecture through the vicissitudes of industrial society, starting from its original privileged position of detachment and pursuing it to the point where it came into contact once more with practical problems and took its place, consciously, in the work of the reconstruction of contemporary society.

# Birth and development of the industrial town

# one

# Changes in building technique during the industrial revolution

At the end of the eighteenth century, the term 'construction' was applied to the end product of a number of technical activities: public and private buildings, roads, bridges, canals, earthworks, water mains and sewers. Roughly, it was used to cover all large-scale items not produced mainly by machinery.

Before the industrial revolution the art of building machines was more closely associated with the art of building houses; now that technical progress had so radically transformed mechanical constructions, they fell increasingly into the spheres of specialist activity and the unqualified word 'construction' tended to mean those activities still connected with the traditional systems and usually associated with the concept of 'architecture'. As soon as one of these activities developed on its own to any extent, it became detached from the others and entered the field of independent specialization; thus for instance until 1830–40 railways figured in treatises on construction, then disappeared and gave birth to an independent literature.

Naturally, the fact that it was relatively faithful to traditional systems did not mean that the art of building remained static during this period, or that many new problems did not arise. The main changes can be summed up under three headings.

In the first place, the industrial revolution altered building techniques even if its effects were less noticeable here than in other sectors. The traditional materials, stone, brick, timber, were now worked in a more profitable way and more easily distributed; to these were now added new materials such as cast iron, glass and, later, concrete; scientific progress made it possible for the materials to be utilized more aptly and for their strength to be calculated; there was better equipment on building sites and machinery began to be used; developments in geometry made it possible for exact and unambiguous plans to be made for every aspect of the construction; the setting up of specialized schools provided society with a large number of specially trained professionals; printing and new methods of graphic reproduction made new contributions readily available.

In the second place there was an increase in the quantities involved; larger roads, wider and deeper canals were built, communication networks on land and water increased rapidly; the increase in population and in movement from place to place made necessary the building of new houses in unprecedentedly large numbers; the growth

**17**    *An English steam-engine (c. 1830, Science Museum, London)*

of the towns demanded larger and more extensive water and sanitary installations; the increase in public functions demanded larger public buildings, while the multiplicity of activities and the sudden intensity of speculation constantly demanded new types of building. The industrial economy would have been inconceivable without a basis of new buildings and installations – factories, stores, warehouses, ports – which

had to be built in a relatively short time, profiting from the lowered interest rate which made it possible to tie up large sums in equipment that would prove profitable only in the distant future.

Finally, these buildings and installations, drawn as they were into the ambit of the capitalist economy, took on a meaning quite different from that which they had had in the past. They were no longer seen as lasting solutions made possible by an outlay of permanently frozen capital, but as investments that could be regularly redeemed, together with the other means of production. As Ashton observed: 'A new sense of time was one of the most striking psychological features of the industrial revolution';[1] formerly, objects which changed very slowly could be regarded as completely immobile, but now more precise functional requirements and the practice of making even quite long-term economic forecasts made this approximation impossible. Now changing values were sharply perceived and men began to concentrate on the dynamic rather than on the static aspects of affairs.

In this respect there is an important distinction to be drawn between the building and its site. As long as a building was regarded as lasting more or less indefinitely and its site as being permanently occupied, the site's value was, so to speak, part and parcel of the value of the building; but if a building's life was regarded as limited, the site acquired an independent economic value which varied according to circumstances, and if the life of a building became sufficiently short, then the concept of a land market could come into existence.

Just at this time, through the influence of liberal economic theories and fiscal requirements, the State and other public bodies lost all their property almost everywhere, and the land on which the cities stood passed into the hands of private individuals. Thus every obstacle to the free sale and purchase of land was removed.

In the next chapter we shall see the effects of these facts on the body of the towns; meanwhile it should be noted that the potential value of a site in view of a possible transformation became an important yardstick for judging the economic potential of the building that was to occupy it; the faster the value of a site changed, the shorter the economic cycle and the life of the building itself became.

In this chapter we shall discuss the advances made in building techniques; the other two points will be taken up again later, because the consequences of the quantitative changes and of the increased speed of the transformations became obvious and presented new problems only after 1830.

## 1 Scientific progress and teaching

The science of building, as we understand it today, studies certain practical consequences of the laws of mechanics and was born, one may say, when these laws were formulated for the first time, in the seventeenth century; in 1638 Galileo devoted a part of his dialogues to a discussion of the problems of stability.[2]

In 1676 Hooke formulated the famous law that bears his name; between the end of the seventeenth century and the beginning of the eighteenth many scientists, including Leibnitz, Mariotte and Bernoulli studied the problem of flexion and in 1684 Mariotte introduced the concept of the neutral axis (the point where fibres in a solid subjected to flexion are neither compressed nor stretched) but defined its position wrongly; the correct solution was found by Parent in 1713.

Meanwhile the spread of the scientific spirit and the desire felt by architects to ascertain the limits of the use of traditional building materials and systems, encouraged various pieces of experimental research.

In Rome scientists began to discuss the stability of the dome of St Peter's, and Benedict XIV commissioned the Marchese Poleni, a physician and archaeologist of the university of Padua, to produce a report on the subject, published in 1748.

In Paris there was a lengthy debate about the building of the church of Sainte-Geneviève (the Panthéon);[3] designed in 1755 by Soufflot with the intention of assigning a precise static function, and the minimal dimensions compatible with this function, to traditional elements. This occasion saw the elaboration of the concept of the maximum safety load and the invention of mechanisms capable of calculating the resistance of the relevant materials.

Almost at the same time Coulomb carried out his studies on torsion, on thrust and drift, and the discovery was made of a general equation for determining the neutral axis, based on that of Parent.

The results of these studies were coordinated and perfected during the first decades of the nineteenth century by Louis-Marie Navier (1785–1836) who is regarded as the founder of modern constructional science; the text of the lectures he gave at the Paris École Polytechnique was published in 1826.

Constructional science, as Nervi said, 'has democratized and popularized statics'[4] since its ready-made formulae enabled many designers to tackle correctly certain matters which had previously been the province of a small number of exceptionally gifted people.

It brought about a separation between theoretical and practical involvement and contributed to the fragmentation of the unity of traditional culture, but also extended the repertoire of methods and forms inherited from antiquity.

Scientific research, too, influenced building technique by modifying instruments of planning; here also the two main innovations came from France: the invention of descriptive geometry and the introduction of the metric system.

The rules of descriptive geometry were formulated by Gaspard Monge (1746–1818) during the last years of the Monarchy and the first years of the Revolution.[5] Generalizing from the methods introduced by Renaissance treatise-writers, Monge gave precise form to the various systems of representing a three-dimensional object by means of the two dimensions of a sheet of paper; designers were thus in possession of a universal process for determining, un-ambiguously, through plans, any arrangement of constructional elements, however complex, and executors had a definitive guide to the interpretation of graphic instructions.

The metric system was introduced by the French Revolution in its effort to change all the institutions of the old society according to rational models.

In 1790 Talleyrand presented the Constituent Assembly with a report deploring the variety and confusion of the old units of measurement, and suggested that a new system be adopted. After long discussion a commission, consisting of C. Borda, A. Condorcet, J. L. Lagrange, P. S. Laplace and G. Monge, was appointed to decide on the most suitable unit; there was much discussion as to whether to adopt the pendulum (whose length, according to Galileo's Law, was proportionate to the time of oscillation) or a predetermined fraction of the equator or meridian, and one forty-millionth of the earth's meridian was proposed. The works on measurement, by a geodetic commission, lasted until 1799, while another commission decided upon the rules to be followed in drawing up the other units, proposing the metric system in 1795. The platinum standard metre, according to the measurements decided upon, was placed in the Paris Musée des Arts et Métiers on 4 Messidor year VII (22 June 1799) and the new system was made obligatory in France in 1801.

Napoleon had no sympathy with this innovation and abolished it in 1812, but the need for unification and certainty that had led the revolutionaries to set up a new unit of measurement became even more pressing, with the development of industry, and many countries adopted the original metric system; Italy in 1803, Belgium and Holland in 1820, after 1830 the South American states; the system was re-established in France in 1840. The definitive standard was made in 1875 and on 20 May of the same year the international convention of the metre was confirmed; and all countries, except the Anglo-Saxon ones and a few others, gradually adopted it.

The adoption of a unified system facilitated the spread of knowledge, and commercial exchanges, and provided building technique with a general instrument whose precision could be extended as far as the ever severer demands of the new techniques required. At the same time it influenced design and 'produced a certain disintegration in architecture' as Le Corbusier[6] says, because it was a conventional measure unconnected with man, whereas the old units – feet, cubits etc. – always allowed some reference to the human body.

France, which was in the vanguard of scientific progress, also acted as guide to other countries in the organization of teaching.

Architecture was first taught, under the *ancien régime*, at the Académie d'Architecture, founded in 1671. This institution enjoyed great prestige, was the guardian of the French classical tradition and the 'grand goût', but was always open to new experiments and to technical progress, discussed rationalist theories and played a lively part in the cultural life of its time.

Meanwhile the increasingly complex and extensive tasks that the State was assuming, created the need for a body of technical specialists; the humanistic traditions of the Académie and the school attached to it made it unsuitable for the teaching of those who were to be pure technicians, so in 1747 the École des Ponts et Chaussées was founded to train the staff of the Corps des Ponts et Chaussées, founded in 1716, and in 1748 the École des Ingénieurs de Mézières was established for the training of civil engineers. The teaching was grounded on rigorously scientific foundations.

Now for the first time the pattern of rivalry between 'engineers' and 'architects' was firmly established; for the moment the lustre of the Académie obscured the prosaic schools of the Ponts et Chaussées and of Mézières, and engineers seemed destined to concern themselves with secondary matters; but scientific progress had the effect of extending the tasks of the engineers and restricting those of the architects. The time came when the Académie realized that the disputes about the role of reason and emotion in art were not just theoretical arguments, but signs of an irresistible cultural and organizational revolution, and it gradually entrenched itself in a position of unwavering defence of art against science.

The Revolution changed the situation still further. The academy of architecture, like those of painting and sculpture, was suppressed in 1793; the school was temporarily allowed to continue, and when the Institut was set up in 1795 to replace the old Académies, the school was attached to the architectural section of the new complex.

Control of works by State administration, however, passed to the Conseil des Bâtiments Civils, which organized a school of its own 'for artists charged with carrying out public works'. Also, with the suppression of the Académie, the title of architect lost all distinctive value; upon payment of a fee, anyone wishing to devote himself to architecture could call himself an architect, independently of the studies he had pursued.

These provisions further weakened the architect's already shaken prestige; at the same time, the engineer's position was strengthened when all specialized teaching was brought together within the sphere of a single organization. Between 1794 and 1795, the École Polytechnique was set up, utilizing for the most part, staff from the École de Mézières; the school accepted a small number of young men, after rigorous examination and after having made certain of their 'attachment to republican principles'; they studied together for two years, then went on to the various advanced technical schools: the École des Ponts et Chaussées at

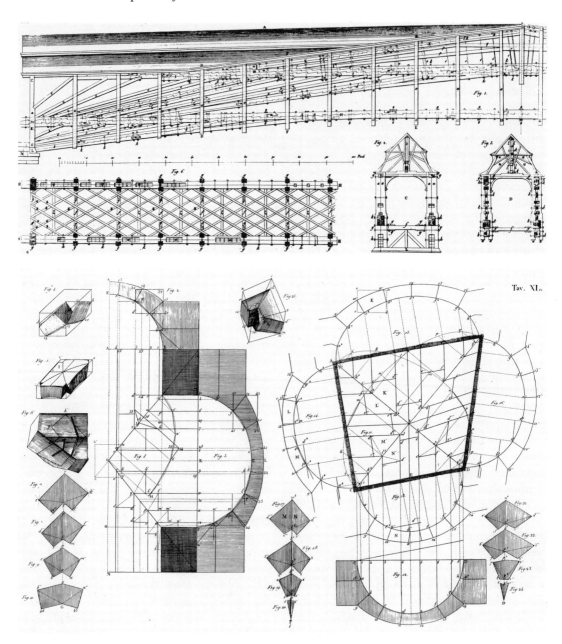

**18**  *The bridge over the Limmat at Wettingen (Johann U. Grubemann, 1777; from Rondelet's* Treatise, *Fig. 103)*
**19**  *Diagram of stone-cutting (from Rondelet, Fig. 40)*

Paris, the École d'Application d'Artillerie et de' Génie Militaire at Metz, the École des Mines in Paris, the École du Génie Maritime at Brest. The organization of studies, based on mathematics and physics, was established by Monge.

The French example was followed by many other countries: in 1806 an advanced technical school was set up in Prague, in 1815 in Vienna, in 1825 in Karlsruhe. The organization of studies – in these and later schools – was modelled on that of the Parisian schools.

The exception was England, where technical teaching was really organized only during the last decade of the nineteenth century. The protagonists of the industrial revolution were mostly self-taught men – like George Stephenson, who learned to read and write at the age of eighteen[7] – or they were the products of academies founded by nonconformists such as Boulton, Roebuck and Wilkinson, Defoe and Malthus.[8] The Institute of Civil Engineers, founded in 1818, had only three graduates among its ten presidents.

For this reason, and because English society was less rigid than that of the other continental countries, the conflict between engineers and architects was less pronounced there; the architects were less jealous of their cultural prerogatives and men frequently moved from one field of activity to the other. Thomas Telford, before concerning himself with bridges and highways, built houses in Edinburgh from 1780 to 1790; John Nash did not think it beneath him to design an iron bridge; Brunel, the designer of the famous Clifton suspension bridge at Bristol, was also a steamship builder and, later, it was not surprising that an important work of public architecture like the Crystal Palace should be entrusted to a gardener, Joseph Paxton.

But even in England technical progress finally restricted the traditional powers of the architect and caused an ever larger proportion of the professional tasks to fall into the hands of specialist technicians; this became particularly apparent after 1830, as society, transformed by the industrial revolution, gradually assumed a definite pattern.

## 2　The perfecting of traditional building systems

One of the main concerns of the ruling-classes and employers in the eighteenth century was the building of new and efficient means of communication: roads and canals.

In France the Monarchy lavished much attention upon the state of the roads; the royal highways, following Colbert's regulations, were often very wide – from thirteen to twenty metres – for reasons of prestige rather than because of the demands of traffic, and extremely regularly built, usually leading from one centre to another in a straight line; a decree of 1720 recommended that their 'alignment should be as direct as possible, for instance from bell-tower to bell-tower'.[9] Their quality, however, was not so perfect; the road-bed, laid according to traditional methods, required constant repair, to be carried out by the inhabitants of the district through which the road ran by means of the 'corvée' system; this was one of the heaviest burdens shouldered by French workers, since they might have to work anything from thirty to fifty days on the roads.

In England, until the middle of the eighteenth century, the roads were well-nigh impassable; they improved from 1745 onwards, when Parliament began to issue the Turnpike Acts allowing private individuals to build and maintain roads at their own expense and demand a toll from the users. Thus the cost of this public service was borne by private individuals who were concerned with keeping the highways in good condition. There were over 450 Turnpike Acts between 1750 and 1775; the planners were still practical men following traditional methods, and one of the most important of these was John Metcalf (1717-1810), one of the most

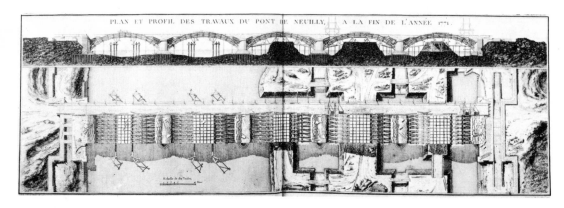

**20**   *The bridge at Neuilly (J.R. Perronet, 1768; from Perronet,* Description des projets et de la construction des ponts, *1788)*
**21**   *Paris, Pont de la Concorde (Perronet, 1787)*

extraordinary of the versatile men of the time. He had been blind from the age of six but this did not prevent him from following various careers: strolling musician, organizer of cock-fights, horse-dealer, recruiting sergeant, dealer in cotton, smuggler of tea and brandy, and coach-driver, until in 1765 he decided to devote himself to road-building, and was personally responsible for over 180 miles of road. A similar figure was James Brindley (1716–72), the illiterate mill-wright who in 1759 built the first navigable canal in England for the Duke of Bridgewater.

Towards the end of the century engineers who had grown up in the new scientific climate began to supplant these more or less amateur designers. In France P. M. J. Trésaguet (1716–96), in England Thomas Telford (1757–1832) and John Macadam (1756–1836) introduced various technical improvements. Trésaguet was a civil servant from Limoges; Telford was the son of a Scottish shepherd, one of the most important personalities in the history of engineering and we shall mention him again when we come to discuss iron bridges. Macadam worked for a merchant uncle, then as an officer during the Napoleonic wars and turned his attention to road-building late on in life; it was he who made the most important technical innovations, by doing away with the bases of big stones and proposing the use of a top layer as water-resistant as possible and consolidated with the dust from limestone materials; these innovations considerably lessened the cost of road-building and macadam – as the method became called – went into general use.

Meanwhile progress in descriptive geometry made it possible to give a satisfactory form to plans which had previously posed insurmountable problems of representation and had practically had to be specified on the spot while the actual building was taking place; men learned how to show the site with contours and in 1791 Monge put forward a scientific method for calculating earthwork.

The building of roads and bridges became more intense during the first years of the nineteenth century; while governments concerned themselves only with the roads, which fulfilled both commercial and strategic functions – Napoleon's great achievements are well-known – canals were often built by private individuals for strictly economic purposes: they were the essential means of transport for the raw materials needed by industry and for the goods that came out of the first factories.

Between the end of the eighteenth century and the beginning of the nineteenth the building of these new roads made necessary a large number of new bridges, often of considerable size. It was primarily this factor that encouraged the progress of traditional methods of building in wood and freestone, and the use of new materials: iron and cast iron.

The new scientific knowledge meant that materials could be used to the limits of their possibilities, and the experience thus gained was utilized in a large number of buildings.

The use of wood for bridges and the roofing of large areas had an unbroken history from the Middle Ages onwards, and had produced impressive and ingenious works, but works which did not move away from elementary static concepts: the beam, the beam reinforced by struts, the truss, the arch. In the sixteenth century Palladio had formulated a theory of truss beams, but it was very little used; now this concept was taken up by Swiss builders, and it enabled Johann U. Grubemann (1710–83) to build bridges of a considerable span: the bridge over the Rhine at Schaffhausen, with two spans of 59 metres each, and the bridge over the Limmat at Wettingen (1777–8) with a single span of 119 metres; unfortunately this was destroyed in 1799 for reasons of war[10] (Fig. 18).

In America in 1804 a bridge 104 metres long was built over the Schuylkill near Philadelphia; in the same year Burr built the Trenton bridge over the Delaware with two spans of 59 and 61 metres. In 1809 Wiebeking – an engineer brought up in France – built the bridge over the Regniz at Bamberg, 71 metres long.

In France, meanwhile, bridges in freestone had reached a peak of perfection; French builders influenced all Europe, as in the Gothic period. Here too the work of the engineers educated at the École des Ponts et Chaussées was of vital importance.

Jean Perronet (1708–94), director of the Parisian school since its foundation (1747), gave new life to the technique of building bridges in masonry; he designed the bridge at Neuilly (1768) (Fig. 20), the Pont de la Concorde (Fig. 21) completed shortly after the Revolution, and of many others in various cities of France; he was also concerned with road-building, built the Bergundy canal and part of the Paris sewers. Many of the innovations introduced by Perronet are still in use: the four-centred surbased arch, imposts higher than flood level and smaller piers functioning solely by means of centred loads; in his attempt to lighten his structures, he also broke the piers up into groups of columns – as in the Pont Saint-Maxence – and planned the same thing for the Pont de la Concorde but was forced to abandon it because of the hostility of his colleagues. His continued attempts to push constructional systems towards their limits made him the object of constant criticism; a report tells how in 1774 a member of the Assemblée des Ponts et Chaussées exclaimed in irritation: 'Ah wretched lightness! Must your cult and your altars be set up for ever in the heart of my country?'[11]

The 'lightness' of Perronet's bridges was achieved by the lavishing of great attention on the perfecting of the freestone structure, the camber and foundations. At this time Rondelet and others gave scientific shape to stereotomy – 'the art of cutting stones according to a given shape'[12] – founded on the principles of Monge's descriptive geometry; absolutely any type of fixing or combination of any stone elements, however complicated, could be represented and carried out most exactly (Fig. 19).

The works of Perronet – bridges and canals, with all their constructional details – were published in 1782, in a splendid series of plates; the volume was reprinted in 1788 with the addition of other plans and two notes on camber and earthwork.[13] During the Revolution, Perronet, now an old man, turned to theoretical studies and in 1793 produced a '*Note on the Research into means for building large stone arches of a span of two hundred, three hundred, four hundred and even five hundred feet*'.

## 3  The new materials

Iron and glass had been used in building since time immemorial, but only now did industrial progress make it possible to extend their uses by introducing completely new concepts into building techniques.

At first iron was used only for secondary purposes: for chains, braces, and to join up the hewn stone in freestone buildings. For instance in the pronaos built by Rondelet for Soufflot's Sainte-Geneviève or Panthéon, in 1770, the real stability of the cornice was ensured by a close network of metal bars, arranged rationally according to the various stresses, like the skeleton of a modern work in concrete[14] (Fig. 22).

At the same time iron was used for certain roofs that did not have to take very much weight, such as that of the Théâtre Français de Bordeaux, designed by Victor Louis (1786). But the limited progress made in the iron industry put an unsurmountable limit to the spread of these methods. It was in England that the decisive progress was made, enabling iron production to increase sufficiently to fulfil the new needs at the end of the century.

Iron ore was smelted, traditionally, with

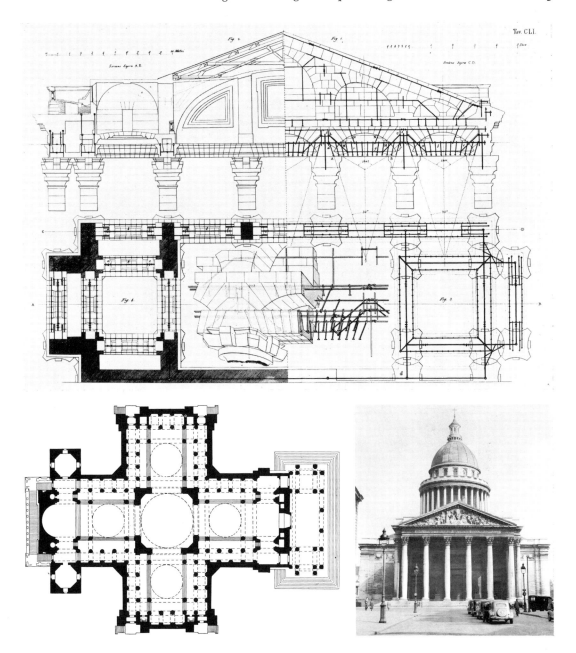

**22, 23, 24**   *Paris, Church of Ste-Geneviève (J. G. Soufflot, 1755): the iron skeleton of the pronaos (from Rondelet, Fig. 151); plan and façade*

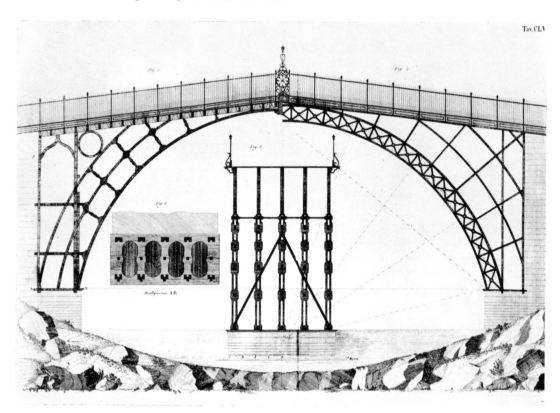

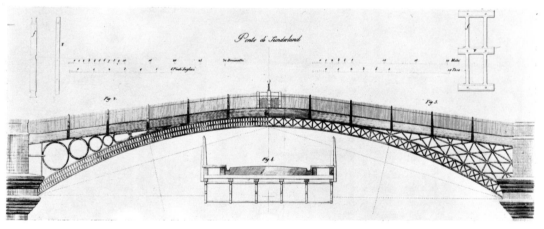

**25, 26**  *Bridge over the Severn at Coalbrookdale (T.F. Pritchard, 1777) and bridge over the Wear at Sunderland (R. Burdon, 1796; from Rondelet, Figs 157 & 158)*

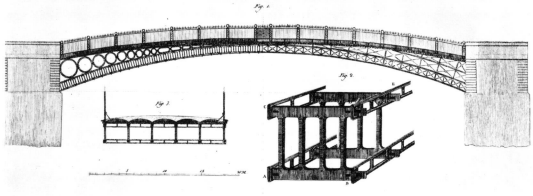

27 *Bridge at Coalbrookdale*
28 *Bridge over the Thames at Staines (R. Burdon, 1802; from Rondelet Fig. 159)*

**29**    *Brighton, Royal Pavilion (J. Nash, 1818)*
**30**    *Berlin, plan for the Marschallbrücke (K.F. Schinkel, 1818)*

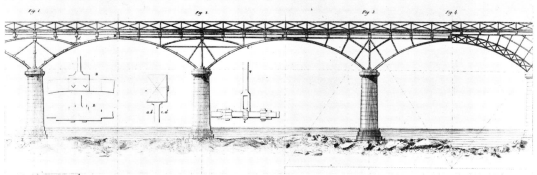

**31, 32**   *Paris, Pont des Arts (De Cessart & Dillon, 1803; from Rondelet, Fig. 160)*

**33**   *Bridge over the Conway straits (T. Telford, 1826; Rondelet, Fig. U)*
**34**   *Clifton bridge over the Avon at Bristol (I.K. Brunel, 1836)*

charcoal; the product was resmelted and poured into moulds, to obtain cast iron, or worked in the forge to obtain ductile iron. At some point in the first decades of the eighteenth century Abraham Darby of Coalbrookdale substituted coke for charcoal, keeping the procedure a secret, entrusting it only to his own descendants. In 1740 Huntsmann, a Sheffield watchmaker, succeeded in smelting steel in small crucibles, thereby obtaining a material far superior to those known hitherto.

After the middle of the century these discoveries were common knowledge, and the need for arms for the Seven Years' War stimulated the setting up of many new works, among which was that of John Wilkinson (1728–1801) at Broseley. Wilkinson is the main figure in the history of the technical application of iron: he helped Boulton and Watt to perfect the steam-engine, using his own patent for shot-boring and applying it to the cylinder of the new machine; he set up the first steam-engine in France and studied further systems of using cast iron for industrial purposes. On his death in 1808 he was buried in a cast-iron coffin and a cast-iron pillar was put up in his memory at Lindale.

It was probably Wilkinson who had the idea of the first iron bridge, built from 1777 to 1779 on the Severn at Coalbrookdale.[15] The design was prepared by the architect T. F. Pritchard of Shrewsbury; the semi-circular arch with a span of 30·5 metres was made by joining two half-arches made in a single piece and cast in Darby's nearby works (Figs. 25, 27).

In 1786 Tom Paine (1737–1809) – who later gained fame as a political writer – designed a cast-iron bridge for the river Schuylkill and came to England to patent it and have the pieces built at the Rotherham Ironworks. The separate pieces were cast at Paddington and exhibited to the public for a fee, but at the outbreak of the French Revolution Paine left for Paris leaving the bridge in the hands of his creditors; the pieces were taken over by Rowland Burdon, who built the Sunderland bridge over the Wear in 1796, with the very considerable span of 72 metres (Fig. 26). In the same year Telford built a second bridge over the Severn, at Buildwas, 39·6 metres long and weighing 173 tons, as compared with the 378 tons of the first bridge at Coalbrookdale.

The bridges of Paine and Telford were built with quite different methods from those of Wilkinson. The arches were made up of a large number of cast-iron pieces, fitted together like blocks of hewn stone; the greater resistance of the new material naturally allowed for larger spans, less weight – the blocks were in fact hollow – and much quicker execution, because the pieces arrived ready made from the foundry.

In 1801 Telford suggested replacing London Bridge with a single span bridge in cast iron, 183 metres long; the project was abandoned not because of doubts about its possibility or economic convenience, but because of the difficulties of compulsorily purchasing the land at the two ends.

During the first three decades of the nineteenth century, Telford used cast iron to build numerous bridges, sewers and aqueducts; with him worked Rennie and Rastrick. John Nash too (1752–1835) ventured to build a bridge for a private client; the bridge collapsed the morning it was finished but the client did not give up the fight, and Nash built him a second bridge, which was in existence until 1905. It has also been suggested that Nash had a part in the design of the Sunderland bridge.

Meanwhile cast iron was being used more and more widely in building; cast-iron columns and girders formed the skeleton of many industrial buildings, and made it possible to roof large spaces with relatively slight and fireproof structures. The plan for the cotton mill of Philip & Lee in Manchester, built by Boulton and Watt in 1801,[16] is well known.

A French traveller, visiting England in 1837, wrote:

'Without cast iron these well-lit and airy buildings, apparently so light and yet supporting enormous weights, such as the six-floor warehouse at St Catherine's dock in London, would be dense and gloomy prisons, with heavy ugly wooden stakes or walls with brick buttresses'.[17]

Nash used cast iron for the Royal Pavilion at Brighton in 1818 (Fig. 29); railings, grilles, balconies and ornaments in cast iron were also used ever more frequently in ordinary building and also in works of public importance, for instance in the Doric columns of Carlton House Terrace in 1827.[18] The cast-iron ornaments of this first period – the last decades of the eighteenth century and the first of the nineteenth – are often excellently made and far superior to the commercially produced ones of the period that followed. The best artists, Adam for example, sometimes supplied the designs.

All these uses were made possible by the extraordinary development of the English iron industry. On the Continent this industry was still in its infancy and throughout the eighteenth century the use of iron and cast iron was limited; there was nothing to compare to the numerous and daring English bridges, only a few modest works like the bridge at Laasan, nineteen metres long, built in 1796 by the Count von Burghaus, and several French garden bridges.

During the first years of the nineteenth century, the Napoleonic régime encouraged the French iron industry; between 1789 and 1812 iron production increased from 115,000 to 185,000 tons. It also became possible to build large-scale works in iron: the Pont des Arts, built between 1801 and 1803 by the engineers De Cessart and Dillon (Figs 31 and 32) and the dome of the circular hall of the Halle au Blé in Paris, built by François J. Belanger (1744–1818) in 1811.[19] Percier and Fontaine, too, like their English contemporaries, were not above using cast iron for many decorative and secondary purposes.

After the Restoration the use of iron was extended in France to a large number of building problems. In 1824 Vignon used iron for the roofing of the Madeleine market; in 1830 Lenoir built an entire Paris store in iron; in 1833 Polonceau (1778–1847) made the cast-iron Pont du Carrousel; in 1837 the wooden roofing of Chartres cathedral was replaced by an iron structure covered with copper. In 1836 Eck's *Traité des constructions et poteries en fer* appeared, and in 1837 Polonceau invented the truss that bears his name.

At the end of the eighteenth century engineers had the idea of suspension bridges with chain cables, since these were better suited than the cast-iron bridges to large spans and less resistent to dynamic stress.[20]

The first known example is a pedestrian footbridge over the Tees, 21·30 metres long (1741). There are several examples in America, dating from the last decade of the eighteenth century. In 1801 Telford had the idea of building a suspension bridge to Anglesey over the Menai straits, but this was realized only after the end of the Napoleonic blockade. In 1813 Samuel Brown, an English naval captain, built a 110-metre bridge across the Tweed which is regarded as the prototype of the European suspension bridge; between 1818 and 1826 Telford built the Menai bridge, 176 metres long, and in the same year a similar bridge was built at Conway, with a lesser span (Fig. 33). In 1823 Navier, amid many difficulties, built the Pont des Invalides; the year 1825 – with the Tournon bridge over the Rhône – saw the beginning of the career of Marc Séguin (1786–1875) founder of a firm which built more than eighty suspension bridges in France; in 1834 the Frenchman Charley completed the bridge over the Saane at Fribourg, 273 metres long and the longest in Europe up to that time; in 1836 Isambard K. Brunel (1806–59) built the 214-metre

**35**   *Paris, Jardin d'hiver at the Champs Elysées (from E. Texier,* Tableau de Paris, *1853)*

Clifton bridge over the Avon at Bristol, regarded as one of the masterpieces of nineteenth-century engineering (Fig. 34).

The glass industry made great technical advances in the second half of the eighteenth century, and in 1806 it was possible to produce panes of 2·50 × 1·70 metres. However in England – the main producer – the fiscal demands of the Napoleonic wars created serious difficulties for glassworks, and it was only after the peace treaty that production could really develop.

Between 1816 and 1829 consumption of glass in England increased from about 10,000 to 60,000 quintals, and prices had dropped; the use of glass for windows, and doors was now universal, and more ambitious uses were being tried out, combining glass

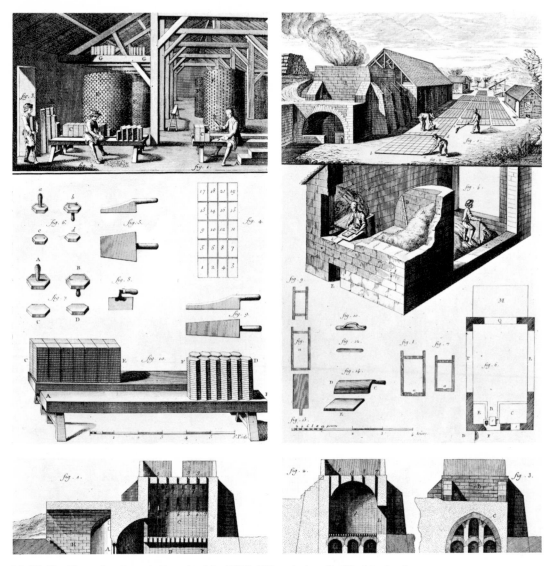

**36, 37, 38**   *Illustrations from the* Encyclopédie *(1751–72) under heading 'Architecture'*

with iron to make roofs that would let in the light.

Great iron and glass skylights were used in many public buildings, for instance in Vignon's Madeleine; in 1829 Percier and Fontaine covered the Galérie d'Orleans of the Palais Royal with glass, and this was to be the prototype of nineteenth-century glass galleries. Glass was used in the construction of some large conservatories: by Rouhault in the Paris Jardin des Plantes in 1833, by Paxton at Chatsworth in 1837, by Burton in Kew Gardens in 1844. Sometimes these conservatories developed into public gathering places, for instance the Champs Élysées in Paris (Fig. 35). The first railway stations needed huge glass roofs and the new shops, with their enormous windows, accustomed architects to planning walls entirely of glass.

Paxton's Crystal Palace of 1851 summarized all these experiments and started the great series of glass exhibition galleries which went on into the second half of the nineteenth century.

## 4 Technical advances in ordinary building

There is a good deal of information about larger scale buildings; but there is little documentation to help one gauge the techniques of ordinary building and in the dwelling houses that the industrial revolution was piling up around the towns.

Most writers on the subject state that building methods remained the same (in Lavedan's history of town-planning: 'while considerable technical advances took place at the beginning of the industrial revolution, there was none, so to speak, that concerned actual houses: the nineteenth century built like the eighteenth century and like the Middle Ages'[21]) and basing themselves on the descriptions of experts in public health and social reformers of the first half of the nineteenth century, they stated that the quality of the dwellings deteriorated as a consequence of haste and speculative demands. Both these commonplaces probably need amending.

The spirit of eighteenth-century enlightenment turned its attention to all technical fields of activity, independently of the importance that cultural tradition assigned to each of them. Famous architects concerned themselves with modest inventions, for instance Boffrand who perfected machines for slaking lime, and Patte who invented devices for diminishing the risks of fire. The *Encyclopédie* (1751–72) published extracts from articles about current building techniques to improve contractors' knowledge (Figs. 36–8).

The use of traditional materials, meanwhile, changed for various reasons. Bricks and timber were produced industrially, and were of better quality, while the network of canals meant that they could be transported anywhere at a low cost, thus levelling out the differences in supply from region to region.

At this time glass began to be used for windows instead of paper (at the end of the eighteenth century in France there were still guilds of *châssessiers* whose task was to cover windows with oiled paper)[22] and slate or tiles for roofs, instead of straw. Iron and cast iron were used wherever possible: for door and window frames, railings, balconies (Fig. 41) and sometimes also for the main structures.

The ceilings of ordinary buildings were usually supported by wooden beams, arranged in various ways (Figs. 39 and 40). J. B. Rondelet, (1743–1829) in his Treatise of 1802, compared ductile iron to wood, claiming that the former could be used in the place of the latter. However, iron in beams in rectangular sections could obviously not be a substitute for wood, because its greater strength did not make up for its greater weight. He continued: 'To avoid the use of thick bars, one might use sort of struts or falsework which would give the iron greater resistance, increasing its strength rather than its weight', and describes a system thought up by M. Ango, consisting of the association of two bars one slightly arched, the other drawn by a bow beneath it.

The commissioners appointed by the Royal Academy of Architecture to examine a floor 5·7 metres long and 4·8 metres wide built in this manner at Boulogne near Paris expressed themselves thus in their report of 13 June 1785: 'We found it extremely solid; it did not crack or shake, whatever force one exerted on it by jumping on it'. There are details about it in the *Encyclopédie* under the headings 'iron vaulting and ceilings'. They end their report as follows: 'It is therefore desirable that the process of M. Ango should be practised by all builders, so that a large number of examples should confirm the good opinion we have formed of the example we have described'.

Rondelet confirmed this opinion with calculations and put forward plans for a floor of iron filled in with brick, with a span of $6\frac{1}{2}$ metres: 'It is clear from these experiments that the calculations connected with them may be applied to all species of framework, for iron flooring, vaulting and other kinds of works' (Fig. 42).

In 1789 N. Goulet tried out a similar system in a house in the rue des Marais, mainly with the intention of avoiding fires: between the iron beams he placed small arches of hollow brick and replaced the traditional parquet floors with tiles. He also proposed that door and window frames should be of copper or iron rather than of wood.[24]

But the economic crisis that followed the French Revolution interrupted these experiments. Metals were unobtainable and in 1793 the architect Cointreaux presented an address to the Convention, asking that the use of iron be forbidden in building, except for fastenings.[25]

In the nineteenth century attempts were again made to use iron for roofing; but a satisfactory solution was not reached until 1836, when factories began to produce H-beams mechanically. From this moment onwards iron roofing gradually began to replace the old wooden structures.

We must now consider the movement taken by prices. The cost of building materials dropped almost everywhere, after the confusion of the Napoleonic wars, so that materials previously reserved for the building of the houses of the upper classes could also now be used for the houses of ordinary people. Workers' wages, on the other hand, were constantly rising; this fact, too, contributed to technical progress, since contractors welcomed any invention that might simplify the work to be done on the site and to save on the actual construction,

even if it meant an ultimate increase in the price of materials.

The houses of the industrial town were, by and large, more hygienic and comfortable than those which had housed the previous generation; the drop in infant mortality leaves no doubt about this. Naturally, things varied greatly from place to place and from period to period; as always, there were also uninhabitable hovels, vividly described by French and English inquiries between 1830 and 1850.

In evaluating these descriptions one must bear in mind that the worst buildings were almost always products of exceptional circumstances, as was the case in England during the Napoleonic wars. Furthermore if complaints about bad housing were more common at this time, it is not so much that it was worse than it had formerly been but that the standards to which it was now being compared were constantly rising. The rise in the standard of living and the new state of mind made intolerable hardships that had been accepted as inevitable just a century before.

One thing that emerged constantly from the inquiries drawn up by Chadwick and the Count of Melun was the conviction that the poverty noted was not an inevitable fate but one that could be eliminated by various means available. As de Tocqueville observed, 'the evil, which was suffered patiently as inevitable, seems unendurable as soon as the idea of escaping from it is conceived'.[26]

To form an impartial opinion of the houses inhabited by the first generation of the industrial age one must distinguish between the quality of the single building and the working of the district and town as a whole; early industrial building entered a state of crisis mainly in connection with town-planning, as we shall show in the following chapter.

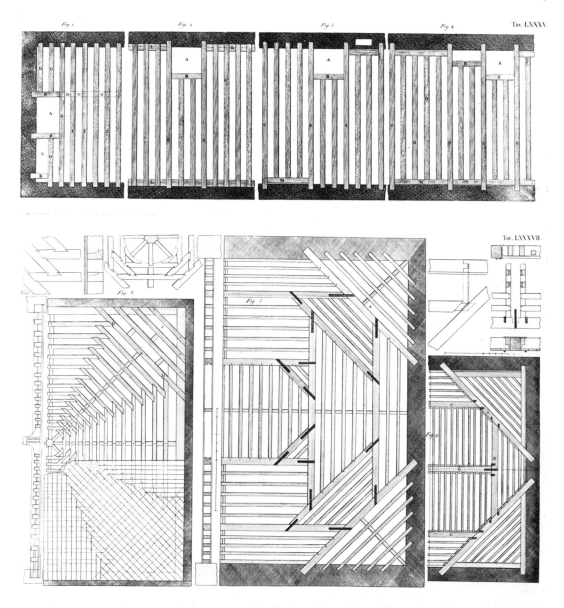

**39, 40** *Wooden roofing (from Rondelet, Figs 85 & 87)*

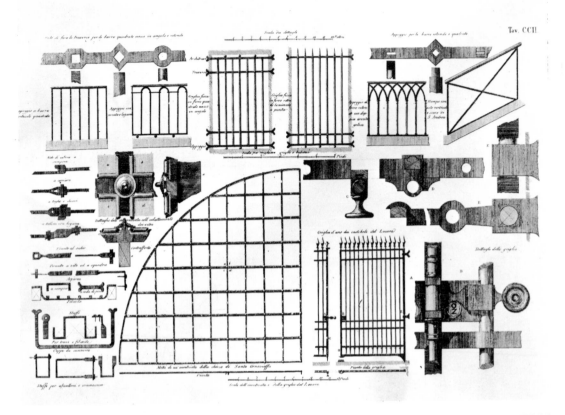

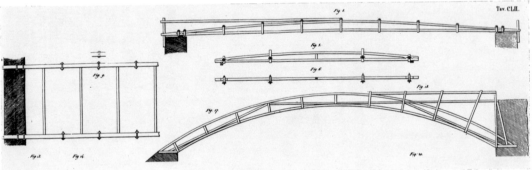

**41, 42**   *Ornaments and supporting structures in iron (from Rondelet, Figs 102 & 152)*

## 5 Engineering and neo-classicism

The period 1760–1830, which economic historians regard as the industrial revolution, corresponds, in art histories, to neo-classicism.

The connection between the two phenomena requires some further explanation. It is rightly said that this period saw the beginnings of the rift between architecture and the problems of constructional practice; the latter fell into the hands of a special category of people, engineers, while architects, once they had lost contact with the practical needs of society, took refuge in a world of abstract forms. The two phenomena therefore proceeded along similar lines, but without meeting, indeed they gradually grew further apart; as Giedion says, the result was 'the gap between science and its techniques on the one hand, and the arts on the other, i.e. between architecture and construction'. [27]

But the word 'classicism' covers a multitude of trends which had varying relations to the development of building techniques.

The spirit of the Enlightenment, applying itself to the repertoire of the Renaissance tradition, recognized in those forms two reasons for their validity: their conformity with the models of ancient architecture, Greek and Roman, and the rational nature of the forms themselves, in that the traditional architectural elements may be equated with certain constructional elements: columns to vertical supports, trabeation to horizontal rafters, cornices to roof projections, tympana to the space between two pitches of a roof, and so on.

Progress in archaeological studies made it possible to define the first relationship with the greatest possible precision: classical antiquity was no longer a mythical age of gold, set at the limits of time, but a historical period to be studied scientifically; thus traditional rules, elastic and approximative, could be transformed into exact references. But this same historical spirit showed that Graeco-Roman antiquity was an age like any

other, and the normative value given to its models was therefore jeopardized. Similarly technical progress made greater precision possible in constructional and functional discussions; the greater attention paid to these aspects led to the amending and limiting of the traditional rules; for instance, the column became permissible only if it was detached, the tympanum only if it actually had a roof behind it, etc. In the *Mercure de France*, 1754, Frézier actually concluded that cornices used in the interior of a church were an absurdity, because they should correspond to roof-gutters, and that 'a savage of any sense' (a typical character in such eighteenth-century disputes) would immediately notice this mistake: 'however little esteemed Gothic architecture may be, he would certainly prefer it, because it does not pretend to such irrelevant imitation'. [28]

The system of traditional architecture was not in a position to take such criticism, and the approximate correspondence between constructional and formal elements, hitherto taken for granted, could not stand up to analytical examination; the idea that classical elements were absolutely necessary could no longer be upheld.

In any case the claims to legitimacy of the ancient classical repertoire were now disputed; the persistence of classical forms, orders etc., now had to be justified in another way, and the possible lines of argument were these: either one had to resort to the supposed eternal laws of beauty, which acted as a sort of legitimizing principle in art (and incidentally it should be noted that explicit recourse to this principle was had only when public opinion was already doubtful about the traditional state of affairs); or, to matters of content, i.e. by claiming that art should inculcate the civic virtues and that the use of ancient forms would remind people of the noble examples of Greek and Roman history; or, more simply, to attribute to the classical repertoire a *de facto* existence by virtue of fashion and custom.

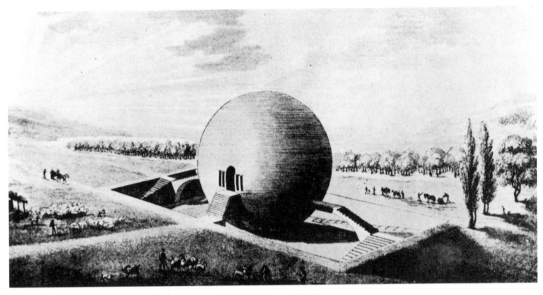

**43** *House for agricultural guards at Maupertuis (C.N. Ledoux, 1806)*

The first position, defended by theoreticians like Winckelmann and Milizia, was that adopted by the most intransigent members of the Academy such as Quatremère de Quincy, who was concerned with safeguarding the independence of artistic culture, and characterized the work of some of the artists most unswervingly devoted to the imitation of the ancients: Canova, Thorwaldsen, L. P. Baltard. The second was typical of the generation involved in the French Revolution, of David and Ledoux, who used art as a profession of political faith; and it produced a particular brand of inspiration which also made itself felt in others of their contemporaries, in Soane and Gilly (Figs. 43–5). The third position was based on the premises of eighteenth-century rationalists, such as Patte and Rondelet, and was theorized about in the new schools of engineering, by Durand in particular, and was adopted, basically, by the most successful designers of the Restoration: by Percier and Fontaine in France, by Nash in England, by Schinkel in Germany, as well as by a host of engineers with no artistic ambitions (Figs. 46–55).

The first and second formed a cultured and pugnacious minority, which attributed an unequivocal cultural value to neo-classicism; theirs could be called ideological neo-classicism.

But for the others, i.e. the majority of constructors, neo-classicism was a mere convention with no special significance but which made it possible to take for granted or to side-step certain problems, thus allowing for the analytical development, as the technical thought of the age required, of the practical, distributive and constructional problems; this could be called empirical neo-classicism.

While the former group charged the old forms with symbolic meaning, and were engaged in an ideological battle over and above practical reality, the latter used the same forms but talked about them as little as possible and, sheltered by this convention, concentrated on the new needs of the industrial town.

The battle between the currents of ideology was the most striking episode of the time, and is normally emphasized as being of prime importance, but it is not so as far

**44, 45**  *Berlin, Design for the monument to Frederick II on the Leipzigerplatz (F. Gilly, 1797)*

as we are concerned. Those who appeared to be the boldest innovators, like the 'revolutionary' architects Étienne Boullée (1727–99) and Claude-Nicolas Ledoux (1736–1806), did not in fact break the bounds of academic convention and did not represent the most *avant-garde* section of the thought of the time. The role that has been attributed to them, that of precursors of the modern movement, is based on abstract formal comparisons and does not stand up to historical investigation.

The limited influence their experiments had can also be explained quite easily. The theses of ideological neo-classicism, despite their rigorous and elaborate justifications, were in fact short-lived, because they could be attacked on the same political and philosophical terrain by other theses, and replaced by them. Just as Boullée interpreted the ancient world according to the secular, progressive ideals of enlightened philosophy, so Chateaubriand, who published his *Génie du Christianisme* in 1802, interpreted the Gothic in neo-Catholic terms and reappraised it by associating it with medieval mysticism: the fortunes of both styles

varied according to the popularity of their respective points of reference.

On the other hand, the association of classical taste with constructional practice, though founded on a conventional premise, had proved very lasting and has an influence even today, as can be seen in the works of certain great builders such as Auguste Perret and Pier Luigi Nervi. One of the reasons for this is a certain similarity in mental equipment: in fact the current methods of structural calculation often led engineers, then as now, towards symmetrical solutions which tend naturally towards certain typically neo-classical effects. This connection can be historically explained, because neo-classical sensibility and methods of calculation both derive, though in different ways, from the analytical mood of the period, but the partial and relative identity of scientific results and principles of the classical style is easily mistaken for a sort of preordained and absolute harmony. Throughout the nineteenth century engineers repeated, with Eiffel, that 'the true laws of force are always in conformity with the secret laws of harmony'.[29]

**46, 47** *London, Regent Street (J. Nash, 1817–19; engravings by T. Shepherd, 1828)*

The origins of this attitude are to be found in the engineering schools where most of the designers of the time were trained. At the École Polytechnique in Paris the architectural course was taught by J. L. N. Durand (1760–1834), a pupil of Boullée and spectator of the doctrinal battles of the revolutionary period; he made use of this complex, mainly theoretical heritage to transmit to the younger generation a system of rational and practical rules well-suited to the vastness of the tasks facing them.

The aim of architecture, he began, was to 'serve public and private utility, and the preservation and well-being of individuals, families and society'.[30] The means at its disposal were *suitability* and *economy*. Suitability demanded that the building be solid, healthful and comfortable, economy that it be as simple, regular and symmetrical in form as possible.

Durand criticized the traditional notion of the orders and confuted the theories of Langier and the treatise-writers who attempted to attribute a supposed universality to the orders, deriving them from the primitive hut or human body; 'one must necessarily conclude that the orders do not form the essence of architecture; that the pleasure one expects from their use and the decoration resulting from it, do not exist; that this very decoration is a phantom, and the expenses to which it leads, are madness'.[31]

But architecture could not be reduced to mere technicalities. Its beauty necessarily derived from the consistency with which the architect achieved his utilitarian goal, and true 'decoration' was the product of the most suitable and economical arrangement of the various structural elements.

So far Durand's programme (apart from the identification of economy with symmetrical forms) would accord even with modern functionalism. But he understood 'arrangement' in a narrow sense, as a combination of given elements. His method involved three stages: first, the description of

the elements, then the general methods for combining the elements with which to make parts of buildings and buildings themselves, and lastly the study of types of buildings. By 'elements' he meant materials with their various properties, and the forms and proportions that these materials assumed when used in building (Fig. 48).

The forms and proportions were of three types: 'those resulting from the nature of the materials and from the use of the objects in the building in which they are to be employed; those which custom has in some way made necessary to us, that is, the forms and proportions imitated from ancient buildings; those which being simpler and more precise, must gain our preference, because of the ease we have in grasping them'.[32]

Like the ancient treatise-writers, Durand drafted a series of constructional observations from which a rough description of the architectural orders can be deduced; but, unlike them, he was rigorously logical and realized that the constructional forms 'are not so firmly fixed by the nature of things that one may not add anything or subtract anything from them, and that, therefore, nothing prevents one from determining them by recourse to forms of the second type, drawn from ancient buildings and which are justified only by habit; and since these vary considerably in Greek buildings, imitated by the Romans and, in their turn, by the modern peoples of Europe, we are free to choose from among these the forms and proportions which, being more simple, are better suited to satisfy the eyes and mind, by benefiting the economy of the buildings'.[33]

Thus he produced a sort of selection of traditional forms, preferring the most simple and basic.

Finally, designers should use the classical forms, but concern themselves with them as little as possible:

'One should also pass quickly over the forms of the first type, deriving from

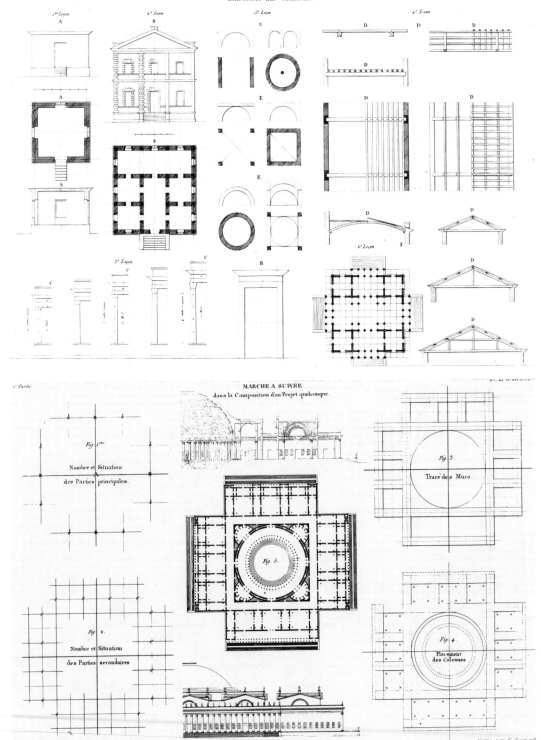

**48, 49** *From the printed text to Durand's course; the elements of building and the method to be followed in the design of any building*

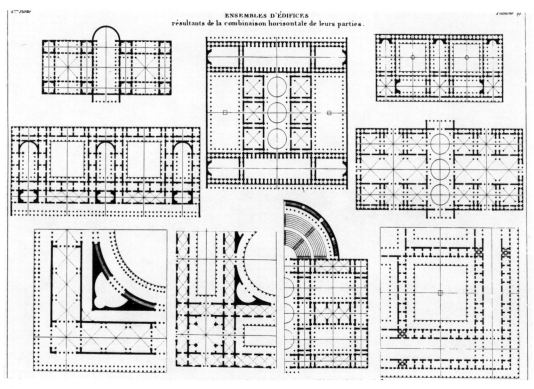

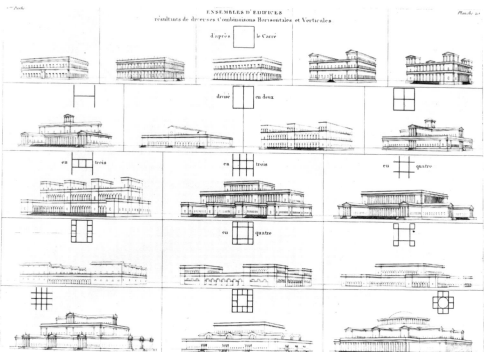

**50, 51** *From the printed text to Durand's course: examples of plans and perspectives obtained with the preceding method*

**52** *Paris, Rue de Rivoli (Percier & Fontaine, 1805)*

utility, although they are the most important, since they are born naturally of the objects and the nature of the materials used to create them; forms of the second type will be considered as purely local phenomena, destined only not to offend our habitudes, so that they would not be used for building in Persia, China or Japan, where they would go against the customs of the country; forms of the third type will be used because they favour economy in a large number of circumstances, and always facilitate the study of architecture. Finally architects will devote themselves mainly to the arrangement of parts which, when convenient and economical and attaining the end architecture sets itself, becomes the source of the pleasing sensation buildings arouse in us'.[34]

What then was this 'architecture' that was being taught to pupils at the Polytechnique, since the technical part had been absorbed into science and the arrangement of the elements was nothing more than a factor in external expediency? Durand makes of it a sort of theory of combination, an exercise in juxtaposing the given elements in every possible way, first theoretically, irrespective of their actual purpose, (Fig. 49), then according to the distributive demands of the various subjects.

The figures from Durand's treatise can be dated by their style, which conforms to the taste of the time (Figs. 50, 51), but they foreshadow the work of nineteenth-century engineers, all of whose typical features are already clearly delineated: the independence of the structural mechanism from the

**53**  *London, Houses in Park Square (J. Nash, 1812)*

decorative refinements and the preference for measurements in round figures and for elementary forms, which reduced the designer's authority to a minimum; both are to be found in the works of Paxton, Eiffel, Contamin, Le Baron Jenney and Hennebique.

Now that the works of these constructors have been re-appraised as constituting one of the sources of the modern movement, (and often excessively admired) it should be remembered that the qualities and defects of their works are closely interrelated and, furthermore, that they were doubly bound up with the work of the architect-decorators.

Both thought that, in design, certain aspects had to be taken for granted so that they could concentrate on others, just as in calculations a certain conventional value is attributed to some variables so that others may be derived from them.

The application of embellishments in certain styles – particularly of neo-classical ones, which were used the more eagerly precisely because the reasons for their use were less clearly felt – served not to resolve but to conceal compositional problems, to isolate constructional problems and to enable the architect to tackle them more easily.

This prevented any real tradition from emerging from the repeated use of new constructional processes. The phrase *functional tradition*, coined by the English who were the first to recognize the incidental architectural values of the nineteenth-century utilitarian buildings, is only half apt; these values emerged, so to speak, only when the designers were intent on some-

**54, 55** *London, Park Crescent & Chester Terrace (J. Nash, 1812–25)*

thing else, and mainly in isolated details of larger wholes, so that they remained fragmentary contributions that could never be added together to constitute a single system. Unity presupposes a synthesis and conscious scrutiny, while at this point habit interfered with stylistic cohesion, and imposed a synthesis that was external and conventional.

Thus, during the nineteenth century, engineers made advances in building techniques and prepared the means which were to be utilized by the modern movement, but at the same time they laid on these means a heavy cultural mortgage, associating them with something approaching indifference for formal definition and linking constructional habits to certain traditional correspondences with styles of the past.

These bonds could be broken only by a really great effort. The modern movement had a long struggle before succeeding, and for some time had to place particular emphasis on purely formal matters, an emphasis whose consequences are still felt today.

# two

# The age of reorganization and the origins of modern town-planning

**1  Political reforms and the first town-planning laws**

The fourth decade of the nineteenth century opened with a series of important political events: the July Revolution in France, Belgian independence (1830), the Polish and Italian risings of 1831, the reform of the English constitution in 1832.

Within the brief space of two years, the political system built up at the Congress of Vienna was shaken throughout Europe. In some places, for instance Poland and Italy, the old order could be restored, but in France the legitimate sovereign was driven out by a revolution which wiped out all the remaining structures of the *ancien régime*, and granted political power to the liberal bourgeoisie; in Belgium the successful uprising created a new state, with a constitution even more liberal than that of the French; in England the Whigs assumed power and undertook a series of substantial reforms in the make-up of the state. The solidarity of European sovereigns and rulers in attempting to maintain the *status quo* diminished, and the original rigid system, based on the principle of divine right, was replaced by a dynamic balance, based on the rivalry of conflicting interests.

In those countries that were economically more advanced, the political consequences of the industrial revolution made themselves felt soon after the event: they included the distribution of political power in ways that were more proportionate with economic power, and the adjustment of the administrative system to the altered make-up of society.

The English Reform Act of 1832, being the result of a bloodless compromise, did not appear to have the features of a revolutionary innovation, but precisely for this reason they were an eloquent witness to the extent of the industrial changes that had taken place.

The industrial revolution had produced profound changes in the distribution of the population over England. In the first half of the eighteenth century England was still basically a rural country, and even industry was carried on mainly in the countryside. As long as iron ore was smelted with charcoal, furnaces grew up wherever there were woods; the textile industry was based on work done in the home, and the peasants and their families took time off from the fields to work at spinning and weaving with hand-worked apparatus that they owned themselves or hired from their employers.

But when iron ore began to be worked with

pit coal, furnaces were concentrated in coal-mining regions; when, in 1768, Arkwright discovered how to apply hydraulic energy to spinning, and Cartwright how to apply it to weaving in 1784, these processes were carried on wherever running water could be utilized as energy; and when Watt's steam-engine, patented in 1769, began to be used to replace water power (between 1785 and 1790) they could be carried on anywhere, even if there was no river available; the network of canals built from 1759 onwards, by lowering the price of transport even for the heaviest and bulkiest of goods, meant that industrial installation was even more independent of outward circumstances.

The places where industries concentrated rapidly became fast-developing centres or, if they grew up near existing towns, produced an enormous rise in their population. It has been estimated that at the beginning of the industrial revolution about one-fifth of England's population lived in towns, and four-fifths in the country; towards 1830 the urban population was roughly equal to the rural, while today the proportion has been reversed and four-fifths of the English population live in towns.

But until 1832 the political and administrative patterns took no account of these changes. The electoral system was based on the old rural organization, and a large number of seats were allotted to under-populated boroughs, whose members were nominated by local landowners, while the towns that had sprung up or grown large because of the industrial revolution had no adequate representation.

The electoral law of 1832 abolished about two hundred such 'rotten boroughs' and re-apportioned the seats in a new way, allotting them mainly to the industrial towns; it also removed the ancient link between political rights and the ownership of real estate, thus putting industrialists and merchants on a par with landowners.

In this way political representation was put in line with the country's economic and social realities; furthermore, by giving the new classes a power proportionate to their economic importance, the electoral law opened the way to a series of reforms of all kinds which were in conformity with the interests of industry and the needs of the new society.

In 1833 came the first really effective factory law, mainly the work of Lord Ashley (later Lord Shaftesbury): working hours reduced to forty-eight for children under thirteen and sixty-five for young people under eighteen, regular meal breaks were fixed and a central body of inspectors was set up to ensure that these rulings were respected. The law was improved in 1842 forbidding the employment of women and children in mines, and in 1844, prohibiting the employment of children under nine in the textile industry; the successive restrictions on child labour were accompanied by extensions in compulsory schooling. Also in 1833 William Wilberforce achieved the abolition of slavery in all the colonies.

In 1834 the old Poor Law was reformed; the current system, set up in 1795 and known as the Speenhamland resolution, guaranteed everyone a certain subsistence level based on the price of bread; if their earnings were less, the difference was made up by a subsidy. Moved by radical theories, the reformers proposed to abolish the subsidy system gradually, but were also averse to fixing any minimum wage and preferred to keep the traditional workhouses, ensuring that conditions there were worse than those suffered by even the poorest workers in the outside world; at the same time they set up a central control body to supervise the working of the law and thus extirpate local abuses.

In 1835 elective municipal administrations were set up in the place of the old institutions with their feudal origins; every town thus had a democratic authority, which from then onwards was responsible for all public intervention in matters of housing, road maintenance, urban drainage and sewerage (hitherto shared by a vast number of special institutions) and, later, for planning in the real sense of the word; these administrations were subject to two complementary pressures: from the electorate below, demanding the fulfilment of local needs, and from the central authorities above, which concerned itself with the general interest. Municipal administrative life was thus forced out of its long period of ultra-conservatism.[1]

This period, from the 1832 Reform Bill to the abolition of the Corn Laws in 1846, has been called 'the Age of Reorganization'[2] by Hilaire Belloc. The conflict between freedom and authority which we mentioned in the Introduction was now right in the open. The Whig reformers, fed on radical ideas, swept away all traces of the *ancien régime* and the old restrictions which had hampered the freedom of the new enterprises; but at the same time they had to solve the organizational problems posed by the new developments and had gradually to adopt a system of rules suited to industrial society, which was finally to restrict free enterprise in a far more energetic and detailed fashion than the old system.

H. M. Croome writes:
'But the more the capitalistic technique grows up, the more complicated economic relationships become, the more people become concentrated in towns, the more each man's prosperity becomes bound up with that of others whom he may never have seen, the more necessary it is that each one's conduct of his life should come up to certain minimum standards. The town-dweller's health, for instance, is no longer only his own concern; in illness he is far more likely to infect his neighbours than the country-dweller in an isolated cottage. Social responsibility – the sense that "we are all members of one body" – becomes more important . . . and so we find, following on the development of capitalism a paradoxical situation; the individualist idea

destroys the old solidarity and makes for the growth of capitalism, and capitalism in turn, by increasing every individual's dependence on his neighbour, demands a return of that same solidarity . . .'.[3]

This period – and particularly the two decades between 1830 and 1850 – was the time when modern town-planning was born. Cohabitation in the industrial town had produced new organizational problems: the old instruments of control proved inadequate and new ones, better suited to the changed conditions, were evolved.

The towns grew from one year to the next, some reaching exceptional proportions: in a absolute sense like London (Figs. 56–8) which had one million inhabitants at the end of the eighteenth century and was the largest town in Europe – or in relation to their original size like Manchester, which had twelve thousand inhabitants in 1760 and about four hundred thousand half-way through the nineteenth century.

The new arrivals were mainly industrial workers; their houses, like their wages and conditions of work, depended solely on free enterprise and were kept at the lowest level compatible with survival.

Groups of speculators – the 'jerry-builders' – built rows of one-storey houses as they were needed, aiming simply at maximum profit: 'provided they would stand [for the moment] and that people who had practically no choice in the matter could be induced to live in them, nobody cared whether they were safe or sanitary, whether they had light or air, whether they were disgustingly overcrowded . . .'.[4]

There still existed numerous ancient institutions and bodies concerned with controlling building activities, drainage, supplies etc.; in London alone there were three hundred such bodies, but they were incapable of intervening effectively in connection with phenomena on this new scale for they were discredited and regarded with

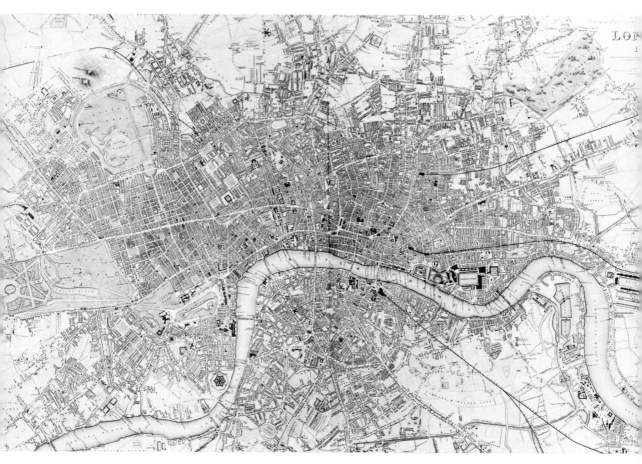

**56**  *Plan of London in 1843 (Bibliothèque Nationale, Paris)*

some suspicion by public opinion as remnants of the *ancien régime* and as stricken with the inertia that had affected all local administration until the law of 1835. Thus in practice there was no public control over private activities.

At the same time as it was renouncing its influence over the quality of private building, authority was also divesting itself of the landed property that could have enabled it to intervene indirectly and at least to control the positioning of the new districts.

As early as 1776 Adam Smith was advising governments to sell their landed property to pay their debts.[5] Thus in many towns building land fell into the hands of private speculators; speculative demands imposed their

laws on the town: densely crowded buildings, the growth of concentric rings around the original town or work centres, lack of open space.

Such a state of affairs was not necessarily detrimental to the single elements – houses, roads, factories – but it did give rise to serious overall difficulties which made themselves felt only after the towns had already grown to a certain size.

Many of the jerry-built houses were bleak and wretched; but the families moving into them at the end of the eighteenth century were probably coming from equally comfortless and crowded country dwellings which were also impregnated with the dust from the hand looms. All in all, the houses built at this

**57**   *View of London in 1851, published by Banks and Co.*

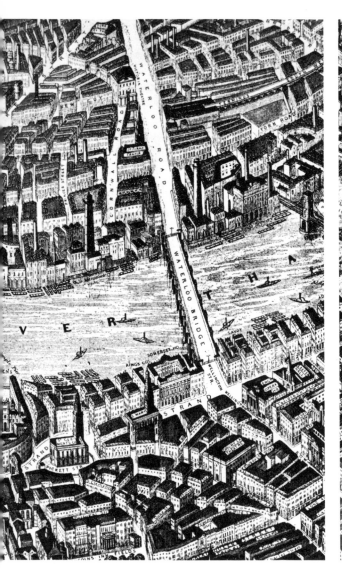

time were probably of a better quality than earlier ones, but such houses were a typical example of the Smithian logic of the age which, after having provided a relatively solid and functional type of building, believed it could continue to pile such buildings together in vast expanses without anything changing. It was precisely this matter of the relationship between the various dwellings that precipitated the building crisis in the early industrial revolution.

Today we would say that the planning rather than the actual building was at fault in these working-class areas, but the men of that time would not easily have been able to grasp such a distinction. Nonetheless, they had the practical results thrust before their eyes, and noses: insalubrious conditions, congestion and ugliness.

The lack of a rational plan for the disposal of solid and liquid refuse might go unnoticed in the countryside, where each house was surrounded by a space where rubbish could be buried or burned and where the more distasteful tasks could be carried out in the open air, but it was the source of serious dangers in urban centres, and became an ever greater problem as the towns grew. It was easy to get water from public fountains where houses were scattered in small groups, but difficult in the new districts which were so extensive and so densely populated; furthermore, industrial needs took priority over private needs. The activities that had formerly been carried out in the open spaces – movement of pedestrians and carts, children's games, the rearing of domestic animals and so on – did not interfere with one another as long as there was enough space, but did so intolerably if all had to be carried on in the narrow allies between the houses. The picture that emerges of these circumstances is hideous and repulsive beyond words, and in no way brightened by the presence of buildings or spaces that were not strictly utilitarian. Nor were these evils confined to certain particular parts of the town;

as in a large aquarium, the infection spread rapidly, and one did not need to be particularly altruistic to be concerned about conditions because the pollution and epidemics that resulted from them spread from working-class to middle- and upper-class districts in all sorts of ways.

Since the evils concerned the town as a whole, remedies, too, needed to be general, and had to be the concern of the public authorities, not the individual ones. Thus this situation, born of the faith in the absolute freedom of the individual and of the absence of traditional means of public control, finally forced the authorities to intervene in another way by placing new restrictions upon individual building enterprises.

But the need for the unified control of the space within which industrial society moved was further demonstrated, as persuasively as possible, by the developments of industry itself and above all by one fact which was particularly characteristic of the age of reorganization: the creation of the railway system (Figs. 59–62).

The first public railway was opened in England in 1825 and Stephenson's first engine ran to Rockill in 1829; soon afterwards the railway appeared in France too and in the U.S.A. (1830), Belgium and Germany (1835), Russia (1838), Italy and Holland (1839) and rapidly formed a network throughout Europe. Thus, in various ways, the need grew for co-ordination among the numerous building enterprises in the industrial town. One might say that the methods of modern town-planning were conditioned by these two facts: by the restricting nature of the new technical developments – particularly railways – and by the provisions demanded by the sanitary experts to remedy the inadequacies of the early industrial centres.

The growth of the first sanitary laws deserves to be described fully, because it illustrates how, setting out from the starting point of a particular section, a whole series of complex regulations was made concerning

**58**  *London docks (from J. Gailhabaud,* Monuments anciens et modernes, *1850)*
**59**  *Work on the London-Birmingham railway, 1836 (from S.C. Brees,* The Illustrated Glossary of Practical Architecture, *1852)*

**60**   *Underground railway in London (from* Universo illustrato, *1867)*
**61, 62**   *London, King's Cross Station (L. Cubitt, 1850–2); from J. Fergusson,* History of the Modern Styles of Architecture, *1873)*

every aspect of town life.

In England, as usual, the action of the authorities was preceded by that of certain private philanthropic associations, such as the Manchester Sanitary Board; quantitatively speaking, their action was negligible but it was nonetheless important because it aroused public interest and showed that the clearance of certain unhealthy districts was possible with the means available to them at the time.

In 1831, when the inconveniences of town-dwelling were already strongly felt, cholera spread from France to England. The following year Edwin Chadwick (1800–90) was appointed secretary of the Poor Law Commission; he played an important part in formulating the new law of 1834 and, through the investigations of the Royal Commission, was able to learn a great deal, and in considerable detail, about the lives of the poorer classes.

Chadwick's particular perspicacity lay in grasping the relation between social problems and the physical conditions of the environment; from now on, until his withdrawal from public life in 1854, he was the instigator of all the government's movements to improve the material conditions in the industrial town.

In 1838 the Assistant Commissioners' report on the conditions of hand weavers described as follows the new roads built in Bethnal Green in the last decades by 'the most unscrupulous private speculators':

'Many of them are the worst that could be imagined, having no common sewers. The houses generally are of two storeys . . . the foundations . . . were often laid upon the turf or vegetable mould, and have no ventilation between the floors of the . . . living rooms and the worst description of undrained soil immediately under such floors. The water . . . makes its way under the houses and, joined by the oozings of the cess-pools, frequently passes off in noxious vapour, and that through the sitting rooms . . .'.[6]

In other places however the picture is different:

'the houses of the best class of weavers [in Coventry] as compared with the cottages of agricultural labourers, are good, comfortable dwellings, some of them very well furnished;[7] [And in Barnsley] their cottages are built of stone for the most part, in the airy and dry situations for which the town and neighbourhood afford abundant space . . . The cellars in which they work are not more damp than is desirable for carrying on their trade. And even when the inhabitants are suffering from extreme poverty, their houses have a look of cleanliness and good order . . .'.[8]

Engels, in his book *Conditions of the Working Classes in England* of 1845, stresses the unwholesomeness of the buildings, the congestion in the towns and lack of any regulations concerning the use of land:

'Single rows of houses or groups of streets stand here and there, like little villages on the naked, not even grass-grown, clay soil . . . the lanes are neither paved nor supplied with sewers but harbour numerous colonies of swine penned in small sties or wandering unrestrained through the neighbourhood . . .[9] [In the old centre] confusion is at its height, because wherever the building programme of the previous age had left a scrap of space, other buildings have been added, so that there is no longer an inch of spare ground between the houses. [In the new districts the situation is even worse because] whereas before it had been a question of single houses, now every courtyard and alleyway was added as the builder wished, without any concern for any other. Now a lane runs in one direction, now in another; each one ends in a blind alley, or runs round an isolated block to bring the visitor back where he started from . . .'.[10]

Refuse disposal was one of the most serious problems:

'[In Bradford, in 1844, the rubbish dump] is in the most public part of town and in the centre of business, and consists of refuse, offal etc. from the butchers' shops, necessaries, ash-places and urinaries . . . This is private property and therefore the surveyors understand that they cannot cause the removal of these nuisances.[11]

In one part of the street [Market Street] there is a dunghill – yet it is too large to be called a dunghill. I do not mistake its size when I say it contains a hundred cubic yards of impure filth . . . it is the stock-in-trade of a person who deals in dung; he retails it by cartfuls. To please his customers he always keeps a nucleus, as the older the filth is, the higher the price'.[12]

In London there was the serious problem of the pollution of the river. There were a whole complex of old regulations and inspectoral bodies, but they worked according to antiquated criteria. For instance drains were conceived mainly as gutters to collect rainwater and it was forbidden to link them to houses or public buildings, though liquid could flow into them from cess-pools. But when private lavatories came into general use, between 1810 and 1840, this prohibition fell into disuse. All drains ran into the Thames, which also provided the city's water; thus London had a permanent cause of epidemics in its very midst.

Numerous methods of improving the situation were studied but to the uncertainty of administrative criteria was added that of technical solutions. Towards 1840 members of Parliament and the potential reformers were 'bewildered by the . . . conflicting opinions of the budding experts on the sizes and shapes of drains, the respective value of gulley-holes, grates and traps, and the mysteries of hydraulics'.[13]

In 1838 a violent epidemic broke out in a place known as the Wellington swamp. Local authorities appealed to the new committee on the Poor Law and a commission of doctors sent to the scene published a report which caused a tremendous stir and thoroughly aroused public opinion.

In the same year the 1837 law on the registration of births, deaths and marriages came into operation, which made it possible to classify deaths according to cause; thus it was possible to set the knowledge of isolated phenomena, as studied by the commissions of enquiry, within a correct statistical framework.

In 1839 the Bishop of London, too, was insistent that the investigations into sanitary conditions carried out in London should be extended to the whole country, and Lord Russell instructed the Poor Law commission to draw up its report which was published in 1842.

Chadwick, the instigator of the report, drew a horrifying picture of conditions in English towns:

'The prisons were formerly distinguished for their filth and their bad ventilation. But the descriptions given by Howard of the worst prisons he visited in England (which he states were among the worst he'd seen in Europe) were exceeded by every wynd in Edinburgh and Glasgow, inspected by Dr. Arnott and myself . . . More filth, worse physical suffering and moral disorder than Howard describes are to be found anywhere among the cellar population of the working population of Liverpool, Manchester or Leeds, and in large portions of the metropolis'.[14]

Meanwhile in 1840 a House of Commons committee published a report on the sanitary conditions in large towns and put the problem on a much larger scale by revealing the lack of all legislation on building and sanitation. A Royal Commission on the state of large towns and populous districts was set up to continue these studies and published its report in 1845, recommending among other things that, before sewers were planned, a

'relief and plan on a suitable scale should be drawn up; that street-paving should be attended to at the same time as the sewers; that local authorities should be able to insist on certain minimum hygienic requirements for houses, such as adequate sanitary arrangements in each apartment; that they should be empowered to force landlords to clean up unwholesome houses and to obtain a licence to draw up tenancy agreements; that they should be able to appoint medical officers; that they should be granted funds to improve and widen roads and open public parks, since the great towns of Liverpool, Manchester, Birmingham and Leeds, and very many others, have at present no public walks'.[15]

Thus the point of departure was sanitary problems, but the point of arrival was a complete programme of town-planning.

Parliament became involved in the problem in 1846; a new cholera epidemic hastened discussion of the problem and public opinion was exercised upon the legislators, but there were many difficulties to be overcome. A first law, put forward in 1847, was withdrawn and only the following year was the first Public Health Act passed, the basis of all subsequent legislation.

The 1848 Act did not include London, but at the same time the Metropolitan Commission of Sewers was set up, with extensive powers. The following year the supervision of this work was put in the hands of the first Board of Health, made up of Lord Shaftesbury, Lord Morpeth, Chadwick and Southwood Smith.

This committee had very broad powers. In 1851 it put forward the question of subsidized housing on a national scale, and succeeded in establishing that towns with over 10,000 inhabitants should be allowed to build economic houses for the working classes, but

with few results, because local administrators did not take advantage of this ruling.

In the same year the publication of census results made it possible to estimate the importance of the phenomenon of movement to the towns. According to official calculations on 3,366,000 inhabitants over the age of twenty, resident in London and sixty-one other towns, only 1,337,000 were born in the place where they were currently living, and of 1,395,000 Londoners, only 645,000.

W. Farr, a disciple of Chadwick's who entered the Registrar General's Office in 1838, wrote the following when presenting these facts:

'Hitherto, the population has migrated from the high or the comparatively healthy ground of the country to the cities and seaport towns, in which few families have lived for two generations. But it is evident that henceforward the great cities will not be like camps – or the fields in which the people of other places exercise their energies or industry – but the birth-places of a large part of the British race'.[16]

In 1866 a new and more progressive sanitary law was passed, and the Artisans' and Labourers' Dwellings Act reverted to the matter of popular housing, introducing the concept of compulsory acquisition with compensation below the market value, which from now on was to be one of the fundamental points of every town-planning programme. Further advances were made in 1875 and 1890, when the Housing of the Working Classes Act brought together all laws on sanitation and popular housing.

But it would be wrong to imagine that the gains implicit in these laws inevitably transformed working-class quarters. They became effective only after a period of adjustment, and after trained staff able to put them into practice had come into existence within public administrative bodies; the restrictions introduced by these laws made houses more expensive, and tenants who could not afford

**63**   *The city of London*
**64, 65**   *Working-class housing in London*

the increased rates were forced to move into new and unsound houses still further from the centres of towns; finally the regulations embodied in the first laws, being purely quantitative, remedied the more serious shortcomings in sanitation but made the streets of working-class areas, if possible, even more dreary and uniform than before and were responsible for the lifeless unlovely rows of houses found in many districts in the second half of the nineteenth century (Figs. 64 and 65).

Nonetheless, just as in politics the Reform Bill sanctioned popular initiative and the possibility of gradually adapting institutions to the development of ideas and material conditions, through parliamentary activity, so the first, imperfect building laws established the precedent for continuous control by local authorities and central supervisory bodies over the development and transformation of the cities.

The respective fields of activity of the two authorities, too, were defined from the beginning, local administrations concerning themselves with actual enterprises, central bodies with the legislative framework and definition of minimum and maximum standards: a distinction that is still valid for planning today.

In France events moved at a different rate, but moved in the same direction. Industrialization was slower, but continued during the Restoration, progressed faster during the July Monarchy protected by customs barriers, giving rise to the need for town-planning and to the usual organizational difficulties, particularly in the departments of the north. But political and administrative activity did not always follow the course of economic and social changes very closely; Louis Philippe's régime rapidly entrenched itself in conservative attitudes and alienated the educated classes; those who sensed the new problems of society that were emerging were therefore mainly found in the opposition and worked out imaginary and generous theoretical solutions but lost contact with the exercise of power and familiarity with practical difficulties.

Only during the brief period of the Second Republic, between the 1848 Revolution and the *coup d'état* of 1851, did the thought of these reformers have a direct influence on legislative activity; this was in fact the period of the most important legal and administrative innovations.

Here too the point of departure was the observation of the sanitary difficulties in the new urban districts. The most famous investigations, like Blanqui's report on the situation of the working classes in 1848 and the studies of the Society of St Vincent de Paul on the inhabitants of cellars in Lille, repeat almost word for word the expressions used by Chadwick and Engels; it is like reading a horror story in which the same situation occurs time and time again, for each time the door of a cellar is opened, in Lille or Manchester, the same scene appears yet again, like the whipping in Kafka's *Trial*;

'Many families in Rouen sleep all together on a pile of straw, like animals in a stable; their crockery consists of an all-purpose vessel of wood or cracked earthenware; the smaller children sleep on a bed of ashes; the parents and other children, brothers and sisters, stretch out together on this indescribable litter. [In Lille the roads in working-class quarters lead to] small courtyards which are used as both sewers and rubbish-dumps. The windows of the houses and the doors of the cellars open out on to the foul passages, at the end of which is a grid placed horizontally over drains that serve as public latrines, day and night. The dwellings of the community are distributed round this hotbed of pestilence, from which local meanness is pleased to draw a small income'.[17]

During the short life of the second republic Count A. de Melun, a member of the society of St Vincent de Paul, député of the Nord, managed to get the first town-planning law passed in 1850. This authorized the Communes to appoint a commission to indicate 'the indispensable measures to be taken concerning unwholesome houses and out-buildings that are rented out or occupied by people other than the owners'; the commission must include a doctor and an architect, and the landlord must be responsible for the work, if he had been responsible for the faults, or alternatively the Commune might take over from the landlord, compulsorily acquiring 'the total of the property included within the perimeter of the work to be carried out'.[18]

This last regulation was the most important, because it gave new meaning to compulsory acquisition. The Napoleonic law of 1810 and the law of 1833, promulgated at the beginning of the Orleanist period, regarded compulsory acquisition as an exceptional measure; the law of 1841 facilitated the procedure but established that an authority could avail itself of it only for the execution of *'grands travaux publiques'*, in fact it acted as a basis for the 1842 law concerning the new railway system. Now compulsory acquisition was contemplated for the improvement of residential districts and was concerned with the whole area covered by the works, therefore with matters that might fall into the hands of private individuals, such as new houses; it thus became a general instrument in town-planning, serving the authorities when they intervened in the transformation of the city, distinguishing between public and private needs.

This was the law that enabled Haussmann, shortly afterwards, to implement his grandiose plans for the transformation of Paris. But its application was carried out in an authoritarian political climate and with a spirit notably different from that of the republican legislators who had promulgated it.

## 2  The neo-Gothic movement

The year 1830, which marks the beginning of social and town-planning reform, also marks the triumph of the neo-Gothic movement in architecture.

The possibility of imitating Gothic rather than classical forms, had been present in architectural thought since the middle of the eighteenth century and its manifestations had hovered at the margins of the whole cycle of neo-classicism, implicitly confirming the conventional character of the choice of neo-classicism.

During the fourth decade of the nineteenth century this possibility developed into a full-scale movement, which was presented with specific technical and ideological justifications and was in opposition to neo-classicism. The outcome of this conflict shed decisive light on the foundations of architectural thought; for the new style neither replaced nor based itself on the preceding one, as had happened in the past; the two styles lived on side by side as partial assumptions and the whole scene of architectural history was soon to appear as a series of multiple stylistic hypotheses, one for each of the styles of the past.

In this way it is perhaps possible to see how the neo-Gothic movement was related to the structural reforms of this period. Reform began when the organizational problems arising from the industrial revolution emerged with some degree of clarity, and when it was completely obvious that the old rules of behaviour could no longer be retained. At the same time, in architecture, it seemed impossible to maintain the ficticious link with the classical tradition, and the conventional nature of a return to the styles of the past was suddenly made plain, although the problem remained in need of a solution that was not purely conventional.

In the eighteenth century the use of Gothic forms appeared as a facet of the taste for the exotic and had a strong literary flavour. In 1742 Langley produced a curious treatise

66   *London, Houses of Parliament (C. Barry, 1836)*
67   *Walpole's house at Strawberry Hill (1753; from J. Gloag,* Men and Building, *1950)*
68   *Sketch for a Gothic Church by K.F. Schinkel (c. 1814)*

**69** *Padua, Pedrocchino (G. Jappelli, 1837)*

called *Gothic Architecture Restored and Improved,* in which he tried to deduce a new set of orders from medieval forms, but his attempt had no influence. In 1753 the novelist Horace Walpole had his house at Strawberry Hill in Twickenham built like a reconstruction in the Gothic style, and in 1796 James Wyatt built Fonthill Abbey for the writer William Beckford, who wanted 'an ordinary building which should nevertheless contain some apartments safe from the inclemencies of the weather'.[19]

In France the so-called 'troubadour' style was equally charged with literary implications; in 1807 Chateaubriand embellished his house at Vallée-aux-Loups with Gothic decorations. Everywhere ornamental garden buildings, interiors, furnishings and decoration and even the odd façade were being designed in the Gothic style. Medieval styles were associated with the mood of Romanticism and were valued not as a new system of rules to replace the classical ones, but on the contrary because they were believed to be without rules and to derive from the supremacy of feeling over reason; for the moment, the Gothic appeared as a confused mass of turrets, pinnacles, wood carvings, shadowy vaults and rays of light filtering through coloured glass.

In the *Encyclopédie Moderne* of 1824, Debret praised the Gothic style, but considered it as 'the raving of a burning imagination which seems to have realized its dreams'.[20] Victor Hugo, in his novel *Notre-Dame de Paris*, of 1831, extolled medieval architecture and criticized classical monuments, but described Notre-Dame as an immense and gloomy cavern whose familiar spirit was the deformed Quasimodo.

Seen in this light the Gothic style soon spread to painting, scenery, publishing and interior decoration, but it appeared as a decorative image remote from constructional practice and inapplicable to large-scale building, while the association between the classical style and engineering was

well established and secure.

The experience which made it possible to introduce the Gothic into current design was the restoration of medieval buildings, which began in the First Empire and gathered momentum during the Restoration. In 1813 Napoleon – with disastrous results – had the interior of Saint-Denis restored so that his family tomb could be placed there; the same architect J. A. Alavoine (1777–1834) restored the cathedral of Sens in 1817 and that of Rouen in 1822.

This same period saw the beginning of the writers' controversy over the preservation of medieval monuments that had been deconsecrated during the Revolution and fallen into the hands of private individuals who were desecrating them at their pleasure. Victor Hugo wrote the *Ode sur la Bande Noire*; in 1834 the Société d'Archéologie was founded, in 1837 the Commission des Monuments Historiques; during the July Monarchy the best-known restorer was J. B. A. Lassus (1807–57) who in 1838 worked on Saint-Germain-l'Auxerrois and the Sainte-Chapelle and who, together with Viollet-le-Duc, was in charge of the work at Notre-Dame from 1845 onwards.

In these works of restoration the relation between medieval forms and constructional problems had naturally to be tackled. After 1830 this experience gradually passed into the designing of new buildings, and designers began to attempt not only outer decoration, or houses for *avant-garde* literary men, but ordinary houses and important public buildings.

In England many medieval buildings were restored and enlarged in this style, for example St John's College Cambridge (T. Rickman and H. Hutchinson, 1825) and Windsor Castle (J. Wyatville, 1826); and when the old Westminster Palace was destroyed by fire in 1834 the competition for the new seat of Parliament prescribed that the submitted designs should be in the Elizabethan or Gothic styles, as of course is the actual building designed by Charles Barry (1795–1860) (Fig. 66).

In Germany, after the works carried out on the completion of Cologne cathedral, Gothic buildings sprang up throughout the country.

In France after 1830, despite the resistance of the Academy, which was largely responsible for the commissioning of public buildings, many private houses and religious buildings were built in the Gothic style; sometimes the clergy positively insisted on Gothic designs, as did the Archbishop of Bordeaux who prescribed this style for all the works in his diocese; in 1852 no less than a hundred Gothic churches were built in France.[21] The church ornament industry took advantage of these preferences; about 1840 the Société Catholique pour la Fabrication, la Vente, la Commission de tous les objets consacres au culte catholique, was founded; this organization and many similar ones flooded France and indeed the whole world with an endless flow (which has still not entirely abated) of chandeliers, statues, chalices and Gothic church ornaments generally.

But the protagonists of the 'Gothic' controversy were intent on distinguishing their own artistic preferences from those of current vulgar trends. The movements for the re-valuation of the medieval, in England, was characterized from the beginning by a polemic against the Gothic objects that had already long been produced in 'those inexhaustible mines of bad taste, Birmingham and Sheffield';[22] we shall come back to this matter in Chapter 6.

One of the most common manuals, the *Principles of Gothic style* by F. Hoffstàdt, which was translated into various languages, begins with this warning:

'Now that the monuments of the Middle Ages are being studied with such care by scholars and artists, the value of Gothic architecture is emerging with ever greater force.

But interest is not limited to the simple recognition of its merit and admiration for the masterpieces of this art, which had been in decline, indeed in complete abandon, for so long; in the face of all antagonism, attempts have been made to revive it and to put it into practice. If in the opinions of connoisseurs few of these attempts have been successful, the reasons are easily explained.

Although we possess a quantity of precious collections, which offer a wide choice of the main Gothic monuments, when it is a question of executing some work in this style men have limited themselves to giving these various models the details considered suitable for composing a complete work, . . . without concerning themselves with the essential, i.e. the basic forms, which give this architecture its fundamental character.

Furthermore if one considers that from the earliest times the style of the ancients alone has laid down the law in the arts; that, despite the much-vaunted multiplicity of studies of the arts, and despite the revival of taste for the Gothic, the study of this style has been excluded from every institution; and, finally, that until now there was no elementary work that might serve as guide to artist or craftsman: without these means they would certainly have tended to repeat those errors which have been committed up to now in the constructions that have been built . . .

The present work aims to remove this stain and to fill up some of these very considerable gaps. Architects should not limit themselves to repeating copies of models of former times, but should also concern themselves with the product and buildings deduced from the principles on which the old masters based themselves, and which constitute the key to the study of this style'.[23]

**70**   *Neo-Gothic wallpaper (from A.W. Pugin,* The True Principles of Pointed or Christian Architecture, *1841)*
**71**   *Chimney in the form of a medieval tower (from R. Rawlinson,* Designs for Factory, Furnace and other Tall Chimneys, *1862)*

**72, 73** *Paris, Castle near Poissy (Bridant, 1840), and country house near Passy (from Normand fils,* Paris Moderne)

The spread of the Gothic style did not take place without provoking serious conflicts; Alavoine was prevented from becoming a member of the Institut because of his medieval restorations, and the study of the Gothic was forbidden at the École des Beaux Arts.

In 1846 the French Academy launched a sort of manifesto in which the imitation of medieval styles was condemned as arbitrary and artificial. The Gothic was a style which might be admired historically, and Gothic buildings should be preserved:

'But is it really possible to go back four
centuries and impose the style of buildings
born of the needs, customs and habits of
the twelfth century, upon a society which
has its own needs, customs and habits? . . .
The Academy agrees that, for whim or
amusement, a Gothic church or castle may
be built, but it is convinced that this return
to antiquated types will remain without
effect, because it is without reason. It
believes that, faced with this plagiary, this
mock Gothic, those who are moved by the
true, ancient Gothic will remain cold and
indifferent; it believes that Christian
conviction is not sufficient to make up for
the lack of artistic conviction; in short,
that for the arts and for society there is but
one natural and legitimate method of
production, and that is to be of their own
time'.[24]

Viollet-le-Duc and Lassus replied that the alternative facing the Academy, i.e. the classical style, was also the artefact of imitation, with the one difference that here the models were even more remote in time and made for other climates and other materials, while Gothic art was a national art. Ruskin, too, was involved in the dispute and wrote in 1855: 'I have no doubt that the only style proper for modern northern work, is the Northern Gothic of the thirteenth century'.[25]

Beneath this dispute, apparently so abstract, several important problems were hidden: theoretically the Academy was right in rejecting the principle of imitation, since in its eyes the classical style was endowed with the quality of actual existence, both in theory and in practice; this thesis was based on an apparently unbroken tradition, and on a series of applications which had led to an interpenetration and almost to an identification of classical forms with the elements of building and the processes of current construction. The supporters of the neo-Gothic were also right, again in theory, because they had revealed that the supposed identity between classical rules and constructional rules was based on pure convention, but in practice they fell back upon another convention, preferable to the first for external reasons, moral, religious and social.

This dispute produced various movements in European architectural thought. The persistence of classical forms could no longer be sustained in the old non-critical way, and the tacit association between engineering and classicism, when called upon to justify itself logically, was weakened and gradually slackened; while the new style inspired by the Middle Ages could not count on any recent constructional experiments to ensure its own contact with contemporary building technique. Thus in both fields the paths of architecture and engineering diverged still further.

While society was concentrating on satisfying the organizational demands that had arisen out of the industrial revolution, and while engineers were vitally involved in this process, providing sanitary reformers and politicians with the necessary instruments – a telling example was Robert Stephenson (1803–59), the builder of bridges and a member of the Royal Commission on large towns between 1844 and 1845, the very period when he was working on his most important work, the Britannia tubular bridge of 1849 – architects became detached from this reality and took refuge in discussion on trends and in the world of pure thought.

Yet on the other hand the neo-Gothic movement did contain within it certain germs favourable to the revitalizing of architectural thought. The neo-Gothic style could not be known, like the neo-classical, simply by appearances because it could not turn to a recent tradition, but to one that had to be resurrected from many centuries earlier. Thus the architects themselves had to reconstruct the 'principles', 'reasons', and 'motives' that stood behind appearances. In doing this they were forced to cross the borders that separated the various styles and to reflect on the basic conditions of architecture and its relationships with the political, social and moral infrastructures.

Also, the neo-Gothic architects were used to considering things in terms of overall symmetry and this was how they interpreted the medieval models. For this reason neo-Gothic buildings are more dissimilar from Gothic buildings than neo-classical ones from classical; irregularities were corrected, approximative imitations made exact. In particular these architects attempted to reproduce the undefined, repetitive and non-uniform structure of certain models, particularly English ones, by combining various individually symmetrical episodes; the result was a 'picturesque' type of composition (used mainly for small detached houses) still conventional in form but bearing within it the seeds from which, later, the basis of the revolutionary experiments of Richardson,

Olbrich, Mackintosh and Wright were to spring. Thus a tension grew up between the original and the copy which gradually exhausted the relationship between them and undermined the foundations of perspective on which all current visual habits depended.

For this reason medievalism marked, on the one hand, a further step in the process of the isolation of the artist and was the product of an élite inspired by literature, but at the same time it was the field of thought from which some of the most important contributions of the modern movement were to come: one has only to think of Morris, Richardson or Berlage.

The main by-product of the quarrel between neo-classicists and neo-Gothicists for the building of the time was a sense of perplexity. As long as there was only one style to imitate, the conventional character of that imitation did not emerge and the faithfulness to those forms was more whole-hearted. Now that there was a choice of so many styles, adherence to one or the other became less certain, more doubtful; style began to be regarded as a covering to be applied, as the occasion demanded, to an unvarying basic pattern, and there were indeed buildings entirely lacking in any stylistic finish; country houses in particular (Fig. 73), where the constructional elements were left brutally in evidence, and where no attempt was made to weld them into a single whole.

# three

# Haussmann and the plan of Paris

## 1 Why Paris was rebuilt

As we have said, the first stirrings of modern town-planning took place between 1830 and 1850, and not in architects' studios – where they were busy discussing whether to model themselves on the classical or the Gothic, and scorning both industry and its products – but amid the inconveniences experienced in industrial towns, through the work of the technicians and sanitary reformers who tried to remedy them. The first sanitary laws were the modest basis upon which the complex structure of contemporary town-planning legislation was to be erected.

For the moment, however, the reformers restricted their attention to certain sectors, and concentrated their activities on eliminating certain specific evils – the inadequacies of the sewerage, the supply of drinking water, the spread of epidemics. It was purely incidental that intervention in one problem brought other problems to light. The building of sewers and water mains depended on a modicum of regularity of plan and elevation in the new buildings; the maintenance of the drains entailed a new complex of technical administrative boards working for the Commune, and the right to demand certain services from landlords. The execution of certain public works, for instance railways

and roads, involved new processes of compulsory acquisition and a series of new technical instruments, among them very exact map-making.

The control of certain aspects of the industrial town involved others so that, inevitably, control gradually spread to new sectors.

The fact that these modes of operation did not develop into a single homogeneous system, and did not manage to affect the whole body of the urban organism, was due mainly to a political difficulty.

The reforms of the two decades between 1830 and 1850 were, on the whole, still dependent upon liberal thought; the need for state intervention in certain specific matters had been recognized, but the nature and extent of the duties of government and local administration with regard to social and economic life generally remained unchanged.

There was no thought of public planning, to co-ordinate and encourage public and private undertakings, and, therefore, there could be no real town-planning.

Those who were aware of the confusion of the industrial town tried to remedy single problems by following the usual specialized administrative channels (like Chadwick and the reformers we mentioned in the previous

**74**    *Caricature of Haussmann as 'artiste démolisseur'*

chapter) or radically criticized not only the town but the whole liberal society that had produced it, and set against this other model towns with model societies that could be realized only far from the existing towns (for instance, the socialist theoreticians to be discussed in Chapter 6).

The 1848 revolution interrupted both these lines of thought and action; the socialist left, after an attempt at coalition with the liberal left, was driven into opposition once more and organized itself on new theoretical grounds which refused all validity to the town-planning proposals of the previous generation.

In most European countries the 1848 revolutions and their consequences brought into power a new kind of conservative right: Napoleon III in France, Bismarck in Germany, the new Tories led by Disraeli in England.

The new right wing, authoritarian and popular, regarded direct state control of many sectors of economic and social life as necessary; it therefore carried out a series of reforms which in part continued those of the preceding two decades but which differed from them by their co-ordinated character and counter-revolutionary bias.

Town-planning played an important part in this new cycle of reform and became one of the most effective instruments of power, particularly in France.

The technical experiments described in Chapter 2, no longer hampered but positively encouraged by the new political climate, made rapid advances during the decades following 1848 and soon began to constitute a coherent system, firmly framed within current legislation and administrative procedure. Thus what we may term 'neo-conservative town-planning' was born, and brought about the reorganization of the European cities, (and of the colonial ones dependent on Europe) in the second half of the nineteenth and the first decades of the twentieth centuries.

The growth of these experiments in town-planning, encouraged by the political factors we have already mentioned, would not have been so rapid without the example of the *grands travaux* in Paris, promoted by Napoleon III soon after he came into power.

A series of favourable circumstances – the advanced nature of the experiment, the opportunity of making use of the republican law of 1850, the high technical standard of the engineers trained in the École Polytechnique, the cultural prestige accruing to everything that happened in the French capital, and above all the personal gifts of Baron Haussmann, prefect of the Seine from 1853–69, and responsible for the whole complex programme – made the transformation of Paris celebrated and influential. For the first time a complex of technical and administrative provisions, covering a whole city of over a million inhabitants, had been coherently formulated and implemented within a relatively short space of time. It is probable that neither the emperor nor the prefect realized the importance of the undertaking. Certain immediate problems – the need to maintain public order and to gain popular favour – had more influence than long-term arguments, building speculation was a more important element than was really desirable. Nonetheless, the problem of an overall plan for a modern city had been posed for the first time on a scale appropriate to the new economic pattern, and the plan existed not only on paper but in reality and had been considered in all its possible consequences, technical and formal, administrative and financial.

Haussmann's personality, like Chadwick's twenty years earlier, had been of primary importance in deciding the course of events: Baron Georges-Eugène Haussmann (1809–91), a professional civil servant, was prefect of the Gironde from 1851. Meeting him at an official dinner Persigny, the Minister of the Interior, described him as follows:

'It was Haussmann who struck me most of

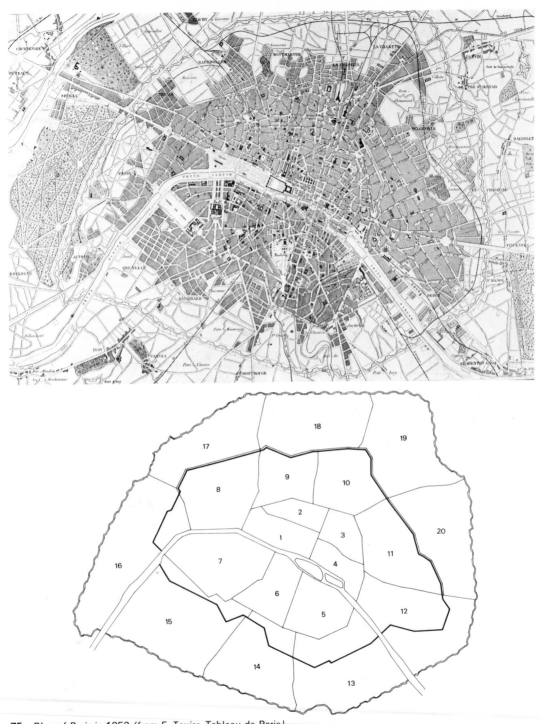

**75**   *Plan of Paris in 1853 (from E. Texier,* Tableau de Paris*)*
**76**   *The administrative limits of the city of Paris before and after 1859, with Haussmann's division into twenty 'arrondissements'*

all. Yet oddly enough it was not his intellectual powers, considerable though they be, but rather the defects of his character that impressed me. I had before me one of the most extraordinary types of our time: big, strong, vigorous, energetic and at the same time perceptive, astute, resourceful; this bold man had no fear of showing himself for what he was. He might talk for six hours without ceasing provided it was on his favourite subject, himself. His forceful personality rose before me with a sort of brutal cynicism. This is the man you need, I said to myself, to fight against astute, sceptical and unscrupulous men. Where a gentleman of finer, more able and nobler character would certainly fail miserably, this vigorous broad-backed athlete, bold and capable, able to counter expedient with expedient, deceit with deceit, would certainly succeed'.[1]

In his memoirs Haussmann tells us how, as soon as Louis Napoleon came to power, he had envisaged the possibility of being elected prefect of the Seine and considered the opportunities offered by this position. The minister had asked him what he could have made of the position, and he had answered:

'Nothing with the present prefect or any other political veteran; everything with a man with enough authority, for his position and in services rendered to the government, to undertake and conclude great works, in possession of the physical and mental energy to fight against custom, so deeply-rooted in France, and to tackle many wearisome tasks personally, let alone the public duties proportionate to the important role he would knowingly have taken upon himself. The prefecture of the Seine reminds me of the great organ of Saint-Roch whose whole register, according to legend, had never been heard because it was feared that the vibrations of the great pipes of the low octave would bring down the roof of the church. Since Napoleon absolutely no government has cared to have a true prefect of the Seine at the Paris Hôtel de Ville, one who could utilize the whole range of this terrible instrument. No-one has understood the advantages that might be derived from that position if it had been occupied with sufficient authority, being honoured personally by the good faith of the head of State'.[2]

Louis Napoleon in his turn built his power on the fears aroused by the socialist revolution of February 1848 and, backed by the army and popular prestige, took up his position against the intellectual bourgeoisie and working-class minority. He thus had a direct interest in carrying out public works, neglected by previous governments, in Paris, to shore up his popularity and make further revolutions more difficult by destroying the narrow medieval streets and replacing them with straight spacious thoroughfares well-suited to troop movements.

Today this second reason may seem out of all proportion to such costly undertakings, but it was perfectly comprehensible if one considers the monarch's anxiety about the recent events of July 1830 and February and June 1848, not to mention his memories of the great Revolution. At every political crisis revolutionary movements originated in the quarters of the old town, the same streets provided the rebels with both defensive positions and offensive means. One need only read this proclamation of 1830 in which the temporary government puts forward means of opposition to regular troops with the coolness of a factory communiqué:

'Frenchmen, all means of defence are legitimate. Tear up the paving stones and scatter them at distances of about a foot to slow down the march of cavalry and infantry, carry as many paving stones to first, second and upper floors, at least twenty or thirty stones to each house, and wait calmly for the battalions to engage in

**77**  *Plan of Paris in 1873 (from A. Joanne,* Paris illustré*)*
**78**  *Diagram of Haussmann's 'percements'*

action in the middle of the road before dropping them down. Let all Frenchmen leave doors, corridors and hallways open, for aid and refuges for our marksmen and so as to be able to help them. The inhabitants must remain calm and not be alarmed. The troops would never dare enter the houses, knowing they would find death there. It would be advisable that someone should remain at every door, to safeguard the entrance and exit of our marksmen. Frenchmen, our safety lies in our own hands; shall we give it up? Which of us does not prefer death to servitude?'

The same methods had been used successfully in the February revolution of 1848, and had hampered the repression of the workers' revolt of June in the same year; also, the emperor had noted the convenience of the *grands boulevards* (Fig. 79) for attacking the mob with bursts of rifle-fire after the *coup d'état* of 1851. It was natural that rulers should be concerned to eliminate, once and for all, the possibility of popular barricades.

Side by side with those political preoccupations were social and economic motives that worked in the same direction. Paris had about half a million inhabitants at the time of the Revolution and First Empire, but under the Restoration and even more under the July Monarchy it began to expand (even if not with the incredible speed of London) and by the time of the accession of Napoleon III it had about one million inhabitants. The centre of the old town was even more plainly incapable of bearing the weight of an organism that had grown so much; the streets, medieval and Baroque, were inadequate for the traffic, the old houses were ill-suited to the sanitary requirements of the industrial city and the concentration of functions and interests in the capital raised the price of building land to such an extent that a radical transformation was inevitable.

As it happened, just at that moment a prefect of exceptional energy and ambition

arrived at the Hôtel de Ville, a man capable of reconciling political and economic motives, creating a complex of organizations that would ensure these *travaux* a certain independence, and of overcoming the foreseeable difficulties by asserting, as a decisive factor, his individual gifts of astuteness and courage.

## 2 Haussmann's achievements

Once established in the Hôtel de Ville, Haussmann reorganized the technical departments according to modern criteria, appointing at their head first-class engineers already experienced in other positions there. After having thus ensured that he had a capable and productive executive instrument, he personally tackled the administrative bodies and civil servants, who were supported by the emperor, making them feel the full weight of his position and completely subjecting them to his own plans.

The works carried out by Haussmann during his seventeen years of power can be divided into four categories:

Firstly, the work on the roads: the building up of Paris outskirts with new networks of roads and the opening up of new thoroughfares in the old districts, rebuilding the houses along them.

The old Paris had 384 kilometres of road in the centre and 355 on the outskirts; Haussmann opened up 95 kilometres of road (doing away with 49 kilometres) in the centre, and 70 kilometres on the outskirts (doing away with 5). The medieval nucleus was cut across in all directions and many of the old districts were pulled down, particularly the dangerous ones in the east, the hotbeds of all the revolts. In practice Haussmann superimposed upon the body of the old city a new system of straight wide roads (Fig. 78) forming a coherent system of communication between the main centres of city life and the railway stations and at the same time providing efficient routes for traffic, crossings and lines of defence; he avoided destroying the most important monuments, but isolated them and used them as focal points for the great new stretches of road.

Building along the new roads was controlled more strictly than in the past: in 1852 it became obligatory to seek permission to build there; in 1859 the old Paris building regulation of 1783–4 was modified and new ratios between the height of the houses and width of the streets were fixed (on streets of twenty metres or more the height had to be equal to the width, on narrower roads it could be greater, up to one and a half times the width) while the pitch of the roofs was limited to 45°.

Bearing in mind the planning criteria, Haussmann's works appear as the continuation, on a larger scale, of the Baroque complexes, based on similar concepts of regularity, symmetry, the *culte de l'axe*. But Haussmann's works resemble those of Mansart and Gabriel as neo-classical buildings resemble those of the classical tradition; apparently nothing is changed, yet the traditional formal repertoire has been used in a conventional way to cover up new solutions dictated by changed circumstances. In this case the new buildings had to be considered within the framework of the technical and administrative transformations now to be discussed.

Secondly, there were the building programmes carried out directly by the prefecture and other public bodies.

The prefect concerned himself with the construction of the public buildings in the new quarters and in the old ones involved in the transformations mentioned above: schools, hospitals, prisons, administrative offices, libraries, colleges, markets. The State, on the other hand, took charge of military buildings and bridges.

For the design of these buildings – illustrated in 1881 in a large publication by Narjoux – the most famous architects of the time were employed, from Labrouste to Baltard, Vaudremer, Hittorf. The stylistic repertoire of eclectic culture was often applied with discretion, particularly by rationalists such as Labrouste and Vaudremer; they managed to define a complete scale of distributive types, to be copied throughout Europe.

The problem of accommodation for the poorer classes, and the need for State intervention, to guarantee certain minimum distributive and hygienic requirements independently of the financial resources of those who were going to live there, now began to play a part (even if not as great a part as the needs demanded) in political and administrative practice.

Louis Napoleon, even as President of the Republic, concerned himself personally with the problem, approved an allocation of 50,000 francs and made a first group of popular houses in the rue Rochechouart, the Cité Napoléon. In 1852, as soon as he was elected emperor, he set aside ten million francs and financed two further complexes, at Batignolles and Neuilly. But these isolated demonstrations of patronage did not noticeably change the situation of working-class housing in Paris, ruled as it was by private speculation which the emperor's power favoured, in other fields, in every way.

The work for the creation of public parks deserves separate discussion. Until now Paris had had only the parks built under the *ancien régime*: the Jardins des Tuileries and the Champs Élysées on the right bank, the Champ de Mars and the Luxembourg on the left bank. Haussmann began to lay out the Bois de Boulogne, the former royal forest situated between the Seine and the western fortifications; because of its position and proximity to the Champs Élysées, this park soon became the centre of the most elegant life in the capital.

On the other side of the city, at the confluence with the Marne, the Bois de Vincennes was laid out, for the eastern parts of town, to emphasize the Emperor's concern for the working classes. To the north and

**79, 80**   *Paris, Boulevard du Temple and Parc Monceau (from A. Joanne,* op. cit.*)*

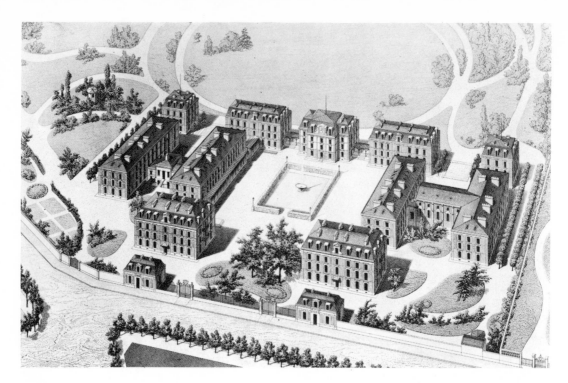

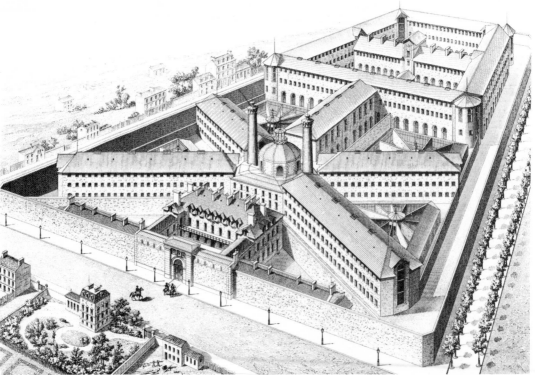

**81, 82** *Paris, Old People's Home of Ste-Perine* (*Ponthieu, 1861*) *and the prison of rue de la Santé* (*Vaudremer, 1864; from F. Narjoux,* Paris, Monuments élevés par la ville, 1850–80, *1881*)

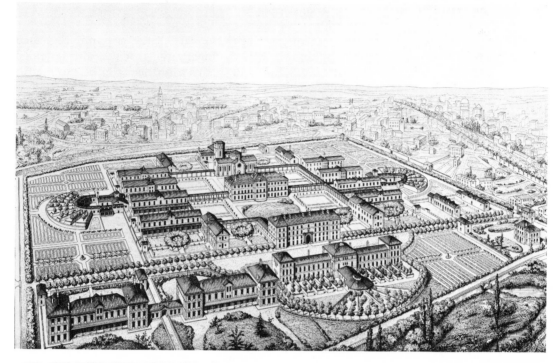

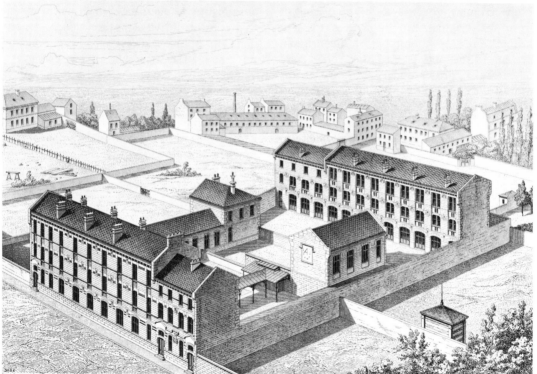

**83, 84** *Paris, Lunatic asylum of Ste-Anne (Questel, 1861) and École Voltaire in rue Titon (Narjoux, 1881;* *from Narjoux,* op. cit.*)*

south, just inside the fortifications, two smaller parks were opened, the Buttes-Chaumont and the Parc Montsouris.

Here Haussmann had an absolutely first-class collaborator, Alphonse Alphand (1807–91); in his memoirs he writes of the parks he made with particular satisfaction, and it is this aspect of his work possibly that seems his most valid claim to fame today.

Haussmann also modernized the water and drainage systems in the old part of Paris.

As far as the water system was concerned, he had an invaluable collaborator in the engineer François Eugène Belgrand (1810–78), an obscure provincial official who was called upon to design the new water-mains and systems for drawing water from the Seine, bringing the water supply from 112,000 cubic metres a day to 343,000, and the system of water-mains from 747 to 1,545 kilometres (Figs. 85 and 86). Belgrand also built the new sewer system, increasing it from the original 146 kilometres to 560, keeping only 15 kilometres of the original system, while outlets into the Seine were taken much further downstream, by means of main sewers. The lighting system was increased three-fold, from 12,400 to 32,000 gas jets. Public transport services were organized, in the hands of a single society in 1854, the Compagnie Générale des Omnibus, and in 1855 a regular public carriage service was set up. In 1866 a site at Méry-sur-Oise was acquired for a new cemetery.

Finally, Haussmann modified the administrative pattern of the capital. In 1859 eleven communes round Paris, lying between the boundaries of the *octroi* and the Thiers fortifications – Auteuil, Passy, Batignolles, Montmartre, La Chapelle, la Villette, Belleville, Charonne, Bercy, Vaugirard and Grenelle – became part of the city of Paris; the twelve traditional *arrondissements* became twenty, and a part of the administrative functions was taken from the jurisdiction of the central administration and put into the hands of the *mairie* of each *arrondissement*.[3]

The boundary of the city thus coincided with the fortifications; it was also intended to add to this a further strip of 250 metres outside them, for a fast ring-road, but it proved impossible to prevent speculative building on this site. Haussmann's thoroughfares were made possible by the law of 13 April 1850, which legalized compulsory acquisition not only of the areas necessary to the roads themselves, but also of the property that fell within the circuit of the works; on 23 May 1852 a decree of the Senate modified the procedure established in 1841, allowing compulsory acquisition to be effected by the executive without recourse to the courts.

The first law was the product of the revolutionary climate of the Second Republic, while the second reflected the new authoritarian mood which was the final outcome of the February revolution. Outwardly the State's decision facilitated administrative planning, but in fact it meant that administrative acts were closely dependent on political directives, i.e. upon the interests of the social classes in power.

These interests tended to limit the interference of the authorities in economic questions; for this reason the laws were interpreted ever more restrictively, seriously hampering the execution of plans (the progress of town-planning is a faithful mirror of the contradictions and ambiguities of the political system of the Second Empire).

After much debate the Council of State decided, on 27 December 1858, that land suitable for building, once acquired and built upon according to the plans drawn up, should be restored to its original owners, i.e. that the increase in value brought about by the Communal works should be pocketed by the landlords themselves, rather than by the Commune.

Haussmann complained that this decision was unjust, but the jurisprudence of the time was all against him. Because of this decision, the city of Paris alone had to bear the expense of Haussmann's works, without being able

**85, 86** *Paris, Wells at Passy and steam engines at Chaillot (from A. Joanne,* op. cit.*)*

to recover anything from the landlords who were the beneficiaries. Nevertheless the productive nature of the works still made itself felt, and Haussmann was able to obtain the necessary funds almost without recourse to the State, by drawing upon free credit available.

In fact the public works not only increased the prices of the surrounding land but had an influence on the whole city, encouraging growth and increasing the overall income. These effects alone ensured the Commune a steady increase in ordinary revenue and made it possible to borrow large sums from banking houses just as any private concern would have done. From 1853 to 1870

Haussmann spent about two and a half milliard francs on public works, received only a hundred million from the State and did not have to impose new taxes or increase existing ones.[4]

During this same period the population of Paris increased from one million two hundred thousand to almost two million; while about 27,000 houses were demolished, about 100,000 new ones were built (and 4·46 per cent of the cost went back into the Commune in the form of taxes); the income per head of the French citizen increased from about 2,500 to about 5,000 francs and the income of the Commune of Paris, according to Persigny, from twenty to two hundred million

**87, 88, 89**  *Paris, The area of the Étoile*

francs. It is therefore evident that the city itself paid for its new lay-out.

If the operation could be considered satisfactory as far as the overall budget was concerned, the same could not be said of the distribution of this wealth. The mechanism set up for compulsory acquisition allowed landlords to pocket the increased value and produced, in practice, a transference of money from the taxpayers to the owners of building land. Furthermore, the amounts of compensation for compulsory acquisition had been fixed by a committee of landowners, and was disproportionately high, so that compulsory acquisition was actually hoped for and sought after as a source of wealth.

### 3 The Haussmann controversy

There has been much discussion as to whether Haussmann was the real author of the transformation of Paris and whether his action followed a comprehensive plan. These two queries can be answered in the affirmative if Haussmann's work is considered in the right way.

Haussmann writes that shortly after he was appointed prefect of the Seine, after an invitation to lunch, the Emperor showed him a plan of Paris 'on which he himself had traced in blue, red, yellow and green, according to the degree of urgency, the new roads he planned to have made'[5] and he never failed to claim that the Emperor himself was the author of the various projects, while he himself remained a mere collaborator. Often these affirmations are taken literally and Napoleon III is acclaimed as the true author of the plan, but it is probable that Haussmann was tactfully exaggerating, to cover his own undertakings with the emperor's name; he himself revealed the nature of this collaboration when writing about his decisive encounter with the Council of State on the interpretation of the laws of compulsory acquisition:

'In vain I have indicated to the Emperor the consequences of this law. The Emperor did not wish to put M. Baroche [president of the Council] in the wrong . . . Furthermore, his Majesty attached only slight importance to problems of administrative procedure until they were translated into visible facts'.[6]

But in the works in Paris these 'visible facts' counted much less than invisible ones; administrative action was the most important aspect of this undertaking and Haussmann performed it alone, warding off both the Emperor and the representative bodies.

With regard to the unity of conceptions, too, appearance must be distinguished from reality. As is well known, Haussmann put forward his programme in three successive stages, the famous *trois réseaux*. It has been observed that most of the work of the first *réseau* had already been planned before Haussmann's arrival on the scene, and that the second and third are a series of unco-ordinated measures; but it would be more exact to say that this method of presentation was in fact a financial device to obtain the necessary funds more easily and that Haussmann had had a coherent plan from the beginning, to which he remained faithful despite all obstacles. This programme was not laid down in the form of a plan, but here lay the modernity and importance of Haussmann's achievement. He did not intend to push the city, by love or force, into the narrow framework of a pre-arranged plan. Others before him had tried to design an ideal Paris; he did much more: in 1859, after the addition of the eleven peripheral Communes, he set up the Office du Plan de Paris, headed by M. Deschamps; year by year this office mediated between work carried out and future projects, taking into account changing circumstances; the machinery survived the death of Haussmann and the Second Empire, ensuring the coherence of Parisian planning for the whole of the second half of the nineteenth century.

Haussmann's plan is interesting today mainly as the first example of action sufficiently sweeping and energetic to follow the movement of the transformations that were already taking place in a great modern city and to regulate them firmly rather than submit passively to them. But at the time this method of procedure was regarded rather as an act of tyranny, and Haussmann was violently criticized on all sides by political and cultural forces.

The liberals reproached him mainly with the unscrupulousness of financial methods, and indeed the functioning of the Caisse des Travaux de Paris, set up in 1858 to pay for the expenses of the second *reseau*, did border on the illegal according to the laws of the time, since it allowed the prefect to take on commitments without any control by central authorities. But the same protests were raised when Haussmann maintained the need to give the benefit of the increased value of the building land along the new roads to the public exchequer; Haussmann might have been wrong in law, but he understood a basic need of modern town-planning and found himself in a position well in advance of his critics.

Intellectuals and artists reproached him with the destruction of the old Paris and with the tastelessness of his new buildings, though without going beyond the usual aestheticist laments based on the dislike of all industrial civilization; here at least Haussmann offset the disappearance of a few picturesque sights with technical and sanitary improvements.

Haussmann appears as less cultured, but more broad-minded and modern than most of his critics. He had an instinctive ability to understand and keep close to the reality of his time, and, therefore, to modify it with such success; the society of the Second Empire found the perfect setting in his schemes, and the echo of his harmony between planning and reality, reached a century ago, can still be felt today, in the fascination and liveliness of the main Paris streets.

Haussmann's ability to project himself whole-heartedly into the reality of his time is also the key to the understanding of both the tremendous success of his methods and their numerous imitations, and the discussions which are still waged over his work and personality.

Haussmann's plan worked well for many decades, because of the plentiful margins allowed by his use of space, but finally it proved inadequate to the growing needs of the metropolis; it was then that his impressive plan revealed its absolute lack of flexibility and its extraordinary resistance to any change; it made Paris the most modern city in the nineteenth century but, in the twentieth, the most congested and difficult to plan.

Basically, Haussmann's understanding of the industrial city took in only its static and not its dynamic aspects; he thought that Paris could be 'laid out' once and for all, and that its lay-out should be sealed with the usual criteria of geometrical regularity, symmetry and elegance. He was particularly delighted at having removed the random element from the old quarters and having replaced it with regular, precise outlines, definitive and unvariable.

Nowadays we regard this as the weakest aspect of his work, since it indicates a passive acceptance of the conventions of academic culture; what is far more interesting is that Haussmann, applying these conventions in new circumstances, did, in fact, move away from traditional models and anticipated a new methodology, however unwittingly.

Though he was naturally authoritarian, Haussmann could not behave like the Baroque town-planners, who carried out their plans with absolute regularity by profiting from the absolute power of their employers; he was acting under the control of Parliament and the municipal council, he was handling public money that had to be accounted for to the central administrative

**90** *Paris, Avenue des Champs Élysées from the Arc de Triomphe*

**91**   *Paris, St-Lazare*

bodies and he had to submit quarrels with private individuals to an independent magistrature; in short, he had to reckon with the separation of powers typical of a modern state, even if the executive was preponderant. Furthermore, political power no longer coincided with economic power and Haussmann, basically, was using not his own money but was organizing private funds for use in a unified programme. For all these reasons his plan does not emerge as a definitive solution but as a continuous process of encouragement and co-ordination of the numerous forces at work in a variety of changing ways on the fabric of the city; thus the similarity between architecture and town-planning ceased, for they were no longer active on the same level, differing only in scale, but on two different interrelated levels.

A similar discussion would also be possible about the formal results of Haussmann's plan; he accepted unquestioningly the traditional precepts of symmetry and regularity, was proud of having provided a monumental focal point for every new road and was eager to impose uniform architecture along the most important roads and squares, attempting to conceal irregularities of layout like those at the Étoile.

But the scale of the street systems in Paris led him to apply the traditional precepts of symmetry and regularity on a scale so large as often to destroy the uniform effect he hoped to gain. The boulevard de Strasbourg, ending at the Gare de l'Est, was 2·5 kilometres long and the architectural backdrop is almost invisible from the other end; at the Étoile, Hittorf's twelve symmetrical façades were each 250 metres apart and they were not large enough to close in the immense void and give an impression of immediate unity; along the rue de Rivoli the elements of Percier and Fontaine's décor were repeated over so great a length that the eye no longer discerned the proportions between the length

**92** *Typical façades in a Paris street (J.F.J. Lecointe, 1835; from Normand fils,* Paris Moderne*)*

of the street and the other dimensions.

In these cases the presence of planned architecture became, so to speak, completely negative, in so far as the walls of the buildings had obviously to be finished somehow, so as not to shock contemporary taste, and ideally in a uniform fashion, so that the eye should not be worried by unjustified anomalies; but the style of the façades was only a tenuous covering, to give an acceptable appearance to a new sort of setting in which roads and squares lost their individuality and melted into one another, while spaces were defined much more by the crowds and vehicles than by the surrounding buildings, i.e. in a way that was always changing (Fig. 91). This was the facet that struck impressionist painters such as Monet and Pissarro, in their views of the Parisian *boulevards* seen from above and crowded with people. The general effect was still rather characterless and abstract, and single shapes could be absorbed into it only by losing their individuality and ming-

ling in a closely-woven fabric of changeable and uncertain appearance; but it was the starting point for the modern conception of an open and fluid urban scene as against the old enclosed one.

This aspect of Haussmann's work – of which he was probably unaware, since he thought of himself as the continuer of the old tradition – did not emerge until later; the great thoroughfares take on their pleasantly familiar character only when the usual paraphernalia of the street is there to mediate between the inhuman scale of the buildings and the tiny human beings who throng them, and when general sensibility has learned to see the elements of the new urban scene in a dynamic way.

The editor of Haussmann's *Mémoires* wrote in 1890: 'For everyone, the Paris of our times is his Paris, perhaps even more so than at the time of the Empire'[7] and indeed the face of the city transformed by Haussmann must have emerged more clearly for

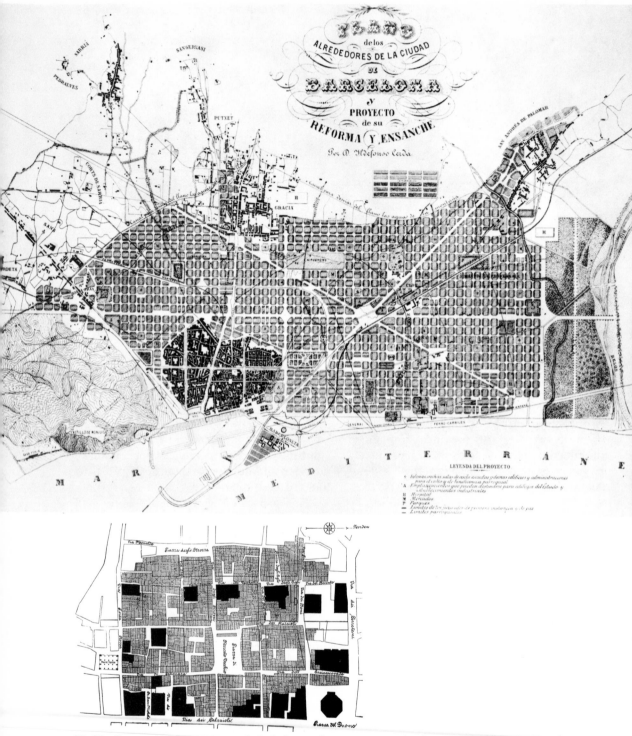

**93, 94** *Two modes of procedure typical of nineteenth-century town-planning extension (plan for Barcelona by Cerda, 1859) and demolition (redevelopment of the old market in Florence, 1885; from J. Stübben,* Der Stadtebau, *1824)*

a visitor to the 1889 exhibition than for a visitor to that of 1867, forced to wander around a city in turmoil, its roads cluttered with building sites from which unknown buildings and complexes were emerging.

## 4  Haussmann's influence

Haussmann's works in Paris were the prototype of what we have called neo-conservative town-planning; this became common practice in all European cities after 1870, but as early as the Second Empire there were already a series of undertakings, in France and elsewhere, following similar lines.

In France many important cities were modified during the reign of Napoleon III. In Lyon the prefect Vaisse, in office from 1853 to 1864, carried out a series of alterations that resembled the Parisian ones in miniature: the widening of the two parallel streets of the rue Impériale and the rue de l'Impératrice, the *quais* along the Rhône and Saône, the park of the Tête d'Or; Marseilles, whose importance increased greatly after the work on the Suez canal, almost doubled its population and was completely transformed by the opening of the rue Impériale (1862–4) from the old port to the Joliette dock; similar straight roads began to be built in Montpellier in 1865 and in Toulouse in 1868, involving the demolition of old quarters and the destruction of many fine buildings; the same was done in Rouen and Avignon, where historic quarters were destroyed with a casualness that seems to us inconceivable.

In Brussels the burgomaster Anspach completely transformed the lower part of the city, channelling the river Senne underground and opening a great thoroughfare in its bed (1867–71) joining the two railway stations of the north and south; in 1864 he also managed to gain for the city the bois de la Cambre, which became the outlying park of Brussels, and built the avenue Louise to join it to the city.

In Mexico City in 1860 the Emperor Maximilian opened the paseo de la Réforme, an imitation of the Champs Élysées, to join the Aztec city to the palace of Chapultepec.

In Italy most important cities had a main road built between the city centre and the railway station: via Nazionale in Rome, via Independenza in Bologna, the 'rettifilo' in Naples, via Roma in Turin. The most important project, however, was the rebuilding of Florence, the capital after 1864, where a serious attempt was made to adapt Haussmann's method to the realities of the newly united state and the particular needs of the ancient city itself.

Giuseppe Poggi (1811–1901) who planned the development, was concerned above all with extending the city to accommodate the new inhabitants that the government was bringing in its wake; he envisaged not so much a new city as a more extensive Florence, and saw no need to transform both centre and outskirts, as Haussmann had done; thus he began to knock down walls, to build a ring of new districts all round the town, except on the hills to the left of the Arno, and put off rebuilding the centre until a later date.

The work was carried out between 1864 and 1877, amid serious economic difficulties, particularly after the capital was moved to Rome; the re-designing of the centre, with the demolition around the *mercato vecchio* (Fig. 94) was carried out from 1885 to 1890 – when interest in the work on the new buildings around the outskirts had more or less petered out – and was inspired rather by the need for prestige than by objective technical or economic requirements. Thus the fabric of the old city was largely saved from destruction, unlike Paris, but, also unlike Paris, the new elements did not merge satisfactorily with the old, and the city had no unity of character but was divided into separate, unconnected districts.

Many other plans of this period were based on the same idea of 'development', for instance Cerda's grandiose plan for Barcelona

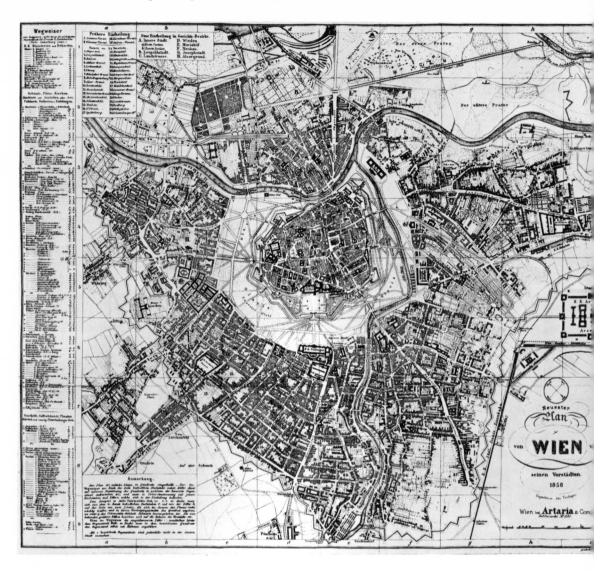

**95** *Map of Vienna in 1856 (from W. Braumüller, Guide de Vienne). The old town is still intact, enclosed within its fortifications, while new districts have developed round it; a strip of public land, the Glacis, runs around the walls; it was not built up, and it was here that the Ring was laid out*

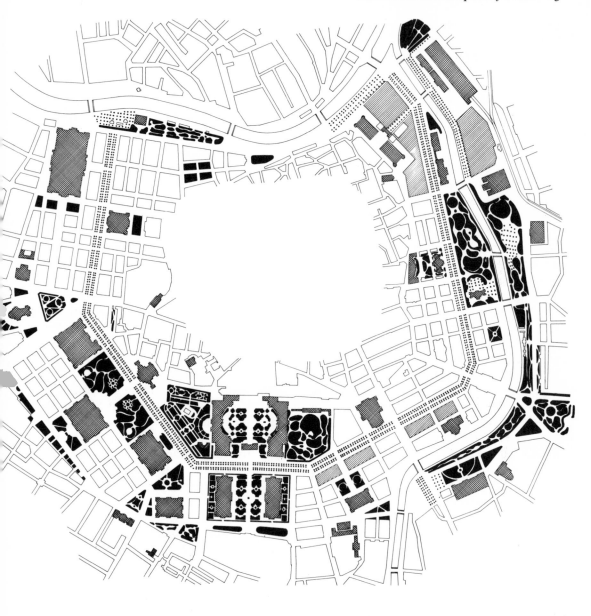

**96** *The Vienna Ring (1859–72); private buildings are shown in white, public buildings in cross-hatching and green zones in black*

of 1859 (Fig. 93) and Lindhagen's for Stockholm, of 1866.

In general the attempts at town-planning based on the Napoleonic plan of Paris were much inferior to their model. Haussmann's plan was important mainly for the consistency and comprehensiveness with which it was carried out; but none of the other planners – except possibly Anspach – had the energy of the prefect of the Seine, and nowhere was there the combination of favourable circumstances which had enabled him to act simultaneously in various sectors, maintaining his unity of purpose over a considerable period. Thus almost all the other plans were abandoned half-way, ruining the old towns beyond repair but without producing efficient modern ones in their stead.

Above all, no administration managed effectively to control the disruptive effects of property speculation; Haussmann worked in the presence of very lively speculation, which profited largely from his improvements, and after 1858 he did nothing to go against the system, but his authority was strong enough to prevent his projected solutions from being deformed by private interests; in this way he managed to proceed with adequate scope and a comprehensive grasp of the problems. In other towns, since it met with no proportionate resistance, speculation frankly triumphed, giving the various enterprises a variable and erratic character deriving from the casual interpenetration of single interests.

Things went differently where the administration owned a sufficient area of building land in places relevant to the transformation of the town. This happened in Vienna, where the old town was still surrounded by a broad ring of fortifications, beyond which the new districts had grown up (Fig. 95). In 1857 the emperor announced his decision to demolish the walls and organized a competition for the use of the area, giving the prospective planners precise instructions: the barracks to the south of the city were to remain, and another group was to be built

to the north, so that troops could move rapidly along a great ring-road, which ran along the Donaukanal for a stretch; the space in front of the imperial palace was to be left free, and nearby there was to be a vast *place d'armes*; along this ring-road various public buildings were to be built: an opera house, a library, archives, a new town-hall, museums, galleries and markets.

The competition was judged in 1858, and was won by Ludwig Förster (1797–1863); then the Minister of the Interior was asked to have a definitive plan drawn up; this was probably done by M. Löhr and was approved in 1859, but discussions of the positions of the various buildings continued until 1872. In practice, the strategic factors were much reduced: the *place d'armes* disappeared, while the number and importance of the public buildings necessary to the ever-growing city, increased (Fig. 96).

The Vienna Ring made it possible to set the old town within the street system of the modern city without cutting into or destroying the old fabric (unlike what happened in Paris) and to build the main public buildings of the nineteenth-century city in airy, spacious surroundings, amid gardens and avenues, but this was made possible mainly by the relative smallness of the old nucleus; the same thing happened in many other northern cities, where the traditional centre remained almost intact within a green belt replacing the original fortification: at Cologne, Leipzig, Lubeck and Copenhagen.

As far as the problem of popular building was concerned, state intervention was organized systematically only during the last decades of the century; on the other hand, from the middle of the century onwards, there were numerous experiments by single employers at building workers' villages, helped and sometimes partly subsidized by the State.

In France the most important was the Société Mulhousienne des Cités Ouvrières, founded in 1853; it was financed by private individuals (for the houses and various basic amenities) and partly by the State (for roads and green spaces). The Société built one-storey or two-storey houses with gardens, to be rented or purchased, putting up over one thousand in fifteen years.

In England, Disraeli, in his early works[8] theorized about the need for such under-takings. His ideas influenced both private contractors and government policy; in 1845 the Society for Improving the Dwellings of the Labouring Classes was founded; in 1851 Lord Shaftesbury had the first laws on subsidized housing passed: the Labouring Classes Lodging Houses Act and the Common Lodging Houses Act; in 1853 Titus Salt began to build the town of Saltaire for his mill-workers, based on a comprehensive plan by the architects Lockwood and Mason; in 1864 Octavia Hill (1838–1912), grand-daughter of Southwood Smith, Chadwick's collaborator in the sanitary enquiry of 1842, became active in this field: with Ruskin's help she bought up and restored some houses in Marylebone and divided them up into small dwellings, renting them out for just enough to cover the initial expenses. In America too, in 1862, the millionaire G. Peabody founded the Peabody trust, to build workers' houses on a non profit-making basis.

In Germany, between 1863 and 1875, the Krupp family built the first group of workers' villages near Essen: Westend, Nordhof, Baumhof and Kronenberg.

Throughout the nineteenth century, through a series of failures and successes, a body of technical and legal experience was built up concerning the planning of cities and the building of working-class quarters; the planning was often unsuitable and con-trived, repeating the geometrical formulae of the Baroque tradition, but now they were put to the test by coming into contact with the material problems of the industrial town, whose diversity invested them with a new character.

In European cities, these systems were used to transform the earlier Baroque or medieval organisms and the success of their results depended upon how closely they retained the traditional character of the various places; in the colonies on the other hand – where the large-scale settlement of Europeans was just beginning – these same systems were applied in a uniform and mechanical way, and no attempt was made to link them with the bodies of local towns and local traditions, so that the implicit cultural contradictions were even more sharply emphasized.

During the two decades of the Second Empire Haussmann's town-planning tech-nique had considerable influence in the colonies. The development of Fort-de-France in New Caledonia began in 1854, in 1865 that of Saigon in Vietnam; also in 1865, at the mouth of the new Suez canal, the new city of Port Said was founded; in Algeria the building of the new towns founded during the first decade after the conquest – Orléans-ville, Philippeville – was intensified, as was that of European districts around native towns. In 1855 the Boers began building their new capital, Pretoria, while the English developed the recently founded cities of Australia (Melbourne in 1836, Adelaide in 1837, Brisbane in 1840 after the abolition of the penal colony).

The history of colonial town-planning remains to be written, though it is one of the most notable aspects of Europe's world-wide expansion during the nineteenth century. Probably an analytical study of this subject would also help to define further the nature of the European prototypes from which it derives.

## 5 Eclecticism and rationalism in Haussmann's time

Architects played a small part in the govern-ing plan of Paris, and restricted themselves to giving acceptable forms to the buildings

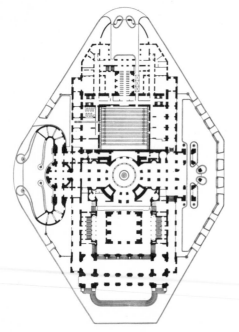

**97, 98, 99**   *Paris, The Opéra by C. Garnier (1861–74): painting by Pissarro, plan and façade*

commissioned by the prefect, without emerging from the ambit of their usual debates on style. But the new tasks and vast experiments made possible by Haussmann's work made urgent, from a cultural point of view, the clarification of those abstract disputes and hastened the crisis of academic thought.

The controversy between the neo-classical and the neo-Gothic – which culminated in 1846, as we have said – naturally could not terminate with the victory of one style or the other. From then on most architects bore in mind either the classical or the Gothic as possible alternatives, and naturally not only these two, but also the Romanesque, Byzantine, Egyptian, Arabian, Renaissance etc.

Thus the attitude known as eclecticism, already virtually contained in the backward-looking tendencies of the neo-classicists and Romantics, emerged and became widespread.

Eclecticism was favoured by an ever-greater knowledge of buildings of other countries and other ages; in 1835 Delannoy published a study on the monuments of Algeria,[9] Coste published his work on Cairo[10] in 1839 and on Persian buildings from 1843 to 1854,[11] in England in 1842 O. Jones published the reliefs of the Alhambra in Granada.[12] The first universal histories of architecture also appeared, for instance that by Gailhabaud.[13]

Philosophers theorized about this vision of art history as a succession of equally valid styles; Hegel tried to interpret the sequence of style dialectically as a succession of thesis, antithesis and synthesis, and considered the cycle closed in his own time; he therefore ended by recommending eclecticism to his contemporaries.[14]

But the practice of eclecticism was everywhere accompanied by a guilty conscience; *avant-garde* writers attacked it from the beginning, for instance T. Gauthier: 'I would like to have been a thief; it is an eclectic philosophy',[15] and more reflective architects expressed their perplexity about the contradictions they observed every day in the exercise of their profession, like R. Kerr:

'In what *style of architecture* shall you build your house? . . .

The architect himself will generally put this query to his client at the outset of their intercourse; and if the client be unlearned in such matters, he may be somewhat astonished to discover what it is he is invited to do. By the exercise of some instinct or some caprice . . . he is expected to make a choice from amongst half a dozen prevailing "styles", all more or less antagonistic to each other, all having their respective adherents and opponents, and all proving to be more and more unintelligible the longer they are examined – the longer, that is to say, they are permitted to contradict each other.

The bewildered gentleman ventures to suggest that he wants only a simple comfortable house, but in the comfortable style, if there be one.

The architect of course agrees: but there are so many comfortable styles – they are all comfortable . . . You must choose the style of your house just as you would the build of your hat; you can have Classical, either columnar or non-columnar, either arcuated or trabeated, either rural or civil, or indeed palatial; you can have Elizabethan, in equal variety; Renaissance ditto; or, not to notice minor modes, Medieval – the Gothic which is now so much the rage – in any one of its multifarious forms – of the eleventh, twelfth, thirteenth or fourteenth centuries, whichever you please, feudalistic, monastic, scholastic, ecclesiastic, archaeologistic, ecclesiologistic and so on.

But really, I would much rather not. I want a plain, substantial, comfortable *Gentleman's house*; and, I beg leave to repeat, I don't want any style at all. I would very much rather not have any; I

**100**   *Paris, cross-section of the Opéra (from* L'Esposizione di Parigi del 1878 illustrata, *Sonzogno)*

**101**   *Paris, Les Halles Centrales (V. Baltard, 1853)*

daresay it would cost a great deal of money
and I should very probably not like it.
Look at myself: I am neither Classical nor
Elizabethan – I believe I am not Renaissance and I am sure I am not Medieval –
I belong neither to the eleventh, nor to the
twelfth, thirteenth nor fourteenth centuries
– I am neither feudalistic, nor monastic, nor
scholastic, nor ecclesiastic, neither
archaeologistic nor ecclesiologistic; I am
very sorry but would you kindly take me
as I am, and build me a house *in my own
style* . . .

Why cannot he (a plain Englishman)
have a plain English house built for plain
English occupation?. . .'[16]

But there were also many open defences
of eclecticism, which certainly echoed the
opinion of a large section of the public:

'Far from deserving the reproach of

slavishness to fashion, art has never enjoyed
so much independence of expression, and
this shall be the honour of our time, which
welcomes all styles, all genres and all
manners, the beauty of every work and
every style is better appreciated, whereas
before everything that did not conform to
the style of the day was despised and
rejected. In those days so little respect was
felt for outmoded styles that an architect
appointed to rebuild the façade of a Gothic
church did not hesitate to build it in another
style, Greek or Roman. Today on the
contrary fashion no longer exists in art;
not only are all old buildings restored to
their primitive state with an awareness and
erudition which does honour to our artists,
but we see the same architect building here
a Renaissance church, there a Romanesque
one, yet elsewhere a town-hall in the
Louis XIV style and a Gothic temple;

**102** *Paris, Les Halles Centrales (engraving from A. Joanne,* op. cit.*)*

another in the same district builds a Louis XV house, a Louis XIII barracks and a fine neo-Grecian lawcourt'.[17]

It is interesting to see how almost all the eclectics, beginning with Garnier, began by protesting against the reproduction of the styles of the past, and claimed that they wanted them freely interpreted and elaborated. In practice their guilty conscience prevented them from being content with current imitations and caused them to seek out new inspiration and new combinations, digging into the least known corners of art history.

J. I. Hittorf (1792–1868) and several pupils of the Académie de France in Rome – Henri Labrouste (1801–75), Victor Baltard (1808–74) – discovered the polychromy of ancient buildings and sent the first coloured reconstructions back to Paris. This gave rise to a controversy, their thesis being supported by Ingres and the Germans Semper and

Hermann, and made known a new aspect of the classical decorative repertoire; Hittorf, a pupil of Belanger, observed that this style was well-suited to buildings in iron, applied it to the Théâtre Ambigu (1827), the Panorama and the Cirque d'Hiver in the Champs Élysées, and drew from it the experience on whose basis he later tackled vast metalroofed constructions such as the Grand Hôtel (1856) and the Gare du Nord (1863).

Hittorf and Baltard were Haussmann's main collaborators in the transformation of Paris. The relations between Haussmann and these architects were very significant; he regretted that his age 'should not have produced any of those artists whose genius transforms art and tempers it to express the aspirations of the new epoch',[18] often reproached contemporary artists for the mean scale of their conceptions (for instance Hittorf for the buildings at the heads of the roads ending at the Étoile) or for their lack of practical sense, and sometimes he changed

**103** *Paris, Interior of the Bibliothèque Ste-Geneviève* (*H. Labrouste, 1843; from E. Texier*, op. cit.)

his designers in mid-task. He had no one favourite style but regarded them all as so many possible finishes, to be used as the occasion demanded; he considered the classical style best suited to important buildings, but when he had to build the *mairie* of the first *arrondissement* next to Saint-Germain-l'Auxerrois, he commissioned Hittorf to design a Gothic building and asked Théodore Ballu (1817–74) to build a Gothic tower between the two buildings for the sake of symmetry.

Sometimes the prefect interfered decisively in the designing, when it seemed to him that the architect was not responding to orders in the desired way. For the Halles Centrales (Figs. 101–2) in 1843 Baltard planned a stone pavilion which was partly built but proved unsuitable; Haussmann had it demolished and asked Baltard to make another design, all in iron, abandoning all concern with style:

'All I need is a vast umbrella and nothing else'. Haussmann describes how, when Napoleon III saw the plans, he was amazed and bewildered: 'How is it possible that the same architect could have designed two such contradictory buildings?' and Haussmann replied 'The architect is the same but the prefect is different'.[19]

In this case Haussmann actually claimed credit for the idea; though in 1874 Sedille gave evidence to the contrary, perhaps with greater justification. After this Baltard designed various other buildings with metal frameworks, for instance the slaughter-house of La Villette and the church of Saint-Augustin, but he never again attained the simplicity and grandeur of Les Halles; indeed in Saint-Augustin he concealed the basic structure in a covering of masonry, with all the traditional ornaments.

It is difficult to understand such incon-

**104**  *Paris, Interior of the Bibliothèque Impériale (H. Labrouste, 1855; from E. Texier,* op. cit.)

sistency in the work of an architect undoubtedly so knowledgeable and so gifted; he passed with ease from serious research into new materials to idle experiments in stylistic combinations or uninspired pastiches to please contemporary taste. He was an apt symbol of the cultural uncertainty at the time, no longer rigidly tied to tradition, open to new ideas, but inconsistent and incapable of choosing one definite path where there was so vast a choice. Some of those who deplored the contradictions of eclecticism realized that the matter went beyond formal appearances and that choices had to be based on objective reasons that could be rationally demonstrated. They were called rationalists and their comments, both of encouragement and of censure, were of considerable influence at the time and to some degree anticipated those of the great modern masters of the 'twenties, to whom the same title was applied. But the analogy is only verbal, since the nineteenth-century rationalists did not know how to

escape from the impasse of eclecticism and could not imagine concrete forms except in relation to one of the styles from the past, classical or medieval.

The most important representative of neo-classicist rationalism was Henri Labrouste; a pupil of the Académie and Grand Prix de Rome in 1824, he spent five years at the Villa Medici studying ancient architecture; in 1830 he returned to Paris and opened a private school of architecture, where he preached strict adherence to constructional and functional needs; in 1843 he designed the Bibliothèque Sainte Geneviève (Fig. 103) and in 1855 the Bibliothèque Impériale (Fig. 104) where he used an iron structure to obtain spacious rooms, though he enclosed it in a stone covering decorated in the ancient style.

Labrouste's ideas were not new. His writing on construction and function is similar to that of Durand, but now these claims acquired a specifically ideological complexion; this was the time when Conte

**105**   *Viollet-le-Duc, Room with dome in iron and masonry, 1864 (from* Entretiens sur l'architecture, *1872)*

published his *Cours de Philosophie* (1845) and his *Discours sur l'Esprit Positif* (1844), when Courbet was preaching pictorial realism and Daumier was attacking bourgeois society with his biting satire. A contemporary of Labrouste, Hector Horeau (1801–72) preached the same ideas with singular ardour and ended up, in the same controversy, by identifying the Académie and reactionary politics, so that in 1872 he joined the Commune, like Courbet, and ended up in prison.

The 1848 revolution marked the peak of these forward-looking hopes, where art, science and politics were more or less identified; the course of successive events, the eventful life of the Second Republic and the coming of the Empire struck a serious blow against these cultural forces, scattering and isolating their most worthwhile supporters.

In 1856 Labrouste closed his school; the pupils went on to the *atelier* of Eugène-Emmanuel Viollet-le-Duc (1814–79) who was the recognized head of the rationalists from now on. Viollet-le-Duc belonged to the younger generation, he had neither the obstinacy nor the ardour of Labrouste or Courbet, was extraordinarily knowledgeable on scientific matters and was concerned not to lose contact with the world of officialdom; he was a friend of the Empress and had a certain influence on Napoleon himself. In 1852 he embarked on a campaign against eclecticism in various reviews, maintaining that architecture must be based on the true functions of and respect for the materials used; this criticism of eclecticism was finally aimed at a specific goal: the Academy which controlled the École des Beaux Arts, the Grands Prix and all important positions. In 1863 the Emperor agreed to a more liberal reform of the Academy.

Viollet-le-Duc was a supporter of the neo-Gothic, as we have said, but he eliminated all Romantic and sentimental implications from his arguments; to his eyes, the eyes of a scholar, there was nothing confused or mysterious about the Gothic, indeed he valued it precisely for the clarity of its constructional system, for the economy of its solutions, for its precise correspondence to distributive needs. Contrasting the Gothic with classicism, Viollet-le-Duc, while remaining within the limits of historicist thought, stressed the arbitrary and conventional character of the alleged general laws of architecture upheld by the Académie, and set against them other laws, less ambitious but more closely in line with reality: the appropriate use of materials, obedience to functional needs. He was also interested in the use of iron, and proposed that it should be used in accordance with its particular characteristics and not to replace traditional materials (Fig. 105).

The fillip given by Viollet-le-Duc to the neo-Gothic movement by associating it with rationalism was very important: he, like his academic adversaries, embarked on the paradoxical task of demonstrating the general and contemporary worth of a style based on past models, though it was less easy, in the case of the neo-Gothic, to present as basic certain precepts which were founded on custom alone, to identify tradition with rationality, because neo-Gothic did not have the continuity of a recent tradition behind it, in fact the first thing it demanded was a struggle against recent traditions.

For this reason the neo-Gothic, wherever it took root, produced a salutary re-evaluation of the artistic heritage of the past and encouraged a more open-minded analysis of modern constructional processes; in fact the books of Viollet-le-Duc, which were read throughout the world, were very important for the formation of the next generation, that of the masters of *art nouveau*.

# four

# Engineering and architecture in the second half of the nineteenth century

## 1  The universal exhibitions

The advances in engineering in the second half of the nineteenth century can conveniently be followed through the universal exhibitions from 1851 onwards.

The exhibitions of industrial products reflected the direct relationship that had been established between manufacturers, wholesale dealers and consumers, after the abolition of the guilds. The Première Exposition de l'Industrie Française was organized in Paris under the Directoire, six years after the proclamation of the freedom of labour.

Throughout the first half of the nineteenth century the exhibitions remained national; this was because almost all countries, with the exception of England, placed strict controls on foreign trade, to protect their emergent local industries. Only after 1850 did the situation change; first France, then the other countries lowered their customs barriers, and the new possibilities of international trade were reflected in the exhibitions, which became universal, showing products from all countries side by side.

The first universal exhibition opened in London in 1851. The initiators of this event were Henry Cole – of whom more will be said in Chapter 6 – and Albert, the Prince Consort; Hyde Park was chosen as the site, and in 1850 an international competition for the building was organized, attracting 245 competitors, including 27 Frenchmen. The first prize was won by Horeau with a huge construction in iron and glass, but none of the designs were regarded as practicable since all, including the winning one, made use of frameworks made up of large separate elements which could not be made use of again after demolition. For this reason the building committee drew up a plan of its own and invited contractors to submit tenders for contract, advising possible modifications. At this point Joseph Paxton (1803–65), the builder of conservatories, intervened with a hurriedly prepared design, sought favour with Robert Stephenson, a member of the Committee, and published the designs in the *Illustrated London News*; but by now the Committee was bound by the decision it had taken, so that Paxton had to associate himself with the contractors Fox and Henderson and present his own plan as an improvement on the Committee's design.

The tender was very risky, because the quantities at stake were enormous and the price of the single elements in iron, wood and glass had to be calculated very exactly, in a very short time. Dickens described the plan

**106, 107** *London, Two views of the Crystal Palace (from the Victoria & Albert Museum and* La Grande Esposizione di Londra, *Tip. Subalpina, Turin, 1851)*

**108**   *London, Interior of Crystal Palace* (*from* La Grande Esposizione di Londra)

**109**   *London, Crystal Palace: an original photo of the interior*

as follows, in *Household Words*:

'Two parties in London, relying on the accuracy and good faith of certain iron-masters, glassworkers in the provinces, and of one master-carpenter in London, bound themselves for a certain sum, and in the course of four months, to cover 18 acres of ground, with a building upwards of a third of a mile long (1851 ft., the exact date of the year) and some 450 broad. In order to do this, the glass-maker promised to supply in the required time nine hundred thousand square feet of glass (weighing more than 400 tons) in separate panes, and these the largest that ever were made of sheet glass; each being 49 inches long. The iron-master gave his word in like manner, to cast in due time 3300 iron columns, varying from $14\frac{1}{2}$ ft. to 20 ft. in length; 34 *miles* of guttering tube, to join every individual column together, under the ground; 2224 girders; besides 1128 bearers for supporting galleries. The carpenter undertook to get ready within the specified period 205 *miles* of sash-bar; flooring for an area of 33 millions of cubic feet; besides enormous quantities of wooden paling, louvre work and partition'.[1]

The offer was the lowest, and the work was in fact carried out, remaining within the limits of the estimated budget; the original plan had not included the transept, which was added to accommodate some large trees. The total cost was 1½d. per cubic foot.

The economy of the plan depended on various stratagems: complete prefabrication, rapid assemblage, the possibility of recovering costs and the technical experience Paxton had gained from building conservatories. The vertical supports, cast-iron tubes, also acted to carry away rain-water, and the horizontal supports, at the base, also acted as gutters; thus in a sense the building was held upright by its own drainage system. The problem of condensation on the glass had been solved by breaking the ceilings up into sloping surfaces so as to prevent the rain dripping through, and by carrying off the water through a groove on the lower cross-beam of each wooden sash-bar to the gutters. The floor was raised four feet above the ground, the spaces below helping ventilation and containing a device for catching the dust.

The Crystal Palace – as of course it was called – aroused great admiration, though eminent critics such as Ruskin had their reservations. *The Times* wrote:
'An entirely novel order of architecture, producing, by means of unrivalled mechanical ingenuity, the most marvellous and beautiful effects, sprang into existence to provide a building'. [2]

E. L. Bucher, a German political refugee, wrote:

'The building encountered no opposition, and the impression it produced on those who saw it was one of such Romantic beauty that reproductions of it were soon hanging on the cottage walls of remote German villages. In contemplating the first great building which was not of solid masonry spectators were not slow to realize that here the standards by which architecture had hitherto been judged no longer held good'. [3]

After the exhibition the palace was taken to bits and put up again at Sydenham in a country setting also designed by Paxton, where it remained until it was burned down in 1937.

The importance of the Crystal Palace did not lie in the resolution of certain problems

**110, 111** *London, Crystal Palace, a detail of its construction and Paxton's sketch* (*Victoria & Albert Museum*)

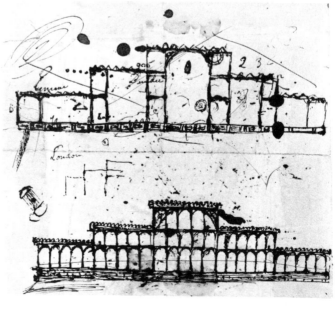

of statics, nor even in the novelty of the pre-fabrication processes and technical devices, but in the new relationship established between the technical means and the desire for prestige and the expressive aims of the building.

Contemporary descriptions, like the famous one by Bucher, stress the impression of unreality and undefined space:

'We see a delicate network of lines without any clue by means of which we might judge their distance from the eye or the real size. The side walls are too far apart to be embraced in a single glance. Instead of moving from the wall at one end to that of the other, the eye sweeps along an unending perspective which fades into the horizon. We cannot tell if this structure towers a hundred or a thousand feet above us, or whether the roof is a flat platform or is built up from a succession of ridges, for there is no play of shadows to enable our optic nerves to gauge the measurements. If we let our gaze travel downward it encounters the blue-painted lattice-girders. At first these occur only at wide intervals; then they range closer and closer together until they are interrupted by a dazzling band of light – the transept – which dissolves into a distant background where all materiality is blended into the atmosphere . . .[4] (Fig. 108).

This impression was due not so much to the use of iron – there were already many buildings of this kind: the conservatories of Paxton himself and of Burton, the Paris Jardin d'Hiver, the railway stations – as more probably to the smallness of the single architectural elements in comparison with the overall dimensions and with the impossibility of taking in the whole building at one glance. Although the total length was over 550 metres, the main nave was only 21·5 metres wide and the cast-iron supports only 7 metres apart; the basic measurement of 8 feet was repeated along the length of the

building, 230 times, and it should be remembered that the transept was not originally envisaged in the design, so that the building did not have a focal centre and would have looked like a sort of endless train. Such a composition, based on the repetition of a simple motif, outwardly resembled the models of the neo-classical tradition, and the recurring elements resembled an architectural order, but the relations and dimensions adopted produced a completely different result and gave the impression not so much of a single finite object as of an indefinite extension defined in an ever-changing way by the objects exhibited there and by the visitors walking in it.

In the same way Haussmann's roads and squares, where regular traditional perspectives were applied to spaces too large for them, were no longer complete in themselves but were transformed into unbounded spaces, qualified in a dynamic way by the traffic and movement taking place in them.

The simple and daring character of the Crystal Palace must be seen in relation to various circumstances: to the training of its creator – who was not an architect, but an engineer and gardener, without the concern for grandiosity which affected the designers of other similar buildings planned later on – with the influence of Sir Henry Cole, the theorist of industrial design who was one of the initiators of the Exhibition and who probably prompted the right attitude to industrial technique: neither pompous over-enthusiasm, with a great show of sensational structures, nor literary bad faith, masking the structure with a traditional series of ornaments, but frank acceptance of mass-produced material and rigid economic limitations which, on this occasion, were of great service to the architectural result.

The Crystal Palace was highly successful: a similar building was planned for the New York exhibition of 1853 – Paxton too submitted a design – but a monumental dome was set in the middle of the nave. In 1854 a GlasPalast was built at Munich by the engineers Voit and Werder.

A similar problem arose in Paris in 1855 over the French universal exhibition. In 1852 Fr. Ad. Cendrier (1803–93) and Alexis Barrault (1812–67) made plans for a big construction in iron and glass, but unlike English industry, French industry was not ready to meet its demands and it was decided to surround the building with a masonry covering, using iron only for the roof; the design for the exterior was by J. M. V. Viel (1796–1863), the roof by Barrault. The building, known as the Palais de l'Industrie, was built on the Champs Élysées and used in all successive exhibitions until 1906 when it was demolished and replaced by the Grand Palais (Fig. 112). The hall measured 48 by 192 metres and at the time was the largest iron covered area without intermediate supports.

The 1855 exhibition, initiated by Napoleon III during the Crimean War, was supposed to strengthen the Empire's prestige and exhibit the advances made in French industry, which was ready to compete on an equal footing with foreign industry. Among the many products exhibited was a strange rowing boat in concrete supported by an internal iron framework designed by J. L. Lambot. But this, for the moment, was only a curiosity. Many other achievements in the building field attracted the attention of visitors: machines, cranes and excavators which had made Haussmann's work possible, foundation piles driven in with compressed air invented in 1841 by Trigier, corrugated sheet iron for roofing already used by Flachet in 1853 at the Gare des Marchandises de l'Ouest, zinc roofing, moulded tiles, blocks of stone hewn mechanically in the quarry, wooden floors and panelling exhibited in the Canadian section, heating equipment functioning by steam and water, ventilation systems already in use in certain theatres and hospitals.

The second universal exhibition in Paris, in 1867, was organized on the Champ de Mars, in a temporary building, oval in shape, consisting of seven concentric galleries; the outer and largest for machines, the others for raw materials, clothing, furniture, the liberal arts, fine arts, the history of labour; in the centre was an open garden, with a pavilion for coins, weights and measures (Fig. 115). Each country had a section with a portion of each of the seven galleries: 'To make the circuit of this palace, circular, like the equator, is literally to go around the world. All peoples are here, enemies live in peace side by side'.[5]

The Galerie des Machines, which had a span of thirty-five metres, was supported by metal arches; stresses were eliminated by prolonging the outside pillars and joining them with tie-bars above the glass roof. J. B. Krantz, the designer of the building, had had the metal framework made in the works that a young engineer, Gustave Eiffel (1832–1923) had just opened at Lavellois-Perret; Eiffel also did the calculations and experimental auditing.

This temporary building was much criticized by the Parisians who were used to monumental projects; Kaempfen wrote for instance:

'Palace? Is this the name to be given to this huge construction which embraces within its perimeter the greatest number of the products of art and industry ever brought together in one place? No, if this word necessarily implies the idea of beauty, elegance and majesty. This enormous mass of iron and brick which cannot be glimpsed at once in its entirety is not beautiful or elegant, nor even grandiose; it is heavy, base, vulgar. But if it is enough that a building, though lacking all this, should contain incalculable riches, then this strange object, without precedent in the history of architecture, is certainly a palace'.[6]

These are remarks similar to those made

**112** *The hall built at the Champs Élysées for the Paris exhibition of 1855 (from Sonzogno,* op. cit.)

about the Crystal Palace, used sometimes as praise, sometimes as blame.

The objects exhibited in this building bore witness to the rapid progress made, in twelve years, in all fields; in building, the most striking novelty was the hydraulic lift presented by L. Eydoux; another exhibit was that of containers in reinforced concrete by J. Monier, patented the same year; iron objects were numerous and testified to the advances made by the iron industry after the invention of the Bessemer converter; shortly afterwards, in 1873, Jules Saulnier (1828–1900) was able to build the first building with a steel skeleton, the Menier factory at Noisiel-sur-Marne.

Six years later the 1873 exhibition was opened in Vienna; the building on the Prater was the work of the English architect Scott Russell and was dominated by a gigantic rotunda with a span of 102 metres (Figs. 116–7). An exhibition was also opened in Philadelphia in 1876 (Fig. 118).

Only in 1878, after the interval of the war

and the Commune, was Paris in a position to stage a new universal exhibition. Two large buildings were put up on this occasion: a temporary one on the Champ de Mars and a permanent one on the other bank of the Seine, on the Chaillot hill: the Palais du Trocadéro.

The temporary building was designed by Leopold Hardy (1829–94); on the façade facing the Seine the outer walls were not of brick but of coloured majolica; the building looked very striking, although it was covered with a variety of eclectic ornament, because it avoided using iron in a traditional style and at the same time did not use it purely functionally, which would have been incompatible with the public nature of the building.

A journalist of the time wrote:

'All this north façade is built of iron, and cast iron; but, as the reader will easily see, at least for the central part of the façade, the architect has brilliantly managed to avoid the usual pitfall awaiting those using

**113** *The Paris exhibition of 1855, a view of the exhibits* (*from A. Joanne,* op. cit.)

metals, of designing a building which looks like a market or factory rather than an exhibition hall. Rejecting conventional forms and eliminating brick and plaster, he has used slabs of coloured majolica to cover the walls; he does not hesitate to present the public with a polychromatic façade where the emblems and crests of the various nations form one of the main decorative motifs' (Fig. 120).[7]

The two Galeries des Machines had spans no bigger than that of 1867, but the engineer De Dion had designed transverse ogee arches which eliminated stress and made external and internal buttresses unnecessary (Fig. 119).

The structures to be used in the vestibules were worked out by Eiffel, who was also working on the grandiose plans for the Portuguese railways, and who started work on the Maria Pia bridge over the Douro that same year.

The Trocadéro was designed by G. A. Davioud (1823–81) and J. D. Bourdais (1835–1915); the idea of a permanent building was naturally associated with that of a structure in masonry, and only the roof was of iron, covered with intrusive eclectic ornamentation. The building was recently demolished and replaced by the Palais de Chaillot.

After 1878 an increasing number of universal exhibitions were held throughout the world: in Sydney in 1879, in Melbourne in 1880, in Amsterdam in 1883, in Antwerp and New Orleans in 1885, in Barcelona, Copenhagen and Brussels in 1888.

The Paris exhibition of 1889, the centenary of the storming of the Bastille, was in many ways the most important of these nineteenth-century displays; it too was organized on the Champ de Mars and consisted of an inter-connected complex of buildings: a U-shaped main hall, the Galerie des Machines and Eiffel's three

**114**  *The outside ambulatory of the building for the Paris exhibition of 1867 (from the international publication put out by the Imperial Commission,* Guide pour les principaux écrivains de France, *1867)*

hundred-metre tower, level with the bridge leading to the Trocadéro.

The building designed by J. Formigé (1845–1926) was a heavy, complicated affair, with an over-decorated dome; but the Galerie and the tower, even if they too were over-burdened with ornamentation that was not always in the best of taste, were the most important works built in iron up to that time, and their dimensions posed new architectural problems.

The Galerie des Machines was designed by Ch. L. F. Dutert (1845–1906) who employed the engineers Contamin, Pierron and Charton (Contamin had the curious fate of being confused by many writers with Cottancin, the pioneer of reinforced concrete, as though he were a medieval master whose identity was in doubt); but for the public of the time the designer was undoubtedly Dutert, *Prix de Rome*.

The great building, measuring 115 by 420 metres, was supported by thrice-articulated arches; this system had already been used in some German stations and made it possible to cover a space almost as big as the Crystal Palace of thirty-eight years earlier without any intermediate supports (Figs. 121–5).

Contemporaries reacted to this building with amazement and uncertainty. Laymen on the whole were enthusiastic, confusing in their admiration the size of the hall, the technical devices and the decorative finish:

'One's gaze can travel over half a kilometre of bright and empty space, revealing from one end to the other the façades of multi-coloured glass and the graceful curve of the supports whose two identical arches, joining at the centre, resemble two enormous trees . . . To avoid the displace-

**115** *A general view of the building for the Paris exhibition of 1867* (ibid.)

ments that would be generated by the inevitable expansion of the metallic parts – an expansion caused by the sun's rays – or their contraction when in contact with the cold, the girders of the arches have been jointed in three places: at the two bases and at the top. By approaching a pillar one may easily see these joints, positive hinges, which allow all the physical properties of the free metal to take their natural courses'.[8]

'The transparent roof is a perfect arch, covered with panes of white glass enlivened with the occasional design in blue, simple and elegant, as are the two walls of glass that close it in to the north and south. While it was empty, the type of building material – iron and glass – gave it such lightness that a poet exclaimed: "What a shame to spoil it by filling it with machines". Now the machines are there; I will not say, like my friend, that it would be better if they were not there; but though I don't say it, I think it'.[9]

'Metal has lent itself to all possible

demands. Until now no-one thought that suitable artistic effects could be produced with iron. The slight and slender appearance of this metal, the difficulty of softening its forms has prevented most architects from using it. The attempt has been satisfactory . . . The columns of the gallery have been built not in cast iron in the usual way but in iron and sheet-metal, with pleasant designs. The railings and balustrades of the stairs are also in commercial iron, T iron or U iron. The whole of the visible framework is likewise composed of similar elements which have opened up new possibilities to architecture in iron . . . Despite the presence of five lateral galleries, the eye has difficulty in adjusting itself to these hitherto unheard of dimensions, and remains disconcerted by the sight of such immensity. The low pointed arches of the roof, too, deceive the eye and do not give an exact notion of the height of the building; the gaze will gradually get used to these huge perspectives: at first surprised, it will end by admiring everything. It is a glimpse into

**116, 117**    *Vienna, 1873 exhibition (from* L'Esposizione universale di Vienna del 1873 illustrata, *Sonzogno)*

**118** *Philadelphia, an interior of the universal exhibition of 1876 (from* L'Esposizione universale di Filadelfia, *Sonzogno)*

immensity, into magnificence'.[10]

The most important writers were admiring, but had reservations; E. Renan wrote:

'I believe that this great effort has produced a work beautiful in its own way, a kind of beauty to which we are not accustomed but which we must acknowledge. The iron domes plainly have nothing in common with those of Santa Sofia or St Peter's . . . Furthermore one must bear in mind that this work is not intended to be permanent. It is all the more surprising because it appears to us, with its ephemeral character, as a prodigious extravagance'.[11]

Many architects, even those of the rationalist school like A. de Baudot, criticized the somewhat squat proportions and the details, particularly the hinged joints which visibly weakened the bases of the pillars. Other experts on the other hand approved of the harmony between the structure and its architectural externals:

'This monument not only states its purpose clearly, but reveals the intention of the builder, offering to the gaze, in their infinite variety, the uses of modern science at the service of the builder. The aim appears fully achieved. Examine the ways chosen to achieve it, the lightness of the structure, the bold soaring of the gracious curve of the arches, which cleave space like the wings of a bird spread in flight'.[12]

The Galerie des Machines was too vast for the spectators to be left to wander as ordinary pedestrians around the great machinery; for this reason two mobile trolleys were installed, running the whole

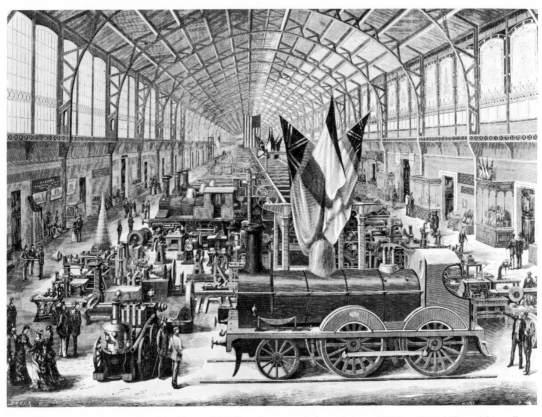

**119, 120**   *Paris, La Galerie des Machines of 1878 and a general view of the exhibition (from* L'Esposizione di Parigi del 1878 illustrata, *Sonzogno)*

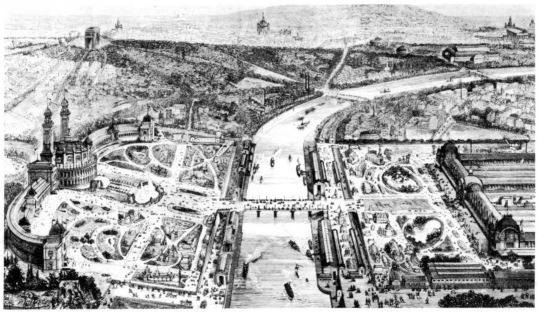

**121, 122, 123** *Paris, La Galerie des Machines of 1889* (*from* Figaro-Exposition, *from* Parigi e l'Esposizione universale del 1889 *by Treves, from Giedion,* Space, Time and Architecture)

124 *Paris, La Galerie des Machines of 1899 (from* L'Esposizione di Parigi del 1899 illustrata, Sonzogno)

length of the Gallery well above ground level, and carrying the visitors above the exhibits (Fig. 124). This device was not only inspired by problems of circulation; it also had a positive effect on the character of the interior, as can be seen from engravings and photographs; in fact the vastness of the empty space was brought down to a human scale not only by the shape of the walls, but by the moving objects and people within it, and was comprehensible only in relation to them. One need only compare one of the usual views of the empty hall (for instance the famous photograph reproduced in Giedion) with the illustration from *Le Figaro* (Fig. 121), imagining the movements of the trolleys, of machinery and of people; when the foreground is crowded with moving objects, the eye no longer sees the whole room as an enclosed empty space, but as an unbounded area limited only by a rhythm which recurs as far as the eye can see, like Haussmann's streets.

It is, therefore, true to say that this building cannot be judged according to traditional criteria, not because of Dutert's design which obeyed traditional criteria, with a ratio of 1:3·6 between breadth and length and an insistent symmetry, but because of the dynamic character that the shape acquires, given its unusual proportions, from its contents and the presence of the crowd.

The Galerie des Machines was unfortunately demolished in 1910, so that it is not possible to put these assumptions to the test. The second famous creation of the 1889 universal exhibition, however, is still standing: Eiffel's three hundred-metre tower.

In 1884 Eiffel entrusted the design to two engineers employed in his works, Nouguier and Koechlin, and remarks that 'they had been drawn to the idea of building an iron tower by their common studies on tall metal bridge piers'.[13] The architectural part was the work of the architect Sauvestre (Fig. 130). The plan was re-elaborated during the two following years and work began at the beginning of 1887.

The outline of the tower was designed so as to resist the action of the wind, and Eiffel saw to it that the forms arrived at by calculations gave the framework a pleasantly curved outline:

'The first principle of architectural aesthetics prescribes that the essential lines of a building should be perfectly suited to its purpose. And what laws have I had to take into account with the Tower? Resistance to wind. Well, I believe that the curves of the four outer ribs, as calculation has determined them, . . . will give a great impression of strength and beauty, because they will convey to the sight the boldness of the whole construction, in the same way that the numerous empty spaces contained within the elements themselves will firmly stress the constant concern not to offer to the violence of high winds, surfaces dangerous to the stability of the building'.[14]

As is well known, a group of artists and literary men made a public protest about the building of this iron tower in an open letter to Alphand, the commissioner for the Exhibition:

'*Seigneur et cher compatriote,*
We writers, painters, sculptors and architects, fervent lovers of the beauties of Paris, hitherto unblemished, protest with all our might in the name of slighted French taste against the erection, in the heart of our capital, of the useless and monstrous Eiffel Tower, which public ill-feeling, often inspired by good sense and the spirit of justice, has already christened the Tower of Babel. Shall the city of Paris associate itself with the grotesque, the commercial fancies of a building (or a builder) of machines, to dishonour itself and disfigure itself irredeemably? For the Eiffel Tower, which not even trade-conscious America would wish to call its own, is the dishonour of Paris, do not doubt it. To picture what is in store for us you must for a moment imagine an absurd and dizzy construction towering over Paris, like a dark gigantic factory chimney, dwarfing and humiliating our monuments and our architecture till they vanish under the impact of this astonishing dream. For twenty years we shall see the hateful shadow of this hateful riveted iron column spread like an inkstain. To you, *Seigneur et cher compatriote,* to you who so love Paris and who have beautified her, to you belongs the honour of defending her once again. And if our cry of alarm is not heard, if our reasoning goes unheeded, then at least we, and you, will have put forward an honourable protest'.[15]

Among the signatories were Meissonnier, Gounod, Garnier, Sardou, Bonnat, Coppée, Leconte de Lisle, Sully-Prudhomme, Maupassant, Zola.

Many technicians maintained that the structure and foundations were bound to give way and that the tower would collapse. The owners of nearby buildings even started legal proceedings, demanding compensation because the danger prevented them from being able to let their houses.

When the tower was finished, on 5 April 1889, many adverse opinions changed to favourable ones; if the press reflected the views of the readers it would seem that public opinion, on the whole, was favourable. Here are some of the comments:

'Before the accomplished fact – and what a fact – one cannot but bow down. I too, like many others, said and believed that the Eiffel Tower was an act of absurdity, but it is a great and proud act of absurdity. Certainly, this immense mass crushes the

**125**  *Paris, view of the Galerie des Machines of 1889 (from Sonzogno,* op. cit.*)*

**126** *Paris exhibition of 1889; an enactment of the 'triumph of the republic' at the Palais de l'Industrie (from Sonzogno*, op. c▸

rest of the Exhibition, and when you emerge from the Champ de Mars, the enormous domes and galleries appear tiny. But what can you expect? The Eiffel Tower seizes the imagination, it is something unexpected, fantastic, which flatters our smallness. When it was first begun the most famous artists and authors, from Meissonnier to Zola, signed an ardent protest against the tower as an insane offence against art; would they sign it now? No, certainly, and they may wish that that document of their anger had never existed. As for the populace, as for the good-hearted bourgeoisie, their feelings may be summed up in a phrase I heard from the mouth of a fellow who had been staring open-mouthed at the tower for five minutes and then said: "Enfoncée l'Europe"!'[16]

'Well set on its arched legs, solid, enormous, monstrous, brutal, it is as if the Eiffel Tower, disdaining whistles and applause, were directly seeking, challenging the heavens, without thought for what is going on at its feet!'[17]

Many great writers remained unconvinced; in the *Journal des Goncourts* the following passage occurs:

'The Eiffel Tower makes me suspect that monuments in iron are not human monuments, that is, monuments of the old humanity which knew only of wood and stone to build its refuges. Furthermore, in iron monuments the flat surfaces are terrifying: take the first platform of the Eiffel Tower, with its row of double look-out posts: one can imagine nothing uglier to the eye of a civilized person!'[18]

The dominant feeling was an impression of novelty; our own is very different and we must, therefore, try to strip away the veil of habit which has made us too familiar with the tower.

The work in itself is not perfect and has certain faults – not only in the decorative superstructure, partly eliminated in 1937, but also in the inconsistency of the general

**127** *Paris exhibition of 1899, the French section of morocco work (from Sonzogno, op. cit.)*

design. On the other hand, the part the tower has taken on in the Parisian landscape is extremely important and forces us to take into account quite different features, probably the most important.

The minister Lockroy, answering the artists' letter, maintained in 1887 that the tower would alter only the insignificant landscape of the Champ de Mars, but he was wrong. The exceptional height and uninterrupted line of the tower between the second and third platforms ensured that it could be seen from every part of Paris and that its relationship was no longer that of an old building with a limited setting governed by a single perspective, but with a whole city and in an endless variety of ways (Fig. 134). As with the Galerie des Machines the unusual proportions changed the significance of its form and gave it a dynamic quality which meant that it had to be considered in

a new light even if the design itself respected the traditional rules of spatial relations.

The tower was Eiffel's last work in the building field. The 1899 exhibition had an Eiffel pavilion which was a sort of personal Eiffel one-man-show and one of whose most striking exhibits was the model of the Garabit viaduct, built between 1880 and 1884. In 1887 Eiffel was commissioned to build the Panama canal, which absorbed all his energies until 1893; after 1900 he devoted himself to aero-dynamic research, making use of his own tower and then of a special laboratory where he worked till 1920.

Iron buildings now seemed to have reached the limit of their possibilities. After 1889 the most important work was the dome for the Lyon exhibition in 1894, with a diameter of 110 metres. During the last decades of the century rapid progress was made, on the other hand, in the new means

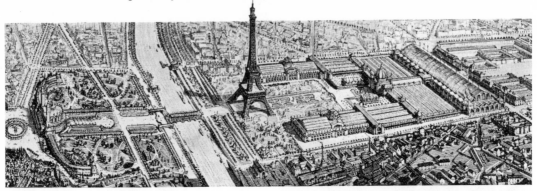

**128, 129, 130** *Paris, 1889 exhibition; general view (from Sonzogno, op. cit.), a caricature of Eiffel and the Eiffel Tower (from Figaro-Exposition)*

of building, reinforced concrete, which soon became very important in ordinary building because it was so economical, particularly after the publication of the building codes. The rapid growth of towns, especially in those countries which were now becoming industrialized, like Germany, put a tremendous strain on the building industry, a strain which could only be borne by a complete revision of the old methods of building.

## 2 The crisis of eclecticism

While building technique was developing so rapidly, the traditional architectural culture of the time was entering a definitive period of crisis.

From 1851 to 1889 the constructions built for the universal exhibitions offered evidence of great progress in building, while the problem of architectural control became increasingly difficult and worrying. As a

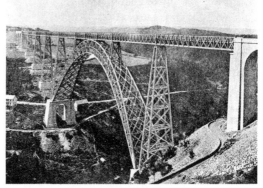

**131, 132, 133** *Three structures by Eiffel: the base of the Eiffel Tower (1889) the Bon Marché in Paris (1876) and the railway bridge over the Garabit (1880)*

work of architecture, the Crystal Palace was greatly superior to later buildings of the same type; the relation between purpose, technical devices and decorative finish was well-balanced, and the designer chose his path with confidence. In the French pavilion, on the contrary – not excluding the famous Galerie des Machines of 1889 – eclectic culture attempted in various ways to give dignity and respectability to the engineers' structures, but without conviction and with an increasing sense of remoteness. It is not surprising if the 1889 exhibition and the discussions it aroused should have produced, as a reaction, an extreme wave of obstinate classicism, with L. Ginain and E. G. Coquart. The old argument about the use of new materials and the relationship between art and science reappeared in learned publications.

Beneath these discussions there was a serious professional concern. In 1863 Viollet-le-Duc and the rationalists obtained from Napoleon III a decree of reform for the École des Beaux Arts, which partly removed the teaching from the control of the Académie and modified the order of studies in a more liberal direction, relaxing the classical bias. The Académie did not accept the new ruling and thus gave rise to a violent controversy which lasted until 1867, when a new decree revoked most of the reforms and gave the Académie back its privileged position.

Outwardly, the argument concerned its attitude towards style and the suitability of including in the syllabus the study of the Middle Ages as well as that of antiquity and the Renaissance, but the real disagreement concerned technical teaching and its relationship with artistic education. Viollet-le-Duc wrote in 1861:

'In our time, the budding architect is a boy of fifteen to eighteen . . . who, for six or eight years, is made to make plans of buildings which usually have only distant connections with the needs and habits of our own times, and which never have to be practicable; he is never given any knowledge, however superficial, of the materials at our disposal, of their use, never taught about the building methods used in all known ages, never given the slightest idea of the conduct and administration of practical work'.[19]

Flaubert, in his *Dictionnaire des idées courantes*, noted this definition: 'Architects:

all imbeciles – always forget the ladders'.

E. Trélat (1821–1907) went even further, and without waiting for reforms founded, in 1864, a private school, the École Centrale d'Architecture, where the teaching was strictly practical and addressed to engineers, contractors and a few architects.

For its part the Academy, keeping to traditional teaching practice, defended the existence of the category of architect. In 1866 C. Daly wrote that by giving too large a part to scientific and technical culture, 'the whole body of architects would finally be suppressed, since it appeared simply to duplicate that of civil engineers'.[20] Furthermore, confrontation could not be avoided in practice; architects could not be regarded as mere artists, they had to define their professional function and to have at least enough scientific education to be able to collaborate with engineers.

The 1867 ruling reflected these uncertainties; it confirmed the traditional trend of their studies, but upheld at least some of the systematic teaching demanded by the rationalists and defined the figure of the architect by instituting a diploma which ended the period of professional freedom begun in 1793.

Plainly, the diploma served to strengthen a dangerous situation but it exposed the architects to the rough winds of the wide world, turning them from artists into professional men, and making inevitable an open confrontation between academic culture and reality.

The rationalists in their turn did not admit defeat, and continued their campaign. In 1886, on the occasion of the competition for the appointment of diocesan architects, the jury observed that the candidates did not have sufficient knowledge of the Middle Ages, and the Conseil Supérieur de l'École appointed Jean-Louis-Charles Garnier (1825–98) to draw up a report on the teaching of architecture, which was published in 1889. Garnier defended the position of the

**134** *Paris, Eiffel Tower in landscape of the city*

**135, 136**   *Paris, Details of Eiffel Tower*

Academy, saying that the school did not have and could not have preference for any particular style because it taught 'the arrangement, composition, reason, ratio and harmony of forms, i.e. the primordial elements of architecture'.[21]

His adversaries replied that these notions were identifiable with classicism, that they were by no means the primordial elements, but remains of an antiquated tradition, and they consistently reproached the École des Beaux Arts for its 'prejudice, narrow-mindedness, pedantry, meanness, despotism, horror of the modern, of movement, of progress'.[22]

In the face of these attacks the Académie took the final step and formulated its programme in a way so broad and liberal as to evade all stylistic controversy once and for all.

Styles were regarded as matters of habit, and any claim of exclusiveness was now regarded as outmoded; the architect's prerogative, which distinguished him from the engineer, was the freedom to choose this form or that, an individual and not a collective prerogative, dependent on feeling, not on reason. Eclecticism was no longer interpreted as a position of uncertainty, but as a deliberate attempt not to limit oneself to any one-sided formulation, to judge as the occasion demanded, objectively and impartially.

This interpretation did in fact avoid the academic controversies between the supporters of the various styles, but by eliminating all tendentiousness in teaching, it renounced the one practical position that kept academic culture anchored to reality – the traditional parallelism between classical precepts and constructional habits – and opened the way

for the dissolution of the entire cultural heritage accumulated by the Académie.

Julien Guadet (1834–1908), a teacher in one of the school's *ateliers* from 1872 and professor of architectural theory from 1894, was a typical representative of this last phase. The programme of his course on theory resembled earlier ones, indeed it resembled that of Durand, mentioned in Chapter 1:

'The object of the course is the study of the composition of buildings, of their elements and their ensembles, according to the two-fold aspect of art and its adaptation to definite problems, to material needs. In the first part we shall study successively the really basic elements, i.e. walls, orders, archways, doors, windows, vaulting, ceilings, roofs etc., then the more complex elements i.e. rooms, entrance-halls, porticoes, stairs, courtyards etc. In the second, after having established the general principles of composition, we shall study the main types of building: religious, civil, military, public and private, adducing for each of them the best-known examples of all ages and countries, showing the needs they answered then and showing how and in what way these needs have altered, so as to arrive at present-day needs and more recent solutions'.[23]

But the spirit of the course was new, and Guadet himself, in the inaugural lecture given on 28 November 1894, explained his attitude as follows:

'What is a course of architectural theory?

The question may seem superfluous, since this course has existed for years and has been taught by men of great worth. It might seem that its tradition is hallowed but yet . . . I shall not conceal from you that I feel around me an impression that this course has still to be created. The point is this: we do not want our course to be in contradiction with the teaching that your professors [the teachers of the various *ateliers*] have the right to give you. The originality of our school can be defined in a word – "the most liberal in the world" – since "the pupil is treated as a man who has the right to choose his master and his artistic bent".'[24]

The theoretical course, therefore, would have no particular bias: 'That which is or could be contested is the province of my colleagues; that which is uncontested, and above all the why, the how, this is my field, this is what I shall talk to you about, and it is very vast'.[25] How can this nucleus of permanent and universal ideas be defined? Guadet stated: 'I am firmly convinced that the first studies must be classical', but soon afterwards he produced this surprising definition:

'Everything that deserves to become classical is classical, without limits in time, space or school . . . everything which has remained victorious in the struggle of the arts, everything that continues to arouse universal admiration' . . .[26]

and resuming the stylistic battle of the nineteenth century, he concluded:

'Fortunately some proud artists – our masters – have seen and have shown that independence does not consist in being a turncoat stylistically speaking, and our art has gradually freed itself from this fossilized view. Everything has not been equally successful, but efforts towards this end have always been fruitful, and today we know and proclaim that art has a right

to freedom, that only freedom can guarantee its continued existence, fecundity and health'.[27]

Theoretically, Guadet's liberalism was more highly evolved than Viollet-le-Duc's rationalism or Garnier's eclecticism, but while he was trying to isolate and safeguard the vital nucleus of the profession, i.e. the freedom of the creative imagination, he eroded and blurred all the traditional notions which had long made up the foundations of academic culture. Those points which had been regarded as incontestable gradually, one by one, revealed themselves to be highly debatable, and the field of theory, far from vast, emerged as almost non-existent.

Guadet, with acute insight, felt this imminent void and wrote: 'Our programmes are prosaic, and could not be anything else, in their formulation. It is up to you to add the poetry, to you to add what I for my part could never put into it: youth'.[28]

This was not mere rhetoric: for in that very year Van de Velde furnished his house at Uccle and held his first lecture at Brussels, Wagner made his opening speech at the Vienna Academy and began his collaboration with Olbrich, and Horta had finished the house in the rue de Turin the year before.

*Avant-garde* artists, turning to the same principles as Guadet, individual freedom and the primacy of the imagination, created a new style independent of historical models and which offered successful opposition to the traditional styles.

This rapid success of *art nouveau* can be explained if one bears in mind the fact that academic culture had been moved to adopt similar theoretical positions of its own accord, and was ill-prepared intellectually to attack the new movement on practical grounds.

Naturally, traditional eclecticism survived for many decades, but it now lacked any inner conviction and was forced increasingly into backward-looking attitudes.

# The debate on the industrial town

# five

# The industrial town and its critics

The events narrated in the first four chapters constitute the official history of the industrial town in Europe until the 1880s. If we were concerned with this period alone, there would be nothing more to add; the particular climate of the nineteenth-century town was the result of just this chain of events, crushing and confusing and yet irreduceable to a common process.

But our aim is to study the formation of the modern movement, which can be defined precisely as the historical alternative to the industrial town we have described so far. In the following chapters we shall therefore concentrate on the debate that took place at this time, and trace in it the points which later – during the last decades of the nineteenth century and the first two of the twentieth – were to lead to the formulation of a plan of action capable of altering the too solid reality of the townscape built until that time.

In this chapter we shall discuss to what degree nineteenth-century thought was aware of the transformation under way in town and country; this awareness was in fact the necessary premise for any conscious attempt at changing things. In Chapter 6 we shall try to give a brief account of the attempts to reform the industrial town, attempts which constitute the background of controversy to the facts described in the first four chapters.

Basically, the experiments of which we shall speak all belong to the sphere of theory, and had no appreciable modifying effect on the course of events; but they were very realistic theories, always on the point of becoming reality, and had only to find the right method in order to take their place in the process of development that had been triggered off by the industrial revolution.

This account can provide only a partial description of our period, but it will serve to emphasize the discrepancy between ideas and their realization – which was precisely the salient contradiction of the nineteenth-century town – and will reveal the tenuous thread linking to one another the activities of the cultural opposition, where future developments were incubating.

After 1830, during the 'reorganization' described in Chapter 2, people began to consider the industrial revolution with sufficient detachment to attempt the first historical accounts of it. In 1835 E. Baines published the first history of the cotton industry in England, and A. Ure the *Philosophy of Manufactures*, a justification for large-scale mechanized industry; in 1838 the first edition of G. B. Porter's *Progress of the*

**137**  *W. Williams, View of the ironworks at Coalbrookdale (1777)*

*Nation,* its successive editions of 1846 and 1850 giving accounts of later developments. F. Le Play carried out a large-scale enquiry into the conditions of the working classes throughout Europe, published in six volumes in 1855. In 1843 and 1845 two other famous works appeared, judging the industrial revolution according to very different political principles: Thomas Carlyle's *Past and Present,* and Engels' *Conditions of the Working Classes in England.* While historians of industry were enthusiastically describing material progress, economic and political writers were generally pessimistic.

Though he noted the evils caused by the industrial revolution, Carlyle did not see the causes of these evils as residing in any particular institutions that should be removed or any particular force that should be attacked; he did not, therefore, put forward any practical remedies but kept his values

safe by placing them above and beyond history. The Catholic Le Play was convinced that the main cause was the unbridled application of Smithian liberalism, the liberal Cobden was convinced on the contrary that they derived from an incomplete application of liberalism and from the continuing existence of the corn laws, while the socialist Engels thought that the most important obstacle to be removed was capitalism, which made possible the exploitation of some classes by others.

All the remedies put forward – whether right or wrong politically speaking – had one common defect: they overlooked the partial problems of single aspects of contemporary society, lumping them all together in the general problem of ideology. Basically, they all regarded reality as simpler than in fact it was, and claimed that they believed the partial problems would solve themselves, by

**138** *View of Coketown (Birmingham)*

a kind of deductive necessity, after certain basic transformations had been effected.

For this reason, deep in ideological conflict, economic and political writers had nothing to say on the narrower problem of the transformations taking place in the towns. Now that there were a certain number of factories, the face of the new city emerged clearly for the first time; it was gloomy and depressing, but no-one had any suggestions for re-introducing order and beauty. The industrial town was completely rejected by conservatives and progressives, by autocrats and democrats; it was not a problem to be resolved but a cumbersome, unlovely fact, it had no logic of its own, to be interpreted and nurtured, but was senseless and mechanical.

A symbol of this conception – so natural that it could be described objectively, like a real thing – was Coketown, where the characters in Dickens' *Hard Times* lived. Here is the first description of it:

'Coketown, to which Messrs. Bounderby and Gradgrind now walked, was a triumph of fact; it had no greater taint of fancy in it than Mrs. Gradgrind herself . . . .

It was a town of red brick, or of brick that would have been red if the smoke and ashes had allowed it; but as matters stood it was a town of unnatural red and black, like the painted face of a savage. It was a town of machinery and tall chimneys, out of which interminable serpents of smoke trailed themselves for ever and ever, and never got uncoiled [Fig. 138]. It had a black canal in it, and a river that ran purple with ill-smelling dye, and vast piles of

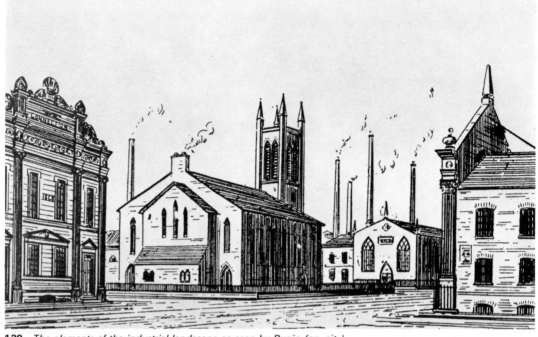

**139**    *The elements of the industrial landscape as seen by Pugin (op. cit.)*

building full of windows [Fig. 140] where there was a rattling and a trembling all day long, and where the piston of the steam engine worked monotonously up and down, like the head of an elephant in a state of melancholy madness. It contained several large streets all very like one another, and many small streets still more like one another, inhabited by people equally like one another, who all went in and out at the same hours [Fig. 141], with the same sound upon the same pavements, to do the same work, and to whom every day was the same as yesterday and to-morrow, and every year the counterpart of the last and the next . . . .

You saw nothing in Coketown but what was severely workful. If the members of a religious persuasion built a chapel there – and the members of eighteen religious persuasions had done – they made it a pious warehouse of red brick, with some-times (but this is only in highly ornamented examples) a bell in a birdcage on top of it

. . . All the public inscriptions in the town were painted alike, in severe characters of black and white. The jail might have been the infirmary, the infirmary might have been the jail, the town-hall might have been either, or both, or anything else, for anything that appeared to the contrary in the graces of their construction; fact, fact, fact everywhere in the material aspect of the town; fact, fact, fact, everywhere in the immaterial. The M'Choackumchild school was all fact, and the school of design was all fact, and the relations between master and man were all fact, and everything was fact between the lying-in hospital and the cemetery, and what you couldn't state in figures, or show to be purchaseable in the cheapest market and saleable in the dearest, was not, and never should be, world without end, Amen'.[1]

The writer's reaction to this reality was instinctive and similar to that of the young Tom Gradgrind, apart, of course, from the

**140, 141** *Two views of Coketown (Colne Valley and Middlesborough)*

violent tone: 'I wish I could collect all the Facts we hear so much about, and all the Figures, and all the people who found them out; and I wish I could put a thousand barrels of gunpowder under them, and blow them all up together!'[2]

But despite its preconceived hostility, Dickens' description is the reverse of superficial; in fact the animosity that inspired it made Dickens' description of the industrial scene more perceptive than the many genuine outpourings in praise of progress, where the new town was presented as an immense cheery hive of industry. Dickens picks upon several features typical of contemporary building, for instance the endless repetition of identical elements and the possible confusion between the types of building. But these facts are given a kind of metaphysical fixity, which turns the observation of reality into a literary myth; thus Dickens' descriptions of townscapes – which are absolute set pieces and the prototypes of numerous other conventional descriptions – are absolutely black, and Coketown is made as unpleasant as possible not only to the eye but also to the ear and nose:

'The whole town seemed to be frying in oil. There was a stifling smell of hot oil everywhere. The steam-engines shone with it, the dresses of the Hands were soiled with it, the mills throughout their many stories oozed and trickled it. The atmosphere of those Fairy palaces was like the breath of the simoom; and their inhabitants, wasting with heat, toiled languidly in the desert. But no temperature made the melancholy mad elephants more mad or more sane. Their wearisome heads went up and down at the same rate, in hot weather and cold, wet weather and dry, fair weather and foul. The measured motion of their shadows on the walls, was the substitute Coketown had to show for the shadows of rustling woods; while, for the summer hum of insects, it could offer, all the year round, from the dawn of Monday to the night of Saturday, the whirr of shafts and wheels'.[3]

Dickens was driven to these exaggerations not so much by the real defects of the industrial town as by the uneasiness he felt in trying to grasp, by means of old mental habits, the image of the new townscape, whose limits were less precise and which changed so much faster than the old.

In previous times the town had been something limited, measurable and relatively static; it could, therefore, easily be conjured up in the imagination. Anyone building a new house could imagine it in relation to the town as a whole, and as long as a common sensibility ruled the actions of every builder, the overall unity was safeguarded even without the intervention of conscious planning.

But now the quantities involved – the greater number of inhabitants, of houses, miles of road etc. – were immeasurably greater, beyond the immediate scope of the imagination. London, Paris and Vienna had grown so much that people could no longer see them in their entirety from any single point, nor cross them at a go, nor reconstruct them completely in their minds' eye, even if they knew their every corner. The speed of growth had increased, and no-one could keep up with the new developments as they took place; the inhabitants themselves were amazed, from time to time, by the sudden changes taking place in their own towns. To-day, too, people living in large towns are continually amazed at the sight of new districts they did not notice being built, or at the transformation of old parts changing so fast that they cannot grasp the various stages, and they have the disturbing feeling that the city moves faster than their awareness of it. Only one great poet in the middle of the nineteenth century commented explicitly on this change and expressed it in the famous couplet:

'Le vieux Paris n'est plus; la forme d'une ville
Change plus vite, hélas, que le cœur d'un mortel!'[4]

In the past the rhythm of the life of a town appeared slower and more permanent than the rhythm of human life and men regarded their towns as a support, a point of reference for their own experience; now the contrary is true and this support has vanished, because the face of the town is shorter-lived even than human memory.

This change – which from a practical point of view meant the abandoning of the old means of control and their replacement by planned intervention – was felt by the writers of the time as a negative limit: it defeated their capacities for mental picturing, and this was perhaps the main reason for their scornful rejection of it.

One subject that was the constant concern of the literature of the time was the great city, the metropolis – London for the English, Paris for the French – which inspired alternately a furious loathing and a morbid attraction.

As early as 1726 Defoe had written of London: 'Whither will this monstrous city extend? And where must a circumvallation or communication line of it be placed?'[5]

When Heine arrived there in 1828 his impression was as follows:

'I have seen the most marvellous thing that the world can show to the astonished soul. I have seen it and am still amazed – my thoughts are still bewildered in this labyrinth of masonry, through the midst of which the surging stream of living men's faces is rushing to and fro, with all their tumultuous passions, . . . That stern earnestness in all things, that mechanical motion, that irksomeness of joy itself, that inexplicable London which stifles fantasy and rends the heart'.[6]

Here, too, the eye of a poet saw deeper than that of other contemporary observers; Heine realized that the grandeur of London was not a matter of architecture in the traditional sense but was derived from the endless repetition of elements on a human scale: 'I expected great palaces and saw only hovels. But it was precisely this uniformity and their incalculable number that left so magnificent an impression'.

For Balzac, Paris was the 'great shaky cancer spread along the banks of the Seine' or the city of a thousand lights, the capital of pleasures. Writers of this period were rarely balanced or objective when writing of a big city; in practice the reality was unknown to them and replaced by a mythical image, coloured by the gilt of enthusiasm or the gloom of mistrust.

Because of the extremity of these viewpoints, writers such as Dickens, and the public opinion they mirrored, were of little help to reformers; indeed they gradually began to confuse Coketown in their scorn with anyone who worked there and accepted this reality at all.

The history of the opposition encountered by the 1848 sanitary laws in England and those of 1850 in France is highly instructive. It might seem that such reasonable provisions must pass without difficulty, yet they encountered obstacles of all kinds: from landlords and land-owners whose interests were affected, from liberals who feared arbitrary limitations placed on the right to private property, from conservatives who were unwilling to accept any technical innovations.

The radical *Economist*, on 13 May 1848, regretted that the Public Health Act had not met with adequate opposition; and not deigning to go into details, since the law concerned 'a great variety of matters which we cannot even enumerate, without crowding our space with a catalogue of somewhat offensive words' (sewers, refuse-heaps etc.)' observed: 'suffering and evil are nature's admonitions; they cannot be got rid of; and the impatient attempts of benevolence to banish them from the world of legislation before benevolence has learned their object and end, have always been productive of more evil than good'.[7] Luckily, as Bertrand Russell observed, 'the "benevolence" of

Parliament was proof against these arguments for not constructing a proper drainage system, because epidemics due to its absence were raging within a stone's throw of the House of Commons'.[8]

Similar conflicts occurred in France over the passing of Melun's law in 1850. The *Moniteur* of 19 December 1849 stated the following: 'the matter is a delicate one . . . the free use, the free availability of the citizen's possessions demands the strictest respect, since it constitutes the basis of all social order'.[9]

These men raising these objections of principle were not moderates but progressives; but they were swayed by the general political concern which John Stuart Mill summed up as follows: 'The third and most cogent reason for restricting the interference of government is the great evil of adding unnecessarily to its power'.[10] The habit of transferring all problems into the sphere of theory hindered progress in planning, which is essentially a question of gradation.

Equally instructive were the criticisms directed at Haussmann's works, and we shall now consider them further, in order to give an idea of appraisals given by educated men of the time, even if they were adverse.

Proudhon, describing the evening of 1 June 1863, drew attention to the Parisian workers' dislike for

'M. Haussmann's new city, monotonous and wearisome, with its straight boulevards, gigantic buildings, magnificent but empty quais, its saddened river now bearing nothing but stone and sand, with railway stations which, replacing the gates of the old city, have destroyed its reason for existence; with its new squares and theatres, its new barracks, its new paving, its legions of roadsweepers and frightening dust . . . a cosmopolitan city, where the native element can no longer be seen'.[11]

Veuillot wrote in 1867:

'Paris is a famous place, where an un-finished city is still growing up. They say that this city will be the wonder of the world, the triumph of modern science, materially and spiritually. The inhabitants are to enjoy complete freedom within a framework of great mutual respect . . . . The Paris streets are long and wide, bordered with huge houses. These long streets grow longer every day. The wider they are, the less room there seems to be. Carriages clutter the vast roads, pedestrians the broad pavements. Seen from the top of the houses, one of these streets looks like a river in flood, carrying away the flotsam of a whole world.

The buildings of the new Paris are of all styles; the whole does not lack a certain unity, because all these styles are of the boring genre, and the most boring of the boring genres, the pompous and well-aligned . . . . The Amphion of this city must have been a corporal!

These great streets, these great quais, these great buildings, these great sewers, with their poorly-imitated and ill-conceived physiognomy, have something about them that points to their sudden and irregular beginning. They breathe boredom . . . The new Paris will never have a history and will kill off the scent of the history of the old Paris. Every trace has already been wiped out for people under thirty. Even the old monuments that have been left standing say nothing, because everything around them is changed. Notre Dame and the Tower of St Jacques are no more in their places than the Obelisk, and seem to have been imported from remote places as vain curiosities'.[12]

Similar judgments must have been circulated in Paris in the 1860s; they are to be found in the *Journal des Goncourts* (18 November 1860), in the *Heures Parisiennes* of A. Delvau (1866) and also in a Sardou comedy of the same year:

'*René* (standing)  But after all, uncle, with

what exactly do you reproach this new Paris?

*Genevoix* My dear boy! The old Paris, the true Paris is getting swallowed up in it! A cramped, unhealthy inadequate city, but picturesque, motley, pleasant, full of memories and so well-suited to our scale! So convenient because of its small size! Our usual walks were a stone's-throw away, our favourite sights so near together; there we had our own little personal revolutions: we loved it.

Walks on foot were not a labour but a joy. The town allowed for that typically Parisian compromise between laziness and activity, *la flânerie*!

Nowadays, for the slightest outing you have to walk whole leagues along a muddy road which women cross without grace, since they no longer have the elasticity of the hard surface. An endless pavement, for the whole length of the road! A tree, a bench, a kiosk; a tree, a bench, a kiosk; a tree, a bench . . . And up above, the sun, the dust, a sickening regularity! A composite, cosmopolitan crowd shouting in all languages, of all colours. No longer any of that quintessence which made us a little world apart, the connoisseur, the amateur, the *bon viveur*, the aesthetic and intellectual élite!

What are we losing, o ye gods, if not everything? It is no longer Athens but Babylon! No longer a city but a station! It is no longer the capital of France but of all Europe, a marvel unequalled, a universe, I grant you. But after all it is not Paris, because there are no Parisians here.

*Claire* But then, uncle, you don't see all that's great, convenient, hygienic about it?

*Genevoix* My dear girl, I've been saying that I am full of admiration for it! It was unavoidable, it had to be done and it has been done. It has been well done! And when all's said and done it's all turned out

for the best! I applaud it, I heartily applaud it, profoundly grateful that the good Lord was unacquainted with this marvellous municipal system and did not plant trees in straight lines and the stars in two rows!'[13]

Haussmann devoted many pages of his memoirs to refuting criticism of this sort, and did not conceal the irritation he felt on seeing his work judged in so vague a fashion; he preferred to go straight to details, countering his adversaries' reasonings with lists, figures and dates.

One very significant exchange took place in 1858, on the occasion of the decision of the Council of State, already mentioned, which limited the right of compulsory acquisition to land destined for public use. Haussmann wrote:

'The new decision, deliberated *motu proprio* by this great assembly, not only imperilled the precious authority already granted to the Cité, to acquire sites outside the routes of the roads that are to be opened up and considered necessary for the construction of adequate and sanitary houses, but it also gave the owners of the relevant buildings the right to retain all the land not destined to public use, after causing the Cité to pay for the value of the buildings originally standing on the land, as well as for the compensation of the former inhabitants. In this way the original landlord was presented, quite gratuitously, with the benefit of the increase in the value of the land, now made available, thanks to the Municipality, for a more profitable use, fronting on to a wide road; while the Municipality was deprived of the opportunity of recovering some part of the considerable expenses incurred as a result of the undertaking, by selling the sites at an advantageous price'.[14]

The liberal J. Ferry replied as follows:

'You might be right, Monsieur le Préfet,

if the decree of 27 December 1858 had constituted a new right for land-owners; but this decree simply regularized the exercise of an old right; it is quite possible that this may have opened the eyes of a great many land-owners; but it is too ingenuous of the Préfet to dare to confess that his calculations included a piece of subterfuge regarding a right consistently recognized by our laws. The whole argument is therefore quite absurd'.[15]

The prefect saw clearly one of the requirements of modern town-planning: the need to secure for the public, wholly or in part, the increase in land value brought about by works built in the framework of a plan, turning them from permanently locked-up funds into productive investments, while Ferry, sticking to the letter of the law, was defending a short-sighted and out-dated conception. Yet at the time of this controversy, over a century ago, Ferry passed for a progressive intellectual and Haussmann for an unlettered and reactionary bureaucrat.

The same disdain of particular problems and the same doctrinal obstinacy can be observed – for different reasons – in Marxist writings.

After 1850, various systems for providing the working classes with better accommodation and better dwellings were studied, sponsored by governments and private philanthropists. Yet in 1872 Engels wrote a series of articles in the Leipzig *Volksstaat*, later collected in a single volume called *Wohnungsfrage*, to prove the irrelevance of all these attempts. In argument with Proudhon and with Sax, who had suggested changing rent into purchase by instalments to allow workers to become the owners of their houses, Engels retorted that this would solve nothing because, as long as capitalists could exploit workers, 'wages would fall on an average corresponding to the average sum saved on rent, that is, the worker would pay rent for his own house but not, as formerly, in money, but in unpaid labour to the factory owner for whom he works',[16] and concluded:

'Only the solution of the social question, i.e. the abolition of the capitalist mode of production, will make possible the solution of the housing problem. To want to solve the housing question while at the same time desiring to maintain the modern big cities is an absurdity. The modern big cities, however, will be abolished only by the abolition of the capitalist mode of production, and when some headway has been made in this direction, it will be far from a question of giving each worker a little house of his own'.[17]

Thus on a purely theoretical basis he dismissed the workers' settlements built round English and German factories, the workers' town of Mulhouse in Alsace created by Napoleon III, the co-operative movement and English Building Societies, English legislation on subsidized building and Haussmann's work based on the French law of 1850.

Engels' criticism did pinpoint the defects in the workings of these various systems, but it concluded, with flagrant injustice, that none of them had ever or ever could have any useful results:

'The breeding places of disease, the infamous holes and cellars in which the capitalist mode of production confines our workers night after night, are not abolished; they are merely *shifted elsewhere*! The same economic necessity which produced them in the first place, produces them in the next place also. As long as the capitalist mode of production continues to exist, it is folly to hope for an isolated solution of the housing question, or of any other social question affecting the fate of the workers'.[18]

Beneath Engels' theoretical obstinacy there was still a note of impatience with (and dislike for) the industrial town, both recurrent

142 *'Now then, make haste, make haste, and pay a visit to Ludgate Hill, and behold, for nearly the last time you will have the opportunity, the vast and celebrated cathedral of St. Paul's, erected by that famous architect Sir Christopher Wren, in the reigns of their majesties the last of the Stuarts. Be in time, be in time. In a very short time this remarkable edifice will be invisible, owing to the great improvements which the march of intellect and the progress of commerce, providentially force upon this Great Metropolis . . . Hurry, be in time, before the view is shut out for ever and ever by the highly ornamented tank in preparation by the Railway company . . . There is no charge, so long as you keep out of the building and in short this is an opportunity which can never occur again in the history of London. Be in time, be in time.'* (from Punch, 8 August 1863; quoted in Gloag, Men and Buildings)

**143**   *London, Ludgate Hill viaduct (engraving by G. Doré, 1870)*

**144** *London, Ludgate Hill viaduct in the nineteen fifties*

themes in nineteenth-century literature on this subject even when the authors admitted, as Engels did, that there was in principle a necessary relationship between industry and contemporary society.

This dislike of the modern town was usually accompanied by nostalgia for the old town, which was presented in an exaggeratedly favourable light, often in flagrant contradiction to historical truth. Engels for instance, writing about the conditions of the working classes in England, paints a falsely idyllic picture of workers' conditions in pre-industrial England:

'Spinning and weaving were done in the workers' homes. The families lived mainly in the countryside, near the towns, and the workers lived a very comfortable existence, a punctual and regular life, scrupulous and honourable . . . They had no need to tire themselves, and in their leisure time they could do healthy work in their field or garden'.[19]

The tone is that of the stories of Dickens, or of Ruskin's essays on the Middle Ages. This contrast between past and present, not impartial but emotional and confused, is another permanent theme of nineteenth-century culture, perfectly expressed in the famous verses by Morris:

'Forget six counties everhung with smoke,
Forget the snorting steam and piston stroke,
Forget the spreading of the hideous town,
Think rather of the pack-horse on the down,
And dream of London, small and white and clean,
The clear Thames bordered by its garden green . . .'.[20]

It is only a literary picture, because if London was small in the Middle Ages, it was certainly never white or clean, and people knew this in Morris's time; but images so emotionally loaded resist all historical repudiation and even Mumford, in his *Culture of Cities*, tried to perpetuate the traditional bucolic conception of the medieval town.

In talking of the universal exhibitions we have seen that the judgment of contemporaries on industrial architecture, and especially on work in iron, varied from arrogant rejection to vague and ingenuous enthusiasm; they were almost always overall judgments carried to extremes, which rarely left space for balanced and worthwhile appraisals of the qualities of the new townscape.

During the last years of the nineteenth century some positive judgments did begin to emerge, based not on uncontrolled admiration but on a reasonable acceptance of the new reality and on an intelligent insight into its specific aspects.

It is a slight thread of thought, for the moment, and limited almost exclusively to England, but its appearance was extremely significant, because it anticipated a change in attitude to the new experimental means, which was to make possible the spread of *art nouveau* during the last decade of the century.

In 1881 Samuel Butler, describing the view down Fleet Street towards St Paul's, wrote as follows:

'It is often said that this has been spoiled by the London, Chatham and Dover railway bridge over Ludgate Hill. I think, however, the effect is more imposing now than it was before the bridge was built. Time has already softened it; it does not obtrude itself; it adds greatly to the sense of size, and makes us doubly aware of the movement of life, the colossal circulation to which London owes so much of its impressiveness. We gain more by this than we lose by the infraction by some pedant's canons about the artistically correct intersection of right lines. Vast as is the world below the bridge there is a vaster still on high, and when trains are passing, the steam from the engine will throw the dome of St Paul's into the clouds, and make it seem as though there were a commingling of earth and some far-off mysterious palace in dreamland'[21] (Figs. 142–4).

The following year George Bernard Shaw, in his novel *Cashel Byron's Profession*, defended railway landscapes in a long passage spoken by Lydia Carew, Shaw's mouthpiece; Lydia and her friend Alice are at Clapham Junction:

'It was a fine summer evening; and Alice, though she thought that it did not become ladies to hide themselves from the public in waiting-rooms at railway stations, did not attempt to dissuade Lydia from walking to and fro at an unfrequented end of the platform, which terminated in a bank covered with flowers.

"To my mind," said Lydia, "Clapham Junction is one of the prettiest places about London."

"Indeed," said Alice a little maliciously. "I thought that all artistic people looked on junctions and railway lines as blots on the landscape."

"Some of them do," said Lydia; "but they are not artists of our generation; and those who take up their cry are no better than parrots. If every holiday recollection of my youth – every escape from town to country, be associated with the railway, I must feel towards it otherwise than did my father, upon whose middle age it came as a monstrous iron innovation. The locomotive is one of the wonders of modern childhood. Children stand upon a bridge to see the trains pass underneath it; little boys strut along the streets puffing and whistling in imitation of the engine. All that romance, silly as it looks, becomes sacred in after life. Besides, when it is not underground in a foul London tunnel, a train is a beautiful thing. Its pure white fleece of steam harmonises with every variety of landscape. And its sound! Have you ever stood on a sea-coast skirted by a railway and listened as the train came into hearing in the far-distance? At first it can hardly be distinguished from the noise of the sea; then you recognise it by its variation one moment smothered in a deep cutting, and the next sent echoing from some hillside. Sometimes it runs smoothly for many minutes, and then breaks suddenly into a rhythmic clatter, always changing in distance and intensity . . . . Abuse of railways, from a bucolic point of view, is obsolete. There are millions of grown persons in England to whom the far sound of a train is as pleasantly suggestive as the piping of a blackbird".'[22]

Both Butler and Shaw rightly connected the new feeling for the countryside with the passage of time, which was gradually refining the raw appearance of the new factories and allowing sensibilities gradually to grasp the new forms.

Prolonged acquaintance with the new urban landscape over a sufficient time, played the same part as shows and exhibitions played in gaining acceptance for the new style of painting and fulfilled the same need, forcefully expressed by Manet as early as 1867:

'To exhibit is vital, is the *sine qua non* of the artist, because it happens that after several viewings the spectator becomes familiar with that which first surprised him, or even shocked him. Gradually it is understood, accepted. Time itself acts like an invisible varnish on a picture, softening the initial hardness. To exhibit is to find friends and allies in the fight'.[23]

This brief summary of the reactions of nineteenth-century thought to the industrial city should be completed by a brief discussion of the reactions of the painters of the time.

Romantic painting, and particularly land-

**145**   *H. Daumier,* Rue Transnonian, 15 April 1834
*'Quick as lightning, a number of soldiers led by an
officer reaches the second floor. A heavy double door
yields to their efforts, a glass door still resists them.
An old man appears: "We are peaceful folk, unarmed,
don't kill us"—but the words die on his lips and he is
transfixed by the three blows of a bayonet. Annette
Besson rushes to his aid from another room, a soldier
turns towards her, pierces her with his bayonet above
the jaw and fires, so that the shattered fragments of
her head hit the wall. The young Henry Larivière who
was following her is hit from such close range that
his clothes catch fire and the lead goes deep into one
of his lungs. But he is only wounded, and a stab of
the bayonet slashes his forehead, baring the skull;
at this point he is also hit from behind and he bears
the marks, on his back, of seven different wounds.
The room is a pool of blood: Monsieur Besson père,
despite his wounds, takes refuge in an alcove and is
followed there by the soldiers, while Mme Bonneville,
her feet in the blood, calls to them while trying to
cover him: "All my family is lying at my feet, there is
no—one else to kill except me"—and five bayonet
blows go through her hands'. (Deposition of
Mme Poirier-Bonneville on facts of 15 April 1834)*

**146**   *G. Doré,* A street in old Paris, *(from Joanne,
Paris illustré)*

**147** *Monet,* Boulevard des Capucines, *1873*

scape painting, so popular during the first half of the nineteenth century, was a means of escape from the confusion and ugliness of the industrial city; this apparent faithfulness to nature concealed an idealization of nature itself in so far as it was still uncontaminated by man and his industry. For this reason the paintings of Corot and Turner are a sort of obverse of Dickens' descriptions; they are not neutral in the face of what they represent, they side passionately with the countryside, trees, clouds and rocks. The passion for exotic settings, in Delacroix, or of local but unusual ones, for instance Alpine scenery, are undoubtedly connected with his rejection of the urban scene as transformed by industry; in the same way the main reason for renewed interest in the past,

typical of the Pre-Raphaelites, was escape from the present, which seemed bleak and prosaic.

Equally concerned with content, but enemies of Romantic escapism, the realists – Courbet, Millet, Daumier – concentrated for the first time on everyday reality at its humblest; nonetheless for them the new landscape – town or country as the setting for human labour – had as yet no clearly defined form: the foreground was occupied by man who incorporated and personified his surroundings; it is this use of the foreground and concentration of expressive meaning in the gestures of a small number of figures that give certain works by Daumier and Courbet their extraordinary vehemence. A well-known example is Daumier's en-

**148** *Monet,* Gare St-Lazare, *1877*

graving 'Rue Transnonain, 15 April 1834' (Fig. 145) which appeared in the *Association lithographique mensuelle.* The ferocious repression of the republican revolt and the various incidents that took place in the rue Transnonain are condensed into the interior of a working-class room seen from ground level and almost completely occupied by the figure of a man seen, dramatically foreshortened, slumped on the ground over the body of a child, while two other corpses are partially depicted at the edges of the picture. The thought and emotions expressed by republican writers in their books are here contained in an elliptical image whose effect is instantaneous. However, Daumier's interest was certainly not limited to the depiction of a single case, however sensational; as its title says, the engraving depicts the rue Transnonain, with several of its inhabitants

murdered by Thiers' troops; so that this work, and many others of the same type, must be regarded as genre paintings, even if in the form of a metaphor. Modern genre painting, based on a conscious faithfulness to a new reality, springs from these works rather than from, for instance, the engravings of Gustave Doré, who at this time was painting the old Paris streets, but regarding them as Romantic backdrops (Fig. 146).

Only with the coming of Impressionism did the townscape of the new cities receive adequate artistic representation. As has sometimes been noted, Impressionism is urban painting *par excellence*, not only because its subjects are normally drawn from the city or its suburbs, but because it grasped the character of the urban scene more clearly than any of the critics or writers of the time: the continuity of its spaces, all

**149**  *Pissarro,* Jardin des Tuileries, *1890*

inter-communicating, each one open to the next and never enclosed within a single self-sufficient frame of perspective; the fact that it was composed of recurrent identical elements, qualified in an ever-changing way and therefore dynamically, in relation to its surroundings; the new relationship between the architectural frame, which was now unbounded and indefinite, and the traffic of men and vehicles; the renewed unity between architecture and the street, and in general the sense of the landscape as a dense mass of objects, all equally important but perpetually in a state of flux (Figs. 147–50).

Often the unfailing perceptiveness of Monet, Renoir and Pissarro reveals not only the positive but also the negative aspects of the new towns: the pedantic façades of Haussmann's roads are reduced, and rightly so, to the rhythmic alternation of dark and light patches, the decorative trimmings resolutely blurred and serving only to give the buildings some sort of conventional finish; the crowds wandering along the *grands boulevards*, rebuffed by the background of indifferent architecture, gather in armies of identical shadows, not unlike the masses formed by trees and vehicles.

The greater, or rather the total, openness of these painters to every natural or man-made object restored the unity of the landscape which had been broken by the emergence of the industrial town; nonetheless, the intensity and emotional involvement

**150**  *Monet,* Parc Monceau, *1878*

typical of the realists was lacking, and in its place was a sort of detachment and impassivity.

Since each shape was reduced to the chromatic elements which made up immediate perception, all interest in the content disappeared, all sentimental associations which might disturb the immediacy of the depiction were renounced, and so was all involvement which went beyond pure contemplation. This receptive attitude was incompatible with the vital commitment that had produced, and continued to produce, this landscape, and therefore with the emergence of an architectural movement suited to the needs of modern society.

Painting can limit itself to reflecting the world, but architecture must set out to change it. Therefore, as Pevsner has remarked, *avant-garde* movements for the renewal of architecture should be related not to Impressionism but to the post-Impressionist crisis and to Cézanne in particular, with his aim to paint 'depths rather than the surface'. But this development, which is fundamental to the explanation of the *avant-garde* movements of the last decade, will be dealt with in Chapter 9.

# six

# Attempts at reforming the industrial town, from Owen to Morris

## 1 The Utopians

Educated men of the nineteenth century were, therefore, moved by a deep mistrust of the industrial town and could not conceive of the possibility of re-establishing order and harmony in Coketown or in the gigantic body of London. Thus when they thought of remedies they believed that the present irrational forms of settlement would have to be replaced by other completely different ones, dictated by pure reason; in fact, side by side with the real city they set the image of the ideal one.

Sometimes the ideal city remained a literary image – the nineteenth century produced a long series of Utopias, from Ledoux[1] to William Morris;[2] but in the first half of the century, and particularly during the optimistic years between 1820 and 1850, some of the builders of Utopias tried to put them into practice. These episodes can be seen within the framework of the tradition of Utopian literature, but our task is to distinguish them from it, because they were the founders of a new line of thought and action, giving rise – even if only in a symbolic and often artificial way – to a conscious movement for the reform of the town and countryside and, therefore, according to Morris's definition, to modern architecture.

## a Robert Owen

Robert Owen (1771–1858) was the first and most important of the Utopian reformers. He was a man of extraordinary character, who lived at the height of the 'hard times', a self-taught shop-assistant, business man and finally successful industrialist and politician. While the politicans and business men of his time took Adam Smith's theories as virtually indispensable norms of behaviour, Owen followed quite a different line of thought, based on an unbiased analysis of economic relations which was so different from theirs that it caused him to be regarded as a dangerous agitator.

His mode of thought can be explained only in relation to his actual experience, first as an employee and then as an employer, and the factory inspired him with a whole set of ideas quite different from those in vogue in his time: an industrial undertaking functioned by organizational controls, which must take into account not only the internal workings but also the outer limits of the enterprise, in relation to the demands of the market. A correct balance, viewed in this way, was by no means automatic, not reached by the play of internal forces, but by harmony between the internal factors and conscious external action, which controlled the method

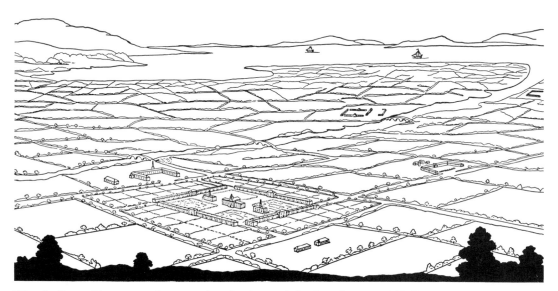

**151**  *A village of harmony and co-operation; drawing made for Owen's report of 1817*

and measure of their deployment.

In 1799 Owen and some partners bought up the spinning-mills of New Lanark, in Scotland, and turned them into a model factory, introducing modern machinery, reasonable working hours, good wages and good living accommodation, building an elementary school and a crèche, the first in England, near the factory. These improvements did not prevent him from making considerable profits and enabled him to withstand the protests of his partners, who were superseded in 1813 by other more broad-minded men, including Jeremy Bentham.

In the first years of the nineteenth century the New Lanark factories became famous and had visitors from all parts of the world. In 1813, when he went to London in search of new partners, Owen came into contact with important English politicians and broadened his field of action: he was one of the pioneers of labour law, of the co-operative movement and of trade unions.

Despite his success as an industrialist, he believed that contemporary industrial production, as a specialized activity, was basically wrong, and was convinced that industry and agriculture should not be separated and entrusted to different groups of workers, but that agriculture should be the main occupation of the English people 'with industry as an appendix'.[3]

To put this idea into practice, in the second decade of the nineteenth century, Owen worked out a pattern for an ideal settlement: a village for a limited community to work collectively on the land and in the factory and to be self-sufficient, possessing all necessary basic amenities.

This plan was put forward for the first time in 1817, in a report to the Committee for the Relief of the Manufacturing Poor;[4] it was defended in various newspapers[5] and more fully developed in a report to the authorities of the County of Lanark in 1820.

Owen specified the following points:

1  The number of inhabitants: he thought that 'all his future proceedings will be materially influenced on this point, which is one of the most difficult problems in the science of political economy',[6] and believed that the ideal number would be between

300 and 2,000 (preferably between 800 and 1,200).

2    The area of the land to be cultivated: one acre per person or a little more, therefore 800–1,500 acres, to be cultivated with the hoe rather than with the plough. Owen was an ardent supporter of intensive agriculture and this is, from an economic point of view, one the the the most important limitations of his theory.

3    Buildings and general organization: according to Owen, in traditional towns

'courts, alleys, lanes and streets create many unnecessary inconveniences, are injurious to health and destructive to almost all the natural comforts of human life. As it will afterwards appear that the food for the whole population can be provided better and cheaper under one general arrangement of cooking, and that the children can be better trained and educated together under the eye of their parents than under any other circumstances . . . a large square, or rather parallelogram, will be found to combine the greatest advantages in its form for the domestic arrangements of the association . . . . The four sides of this figure may be adapted to contain all the private apartments or sleeping and sitting rooms for the adult part of the population; general sleeping apartments for the children under tuition; store-rooms or warehouses in which to deposit various products; an inn, or house for the accommodation of strangers, an infirmary etc. In a line across the centre of the parallelogram, leaving free space for air and light and easy communication, might be erected the church, or places or worship; the schools; and kitchen and apartments for eating . . .'.[7]

The private apartments, which were to occupy three sides of the parallelogram, might have from one to four storeys; they would not have their own kitchens, but would be well ventilated, and if necessary heated and cooled.

'To heat, cool and ventilate their apartments, the parties will have no further trouble than to open or shut two slides or valves, in each room, the atmosphere of which, by this simple contrivance, may always be kept temperate and pure.

One stove of proper dimensions, judiciously placed, will supply the apartments of several dwellings, with little trouble and at very little expense, when the buildings are originally adapted for this arrangement of the association . . .'.[8]

4    The proposal to build such villages, being economically productive, might be acceptable to the land-owners, capitalists, local authorities and co-operative associations. 'Many errors will at first be committed; and experience will suggest a thousand improvements';[9] the cost of setting up such a village would be about £96,000.

5    The surplus produced by the work of the community, after basic needs had been satisfied, could be freely exchanged, using the labour employed as a term of monetary comparison.

6    The duties of the communities towards local and central authorities would continue to be regulated by common law; they would pay taxes regularly in cash and the men would do military service; but they would do without courts and prisons, since they would not need them, and would thus lighten the government's task.

Owen made several attempts to put his plan into practice, first at Orbison in England and then in America. In 1825 he purchased the village of Harmony, in Indiana, from a Protestant sect and settled there with about nine thousand followers, after having appealed to the President of the United States and to Congress.

In neither case did the architectural form of the village correspond to the theoretical parallelogram, and Owen was not very concerned about this, for he was absorbed by the social and economic problems. Naturally enough, the passage from theory to practice was not successful, and the enterprise failed almost immediately; Owen lost his capital and was greatly impoverished.

However, many of those who had gone to America with him, including his sons, stayed there and made valuable contributions to the colonization of the West. Thus the Owenite village began to fulfil a function directly opposed to that envisaged by its inventor, failing as a self-sufficient community but becoming an important centre for the surrounding territory.

In 1906 Podmore passed the following judgment on the results of the experiment:

'Thus, though Owen's great experiment failed, a quite unlooked for success in another direction rewarded his efforts. New Harmony remained for more than a generation the chief scientific and educational centre in the West; and the influences which radiated from it have made themselves felt in many directions in the social and political structure of the country. Even to this day the impress of Robert Owen is clearly marked on the town which he founded. New Harmony is not as other towns of the Western States. It is a town with a history. The dust of those broken hopes and ideals forms the soil in which the life of the present is rooted'.[10]

After the American experiment Owen's thought became increasingly radical; between 1832 and 1834 he was the leader of the English trade union movement, then began to devote himself to propagating his unorthodox ideas on marriage and religion, and ended his life shunned by English society as a mad visionary.

In many ways Owen was the most important of the nineteenth-century Utopians, even if he was not the most successful; his personal qualities, his love of humanity, his confidence in the world of industry and of machines gave him a firm grasp of social and town-planning problems to which his contemporaries were blinded by the veils of conventional theory. Yet his boundless faith in the efficacy of upbringing and persuasion hampered his contacts with the rest of the world and brought about the failure of all his practical enterprises after New Lanark.

### b   Charles Fourier

Charles Fourier (1772–1837), a close contemporary of Owen's though lacking his financial means and personal gifts, was a shop clerk from Besancon.

He based his thought on a philosophico-psychological theory which derived human actions not from economic gain but from personal attraction. He distinguished twelve basic passions and interpreted all history in terms of their combinations: at present humanity was passing from the fourth period (barbarism) to the fifth (civilization); the sixth would follow (guaranteeism) and lastly the seventh (harmony). While civilization was characterized by limited personal property, guaranteeism would submit it to a series of restrictions and limitations which Fourier describes in great detail.

Unlike the shapeless forms of present-day towns, the towns of the sixth period would be built on a concentric pattern: in the middle would be the commercial and administrative town, surrounded by the industrial and then by the agricultural ones. In the inmost zone free space would have to equal that occupied by buildings, in the second it would have to be double and in the third triple. The height of the houses would be regulated according to the width of the streets, while walls would be abolished and replaced with hedges; land-owners' rights would have to be 'reconciled' with the rights of others, and the increased value produced by public works in the sites surrounding them would go in part to the community.

But Fourier considered these advances as mere stepping-stones towards the seventh and definitive stage, when life and property would be completely collectivized; leaving the towns, men would settle in 'phalanges' of 1,620 individuals and would live in special buildings called 'phalansteries'.

Unlike Owen, Fourier did not envisage separate accommodation for the inhabitants of the phalanstery; life would be completely communal, like that in a big hotel, with old people housed on the ground floor, children on the mezzanine and adults on the upper floors. The phalanstery would have collective equipment and centralized water and drainage systems. For the actual building, Fourier envisaged the stately form of grand French architecture; it would be symmetrical, with three courtyards and numerous entrances, on the axes of the various parts of the building; the central court, known as the Place de Parade, would be overlooked by the Tour d'Ordre, with a clock and semaphore. His description contains surprisingly minute detail:

'The "street-gallery" is situated on the first floor; it could not be on the ground floor, which is crossed at various points by passages for vehicles.

The street-gallery does not receive light from both sides, because one side of it adjoins the building; throughout the phalanstery there are two series of rooms, one getting its light from the outside, the other from the street-gallery, which must be as high as the three floors that look on to it. The doors to the apartments on the first, second and third floors open on to the street gallery, which has stairs leading to the second and third floors. The main stairs, as is customary, lead only to the first floor; but two lateral stairways will lead to the fourth floor . . . . The street-gallery will be six *toises* wide throughout the central

building and four in the wings when the final constructions are built in about thirty years' time; but for the moment, since the financial situation is modest, the buildings will be as economical as possible, particularly since in thirty years they are to be rebuilt on a much larger scale. The street-gallery will therefore be four *toises* in the centre and three in the wings. The buildings will be twelve *toises* wide, divided up as follows:

gallery 18–24 feet;
room opening directly on to gallery
    20 feet;
room directly by outer wall 24 feet;
two outer walls each 4 feet;
in all 72 feet, i.e. 12 *toises*; some of the public rooms will be 8 *toises* wide, stretching from the gallery to the outer wall . . .'.[11]

There were various attempts at realizing the phalanstery, first in France, then in Algeria and New Caledonia, but they were always unsuccessful. During the Second Empire a rather similar enterprise was realized at Guise by J. B. Godin (1817–89) a former worker who had become an employer, like Owen, and the experiment, against all expectation, lasted a long time. But Godin altered Fourier's plans in two essential ways; he based the enterprise on industry and abolished communal life, giving each family a separate apartment in a large building with courtyards, as well as a crèche and assembly room. This complex was called the *familistère* and it ran Godin's industry over a long period of time, after his death, as a fully co-operative productive society[12] (Figs. 152–4).

### c *Étienne Cabet*

During the July Monarchy various writers discussed the ideal city to replace the confused and gloomy reality, and they produced often naïve mixtures of town-planning considerations and social vindication. There was completely unrealistic talk of the trans-

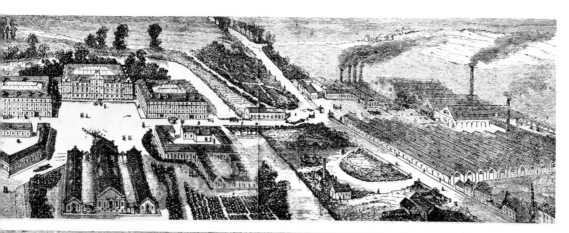

**152, 153** *General view of the 'Familistère' at Guise and the interior of the crèche (from Godin,* Solutions Sociales)

formation of Paris, for instance by the Saint-Simoniens in the Globe; C. Duveyrier conceived of the new Paris based on a plan shaped like a man about to take a step[13] and M. Chevalier provided the following astonishing description:

'The king and his family, the ministers, the Court of Cassation, the Royal Court, the two Chambers will man the pick and the shovel; the old Lafayette will be present; the regiments, musical bands and bands of workmen will be overseen by engineers and polytechnicians in full dress; the most brilliant women will mingle with the workers to encourage them'.[14]

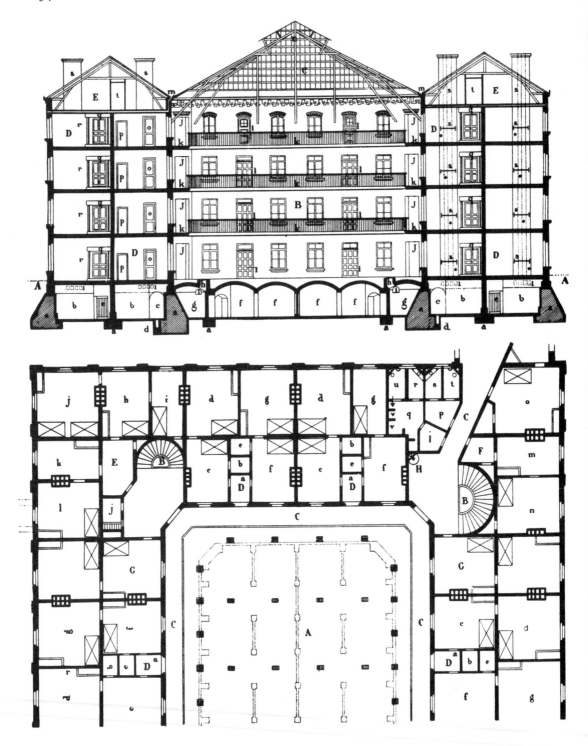

**154** *Plan and section of the residential building of the 'Familistère' (from Godin,* op. cit.*)*

Then came the suppression of working-class movements, the rue Transnonain and the censorship of the press, and it seemed unlikely that Louis Philippe and his court would go to work on a building site. So yet again these aspirations were diverted to the realms of fancy.

In 1840 Étienne Cabet (1788–1856) published the description of a new ideal town, Icaria, based on a socialistic organization of property and production; like Fourier, Cabet gives a minute description of his town, but he thinks in terms of a great metropolis combining all the beauties of the most famous cities; the plan was to be rigidly geometrical, with straight roads crossing one another at right angles and a straight river running through the middle. All the roads were to be identical; numerous measures were to be taken to facilitate the flow of traffic, and particularly of pedestrians, and to keep it separate from that of vehicles.

The architecture of Icaria was to be the perfect realization of the ideals of eclecticism, because each of the sixty districts was to reproduce the characteristics of the sixty great nations of the world, and the houses (all identical inside) were to be decorated according to every stylistic pattern.[15]

In 1847 Cabet launched a manifesto called *Allons en Icarie*, announced that he had acquired the necessary land in Texas and collected about five hundred followers; the Icarians, eager to depart, left Paris in 1848, against Cabet's wishes and without him, earlier than the pre-arranged date, but when they arrived in the United States they realized that the land was too extensive and was divided up into various separate pieces; so they withdrew to New Orleans, decimated by illness and defections.

Cabet joined them in 1849, but his arrival caused an immediate schism; the minority attempted to settle in Cheltenham in 1856, in a one-time bathing establishment, and went bankrupt in 1862, while the majority went west once more and finally founded the ideal city of Corning, in Iowa, in 1860, this time with success. The buildings were set in the middle of a 3,000-acre estate and were arranged in a way reminiscent of Owen's parallelogram. Icaria was described on various occasions, and the following is a description of it in 1875:

'The Icarians call their dwellings collectively the "city" [ville]; in the centre is the refectory, set in the middle of a huge square. Three sides of this square are occupied by detached houses, the gaps between them being filled by decorative gardens. The fourth side is devoted to common amenities, the laundry, bakery etc. . . Icaria is a most delightful-looking place. The great building of the refectory, surrounded by a clustering semi-circle of small houses, backs on to a great dark wood which emphasizes the little white-painted houses. Fruit-trees and exotic flowers and trees, and meadows, separate the various parts of the village'.[16]

But the success of the enterprise was closely linked with the extremely small number of participants, thirty-two in all. And even they could not manage to live together so closely for long, despite the flowery gardens and little white houses. In 1876 the community divided up into two groups: the young Icarians – thirteen – who emigrated to California and founded Icaria-Speranza; and the old Icarians – nineteen – who founded New Icaria not far from the original settlement, and with the same architectural lay-out. The two villages lasted some years, then dissolved in 1887 and 1895 respectively.

Cabet's idea of founding a metropolis ended as a kind of *reductio ad absurdum*, and led to the foundation of ever smaller rural villages, dwindling to the size of an ordinary farm complex.

The scientific Socialists of the second half of the nineteenth century levelled a well-known criticism at these naïve forerunners, the Utopian socialists: it was that of believing that the obstacles in the way of the realization of the new society lay solely in ignorance and not in the interests of the ruling classes, and therefore to have recourse to persuasion and not to class warfare.

In the 1848 Manifesto of Marx and Engels we read:

'The undeveloped state of the class struggle, as well as their own surroundings, cause Socialists of this kind to consider themselves far superior to all class antagonism. They want to improve the condition of every member of society, even that of the most favoured. Hence, they habitually appeal to society at large, without distinction of class; nay, by preference, to the ruling class. For how can people, when once they understand their system, fail to see in it the best possible plan of the best state of society?'[17]

Fifty years later W. Sombart judged Owen and the others with equal harshness. They started from an eighteenth-century faith in the natural goodness of man and in the natural order of society, which 'may perhaps have existed somewhere, and which, in any case, should exist everywhere, where there are no artificial obstacles'; when these obstacles were removed, 'the new society could come into existence at any moment'; socialism could seize the world 'like a thief in the night' as Owen says.[18]

For this reason they agree, basically, with the liberals because 'they too believe in the natural order, though they think it has already been realized' through free trade. In short, everything was regarded as depending on knowledge; the Utopians believed that 'the present order of things derived only from error and that men were at present wretched only because they had not known, hitherto, how to find anything better . . . . The typical demonstration of this ingenuous conception is the well-known example of Charles Fourier, who every day stayed at home from twelve to one awaiting the millionaire who

was to bring him the money to build a first phalanstery'.[19]

Politically speaking this criticism was pertinent; but despite their errors, indeed in a certain sense because of them and because of their political *naïveté*, Owen and the others made a most important contribution to the modern movement in architecture.

They were immune from that other error, which poisoned all the political thought of the time, whether liberal or Marxist, that of thinking that attention should not be focused on single problems – for instance that of the form of settlement – before basic political problems had been resolved, and that solutions to all partial difficulties would emerge naturally once the answers to general difficulties had been found.

For this reason they embarked upon partial experiments with almost exaggerated conviction and they sometimes thought – reversing current ideas – that they could solve social problems through architecture, and could improve men simply by housing them in a phalanstery or co-operative parallelogram.

Their practical experiment failed, but the ideal city that they envisaged had found a place in modern thought as a model charged with sympathy and generosity, quite different from the ideal city of the Renaissance, and it has continued to act as a spur to the progress of town-planning institutions until the present day, even if we no longer take it literally.

There is a striking similarity between many suggestions put forward by Owen and Fourier – for instance the 'unité d'habitation' with a limited number of inhabitants, centralized amenities, the 'rue intérieure' etc. – and certain solutions which constantly appear in contemporary planning. Even the number of inhabitants of Fourier's phalanstery – 1,620 – corresponds to the number of people housed in Le Corbusier's first 'unité d'habitation', and the population density advocated by Owen, one inhabitant per acre, is that suggested by Wright for Broadacre. Integration between agriculture and industry, town and country, was resolved in an unrealistic and inadequate way, and took no account of the large modern factory, which often causes several tens of thousands of workers to be gathered together, nor of certain tendencies of extensive and mechanized modern agriculture. Nonetheless, it is certain that harmony between these two different realities is an indispensable condition for the reconstruction of the unity of the modern urban scene and the modern countryside.

## 2 The movement for the reform of the applied arts

The 1848 revolution marked the peak of the period of those hopes of social regeneration which had inspired the Utopians, but the rapid ascendancy gained by the reactionary opposition produced general discouragement; the gap between theory and practice suddenly appeared too wide for any serious hope of immediate reform of the urban scene.

This was a time of ideological revision, when the European left elaborated a new line of action – announced in 1848 in Marx and Engels' Manifesto – and opposed all idea of partial reform with proposals for total revolution. Political discussion moved to questions of principle and allowed traditional links with town-planning technique to slacken, while the new European conservatism – Bonapartism in France, Disraeli's movement in England, Bismarck's régime in Germany – though withdrawing from the theoretical debate, did in fact seize upon the experiments in and proposals for town-planning elaborated in the first half of the century and used them as an important *instrumentum regni*: an obvious example was that of Haussmann's *grands travaux* in Paris.

As we have said, the sanitary laws passed before 1850 were applied by the new régimes in a spirit quite different from that in which they were originally elaborated, and made possible the great town-planning programmes of the second half of the century. At the same time theoretical models, conceived by socialist writers as alternatives to the traditional town, were largely absorbed into the sphere of the activities of the neo-conservative planners; their political implications were dropped and they were interpreted as mere technical proposals, for the re-organization of existing towns.

The ideal towns described after 1848 – the Victoria of J. S. Buckingham, published in 1849, the Hygeia of B. W. Richardson, published in 1876 – were no longer effective as a spur to any real transformation of the countryside; now at most it was a case of rationalizing the existing picture, of eliminating certain visible signs of urban disorder while leaving the causes untouched.

Thus the line of thought described in the previous paragraph, which may rightly be regarded as the first source of modern architectural thought, was swallowed up by the activities of technical departments and distorted by the paternalistic interpretations put upon it by the new authoritarian régimes. Indeed, it was precisely because of this inability of town-planners to resolve the basic contradictions of the industrial city that the need for a cultural re-thinking continued to exist, and this became urgent at the beginning of the following century.

While all this was happening, the dissatisfaction of nineteenth-century thought with the contemporary town discovered a new *raison d'être*, since the confusion and vulgarity of industrial production, including ordinary everyday household objects and utensils, were now reflected in every aspect of communal life.

In this way a movement emerged to improve the form and character of these objects – furniture, tools, textiles, clothes, utensils of all kinds – and this movement was the spearhead of the cultural debate of the second half of the nineteenth century, for as

**155** *Percier and Fontaine, Bed for Madame M. in Paris (from* Recueil de décorations intérieurs, *1801)*

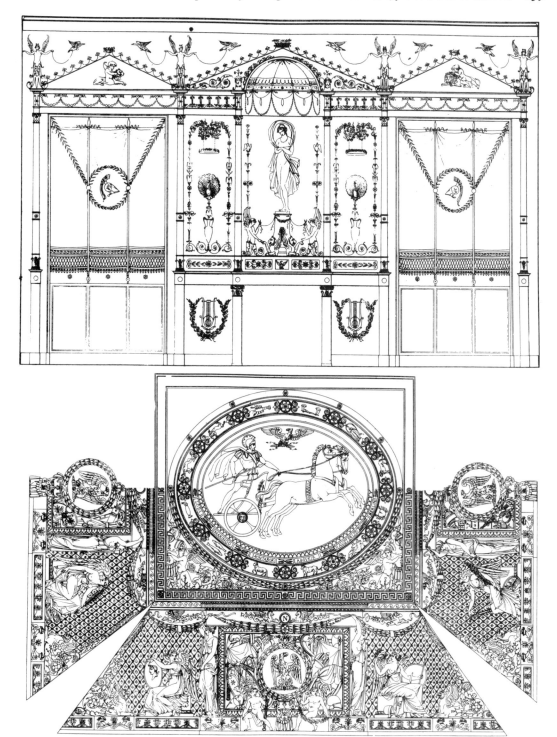

**156, 157**  *Percier and Fontaine, Wall of salon in house of C.C. in Paris and ceiling of the guardroom at the Tuileries (from* Recueil*)*

long as Morris made it possible for this line of thought to be linked to that of urban utopias.

The concept of 'applied arts' and their separation from the major arts was one of the consequences of the industrial revolution and of historicist thought.

Those who considered themselves as 'artists' and regarded themselves as the depositaries of the cultural tradition, gradually limited their activities to an ever narrower field of production, i.e. to those objects least connected with everyday use and which could be regarded as pure art; all the rest, and particularly mass-produced objects made in factories, were beyond their control and abandoned to the mercies of obscure designers, almost always motivated by strictly financial aims and mostly completely lacking in artistic education. Naturally this minor production, which was far greater in quantity than that of 'major' art and which played so vital a part in the formation of the industrial landscape, would finally reflect official artistic trends, but where this relationship had previously been direct and continuous, it now became indirect, erratic and casual.

In practice current forms of industrial production were determined by a small minority of fashionable artists – indeed, this dependence was even closer than in the past, since their execution was now a mainly mechanical action, a matter of passively executing ready-made models – but they could not exert any influence on the diffusion and interpretation of the form they had put into circulation; thus a one-sided relationship grew up between art and industry, rather than a real interchange of experience, and production broke up into various strata which moved separately, according as to whether this relationship was more or less direct.

One example will suffice: the spread of the so-called 'empire style' at the beginning of the nineteenth century. Two young architects, Charles Percier (1764–1838) and Pierre

François Léonard Fontaine (1762–1858) were largely responsible for it; they had studied together, first in Paris and then in Rome, following the classical path of French academic teaching. Fontaine lived for some time in London, where he was probably influenced by Robert Adam; they worked together from 1794 and assumed a position of great importance at Napoleon's court; Percier was concerned mainly with actual designing, Fontaine with dealing with clients and craftsmen. Together they designed the rue de Rivoli, furnished the Emperor's various residences and translated his ideas for town-planning into actual designs; in 1801 they were appointed to design the residences of the first and second consuls, and in 1804 Fontaine was appointed architect of the imperial palaces.

With the advantage of their official position and excellently organized studio, they modified the whole of French, and European, architecture and furnishing, and their influence is comparable to that of Lebrun, at the time of Louis XIV, although the respective ways in which their influence was exerted were completely different. Lebrun acted through the corporative structure of his time, and his directives affected both design and techniques of building together; there was a close relationship, organizational as well as informative, between the artists who supplied the models and the workmen who realized them, and it was the same organization that sustained relations between the two categories of craftsmen and decorators, as between interior decoration and architecture.

Percier and Fontaine, on the other hand, had no means of controlling the activities of those working outside their own sites. They provided a series of formal prototypes and validated them by the prestige of their position; from 1801 numerous editions appeared of their *Recueil de décorations intérieures*, which became the manual of all interior decorators of the first half of the nineteenth century (Figs. 155–7). The en-

**158** *Vases exhibited at the universal exhibition in London, 1851 (Victoria & Albert Museum)*

**159, 160**   *Objects exhibited at the Paris exhibition of 1878 (from Sonzogno,* op. cit.*) and at the 1851 London exhibition (from Tallis,* History and description of the Crystal Palace, *1851)*

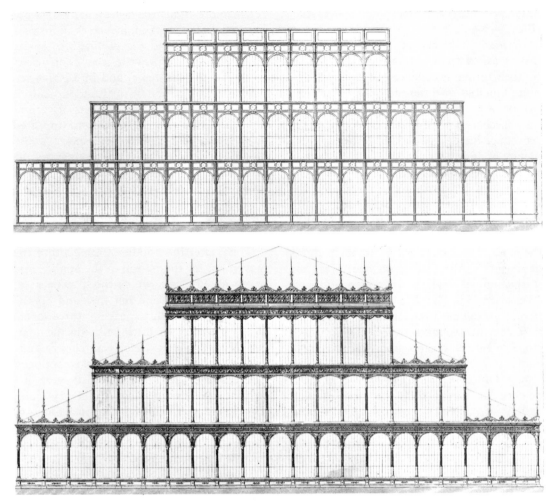

**161** *Suggestion by L. Canina for the improvement of the decoration of the Crystal Palace* (*from* Particolare genere di architettura domestica . . . proposto all'applicazione delle fabbriche moderne, *1852*)

gravings of which these volumes consist are the only real link between Percier and Fontaine and their imitators: a series of shapes, isolated from the circumstances in which they were conceived and even from the materials from which they were originally made, and endowed with an abstract and impersonal life of their own; machines, meanwhile, were ready to translate these forms, equally impersonally, into realities on any scale, in any material and in any quantity.

In this way two important artists, who for their own part maintained the close relationship between interior decoration, architec-ture and town-planning, gave rise to the first style of *décor* in which the furnishings of a room were regarded as a separate entity from the architecture. From the first decades of the nineteenth century onwards the empire style followed a course independent of the rest of official artistic culture and throughout the century remained an abstract possibility which could be adopted any time as an alternative to every other style. A limited number of fine craftsmen produced works of considerable artistic merit, particu-larly at first, but these were exceptions hard to recognize in the flood of shoddy goods that industry was showering upon the market (Figs. 158–65).

Formerly, objects of quality could be distinguished from ordinary goods not only by their formal excellence but also by other more tangible qualities: richness of design, executive precision and precious materials; but mechanized production could easily reproduce the first two characteristics; complexity of design was no longer an economic problem, because all that was needed was a mould, which could produce an indefinite number of objects, and the precision with which machine-made objects were finished was greatly superior to that with which even the finest craftsmen of old could finish off his handiwork. All that remained was the distinction of materials, though industry soon learned to simulate a great variety of these with the most ingenious processes; the taste for the straightforward use of wood, stone and metal disappeared. Between 1835 and 1846, according to Giedion, the English Patent Office registered at least thirty-five patents for the covering of surfaces in a variety of materials, so that they should look like others; in 1837, for instance, a process was invented for covering plaster with a layer of metal so that it should look like bronze.[20]

Thus not only did mechanical production overwhelm quality with quantity, but it also made it impossible for the latter to be distinguished from the former by any means apart from basic artistic worth, which could be judged only by a connoisseur.

This was why, in the first half of the nineteenth century, the average standard of the production of everyday implements fell rapidly. There were exceptions, of course, like the Wedgwood pottery (in England) and it is also notable that the decline in taste occurred a little later than industrialization, so that the standard of mass-produced objects was still high in many cases until the first decades of the nineteenth century – probably until the death of the generation which had retained pre-industrial tastes and habits – but on the whole the phenomenon is quite self-evident. After 1830 the decline was so far advanced as to provoke the controversy discussed in Chapter 2, and in 1851, when the universal exhibition in London made it possible to compare the products of various countries, the overall situation appeared alarming to people of discernment.

This realization was not limited to the field of art criticism: it forced a number of critics into action to try and remedy this state of affairs and to raise the quality of production by re-establishing the links between the major and minor arts.

Thus, after the middle of the century the movement for the reform of the applied arts began, in England, where the drawbacks of mass-production were felt first and on the largest scale. Roughly speaking, three separate phases can be distinguished: the first, between 1830 and 1860, was closely connected with the 're-organization' mentioned in Chapter 2, and its protagonists were far-sighted civil servants like Sir Henry Cole; the second was linked to the teachings of Ruskin and the activities of Morris, and was strongly ideological and literary; the third saw Morris's disciples – Crane, Ashbee, Voysey etc. – in action, and the movement's connection with architecture emerged more clearly.

The movement for the reform of the applied arts, too, moved from a Utopian standpoint to a more practical and realistic one; this was the meeting point, in fact, for industry and artistic culture with their respective traditions and prejudices which had to be overcome, with great difficulty, before any apposite solution could be found.

*a   Henry Cole and his group*

At the time of the Reform Bill the public authorities were forced to intervene in various fields of social activity, where the new problems raised by the industrial

**162**  *Printed English cotton, c. 1830 (Victoria & Albert Museum)*

revolution demanded a new institutional framework.

In April 1832, shortly before the voting on the electoral law reform, the House of Commons debated the subject of the institution of a National Gallery; during this debate the social importance of the problem of applied art emerged for the first time.

Sir Robert Peel declared:

'Motives of public gratification were not the only ones which appealed to the House in this matter; the interest of our manufactures was also involved in every encouragement being held out to the fine arts of this country. It was well known that our manufacturers were, in all matters connected with machinery, superior to all foreign competitors; but, in the pictorial designs, . . . they were, unfortunately, not equally successful'.[21]

The supporters of the neo-Gothic movement, who came into the field between 1830 and 1840, criticized both the academic classicism and the conventional neo-Gothic forms adopted at the time by manufacturers of everyday implements; Augustus Pugin (1812–52), one of the main advocates of the return to the Middle Ages, published a brilliant polemical work[22] in which he accused industry of having contaminated both the townscape with its enormous factories and the home with its vulgar products; in a lecture in 1841 he gave an ironic description of industrially produced

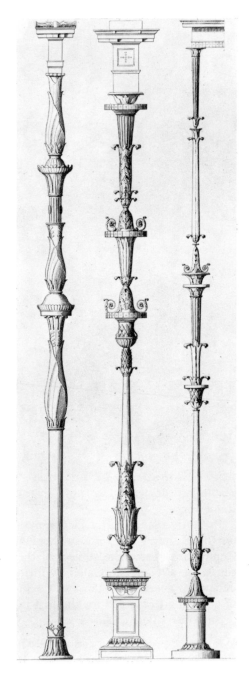

**163, 164**   *Furniture exhibited at the Great Exhibition, London, 1851 (from Tallis,* op. cit.*)*
**165**   *Decoration for cast-iron columns (from Canina,* op. cit.*)*

**166** *Neo-Gothic furniture (from Pugin, op. cit.)*

objects in imitation Gothic:

'staircase turrets for inkstands, monumental crosses for light shades, gable ends hung on handles for door-porters, and four doorways and a cluster of pillars to support a French lamp; while a pair of *pinnacles* supporting an arch is called a Gothic-pattern scraper, and a wiry compound of quatrefoils and fan-tracery an abbey garden-seat. Neither relative scale, form, purpose nor unity of style is ever considered by those who design these abominations . . . if they only produce a quatrefoil or an acute arch, be the outline and style of the article ever so modern and debased, it is at once denominated and sold as Gothic'.[23]

This trend of opinion led to the appointment of a committee of enquiry to hear the opinion of industrialists, of industrial designers, of artists and members of the Royal Academy, and it concluded that there was no suitable organization for the teaching and spread of the arts; art schools were set up in London, Birmingham and Manchester, and examples of works of pure and applied art, ancient and modern, were collected and donated to these schools to influence the pupils' taste.

These activities were promoted mainly by the Prince Consort, who had as his main collaborator a young civil servant Henry Cole (1808–82) whose untiring and far-sighted work in the field of the applied arts was comparable to that of his contemporaries Chadwick and Farr in the field of social welfare. ·

Cole was deeply convinced that the low standard of current production was due to the separation between art and industry, and therefore that it could be improved by action on an organizational level and by directing artists' activities towards industrial design.

In 1845, under the pseudonym of Felix Summerly, he won a competition organized by the Society of Arts for the design of a tea service; from 1847 onwards he organized a series of exhibitions of industrial products at the Society's headquarters – the 'Felix Summerly Series' – and from 1849 onwards published a *Journal of Design*, where he reproduced and criticized examples from all branches of industry. In 1848 he tried in vain to organize a national exhibition of English industry; in 1850, however, he gained Prince Albert's approval to organize the first universal exhibition and played an important part in the layout of the building – Paxton's Crystal Palace – and in the arranging of the exhibits.

The 1851 exhibition gave him the opportunity of weighing up the respective merits of the industrial productions of all the countries of Europe; compared with Oriental art, or with American utensils, European decorative art offered a distinctly decadent spectacle. 'The absence of any fixed principles in ornamental design is apparent in the Exhibition ... It seems that the art manufacturers of Europe are thoroughly demoralized'.[24]

Cole tried to draw the greatest profit from this comparison, never tiring of illustrating the problem in newspapers and journals, and in 1855 was instrumental in founding a museum of applied art in South Kensington, where the finest examples from past and present were exhibited side by side with examples of current production; this was the nucleus of the present day Victoria and Albert Museum.

Towards the end of his life he was concerned mainly with teaching (Fig. 168), gathering round him a group of artists who made a direct contribution to the improvement of the applied arts.[25]

The best-known was the painter Owen Jones (1806–89), son of the archaeologist of the same name; as a young man he travelled widely in Italy, the Orient and Spain, and was struck by the decorative perfection of Moslem art. In 1842–5 he published the geometrical designs and details from the Alhambra in Granada, drawn by himself and other scholars on the spot, then a volume on tessellated pavements, one on illuminated medieval books and one on Italian polychromatic ornament.[26]

In 1851 he was involved in the universal exhibition, painting the metallic structure of the Crystal Palace, and the following year he published a theoretical work on the use of colour in decorative art.[27] In 1856 he published his main work, the *Grammar of Ornament*, a collection of examples of ornament of all times and countries, though not with the mere intention of providing models for his contemporaries to copy. 'I have ventured to hope that in thus bringing into immediate juxtaposition the many forms of beauty . . . I might aid in arresting that unfortunate tendency of our time to be content with copying, whilst the fashion lasts,

**167, 169** *(above)*  O. Jones, Wallpapers for Jeffreys & Co.
**168** *(below)*  H. Cole, Designs of implements for formal education of children *(from* Journal of Design, *1849)*
**170** *(below on right)*  O. Jones, Chestnut leaves *(from* Grammar of Ornament, *1856)*

the forms peculiar to any bygone age'.[28] In fact in the last chapter he tried to draw a conclusion and to deduce, from these examples, some general rules of ornamental design, with reference to natural objects such as trees, leaves and flowers, and tried to abstract the geometrical laws of their structure; as an example he would draw the flowers of an iris in plan and elevation, and a group of chestnut leaves in a strictly two-dimensional form (Fig. 170).

After this Jones published a series of initial letters, one of monograms and a volume of Chinese decorative art, taken from the originals in the museum founded by Cole.[29]

Richard Redgrave (1804–88), whom Giedion considers the group's finest theoretician, developed the concept of 'utility' as a basic factor of applied art and showed that all the demands of artistic culture derived from this term;[30] there is an obvious connection with the utilitarianism of J. S. Mill, who was in contact with Cole and his group.

The German archaeologist Gottfried Semper (1803–79) worked with Cole's group for a time; from 1855 onwards, when he returned to the continent and was appointed professor at the Technische Hochschule in Zurich he made the activities of the English movement known in German-speaking circles, in particular with his book *Der Stil in den technischen und architektonischen Kunsten* which was widely read until the time of the Werkbund.

In 1856 L. De Laborde published a report on the activities of the French commission for the universal exhibition of 1851 where, like Cole, he expressed a hope that there would be a 'reconciliation' between industry and art, the vessel of traditional values.

The most important positive feature of the work of Cole and his colleagues was his confidence in the world of industry. Cole was inspired by the same spirit of daring and broad-mindedness that had animated Cobden, Chadwick, Robert Stephenson and other personalities of the early Victorian era.

A defect, on the other hand, was the excessive simplification of the problem. Art and industry had to be made to meet, but all that Cole and his colleagues did to obtain this result was to offer examples of good decorative design, culled from the past or from remote countries, to encourage emulation by contemporary artists; basically, they thought that the problem could be resolved on a purely formal level and, like the Utopians, thought that it was simply ignorance that hindered good design in the applied arts.

It remained for Ruskin and Morris to take the decisive step, by demonstrating that the quality of design is connected with the moral and intellectual attitude of the designer and the consumer, and with the social organization that conditions their relationship.

### b John Ruskin and William Morris

John Ruskin (1819–1900) was the teacher of Morris and his generation; he never concerned himself directly with the problem of the applied arts, but his teaching – in both its positive and negative aspects – was a decisive factor in the movement's subsequent course, and must be considered briefly before any discussion of Morris and his followers can take place.

Ruskin was a very different character from Cole and the reformers of the time who were almost his contemporaries. They were positive people, qualified in certain fields and acting in constant contact with reality; their interests were always restricted to matters which they thought they could modify by direct intervention. Ruskin on the other hand was a man of letters and his interests, theoretically, were as broad as life itself: he therefore concerned himself with politics, economics, art, geography, geology, botany and many other subjects: 'the matters he dealt with were almost as various as are the interests of human life'.[31]

In all fields, however, his attitude was always somewhat detached and sometimes superficial as compared with that of those who were practically involved, but the breadth of his cultural horizon enabled him to grasp certain relationships between one field and another which went unnoticed by those involved in only one or another of these fields.

Ruskin realized that art was a phenomenon far more complex than it seemed to his contemporaries. The so-called work of art, i.e. the image created by the artist and contemplated by the art critic, was an abstract entity isolated from a continuous process, which took in the painter's economic and social starting point, his relationship with his client, and the methods of execution, as well as the destination of the work, changes in ownership and possible material modifications.

The critic could isolate this entity, as a temporary measure, but anyone actively working in the field of art had to bear in mind the sum total of all these interconnected factors because it was impossible to alter one without affecting all the others at the same time. The work of art was like an iceberg, where the top fragment, the only part visible, moved according to laws which were incomprehensible unless one took into account the submerged, invisible part.

This view was a decisive factor in the initiation of a real movement of reform in the field of art, completely changing the course of nineteenth-century thought, since it revealed the inadequacy of the analytical attitude and the need to aim for integration between the various problems. Today this is one of the basic principles of our own culture, but towards the middle of the nineteenth century it was very hard to accept or even to grasp, and Ruskin found himself in disagreement both with his readers and himself, in as far as he shared the prejudices of his time.

The basis of his teaching, then, was important and fruitful, while the specific doctrines he put forward appear less satisfactory, even

reactionary in comparison with those of Cole and his group.

Ruskin was conscious of the disintegration of artistic culture and realized that the causes should be sought not in the field of art itself but in the economic and social conditions in which art is produced; however – because of a tendency to excessive generalization – Ruskin located the causes of these evils not in certain incidental defects in the industrial system but in the system itself, and he became antagonistic to all the new forms of life introduced by the industrial revolution. Making an error in judgment common to the thought of his time, he transformed a historical judgment into a universal one and set himself to fight not the concrete and detailed conditions of the industry of his time, but the abstract concept of industry. And since he saw that a harmonious relationship between the processes of production had been satisfactorily realized at certain times in the past – in the late Middle Ages for instance – he thought, in an equally antihistorical way, that the remedy lay in returning to the forms of the thirteenth century, and became the champion of the neo-Gothic revival.

This narrowness of outlook prevented him from making the most of his many brilliant intuitions, and he habitually shied away from any detailed, concrete discussion.

In *The Seven Lamps of Architecture*, of 1849, Ruskin began a detailed criticism of the falsifications common in contemporary production, and distinguished three types:

(i)   the suggestion of a mode of structure or support other than the true one . . .

(ii)   the painting of surfaces to represent some other material than that of which they actually consist . . . or the deceptive representation of sculptured ornament upon them . . .

(iii)   the use of cast or machine-made ornaments of any kind . . . [32]

With regard to the first point, he referred mainly to structures in iron:

'Perhaps the most fruitful source of these kinds of corruption which we have to guard against in modern times, is one which, nonetheless, comes in a "questionable shape" and of which it is not easy to determine the proper laws and limits; I mean the use of iron. The definition of the art of architecture, given in the first chapter, is independent of its material: nonetheless, that art having been, up to the beginning of the present century, practised for the most part in clay, stone or wood, it has resulted that the sense of proportion and the laws of structure have been based, the one altogether, the other in great part, on the necessities consequent on the employment of these materials; and that the entire or principal employment of metallic framework would, therefore, be generally felt as a departure from the first principles of the art. Abstractedly there appears no reason why iron should not be used as well as wood; and the time is probably near when a new system of architectural laws will be developed, adapted entirely to metallic construction. But I believe that the tendency of all present sympathy and association is to limit the idea of architecture to non-metallic work; and that not without reason'.

In fact, Ruskin goes on, since architecture was the first of the arts, it was necessarily linked to the conditions of primitive societies, where the use of iron was unknown, and consideration of these historical antecedents was inseparable from its dignity as an art; he therefore concludes that iron 'may be used only to bind, not as a support'.[33]

Ruskin naturally made a number of exceptions to the second point: covering bricks with plaster and plaster with frescoes is not reprehensible, and the expedient of gilding less precious metals is also tolerated because custom has familiarized us with it. The rule was to avoid deliberately deceiving the observer, and deceit depended upon the habits he had acquired.

Lastly, machine-made objects were rejected as follows: 'Ornament, as I have often observed, has two entirely distinct sources of agreeableness: one, that of the abstract beauty of its forms, the same whether they come from the hand or the machine; the other, the sense of human labour and care spent upon it'.[34] Mechanical production completely falsifies the second feature and therefore introduced an element of untruth and a deception.

It should be remembered that in Ruskin's time the current tendency was to attempt to reproduce, mechanically, the look of elaborate handmade work, without the relative expense; for instance, in the case of cast iron, as early as 1756 an Englishman wrote candidly:

'Cast iron is very serviceable to the builder and a vast expense is saved in many cases by using it; in rails and balusters it makes a rich and massy appearance when it has cost very little and when wrought iron, much less substantial, would cost a vast sum'.[35]

In reply Ruskin wrote reproachfully:

'You use that which pretends to a worth which it has not; which pretends to have cost, and to be, what it did not, and is not; it is an imposition, a vulgarity, an impertinence and a sin. Down with it to the ground, grind it into powder, leave its ragged place upon the wall rather; you have not paid for it, you have no business with it, you do not want it'.[36]

In order to be able to continue these arguments correctly one would have to go more deeply into the concept of habit, to place these judgments on a historical level; all the processes condemned by Ruskin were in fact objectionable only in terms of con-

**171, 172, 173**   *John Ruskin, Studies of leaves and clouds (from* Modern Painters, *Vol. V, 1860)*

**174**    *William Morris, Ornamental design, 1891 (Victoria & Albert Museum)*

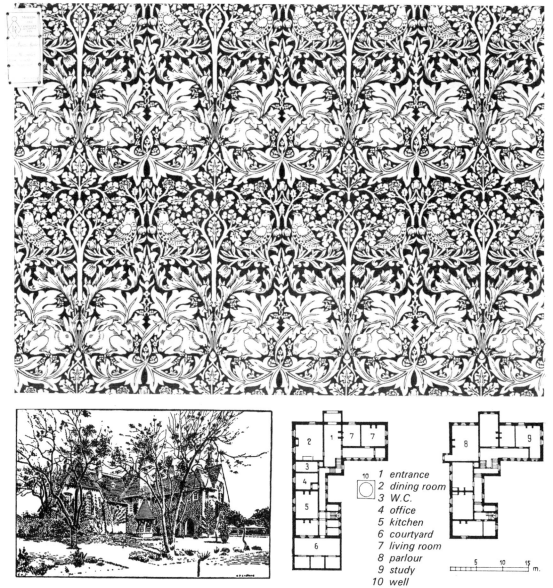

**175** *William Morris, Chintz, 1883 (Victoria & Albert Museum)*
**176, 177** *Morris's Red House (Philip Webb, 1859; drawing from Crow,* William Morris Designer, *1934)*

1 entrance
2 dining room
3 W.C.
4 office
5 kitchen
6 courtyard
7 living room
8 parlour
9 study
10 well

temporary custom, including that of machine-made products, because only someone not accustomed to machine-work compares a mass-produced object to a hand-made one. Ruskin was aware of this need and sometimes expressed it, for instance when he talked about iron, but then immediately returned to theorizing and the literary channels with which he was familiar; thus his teaching went no further than the conventional enthusiasm for the Middle Ages and the rejection of the present.

But despite its faults, Ruskin's thought was of primary importance; the defects, one might say, were glaring but superficial, while his real thought lay deeper and was less obvious, but was at the basis of all subsequent progress. Laver wrote: 'The modern world owes to Ruskin in many departments of life more than it is always ready to admit. He set out to move a mountain, and he did move it, even if ever such a little. Is it to be wondered at that he scarred his hands and spoiled his temper in the process?'[37]

A secondary contribution that Ruskin made to the movement for the reform of the applied arts were his scientific and formal studies on certain elements in nature – rocks, trees, clouds – which were examined not only from the viewpoint of natural science nor merely from an aesthetic one, but in an attempt to try and abstract, with the help of science, that basic structure which was at the heart of their artistic effect; his designs, though executed in the style of Turner and the Romantic painters, are sometimes curiously abstract, anticipating both the repertoire of Morris and certain effects of *art nouveau* similarly based on the stylization of natural objects (Figs. 171–3).

William Morris (1834–96) was a faithful follower of Ruskin and did not disagree with him on any important point. His originality lay in the nature of his interests, which were not only theoretical but also practical: he contributed a number of practical details drawn from his own working experience to Ruskin's line of thought, and he bequeathed to the modern movement not only a wealth of ideas but an active experience of infinitely greater importance.

Morris came of a wealthy family; he studied at Oxford and there met Edward Burne-Jones and other young artists with whom he formed the group known as the Brotherhood, which met to read theology, medieval literature, Ruskin and Tennyson.

In 1856, at the age of twenty-two, he entered the studio of the neo-Gothic archi-

tect George Edmund Street, a pupil of George Gilbert Scott, but found the work unsatisfying; the following year he met Dante Gabriele Rossetti, began to paint, to write poetry and also to publish a magazine.[38] In 1859 he married and decided to build himself a house in which his own artistic ideals would be put into practice: this was the famous Red House at Upton (Figs. 176–7). Philip Webb (1831–1915) made the architectural plan, Morris and his friends designed and made the furnishings; it was then that he decided to set up a workshop for decorative art, with Burne-Jones, Rossetti, Webb, Brown, Faulkner and Marshall; in 1862 the group went into business as Morris, Marshall, Faulkner and Co., and moved to London in 1865.

The firm produced carpets, fabrics, wallpaper, furniture and glass (Figs. 175, 178 and 179); Morris's intention was to give rise to an art 'of the people for the people', but like Ruskin he rejected machine manufacture with the result that his products were expensive and therefore available only to the rich. Furthermore, his enterprise never managed to expand and influence contemporary production as a whole; the firm therefore had rather a difficult existence until it was finally dissolved in 1875, when Morris became the sole owner of the workshops.

This was the beginning of his most intense and varied period of production; Morris became ever more convinced of the vital link between art and social structure and his logical development of Ruskin's principles led him to feel the need to take analogous action in the political field; in 1877 he became a member of the Radical section of the Liberal party, in 1883 went over to the democratic federation and became party treasurer; the following year he founded the Socialist League, edited its newspaper the *Commonweal* and played an important part in the workers' movements of those years; but since in 1890 the League was predominantly anarchist, Morris left the paper and, subsequently, political life altogether. Soon afterwards he published the novel *News from Nowhere* in which he described the world as transformed by Socialism as he himself understood it.

At this time he was involved in numerous other activities: in 1877 he founded the Society for the Protection of Ancient Monuments and carried on Ruskin's fight against restorations that were too radical, like those of Viollet-le-Duc; in 1878 he left London for Merton Abbey, in Surrey, where he set up a carpet factory in 1881 and a printing press, the Kelmscott Press, in 1890 (Fig. 180). In 1883 he organized the Art Workers' Guild, and from 1888 onwards organized exhibitions under the name of the Arts and Crafts Exhibition Society.

During all this time Morris also continued to propagate his artistic and political views: two volumes of essays appeared during his lifetime: *Hopes and Fears for Art* in 1882, *Signs of Change* in 1888; a third volume, *Architecture, Industry and Wealth* appeared in 1902, six years after his death.

It is difficult to summarize Morris's contribution to the debate over modern art in a few pages, because it gains its efficacy from practical experiment, while his thought received somewhat fragmentary expression in various occasional writings.

His contact with the practical world enabled him to transcend some serious limitations by which his master Ruskin was still bound. At the beginning of *The Seven Lamps of Architecture* Ruskin gives this definition: 'Architecture is the art which so disposes and adorns the edifices raised by man, for whatever uses, that the sight of them may contribute to his mental health, power and pleasure'.[39] This still contains the traditional dualism of beauty and utility, and soon afterwards Ruskin embarked upon a subtle and thoroughly academic distinction between architecture and building.

Morris, even if he does not explicitly confront the dilemma, does not like these distinc-

tions and defines the idea of architecture in a surprisingly broad way:

'Architecture embraces the consideration of the whole external surroundings of the life of man; we cannot escape from it if we would, so long as we are part of civilization, for it means the moulding and altering to human needs of the very face of the earth itself, except in the outermost desert. Neither can we hand over our interests in it to a little band of learned men, and bid them seek and discover, and fashion, that we may at last stand by and wonder at the work, and learn a little of how 'twas all done; 'tis we ourselves, each one of us, who must keep watch and ward over the fairness of the earth, and each with his own soul and hand do his share therein, lest we deliver to our sons a lesser treasure than our fathers left to us'.[40]

This definition is still fully acceptable to-day; this all-embracing vision contains all Morris's experiments in the field of the applied arts, and also in a certain sense of the political ones as well.

He believed that the distinction between art and utility could be overcome by keeping the two ideas closely united in the act of the man working to produce the relevant object. Here too the difference of tone between Ruskin and Morris derived, partly, from the way in which each approached the work of art; Ruskin saw the finished object, and had to reflect carefully to separate its various aspects, while Morris concerned himself with the production of the object, and the experience of the unity of this act persuaded him that the various facets should spring from a single reality.

Morris defined art as 'the way in which man expresses joy in his work',[41] denied that there was such a thing as 'inspiration' and fused it with the idea of 'craft'. But it was in these very concepts that he saw the justification of his rejection of mechanical production; the machine, in fact, destroyed the 'joy

**178**   *William Morris, Chintz, 1896 (Victoria & Albert Museum)*

**179** *William Morris. Chintz, 1891 (Victoria & Albert Museum)*

in work' and killed the very possibility of art. Like Ruskin, he condemned the whole economic system of his time and took refuge in the contemplation of the Middle Ages, when 'every man that made anything made it a work of art as well as a useful piece of goods'.[42]

From a political point of view, Morris associated mechanical production with the capitalist system and for this reason thought that the socialist revolution would bring to an end the mechanization of labour and, simultaneously, would replace the great urban centres with small communities, where tools would be produced by hand. Thus his socialism too became Utopian and ill-suited to the solving of the real problems of the last decades of the nineteenth century.

But here, too, practical experience did in fact partly modify his theory: despite Morris's efforts to allow only medieval processes to be used in his workshops, certain products – particularly fabrics – had to be machine-made, and in his last writings Morris slackened his absolute rejection of machines, admitting that they could all be used to good ends provided that they were dominated by men's minds:

'I do not mean that we should aim at abolishing all machinery; I would do some things by machinery which are now done by hand, and other things by hand which are now done by machinery; in short, we should be the masters of our machines and not their slaves, as we are now. It is not this or that tangible steel or brass machine which we want to get rid of, but the great intangible machine of commercial tyranny, which oppresses the lives of us all'.[43]

The theoretical and practical ambiguities in Morris's works can be further explained, not only by the origins of his thought, but also by certain aspects of his character. Despite his democratic aspirations, Morris was at heart – and particularly in his early life – an aesthete in love with beauty at its rarest and most exquisite; for this reason his objects always tended to be highly ornate, because of the intense delight Morris felt in the wealth of forms and colours. It has been said[44] that his work is all firmly two-dimensional, without any attempt at depth, and this limitation gives most of it a conventional character.

Morris's sensibility led him not to the direct appreciation of reality, but to that of the image of reality as reflected in certain forms of art; his friend Swinburne said of him that he was 'always more truly inspired by literature than by life'.[45]

It was quite natural, for him, to turn to the Middle Ages when expounding his ideas on the organization of labour, or to imitate medieval motifs in his tapestries and wall-papers, since only historical reference allowed him to become familiar with ideas and forms. In this he was entirely at one with the culture of his time, with Ruskin, Tennyson, Browning, Burne-Jones and even Gilbert Scott.

His great merit, as far as Victorian culture was concerned, was that he carried a courageous and revolutionary argument through to its conclusion, in both theory and practice, without seeking refuge in compromise, and suffering personally for the partial contradictions between his line of reasoning and his natural and acquired inclinations.

It was here that his practical experience was of vital importance: in theory all solutions can be made to work, suitably adjusted, but Morris was so sincerely committed to his intellectual choices that he did not hesitate to put them to the test of reality, that unforgiving touchstone, knowing that sooner or later their faults would have to appear.

This basic attitude also explains the development of Morris's thought. As a young man he gave up the idea of becoming an architect because he realized that the architecture of his time was a stylistic exercise, that had nothing to do with the basic relationship between man and building, and he devoted himself to the clarification of this relationship at its beginning, in the field of the applied arts.

Later he wrote:

'I found that the causes of the vulgarities of civilization lay deeper than I had thought, and little by little I was driven to the conclusion that all these uglinesses are but the outward expression of the innate moral baseness into which we are forced by our present form of society, and that it is futile to deal with it from the outside'.[46]

This led him to play an active part in political life, and to work within the socialist movement.

Today, Morris strikes us in a sense as old-fashioned, but also as alive and of our own time. His artistic production is admirable but remote from present-day tastes not only because of its stylistic imitativeness, dark colours, excessive ornamentation, but also because of the literary flavour that detaches it basically from real life. According to a recent critic of Morris's, 'his tapestries, books, tiles, carpets, illuminated manuscripts and stained-glass windows were museum pieces from birth';[47] the visitor to the Victoria and Albert Museum going from the medieval section into the room devoted to Morris is not aware of any gulf between them or of having come any nearer to our own time.

His writings are full of illuminating phrases and penetrating judgments, but they seem to come from a world remote and different from our own; the prophetic tone, the continual appeal to emotion, the tendency to make generalized judgments, all hinder any real communication between Morris and the general reader. Problems are formulated in an over-literary way, solutions are sometimes purely verbal: for instance Morris expresses a hope that all art will be killed off by industrial civilization and that humanity will return to barbarism so that the world will once again become 'beautiful and dramatic withal'.[48]

For us, his example is of more value than his works or writings: Morris was the first thinker in the field of architecture to see the relationship between life and culture in a modern way, and consciously to bridge the gap between theory and practice, though he had many predecessors in each separate field. If he made certain mistakes, he nonetheless pointed out the path along which the correction of his mistakes would necessarily lie; in this sense he (more than anyone else) deserves to be considered as the father of the modern movement.

### c  Morris's successors

Because of its anti-industrial bias, Morris's work was not immediately successful in influencing English production as a whole, but remained an experiment limited to an aristocratic élite.

However, through the Art Workers' Guild and particularly through the Arts and Crafts Exhibition Society begun in 1888, Morris did attract a large number of English craftsmen and industrialists; during the last fifteen years of his life he could no longer be regarded as an isolated innovator, but as the instigator of a widespread movement.

The gulf between the world of art and that of industrial design had certainly diminished, thanks to his work. 'What for half a century had been considered as an inferior occupation' – writes Pevsner – 'became once more a noble and worthy task'.[49] At the same time another basic idea of Morris's was also taking root – that of the corporate spirit – and each artist who entered the movement did not shut himself up within his own experience but was eager to broadcast and communicate it through appropriate channels.

In 1882 A. H. Mackmurdo's Guild came into existence, in 1884 the Home Arts and Industries Association and in 1888 (the year of the first Arts and Crafts Exhibition) Ashbee's Guild and School of Handicrafts.

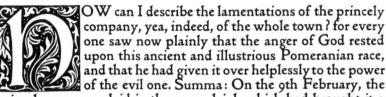

OW can I describe the lamentations of the princely company, yea, indeed, of the whole town? for every one saw now plainly that the anger of God rested upon this ancient and illustrious Pomeranian race, and that he had given it over helplessly to the power of the evil one. Summa: On the 9th February, the princely corse was laid in the very sleigh which had brought it a living body, and followed by a grand train of princes, nobles, and knights, along with a strong guard of the ducal soldateska, was conveyed back to Stettin; & there, with all due & befitting ceremonies, was buried on Palm Sunday, in the vault of the castle church.

CHAPTER XXII. HOW BARNIM THE TENTH SUCCEEDS TO THE GOVERNMENT, AND HOW SIDONIA MEETS HIM AS SHE IS GATHERING BILBERRIES. ITEM, OF THE UNNATURAL WITCH-STORM AT HIS GRACE'S FUNERAL, AND HOW DUKE CASIMIR REFUSES, IN CONSEQUENCE, TO SUCCEED HIM.

OW Barnim the Tenth succeeded to that very duchy, about which he had been so wroth the day of the Diet at Wollin, but it brought him little good. He was, however, a pious prince, and much beloved at his dower of Rugenwald, where he spent his time in making a little library of all the Lutheran hymn-books which he could collect, and these he carried with him in his carriage wherever he went; so that his subjects of Rugenwald shed many tears at losing so pious a ruler. Item, the moment his Grace succeeded to the government, he caused all the courts to be re-opened, along with the Treasury and the Chancery, which his deceased Grace had kept closed to the last; & for this goodness towards his people, the states of the kingdom promised to pay all his debts, which was done; & thus lawlessness and robbery were crushed in the land. But woe, alas! Sidonia can no man crush! She wrote immediately to his Grace, soliciting the præbenda, and even presented herself at the ducal house of Stettin; but his Grace positively refused to lay eyes on her, knowing how fatal a meeting with her had proved to each of his brothers, who no sooner met her evil glance than they sickened and died. Therefore his Highness held all old women in abhorrence. Indeed, such was his

s 1                                                                                      257

**180**  *Page from a book printed at the Kelmscott Press*

Among the most important of Morris's successors were Walter Crane, the most faithful of his disciples and direct continuer of his activities in the Arts and Crafts Exhibition Society, Ashbee, Lethaby and Voysey who were also interested in architecture. Richard Norman Shaw had no working relations with Morris and his successors but followed the same cultural inspiration and was the dominant figure in English architecture during the last decades of the nineteenth century. Around them a host of other figures – Barnsley, Benson, Cobden-Sanderson, Day, De Morgan, Dresser, Gimson, Gordon

**181-184** *Walter Crane, Decorative motifs from* Line and Form, *1902*

**185**   *Voysey, Printed material, 1905 (Victoria & Albert Museum)*

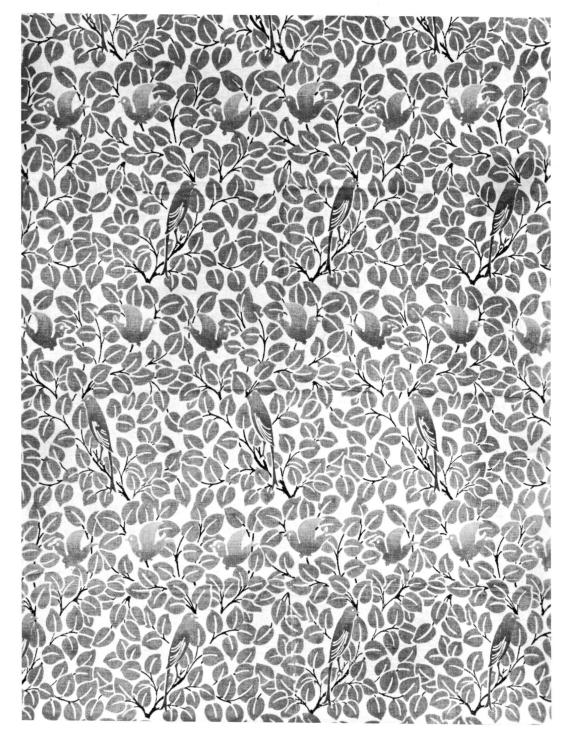

**186**  *Voysey, Printed material, 1900 (Victoria & Albert Museum)*

Russell, Powell, Walker – gave new impetus to every branch of the applied arts, from weaving to printing, furniture-making, pottery and glass.

Walter Crane (1845–1915) (Figs. 181–4) the son of a painter, was influenced by the Pre-Raphaelite group; from 1859 to 1862 he learned the art of wood-engraving in the studio of W. J. Linton and designed the illustrations for numerous books, some of which were printed at Morris's Kelmscott Press; for a long time he did regular weekly cartoons for the socialist journals *Justice* and the *Commonweal* (edited by Morris between 1884 and 1890), later collected in the volume *Cartoons for the Cause* (1896). From 1888 onwards he devoted a large part of his energies to the Arts and Crafts Association and to the spread of the movement's ideas. In his writings Crane faithfully accepted all Morris's theses, including the respect for craftsmanship and distrust of industry, but in his personal architectural work Morris's heavy medievalism was lightened, partly because of the influence of Japanese prints.

Richard Norman Shaw (1831–1912) was a contemporary of Morris; in his youth, after a period of apprenticeship, he travelled for several years on the continent and in 1856 published graphic material collected in France, Italy and Germany;[50] then he entered Street's studio, where he met Morris. From 1863 he practised architecture independently and soon became one of the best-known designers in England. Basically Norman Shaw did not give up the principle of stylistic imitation, but selected the simplest styles from the traditional repertoire, those where the ornamental trimmings were least in evidence: first the Tudor, then Queen Anne. In some of his later works the style is really reduced to the thinnest possible veil, just as much as was needed to make the appearance acceptable to the Romantic culture of the time, while what count are the unbroken surfaces of well-laid tiles, the white surrounds of the doors and windows, the perfectly arranged functional elements. Norman Shaw was also important for the influence he exerted on the generation of younger architects, many of whom entered his studio as apprentices.

William Richard Lethaby (1857–1931) learned the craft of architect in Shaw's studio from 1880 to 1892 and later taught design and the history of architecture. He played an important part in founding the Central School of Arts and Crafts and became its first director, from 1893 to 1911. He was also professor of design at the Royal College of Art until 1918.

Charles Robert Ashbee (1863–1942), architect and decorator, founded a guild and school of handicraft in 1888; this enterprise, like Morris's, met with serious economic and organizational difficulties; it was probably as a result of this experiment that Ashbee's attitude changed, and he was the first to recognize that the movement for the rebirth of the applied arts could succeed only by abandoning the attempt at reviving medieval craftsmanship. In 1911 he wrote: 'Modern civilization rests on machinery and no system for the encouragement or the endowment of the teaching of the arts can be found that does not recognize this'.[51]

Charles F. Annesley Voysey (1857–1941) was the least committed theoretician, but the most gifted artist. In his architecture, as in the numerous designs for furniture, tapestries, objects in metalwork etc., there was a freshness, a freedom from stylistic imitation which detached them completely both from Norman Shaw's Queen Anne style and from the medievalism of Webb and Morris. He had no use, either, for the graphic detail which in Morris's designs was more or less the symbol of manual accuracy and excluded mechanical processes: Voysey's designs were precise, bold and simple, using only outline, absolutely consonant with mechanical processes of production (Figs. 185–6).

The two most important steps achieved by Morris's successors were the conquest of the prejudice against industry and the rejection of stylistic imitation, particularly in industrial design. It is noteworthy, within the present context, that the acceptance of mechanical means of production was not brought about by any development of theoretical thought, but as a result of practical experiment; it is also significant that some of the most convinced supporters of industry – Ashbee in particular – were also active as architects.

The rejection of medievalism and of the heavy, compact style of Pre-Raphaelite decoration was linked with the abandoning of the bias in favour of handicraft; but it probably had other causes as well: the influence of Whistler, the vogue for Japanese art and the art of the far east and, later, that of *avant-garde* movements on the continent.

Whistler was harshly criticized by Ruskin and Morris, and in 1878 even brought legal action against the author of *Fors clavigera* for slander. It was mainly a controversy about principles, since Ruskin and the Pre-Raphaelites extended artistic involvement to the fields of morality and society generally while Whistler, like the Impressionists, believed in art for art's sake and mocked Morris's concern with reform; ('It is as if I were to embark on a painting to persuade drunkards to become teetotallers'.[52]) To Morris, Whistler's simplicity and brevity were indistinguishable from his ambition to be a 'pure' artist. However, after some time, Whistler's preference for light colours, simple forms and sober decoration was assimilated by Morris's successors when his and Burne-Jones's medievalism began to appear out-dated. Decorating the White House in Tite Street in 1878, Whistler left the walls blank, painted white or yellow,

with a few pictures and prints in dark but unobtrusive frames; Voysey's interiors were closer to these than to those of the Pre-Raphaelites, whose walls were hung with tapestries and densely ornamented wallpaper. The vogue for Chinese and Japanese art can, generally speaking, be regarded as a facet of late nineteenth-century historicism; but the gulf between the principles of far-eastern art and those of the European tradition is such that examples of this genre had a far more liberating effect on the visual habits and the taste of western artists than did examples of ancient European art. Its basically negative function, that of hastening the end of dependence on historical styles, is further demonstrated by the fact that every school used the stimulus of eastern art to its own ends, which were often mutually incompatible: Impressionists, post-Impressionists, creators of *art nouveau*.

Finally, the relationship of the English movement with European movements must be carefully considered. There is no doubt that the English movement developed in its own particular direction, quite differently from continental movements, and that the most important influence was that of England on the continent, not vice versa, at least until the end of the nineteenth century. This is why we have spoken so far of Voysey and Ashbee even thought they were both younger than Van de Velde and Horta and though they were working at the same time as the masters of *art nouveau*. Nonetheless, Belgian and German production did undoubtedly influence the applied arts in England after 1900, and this will be discussed more fully in Chapter 9, where I shall try to define the limits of the European influence on *art nouveau*.

# The industrial city in America

# seven

# The American tradition

In 1781 the United States gained independence and cut off their political fate from that of the countries of Europe. But from then on cultural relations, on the contrary, became much more important; America was no longer thought of as a simple open space to accommodate the interests and rivalries of the Old World, but as a new reality, at least as much alive in European culture as Europe was in the memory of the former colonists.

Indeed what happened beyond the Atlantic could not be considered a simple echo of European events; the elements of the common tradition, imported into a new setting, developed quite differently, and often much more rapidly, anticipating certain consequences which were afterwards to prove universally valid. American architecture, despite its traditional respect for European models and the apparent disproportion between what it took from and what it gave back to Europe, was in fact in advance of European architecture on at least two occasions: during the decade 1880–9 and today, after the Second World War.

It is therefore vital to summarize what happened in America up to the nineteenth century (Chapters 7 and 8) before considering the European *avant-garde* movements of the last decade of the century (Chapters 9 to 11).

## 1 Colonial architecture

The elements of the American tradition, as is obvious, came from the original countries of the immigrants and particularly from England, but they were profoundly modified in the process of adaptation to their new surroundings.

Seventeenth-century colonists found no suitable building tradition on the spot, and so tried to reproduce the building methods used in their native lands: the walls in stone or brick and the structural work in wood (Figs. 189–90).

Materials were plentiful, but labour and tools were short. For this reason every effort was made to simplify the processes, both by organizing the preparation of the material industrially – from the mid-nineteenth century, mechanical saw-mills were set up along the rivers in the east, which could provide ready-dressed timber in large quantities, and the production of bricks was soon concentrated in a few large brickyards – and by selecting the most economical building methods and repeating them without any concern for monotony.

Building in wood proved the best solution, since it meant that a maximum number of processes could be carried out in the factory and a minimum number on the site, thus

**187, 188**   *San Francisco at the time of the pioneers and today*

**189** *Wakefield, Virginia, Washington's birthplace*

reducing to a minimum the time involved and the man-hours expended. But European building systems soon proved inadequate to less clement climatic conditions: European houses were made of a braced wooden framework, visible from the inside and out and filled in with panels of light masonry; but an exposed structure could not stand the hard winters and hot summers of the New World, nor could the light outer walls protect the inhabitants from the rigours of the climate, so that the supporting structure was covered on the outside by a layer of overlapping boards and sometimes on the inside as well by a second lighter layer; the intermediate wall gradually disappeared, to form an air-chamber, and finally the system of supports, beams and boards was treated as a single constructional whole by reducing

supports and beams and utilizing the boards themselves to increase the stability of the building.

Openings were still small and far apart so as not to weaken the structure and because of the difficulty of obtaining glass; winter heating demanded large chimneys which were also used as structural supports, as an anchor for the light wooden structure; porticos and loggias appeared as protection against the summer heat (Fig. 191). The problem of heating and ventilation continued to be a source of concern to colonists; in 1744 Benjamin Franklin invented a cast-iron stove – one of whose advantages was that it could be mass-produced – and turned his attention several times to the possibility of real air-conditioning.

When there was any margin for stylistic

**190**  *Williamsburg, Virginia, Raleigh Tavern (1742)*

expression, builders turned to the classical repertoire, in its current English form; various public buildings of the colonial era are still standing in the east, for instance Independence Hall (1730), stylistically very correct and comparable with the best English works of the time; but American cities had no medieval buildings to remind people of other possibilities, nor was there any cultural debate to institute parallels between the various historical styles; architectural forms were affected by this situation and acquired a sort of certainty and spontaneity, just at the time when, in Europe, they were weighed down with the element of doubt produced by historicist thought.

The tendencies already present in American architecture can best be evaluated by considering the organisms of the colonial towns. Many were built on regular geometrical plans, like that drawn up by Penn for Philadelphia (1862), similar in appearance to the usual chess-board Baroque plans (for example that of Mannheim of 1699) and

probably generically inspired by these models (Fig. 197).

But the difference between the two ways of thinking was quite plain. In Europe the Baroque plans were based on the idea of extending the criteria of spatial relations that regulated the composition of a building to the whole body of the town; often it was in fact a dominant building that acted as a focal point for the composition and the town or district was based on the axes of this building. This meant that the ensemble must be not only geometrically regular but also immediately comprehensible as a precise entity, one which usually coincided with the circle of the town walls. American towns had the same regularity but not the sense of perspective unity; the street system was undifferentiated, the few distinctive elements – a wider street, a square or important building – simply interrupted the uniform texture, without producing any related intensification in the adjacent buildings; the organism was temporarily bounded by natural limits or geo-

**191** *Bethlehem, Pennsylvania (founded in 1741)*

metrical lines, but was open in all directions, the streets running in a way that suggested that they might vanish gradually into the surrounding countryside.

Rather than the Baroque town, the most obvious European term of comparison that comes to mind is that of the late medieval *bastide* towns such as Montpazier; naturally there is no direct connection, but a noteworthy coincidence of circumstances: in thirteenth-century Europe, as in seventeenth-century America, there was a problem of colonization and a desire for material and spiritual economy which have produced partly similar results.

The true nature of these American plans can be discovered not so much by considering the designs themselves as by the process of their application. A European immediately

translates the design into architectural terms, as though it were a plan for a whole complex of buildings, whereas Penn was concerned not with designing a definite complex of buildings, but only with a two-way correspondence between certain numbers and certain plots of ground. The objects and activities to be concentrated on certain particular spots were not laid down or fixed in advance, and might in fact vary continually; what was fixed was the squaring up of land according to a given pattern, and the application of a certain constant number to each little square (Fig. 198). This system was used to lay out the blocks of a city, but after the Land Ordinance of 1785 it was also used – with an increase in the basic units – to divide up agrarian property (Fig. 200) or – using meridians and parallels as a grid – to

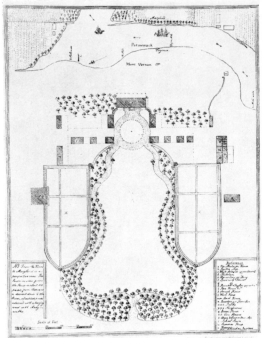

**192, 193, 195** *(below)   Washington's house at Mount Vernon*
**194** *(above right)   Boscobel in the county of Westchester, N.Y. (M. Dyckman, 1792)*

delimit the states of the Confederation.

These plans afford an immediate clue to one of the characteristics of American tradition. Certain elements are laid down rigidly and invariably, but only in so far as is necessary to provide a common and indisputable frame of reference; everything else beyond this basic pattern is free to vary

indefinitely and continually.

## 2  Thomas Jefferson and American classicism

The breaking away of the American colonies from England, between 1773 and 1781, had major consequences in the fields of

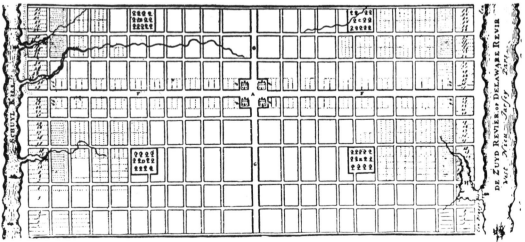

**196** *American public building was still inspired by European models. Here are some buildings in Cambridge, Mass., of 1699 (from L.C. Tuthill,* History of Architecture, *Philadelphia, 1848)*
**197** *Penn's plan for Philadelphia (1682)*

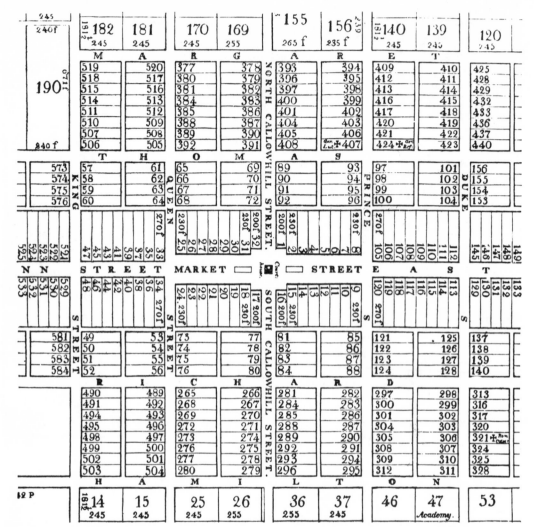

**198**   *Detail of the plan for Reading (1748, from H. Hegemann,* Amerikanische Architektur und Stadtbaukunst, *1925)*

building and architecture.

Firstly, the country's new organization demanded a series of new buildings: the seats of the new political and administrative bodies in the thirteen states, and indeed a new capital, Washington. There were also pressing needs to be satisfied in private building because of its prolonged suspension during the war, but for the moment the economic conditions of American society were not sufficiently improved to allow for recovery and only the state was in a position to carry out a building programme in the

teeth of difficulties of all kinds.

There were reasons of a political kind that confirmed the choice of the classical style. The classical forms were charged with ideological significance, as they were for Frenchmen of the same period, and they became the symbol of republican virtues; they also acquired a prestige value all the greater now that the new state had to step on to the international stage, encumbered by a series of economic, organizational and military difficulties. This aspect cannot be over-estimated when one bears in mind the

**A SECTION OF LAND = 640 ACRES.**

*A rod is 16½ feet.*
*A chain is 66 feet or 4 rods.*
*A mile is 320 rods, 80 chains or 5,280 ft.*
*A square rod is 272¼ square feet.*
*An acre contains 43,560 square feet.*
*"    "    "    160 square rods.*
*"    "  is about 208¾ feet square.*
*"    "  is 8 rods wide by 20 rods long,*
*or any two numbers (of rods) whose*
*product is 160.*
*25x125 feet equals .0717 of an acre.*

10 chains.    330 ft.

80 rods.

5 acres. 5 acres.

20 acres.

5 ch.   20 rods.

40 rods.   10 acres.   660 feet.

660 feet.   10 chains.

80 acres.

40 acres.

80 rods.

**CENTER OF SECTION.**

20 chains.

1,320 feet.

Sectional Map of a Township with adjoining Sections.

| 36 | 31 | 32 | 33 | 34 | 35 | 36 | 31 |
| 1 | 6 | 5 | 4 | 3 | 2 | 1 | 6 |
| 12 | 7 | 8 | 9 | 10 | 11 | 12 | 7 |
| 13 | 18 | 17 | 16 | 15 | 14 | 13 | 18 |
| 24 | 19 | 20 | 21 | 22 | 23 | 24 | 19 |
| 25 | 30 | 29 | 28 | 27 | 26 | 25 | 30 |
| 36 | 31 | 32 | 33 | 34 | 35 | 36 | 31 |
| 1 | 6 | 5 | 4 | 3 | 2 | 1 | 6 |

160 acres.

40 chains, 160 rods or 2,640 feet.

**199**  *Diagram of Jefferson's Land Ordinance (from C. Tunnard,* The City of Man*)*

political realism of the rulers involved:

'America had to have time to grow and room to expand in; and no stratagem which held at bay the arrogant nations of the Old World was too small to be overlooked. A handsome capital city in which to receive foreign diplomats decently – this was a real necessity in the tricky, shark-filled shoals of international diplomacy. A "tasteful" dinner party in well-designed and well-furnished rooms would serve to blur, if not conceal the complete absence of a naval fleet. A lavish table with choice wines would contradict ugly rumours of bankruptcy; and public buildings like the classic State House at Richmond would partially correct the rude impact of the log cabins in the pinelands'.[1]

Thomas Jefferson (1743–1826), the father of American democracy, personified this

**200**   *Stretch of American countryside seen from the air*

situation in his dual role of statesman and architect. A member of a wealthy family, Jefferson knew Europe well, was ambassador to France from 1774 to 1779 and in contact with the French artists of the Revolution, whose ideological classicism he shared; he was no mere amateur in the field of art, but was well-acquainted with ancient monuments and had first-hand knowledge of the advances made in historical and architectural thought. He adhered to these models unreservedly, but this did not prevent him from distinguishing clearly, on every occasion, between what was and what was not utilizable in his country, which was always in the forefront of his mind; he was concerned about both classicism and technical propriety, and he had apparent doubts about the function of them both in the American architecture of the future.

The relation between classical rules and technical rules was the central problem of neo-classical culture, and Jefferson's conception belonged, broadly speaking, within this cultural setting. Nonetheless the problems he grappled with were different, simpler than those around which European culture turned; it was almost as if the classical rules too were conceived materialistically, as given facts, and as if the problems of making them agree with technical necessities involved not mediation between the two orders of facts, but only a prudent choice of material data of a single order.

Two examples should suffice: while travelling in France, Jefferson was requested by the Virginia authorities to draw up a plan for the new Capitol, and he sent them instead the measured drawings of the Maison Carrée in Nîmes, regarding the request as 'a favorable opportunity of introducing into the State . . . the most perfect model of Roman architecture'.[2] Then when he built the University of Virginia he designed it in the Corinthian style, and subsequently changed it to the Ionic, since he was having to teach Negro slaves to carve the columns and regarded the Corinthian capital as too difficult.

In 1782, describing the conditions in Virginia, he complained about the rough and irregular appearance of its architecture and expressed the hope that the classical style would soon be introduced:

'To give these buildings symmetry and taste would not increase their cost. It would only change the form and combination of the members. This would often cost less than the burthen of barbarous ornament with which these buildings are sometimes charged. But the first principles of art are unknown, and there exists scarcely a model among us sufficiently chaste to give an idea of them . . .'.[3]

Jefferson's most important works – which were in fact to be used as 'pure models' for many decades – were the Capitol at Richmond, already mentioned, (Fig. 11), the University of the same state and his own villa at Monticello (Fig. 201). The spontaneity with which Jefferson adhered to this formal world gave his buildings a special grace, unknown to the restless European compositions of the same period: they are spacious without grandiosity, and the correctness of the design does not interfere with the convenience of the building. The distributive plan is outlined with great clarity and is simplified in such a way that the application of the classical canons is carried out effortlessly and easily. The adaptation of the ancient repertoire to the American way of living was as successful as it could be, and at this point, with an instinctive sense of moderation, Jefferson stopped. But as much could not be said of his successors, who promptly multiplied columns, pediments and domes for better and for worse throughout America.

Jefferson influenced American architectural thought in many other ways apart from his personal works.

In 1785 he passed the Land Ordinance for the colonization of the Western territories,

**201**   *Charlottesville, Virginia, Monticello (Jefferson, 1796–1809)*

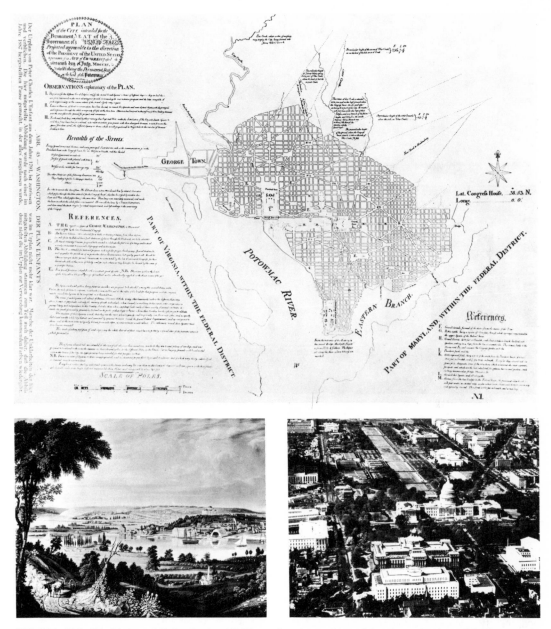

**202, 203, 204** *Washington, L'Enfant's plan (1887 copy) and two views of the city at the time of Jefferson and today*

and from 1789 to 1794, as Secretary of State, he inaugurated the foundation of the city of Washington and the competition for the Capitol. Later as Vice President and from 1801 as President, he was in charge of public works throughout the Confederation and

was closely connected with the architect Benjamin H. Latrobe (1764–1820) for whom he created the post of Surveyor of Public Buildings.

The 1785 Land Ordinance established that the new territories were to be subdivided

1 portico
2 vestibule
3 east living room
4 green room
5 blue room
6 red room
7 official dining room
8 family dining room

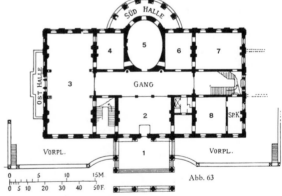

**205, 206** *Washington, The White House (J. Hoban, 1792)*

according to a grid corresponding to meridians and parallels; suitable multiples and sub-multiples of the main network (made up of squares a mile across) served to define the lots of agricultural and building land (Fig. 199). Jefferson would have liked the grid to

have been extended on a geographical scale, to establish the borders of the new states, and this was done in certain cases, but often a natural boundary, such as a watercourse, was preferable. This basic measure has left an indelible trace on both the urban and rural landscapes in the United States, generalizing the chess-board system tried out in the colonial period.

The plan designed in 1791 by Pierre Charles L'Enfant (1754–1825) for Washington, on the other hand, was an attempt at introducing Baroque concepts of circumscribed spatial units into the traditional uniform network, subordinating the composition to two monumental axes meeting at a right-angle on the banks of the Potomac, while numerous radial thoroughfares, cutting the network diagonally, lead up to the Capitol and White House (Fig. 202). L'Enfant's intention was expressed in a letter to President Washington:

'Having determined some principle points, to which others were to be made subordinate, I made the distribution regular, with every street at right angles, north and south, east and west, and afterwards opened some in different directions, as avenues to and from every principal-place, wishing thereby not merely to contrast with the general regularity . . . but principally to connect each part of the city, if I may so express it, by making the real distance less from place to place by giving them reciprocity of sight and making them thus seemingly connected'.[4]

It was a somewhat academic intention, deriving from classical European culture, like the 'symmetry' and 'taste' that Jefferson wanted to introduce into architecture. The colossal dimensions – the axis of the main esplanade, from the Capitol to the river, is more than four kilometres long, longer than that of the park at Versailles – mean that the effects of overall unity are felt chiefly in the plan but are dispersed in reality over an impossibly large area, though they do give L'Enfant's plan a noteworthy margin of permanency: the street system designed in 1791 was to meet the needs of the federal capital for over a century (Fig. 204). Baron Haussmann obtained similar results in Paris

a century later; it is interesting to note that in America certain potentialities found in borrowings from Europe, at work in a simpler, more open environment, came to fruition in America before they did in Europe.

It should be remembered that all American architects active at this time either came from Europe, like Latrobe and L'Enfant, or had studied in European universities; the relative independence of American architecture from European was therefore not the result of isolation, but of a particular limitation in cultural relations; American architects assimilated European experiences but took to America only what they regarded as useful, with a sense of moderation which is, in a sense, the real core of their national tradition.

In 1768 Jefferson wrote a sort of guidebook for the American tourist in Europe, where he listed subjects worthy of interest and others unworthy of it. There were six points he considered important:

(i)   Agriculture. Everything belonging to this art.

(ii)   Mechanical arts, so far as they respect things necessary in America, and inconvenient to be transported there ready-made, such as forges, stone quarries, boats, bridges (very especially) . . .

(iii)   Lighter mechanical arts and manufactures. Some of these will be worth of superficial view; but . . . it would be a waste of time to examine these thoroughly.

(iv)   Gardens. Particularly worth the attention of an American.

(v)   Architecture. Worth great attention. As we double our numbers every twenty years, we must double our houses . . . Architecture is among the most important arts; and it is desirable to introduce taste into an art which shows so much . . .

(vi)   Painting. Statuary. Too expensive for the state of wealth among us . . . worth seeing but not studying . . .[5]

This materialistic list, where arts and techniques are listed together like wares in a big store, to be bought or rejected, is more revealing than any lengthy discussion about the relationship between America and Europe. From the European point of view it is easy to conclude that Jefferson and the Americans understood nothing; nonetheless their attitude reveals a serenity, a detachment from the ferocious European battle – exactly the quality that appeared in Jefferson's architecture as breadth, freedom, spontaneity – which hinted at the possibilities of a new development, less subtle but freer and more open.

As far as organization was concerned, American architecture remained dependent on Europe throughout the first half of the nineteenth century. The professional figure of the architect emerged only with the founding, in 1852, of the American Society of Civil Engineers, and in 1857 of the American Institute of Architects. In 1866 the Massachusetts Institute of Technology offered the first universal course in architecture, (until then American architects had had to study in European universities, as did Richardson and Sullivan who had studied at the École des Beaux Arts in Paris) and only in 1868 was the first American architecture journal produced at Philadelphia. In the meantime American architecture faithfully mirrored the images that had come to light during the European controversy (in the first decades there was the Greek revival; about 1840, with Walter Scott's novels and Pugin's writings, the neo-Gothic and so on, through the whole repertoire of European eclecticism) but regarded them as formal alternatives, without paying any attention to the particular cultural themes and considerations from which they derived: certain albums of architectural plates were popular at the time, for instance *The Beauties of Modern Architecture* by M. Lafever and *The*

*Practice of Architecture* by A. Benjamin; they made no attempt to set the images they offered within a historical framework but simply aimed to keep their readers informed of current trends, like ladies' fashion magazines.[6]

During the first half of the nineteenth century American advances in building were not comparable to those made in Europe, since they were based upon much slighter industrial development. In 1850, for instance, American steel production totalled only a sixth of English production, about the same as that of France; only between 1830 and 1840 did the use of cast-iron supports spread, and it was not until 1855 that rolled iron girders and rails were made in Pittsburgh.

On the other hand after 1850 the use of cast iron spread rapidly; James Bogardus (1800–74) built a large number of commercial buildings in cast iron in New York and elsewhere, and became an unwearying advocate of this new material, for which he was constantly proposing new uses. His ideas were more similar to those of Wilkinson, the 'ingenious iron-master' of the eighteenth century, than to those of his contemporary Labrouste; he took pleasure in replacing the old materials with the new while leaving stylistic forms unchanged, without pausing to reflect on the cultural significance of the operation.

American engineers made certain important contributions in sectors connected with particular environmental needs: means of communication – railways, telegraph, telephone – and heating and ventilation systems. The development of the railways, from 1830 to 1869 (when the Atlantic and Pacific were linked) is one of the most famous episodes in American history. In 1840 R. Mills began the study of air-conditioning for the Capitol in Washington; in 1848 a system of air cooling was put into action in a hospital in Florida; in 1844 there appeared two basic treatises on central heating[7] and ventilation.[8]

The practical bias of American culture

prevented any proportionate battle of ideas from emerging from these advances. The first American author to consider the problems of architecture in a critical spirit and to be aware of the methodological difficulties lurking behind the use of historical styles was probably Horace Greenough (1805–52). A graduate of Harvard in 1824, he spent several years in Italy where he studied sculpture and was in contact with ancient models, participated with other American intellectuals in the Mazzinian movement and returned to America in 1851, after the defeat of the Italian revolution. He accepted the formal discipline of classicism, but like Labrouste and other European contemporaries he wanted to go beyond its forms and to follow up the intellectual rationale of planning by drawing the contributions of industry and modern engineering into the ambit of rationalized classicism. He wrote: 'By beauty I mean the promise of function. By action I mean the presence of function. By character I mean the record of function',[9] and summarized his thoughts on architecture as follows in a letter to Emerson:

'This is my theory of structure: a scientific disposition of spaces and forms, suited to place and function; accentuation of the elements in proportion with their degree of importance and in relation to their function; colour and ornamentation to be decided, arranged and varied according to strictly organic laws, giving a precise justification to every single decision; the immediate and complete banishment of all pretence'.[10]

From Greenough onwards the course of American architecture and its relations with Europe began to alter; while culture began to be organized locally (journals, schools, associations etc.), people began to feel the need to find an ideological justification, autonomous and national, for American architecture, and looked towards European culture not with the unruffled confidence of Jefferson, but with an anxious desire for emulation. Meanwhile the rapid growth of industry was suddenly faced with organizational difficulties no less great than those currently facing industry in Europe.

## 3  The 1811 plan for New York

Between the War of Independence and the Civil War, the American Confederation grew stronger and spread as far as the Pacific; at this time the United States' economy was based on a relative but lasting balance between agriculture and a moderate degree of industrialization. American town-planning now settled into patterns that were to remain stable for a long time, without ever experiencing the vital conflicts that were shaking Europe at that time.

The founding of new cities was always a current problem as colonization proceeded. Some of L'Enfant's collaborators tried to transplant the panoramic criteria of the plan of Washington to the Middle West in an ambitious form and on a large scale, as did Woodward with his 1807 plan for Detroit (Fig. 212) or in a simple form as Ralston did with the 1821 plan for Indianapolis (Fig. 213). The results were curious compromises between the Baroque concept of radial composition and the native concept of an undifferentiated street system; Ralston superimposed on this network four diagonal streets meeting in the centre at a circus; Woodward envisaged an indefinite series of radial systems, i.e. he used the star-shaped pattern of converging streets an an element to be repeated at will but his intention, over-contrived, was only partly carried out.

It was during these years that the monumental plan for the development of New York was made; here L'Enfant's panoramic schemes were firmly put aside and the uniform grid system was applied on a hitherto unknown scale (Figs. 214 and 215).

At the beginning of the nineteenth century New York had almost 100,000 inhabitants gathered together on the tip of the Man-

**207, 208**   *Two further examples of American public building: the first Capitol at Washington (W. Thornton, C. Bulfinch and others, completed in 1827) and the Yale University Library (from Tuthill,* op. cit.)

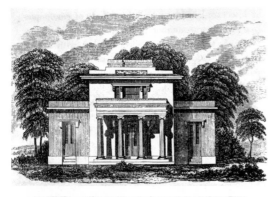

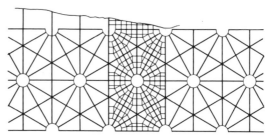

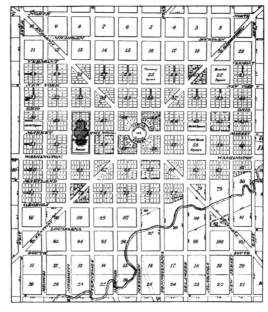

**209, 210, 211** *(left)    Cottages in the Greek style, the Gothic style and the Swiss style (from Tuthill,* op. cit.*)*
**212, 213** *(right)    Diagram of Woodward's plan for Detroit (1807) and Ralston's plan for Indianapolis (1821)*

hattan peninsula. So far the city had developed rapidly with no pre-arranged plan, but now the speed of its growth made some kind of overall plan for the whole peninsula vitally necessary.

Since the municipality was unable to solve the problem on its own, it turned to the State administration, which appointed a commission consisting of Governor Morris, S. De Witte and J. Rutherford. The commission

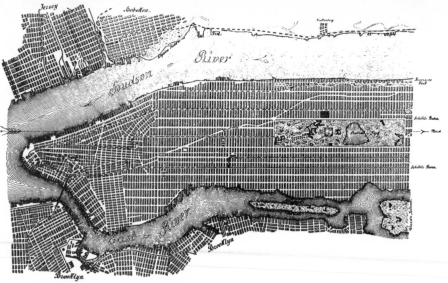

**214, 215** *New York, Aerial view and plan (from K. Stubben,* Der Stadtebau)

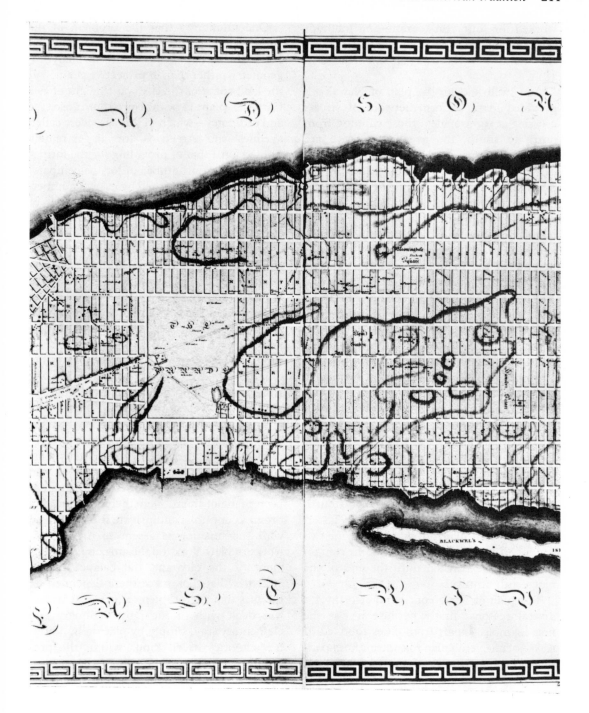

**216** *A portion of the 1811 plan for New York; the chess-board was imposed on the projections and unevenness of Manhattan without losing its uniformity (from the original preserved in the public library)*

worked for four years, examining methods of planning and possibilities of effecting them, and the definitive plan was passed in 1811.

As is well known, the plan of New York provided for a uniform network of streets crossing at right-angles: those running from north to south, the avenues – there are twelve of them – and those running from east to west, the streets, designated by the numbers 1–155. The only irregular street crossing this network diagonally is Broadway, an already existing street which the members of the commission wanted to have demolished but which they had to retain because of the interests people had in the buildings that had grown up along it. The only free space was a rectangle between Fourth and Seventh Avenue and Twenty-second and Thirty-fourth Streets which was to serve as a *place d'armes*. Later this space was filled up, while further upstream another larger rectangle was cleared for the laying out of Central Park (1858).

The dimensions of the plan were enormous, the avenues running straight for almost twenty kilometres and the streets for five; the commissioners foresaw that by fifty years later, in 1860, the city's inhabitants would have multiplied fourfold and would occupy the network up to Thirty-fourth Street; in fact, growth proved much faster, but the overall plan provided space for two and a half millions, and was able to contain New York's expansion until the end of the nineteenth century.

The plan of New York is noteworthy for several reasons: firstly because it was the first example – apart from cities founded *de novo* – of an overall plan to control the expansion of a modern city of this size, while in Europe this same problem had not yet made itself felt. Secondly, the scale of application made the comparison with Baroque plans irrelevant once and for all and revealed a new conception of the city, based on a specifically American tradition.

One might say that the problem of the commissioners appointed by the State of New York was a problem of analytical geometry rather than of projective geometry; the land space of the city was thought of as a Cartesian plane to be measured with abscissae and ordinates – which in this case were called avenues and streets – for an extremely limited aim: that of providing for the formation of a certain number of lots or compartments, each distinguished by its own number, to accommodate various future activities of all types without mutual hindrance, and each within easy reach of public amenities. The problem of the modern city was one of co-ordination; here, making use of the relatively plentiful space, the idea was to organize the least restrictive type of co-ordination, that is, to reduce rules to the minimum compatible with the technical necessities of community life, while making those few extremely rigid and unvarying. The plan of New York was not unlike the American Constitution, where the rules of political life were formulated in such a way as to occasion minimal limitations to the citizens' private activities, being therefore reduced to a series of formal statements whose meaning was comprehensible only in relation to the application that is and has been made of them. Nonetheless the orderly progress of public and private life was linked with the unanimous assent to this framework; in New York too the amazing development of the city and the balance of the activities that took place there depended on the fact that the problem of urban structure was dealt with in the most summary and elementary way, simply by placing buildings for activities of all kinds within the pre-arranged network of the regular chess-board (at least until recent decades, when the scale of the problem increased to such a degree as to render the chess-board itself restrictive and inadequate and to pose certain problems of structural transformation, all the more difficult because of the strong resistance put up by the old scheme; but this will be more fully discussed further on.)

In their conclusive report of 1811, the commissioners said that they had hesitated between the chess-board system and a design similar to that of L'Enfant, with circuses and radiating streets; they had chosen the first way because 'a city is made up of houses, and when streets cross at right angles houses are less expensive to build and more convenient to live in'.[11] The lack of squares and open spaces was justified in an equally off-hand manner: 'squares are not necessary; people live in houses, not squares'.[12] To understand these statements one should bear in mind that the building of houses was not here envisaged, as in the Baroque plans, as being contemporaneous with the creation of the street system – and therefore as part and parcel of a single unified and large-scale plan – but was to be put off until some future date; the building to occupy a certain block might be either a single-storied shack or the Rockefeller Center. For this reason the designers of the plan chose a layout that would offer as little hindrance as possible to any kind of building.

It was natural that Europeans, judging Americans by their own standards, should consider this procedure absurd, and mistake this suspension of judgment for a lack of it. For example Sitte wrote:

'Artistically satisfactory parcelling of a new section of town cannot be attempted without first having some idea as to what purpose this section will serve in the long run and what public buildings and plazas might be intended for it. Without any idea at all what buildings and plazas are to make up a part of town or what purpose it is ultimately to serve, one cannot begin either to make a distribution in keeping with the site and its conditions or to attain any measure of artistic effectiveness. It is just as if a patron were to show a building lot to his architect

and say to him: "Build something on this for me for about 100 thousand florins." "You mean an apartment house?" "No!" "Or a villa?" "No!" "Perhaps a factory?" "No!" etc. This would be simply ridiculous, indeed crazy, and could not really happen because nobody approaches a builder without very definite intentions or without a building programme.

Only in town-planning is it considered reasonable to go ahead with a building plan without a definite programme, and this derives from the fact that one simply does not know how any specific new district will develop. The consequence of this absence of a programme is the familiar building-block system, which tells us in all bluntness: "We could perhaps create something beautiful and useful here, but we do not know just what", so we humbly decline to deal with such a vague problem and therefore present merely a division of the surface area so that its sale by the square metre can begin.

Our assumption that a lack of programme is one of the reasons for unimaginative layouts is confirmed by the very latest parcelling known – the division of North America into states. This vast new land has been everywhere divided according to the same rectangular system, its straight lines corresponding to latitude and longitude. This is obviously due to the fact that the terrain was not well-known at the time and its future development could not be predicted, since America lacked a past, had no history and did not yet signify anything else in the civilization of mankind but so many square miles of land. For America, Australia and other unopened lands, the gridiron plan may for the moment still suffice. Wherever people are concerned merely with colonizing land, live only for easy money and earn money only in order to live, it may be appropriate to pack people into buildings like herring in a barrel'.[13]

**217**  *View of Broadway at the level of Canal Street (print by T. Horner and J. Hill)*

Camillo Sitte was a far more educated man than the three commissioners of 1811, but writing this, eighty years after the plan of New York, he was nonetheless further than they from an understanding of the problems of modern town-planning. He thought that a plan of a town should be like an architectural plan on a larger scale and did not realize that a modern town-planning scheme – precisely because of the difference in scale and speed of changes – was always a 'vague problem'. The problem lay precisely in distinguishing the terms posed from those not to be posed on the various scales. Governor Morris and his collaborators were convinced from the start that their job was not to design the future city but only to give it certain rules, the simplest ones possible. Their mistake was one of degree, because they thought that they were taking a decisive step by fixing the street system once and for all and leaving all the rest free.

The result was not an over-monotonous or over-orderly city, but one that was not orderly enough; in fact it later transpired that the modern city was not 'composed chiefly of houses' but of many other things: railways, markets, warehouses, offices, hospitals, theatres, cinemas, parking lots etc., which had different scales and different needs, and which could not be accommodated at random in the orthogonal system but which required an entirely different kind of organization. The new city fitted over the old plan like a piece of tight clothing; in order to continue to live, it had either to burst out of the old lines of demarcation – encountering tremendous resistance, because until now everything had been regulated as if it were to last for ever – or by trying to escape from the old traces by going underneath or above them with roads running above or beneath. But this is recent history and does not lessen the value of the 1811 plan, which

NEW YORK FROM BROOKLYN

**218**  *The Manhattan skyline from Brooklyn (print by T. Horner and W. Neale)*

despite its faults was one of the main contributions to modern town-planning thought, and which, because it was implemented in its entirety, brought to light all the technical, legal, economic and formal consequences of the criteria on which it was based; the best way to understand its value is to look at New York itself, 'the first place in the world to be in scale with the new era',[14] and perhaps the city where man's ability to transform nature as he wishes is most in evidence.

This same combination of formal rigidity on some points and of liberality on all others characterizes the building legislation of the city of New York; here too in some ways American experience was ahead of European, though it lagged behind in others. From the beginning of the nineteenth century the price of building land rose rapidly on Manhattan, forcing landlords to exploit it intensively, and from then onwards laws were passed prohibiting the erection of buildings covering a whole block, without leaving courtyards; it was also established that the municipality could purchase buildings that did not comply with these rules, demolish them and use the land as it thought fit (apparently during the first decades of the

nineteenth century this right was used on various occasions.)[15]

But crowding did not diminish; the only form of economic accommodation in the first half of the century was that of old decaying houses whose original rooms were further divided by partitions. In 1834 a report on the sanitary conditions of New York building drew the attention of the authorities to this problem, but it was only in the second half of the century that any measures were taken; in 1866 the Board of Health was set up, and in 1867 the first law on rented houses was passed, followed by another harsher one in 1901. These were simple regulations, embodying certain minimum standards for new buildings (Fig. 222) but they did not provide for any direct intervention on the part of the authorities.

From 1850 onwards, however, there were numerous private concerns providing decent popular housing. In 1847 the Association for Improving the Conditions of the Poor put forward a plan for a model popular dwelling, and in 1855 decided to build 'one or more model tenement houses for the labouring classes, in order to solve the problem of providing commodious well-ventilated apart-

**219** *Brooklyn Bridge (J. Roebling, 1867–73; from M. Schuyler,* American Architecture and other writings*)*
**220** *View of Manhattan in the middle of the nineteenth century*

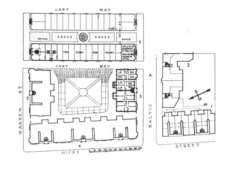

**221, 223** *(above)   New York, Brooklyn Bridge and buildings in Manhattan*
**222, 224** *(below)   New York buildings according to successive regulations and the first popular houses built by White in Brooklyn (W. Field & Sons, 1878–80; from Gray,* Housing and Citizenship, *1946)*

ments, supplied with most modern conveniences, at a price within the means of the poorer classes, which should, if practicable, defray interest on the outlay . . .'.[16]

In 1876 A. T. White organized a building society based on the principle of conserving the capital invested without speculative profit or philanthropic loss; the first group of houses built between 1878 and 1880 at Baltic Street (designed by the firm W. Field

and Sons) marked a great advance on the previous ones, because they were grouped round adequate open spaces (Fig. 224); in their next enterprise – the Riverside Dwellings in Brooklyn, of 1884 – the open space became a garden with a children's playground, garden for adults etc. In 1881 the Improved Dwellings Association – in which White was still involved – built a block of houses (designed by Vauw and Radford) using the land more intensively; another solution making very economical use of land was studied in 1896 by the architect E. Flagg for the City and Suburban Homes Co.

It is interesting to note that the public authority took many suggestions from these experiments for the determining of the standards to be introduced into the regulations, but took no definite steps to implement them and even less to intervene directly in the building field; it was not until the crisis of the First World War that the state began to intervene for popular building.

At the same time, however, the simple rules which had safeguarded the life of the city until then, began to prove insufficient to contain the new technical and social needs; this was the moment when the whole basic town-planning of New York – hitherto based on the 1811 plan and the liberalism connected with it – was to be reviewed.

# eight

# The Chicago school and the American avant-garde

In 1804, at the point where the river Chicago flows into Lake Michigan, the American army founded Fort Dearborn, destroyed by Indians in 1812 and rebuilt again soon afterwards. Several pioneers settled around it, and in 1830 the new settlement became a city; not as in the time of Romulus, by the ploughing of a furrow, but with a mathematical and economic operation in the American tradition, the division of an area of half a square mile into small regular squares near the mouth of the river and by their subsequent sale as separate sites.

The network was such that it could be extended indefinitely and by successive additions – by simply prolonging the original streets over mile after mile – and the city gradually grew, by the end of the century, to the size of 190 square miles and 1·7 million inhabitants.

During the first decades buildings were mainly of wood. From the beginning, this material was used with a particular technique which became known as the 'balloon frame'; Giedion has established that the invention of this technique was probably due to G. W. Snow (1797–1870) who from 1833 onwards occupied various technical posts in the administration of Chicago but was also a contractor and lumber dealer.[1]

This was a structure that did not have the usual hierarchy of primary and secondary elements, mortised together, but one in which numerous thin plates or studs of standardized size were placed side by side at set distances and simply nailed together; the openings, doors and windows, were necessarily multiples of the basic module; a layer of diagonal boards ensured the rigidity of the structure, while a second layer of overlapping boards protected it against the weather.

This structure made possible the exploitation of the industrial working of timber, in standardized sizes, and was itself made possible by the low price of steel nails; also it minimized the time it took to put a building up and demanded no special skills; indeed it meant that people could build their own houses with little or no equipment.

The germ of the principle of this system was contained in the framework of colonial buildings; Snow's invention was another typical application of the American concept of the *standard* in architecture, and is still widely used, with certain improvements, in the American building industry.

Chicago was almost completely destroyed by a fire in 1871, when it already had 300,000 inhabitants. Rebuilding, hesitant at first, for fear of further disasters, was intense

**225** *Aerial view of the Chicago Loop*

during the two decades from 1880 to 1900, and on the site of the old village a modern business centre grew up, with offices, large warehouses and hotels, where new building methods were tried out, with unusual boldness, to answer new needs. Throughout the nineteenth century the old chess-board system was regarded as sufficient to contain the development of the city, but in the first decade of the twentieth century the need was felt for town-planning control proportionate to the new scale of the town; the town-planning scheme of Burnham and Burnett, in 1909, was the first attempt at introducing order, if only with formalistic criteria, into the sprawling body of the city, and marked the end of this phase of the explosion of uncontrolled building.

## 1  The Chicago school

The protagonists of these events were known collectively as the 'Chicago school'.

The first generation, working immediately after the fire, included excellent engineers many of whom had been trained in the Corps of Engineers during the Civil War: William Le Baron Jenney (1832–1907); William W. Boyington (1818–98); J. M. van Osdel (1811–91). Of these Le Baron Jenney was the

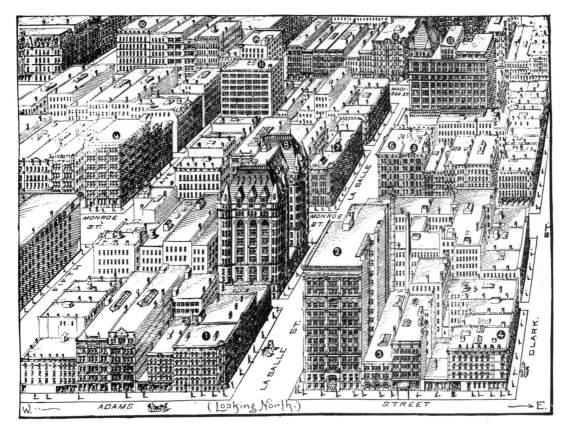

1  Schlosser Block, 1872
2  Home Insurance building (W. Le Baron Jenney, 1884)
3  Edison Company Power House, 1887)
4  Porter Block (J.M. van Osdel, 1873)
5  Kent Block, 1871
6  Nixon building (before the fire)
7  Bryan Block, 1872
8  Woman's Temple (Burnham & Root, 1892)
9  Wells building, 1884
10  Galbraith building (Cochrane & Miller, 1873–92)
11  Lees building (J.G. Rogers, 1892)
12  La Salle building (Dixon & Hamilton, 1874)
13  Y.M.C.A. building (Jenney & Munde, 1893)
14  Security Deposit Company building (C.J. Warren, 1892)

**226**  *Chicago, View from Adams Street northwards (from Rand, McNall & Co.,* Bird's-eye views and guide to Chicago, *1898)*

1  *Owings building (O.J. Pierce, 1886)*
2  *Marshall, Field & Co. building (H.H. Richardson, 1886)*
3  *Phelps, Dodge & Palmer buildings, 1888*
4  *Williams Block, 1874*
5  *C.B. & Q. Railway building, 1882*
6  *Hovey building, 1873*
7  *Carson, Pirie & Scott building, 1899*
8  *Mercantile Company building (Bauer & Hill, 1886)*
9  *Robert Law building (J.M. van Osdel, 1887)*
10  *Willoughby building, 1887*
11  *Boddie Block, 1883–93*
12  *McCormick Block, 1887*
13  *Chalmers building, 1889*
14  *McCormick, 1887 building*
15  *Yondorf building, 1874–92*
16  *Mallers building (Flanders & Zimmermann, 1892)*
17  *Ryerson building (Adler & Sullivan, 1888)*
18  *Farwell building (J.M. van Osdel, 1886)*

**227**  *Chicago, View from Fifth Avenue westwards (from Rand, op. cit.)*

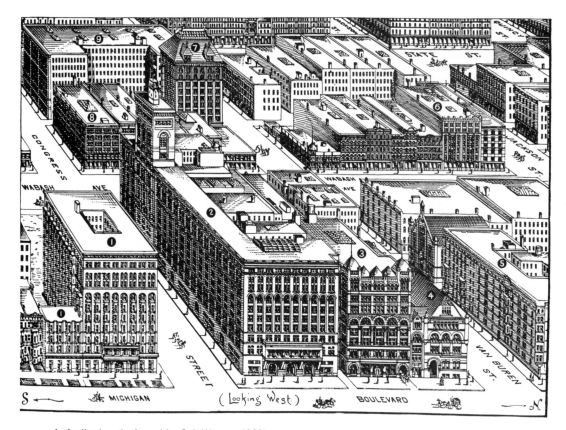

1 *Auditorium (enlarged by C.J. Warren, 1892)*
2 *Auditorium (Adler & Sullivan, 1887–9)*
3 *Studebaker building (S.S Beman, 1884)*
4 *Chicago Club building (Burnham & Root, 1885)*
5 *Victoria Hotel (G. Vigeant, 1882)*
6 *Kimball Hall (F. Baumann & J.K. Cady, 1882)*
7 *Isabella building (Jenney & Mundie, 1893)*
8 *Richardson building, 1886*
9 *Siegel, Cooper & Co.'s building (Jenney & Mundie, 1891)*

**228** *Chicago, View from Michigan Boulevard westwards (from Rand, op. cit.)*

most important, and the chief designers of the next generation emerged from his studio: Daniel H. Burnham (1846–1912), who worked with John W. Root, born in 1850, till the latter's death in 1891, William Holabird (1854–1923), Martin Roche (1855–1927) and Louis Sullivan (1856–1924) who went into partnership with Dankmar Adler (1844–1900). Closely connected with them were specialist technicians, e.g., W. S. Smith and C. L. Strobel, who collaborated with them in certain structural problems.

The work of these architects had a notably uniform character, particularly between 1879 (when Le Baron Jenney built the first multi-storey building with a metallic framework) and 1893 (the date of the Columbia Exposition) on which the particular physiognomy of the Loop, Chicago's commercial centre, depended; contemporaries were quick to notice it, and could find no other way of designating it than that of using the name of the city itself. The protagonists of this period were men of extremely divergent temperaments: some were business men like Adler, others pure technicians like Strobel, discontented artists like Root and ambitious ones like Burnham. Sullivan's case was rather different; he criticized his contemporaries, aimed at originality and at evolving a personal style of architecture, an alternative to the current version, illustrating his ideas not only with actual buildings but also with theoretical writings; for this reason Sullivan may be considered in another light, together with H. H. Richardson and F. L. Wright, i.e. among the *avant-garde* artists in disagreement with the dominant trends of their time and country, who looked towards Europe and the controversy being waged there but who also hoped to distinguish themselves from Europeans and to produce a truly 'American' art.

The high buildings of the Chicago Loop were made possible by certain technical inventions. The steel skeleton construction perfected mainly by Le Baron Jenney made it possible to increase height without needing to fear excessive strain on the piers of the lower storeys, and to have almost unbroken glass in the walls so as to be able to illuminate large expanses of building; in 1872 F. Baumann[2] suggested new systems of stone piers to support the concentrated weight of the pillars; they were gradually perfected until the appearance of the 'Chicago Caisson', in 1894. The steam lift, the first safe model, was installed for the first time in 1857 by E. G. Otis in New York and appeared in Chicago in 1864; in 1870 in Chicago, C. W. Baldwin invented and built the first hydraulic lift, while in 1887 the electric lift went into use.[3] Lifts, telephones and the pneumatic post made possible the running of hotels, warehouses and offices of any size whatever and with any number of storeys; thus, in Chicago for the first time, the skyscraper appeared. An observer wrote in 1895:

'The construction of enormously high office buildings with frameworks of iron and steel carrying the exterior and interior walls and partitions, has become an established feature in nearly all large American cities. This style of construction originated in Chicago, in its practical application, at least, and that city has at the present time more buildings of the steel skeleton type than have all other American cities together'.[4]

The skyscraper is another application of the abstractive process typical of American culture, like the chess-board. It has always been judged harshly from the point of view of overall composition, since it is an indefinite device lacking both proportion and unity; as Wright said, it is a 'mechanical device' to 'multiply by as many times as it is possible to sell over and over again the original ground area'.[5] But setting aside the disparaging view which derives from comparison with traditional visual habits, one realizes that these judgments do in fact point to a new mental process, which contains –

for the moment in rough and embryonic outline – a new way of seeing architecture, and which must be judged according to new formal criteria.

Emilio Cecchi has written observantly: 'The skyscraper is not a symphony of lines and masses, solid walls and openings, forces and obstacles; it is rather an arithmetical operation, an act of multiplication',[6] just as the method of dividing up the ground on which it stands is basically another mathematical operation, an act of division. Neither are architectural realities, but they contain the seeds of a radical transformation of the traditional architectural scene, and the principle on which they were based, being the same as that which governs industry itself, could help to move the new townscape in the direction of the needs of industrial society.

Seen in this light, the experiments of the Chicago school were an important contribution to the formation of the modern movement; but the promising results attained during the 1880s were dispersed soon afterwards, because none of the protagonists was really aware of the problems they had brought into existence. Each was caught in a cultural dilemma from which there were only two ways of escape: either a return to the conformity of historical styles (the way Burnham took) or individual *avant-garde* experiment (the way taken by Sullivan and, later, by Frank Lloyd Wright).

Le Baron Jenney was an engineer educated at the Paris École Polytechnique; he was a major in the Corps of Engineers during the Civil War and opened his studio in Chicago in 1868 together with S. E. Loring; in 1869 he published a book of plates, *Principles and Practice of Architecture,* and taught architecture at the University of Michigan from 1876 to 1880. Burnham confirms that 'the principle of carrying the structure on a carefully balanced and braced metal frame, protected from fire, is precisely what Mr. William Le Baron Jenney worked out. No one antici-

pated him in it, and he deserves the entire credit belonging to the engineering feat which he was the first to accomplish'.[7]

This principle was applied for the first time in 1879 on the Leiter building, supported from the outside by widely spaced brick pillars and on the inside by cast-iron columns, and again more consistently on the Home Insurance building of 1885 (Fig. 226), considered the first Chicago building to have a complete metal skeleton, though a portion of the party walls did still have a load-bearing function. In 1889, with the second Leiter building (Fig. 229) and the Fair building, Jenney perfected his constructional principle, reducing the façades to light screens, carried by the internal metal skeleton; however, he did keep some sections in full stonework, designed as pilasters with classical bases and capitals – though naturally beyond all canonic proportion – and also treated the metal supports as small columns where possible. The Manhattan building of 1890 rose to sixteen storeys for the first time ever to seek light above a narrow street; this time the windows, some set flush with the façade and others at an angle, opened out of continuous masonry which itself was supported, floor by floor, by the steel skeleton.

Jenney's contemporaries had greater artistic ambitions and tried to eliminate allusions to historical styles, but were less consistent in structural invention.

In 1889 Holabird and Roche built the Tacoma building, twelve storeys high, using a mixed structure with some internal and party load-bearing walls; here there were no architectural elements running from one floor to the next, but a gradation of architectural features was obtained by a gradual decrease of ornament and an attic floor with open galleries (Fig. 231).

In 1891 Burnham and Root built the Monadnock block, sixteen storeys high with load-bearing outer walls in masonry; the stonework was smooth, without any ornament and the surfaces were curved at the

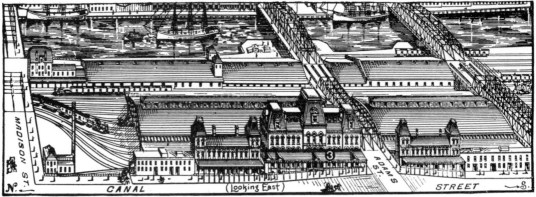

**229, 230**   *Chicago, Leiter building (Le Baron Jenney, 1885) and the Canal Street station (from Rand,* op. cit.)

**231**  *Chicago, Tacoma building (Holabird & Roche, 1889)*

corners, to emphasize the volumetric effects of the impressive box-shaped building and the columns of bow-windows.

This exceptional simplification of the outer covering was the result of the insistence of the financier who was taking a great risk by building on the outskirts of town,[8] and only later was it adopted by Root for purely aesthetic reasons; in any case the simplicity was more apparent than real, because 'the brick . . . was carried across openings on concealed steel angles and the flowing contour, unnatural to brick work, was got by forcing the material – hundreds of special moulds for special bricks being made – to work out the curves and slopes'.[9]

In 1892 Burnham and Root built the Great Northern Hotel – the structural methods normally used for office blocks were here adapted for a large hotel – and the tallest building in old Chicago, the Capitol, also known as the Masonic Temple, which was twenty-two storeys and 91·5 metres high (Fig. 233). Here the architecture was more complicated; the impressive whole was set on an arched base and topped by a steeply inclined roof, Romanesque in appearance and revealing the influence of Richardson.

The Reliance building is probably Chicago's finest skyscraper and its history is extremely instructive. It was built by Burnham and Root in 1890 as a five-storey building; in 1895, after Root's death, Burnham and the engineer E. C. Shankland added another ten floors, repeating the motifs of the lower architecture without any variation (Fig. 232). The reason for the charm, for the modern observer, of this slender tower of glazed white tiles and glass, lies probably precisely in this accident of construction, i.e. in the fact that the whole was not designed as such, but was the result of a 'multiplication' as Cecchi says; thus the simple motif of expanses of glass and decorative strips was repeated identically thirteen times over above the base of the first two floors, and no attempt was made at gradation

towards the top. The most enthusiastic critics of the Reliance building, from Giedion onwards, make no mention of this. Yet what better evidence could there be of the cultural conflict underlying the experiments of the Chicago school?

The architects of the generation after Le Baron Jenney were involved in the development of a new type of building, which contained certain formal potentialities completely different from those inherited from past culture; they wanted to master this type of building architecturally, but had only the instruments of that culture at their disposal to do it. Thus the results which seem to us most important were obtained at just those moments when, for one reason or another, concern for compositional detail slackened. Root was partly aware of this contradiction when he wrote:

'To lavish upon [modern multi-storey buildings] profusion of ornament is worse than useless . . . Rather should they by their mass and proportion convey in some large elemental sense an idea of the great, stable, conserving forces of modern civilization. One result of such methods as I have indicated will be the resolution of our architectural designs into the essential elements. So vital has the underlying structure of the building become, that it must dictate absolutely the general departure of external forms; and so imperative are all the commercial and constructive demands, that all architectural detail employed in expressing them must become modified by them. Under these conditions we are compelled to work definitely with definite aims, permeating ourselves with the full spirit of the age, that we may give its architecture true artistic forms'.[10]

Nonetheless, the problem was formulated in the usual terms for a renewal of architectural thought (masses, proportions, ornament, internal structure and external forms

**232**  *Chicago, Reliance building (Burnham & Root, 1890–5)*

etc.); revivifying energies were thus dispersed in so many isolated attempts inspired by certain less common, more peripheral aspects of the eclectic tradition, as when Root compared the Monadnock building to an 'Egyptian pylon'.[11]

Jefferson's type of realism, which led Americans to attribute cultural values with a sort of material and independent existence, enabled Chicago architects to interpret certain of the needs of a modern centre in an extremely open-minded way, and therefore to make advances in the direction of the 'pure forms' mentioned by Giedion, anticipating the work of European architects by several decades; at the same time, however, it prevented them from systematizing these results, because that involved a consideration

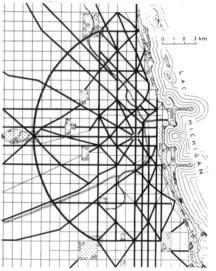

**233, 235** *(above)   Chicago, Masonic Temple (Burnham & Root, 1892) and People's Gas buildings (Burnham & Co.; from Greber,* L'Architecture aux États Unis, *1920)*
**234, 236** *(below)   Chicago, Plan by Burnham and Bennett, 1909 (from Greber,* op. cit.*) and diagram of the new street network (from Lavedan,* Histoire de l'urbanisme*)*

of the connections between the various values, which American thought was not inclined to assess. So at the juncture when the need for town-planning made it necessary to review these experiments and to order them into a system, the architects could only turn to classicism, i.e. to a ready-made system which did not need to be adapted.

It is in this context that the Columbian Exposition of 1893 and Burnham's so-called 'betrayal' must be judged.

The architectural Commission for the exhibition included some architects from the East Coast, George B. Post (1837–1913), Richard Hunt (1827–95) and Charles F. Mackim (1847–1909); Burnham, the most authoritative of the Chicago architects, was easily persuaded by them to give the complex a classical bias. The Exposition was very successful and from that moment onwards the taste of clients and the public gradually veered towards classicism, while the original innovations of the Chicago school were regarded as old-fashioned; thus many important figures from the preceding decade adapted themselves to the new atmosphere, including Burnham who founded a new firm in 1894 (D.H.B. and Co.) and became increasingly active (Fig. 235) while others, for instance Sullivan, were intransigent and therefore unpopular.

Current opinion on these matters is based on the evaluation of Sullivan and Wright who, with customary American realism, saw things in terms of the particular and considered the neo-classical trend as the result of an unfortunate choice made by a few people, and which had been enough to interrupt the course of earlier experiment. This negative judgment is correct in a sense, but it refers to a limitation that was inherent in the whole cycle of the work of the Chicago school; indeed the activities of Jenney, Root, Holabird and Roche did not leave the sphere of eclectic culture of their own accord, but broke through the frontiers of this culture in the attempt to annexe certain new themes for

it, which contained revolutionary formal implications; this was made possible by the various favourable circumstances existing in Chicago in the 1880s: an advanced degree of economic development, the availability of good technical education, absence of a restricting tradition like that of the eastern cities, and indeed the absence of any pre-existing setting, owing to the fire of 1871. But the results attained could be neither standardized nor diffused, and the only consistent way of abstracting a general norm from them, when changed economic and functional needs made this necessary, was to go back from the single experiments to common cultural premises, though it was precisely the original element of these experiments that was lost during this operation; what was left was, of course, the basic eclecticism, and the necessary lowest common denominator could be none other than classicism.

Burnham's behaviour was therefore quite logical; he interpreted in the only way possible the organizational demands that arise when a city reaches a certain density, whereas Sullivan remained entrenched in his individualist position which was soon to be by-passed by events.

The normative value of Burnham's classicism emerges clearly when one considers his town-planning activities. In 1900, the anniversary of the transference of the capital to Washington, Burnham, together with Frederick L. Olmsted (1822–1903), designer of New York's Central Park, were members of the Commission set up to look into the city's town-planning problems, and advised a return to L'Enfant's plan, eliminating any subsequent irregularities; he then began work on a plan for San Francisco, but his work was interrupted by the earthquake in 1905, which forced the administration to give up any large scale projects; from then on he and his partner E. Bennett devoted themselves entirely to the new Chicago Plan, promoted by the Chamber of Commerce.

The uniform network of the original city

**237**   *Plan of Burnham and Bennett for San Francisco (from Greber, op. cit.)*

had grown to such a degree that some roads were as many as forty kilometres long, and it no longer served its original purpose. Burnham provided a formalist solution, for he superimposed over this network a symmetrical system of new diagonal roads contained within a semi-circle thirty-two kilometres in diameter (Fig. 236), but behind this solution lurked serious problems of traffic circulation, zoning and distribution of public buildings. As in Berlage's contemporary plan for Amsterdam, no way could be found of solving these needs definitively without borrowing from traditional panoramic rules.

The importance of the problems touched upon by Burnham was demonstrated by the popularity of these operations: W. Moody, director of the Plan Commission, prepared an explanatory booklet about it for schoolchildren which was distributed in 1909, on the occasion of its approval; lectures and

**238**　*North Easton, Mass., detail of the house of F.L. Ames (H.H. Richardson)*

meetings were organized to discuss it, and there was even a special day in its honour, Plan Day.[12]

The days of the Chicago school were far away by now; everyone saw that the city could not be developed in a series of isolated enterprises but only with appropriate co-ordination, even if the instruments of this co-ordination were as yet weak and uncertain.

## 2   Louis Sullivan

In 1885 Henry H. Richardson (1838–86) went to Chicago to design the great Marshall Field Wholesale Store, opened in 1887, a year after his untimely death (Fig. 227). This building made a great impression on Louis Sullivan (then thirty years of age) as he said himself, and was decisive in his artistic vocation.

Assessment of Richardson today is largely dependent on this episode and on what Sullivan and Wright have written about it. Richardson studied in Paris from 1860 to 1865 and worked mainly in Boston, for the most highly educated and modern sector of American society; he belonged to the generation which became active after the Civil War and which brought to America first-hand knowledge of European artistic thought: the generation of R. M. Hunt and C. M. Mackim, who was responsible for the Philadelphia Centennial Exhibition of 1876.

In France, in the current neo-Romanesque style of Leon Vaudoyer (1803–72) Richardson found a style that was adaptable to the building tradition of Massachusetts where, from the first half of the nineteenth century, builders had used massive masonry in un-dressed stone, small, isolated and rhythmic-ally coupled openings, rusticated walls and simply-hewn surrounds for doors and win-dows.[13] Reference to medieval models helped him to give order and dignity to the local tradition, while faithfulness to traditional methods and the native love of stone made it possible for him to enliven stylistic patterns, and sometimes obtain effects of extraordinary power, without departing from the cultural ambit of eclecticism (Fig. 238).

Richardson deserves to be studied more objectively within the framework of the limits of his academic education; but hitherto he has always been romanticized about along the lines suggested by Sullivan; in the present state of studies it would be unwise to attempt an overall judgment of his work, so that I have discussed only his activities in Chicago and its consequences for the Chicago school.

Sullivan too, like Richardson, had studied in Paris from 1874 to 1876; in 1879 he entered the studio of D. Adler and in 1881 became his partner, an association that lasted until 1895.

Adler was a practical man, who conceived of a building as a technical problem and a business proposition. Wright described him as 'squat and solid as an old Byzantine Church . . . He could gain the confidence of both contractors and clients, dealing with both in a masterly fashion; he could pick up a contractor like a mastiff seizes a cat, and let him fall again; there were people who had got into the habit of having a stiff drink before going up to speak to him';[14] Adler had a great respect for Sullivan, who was 'a little man in an impeccable brown suit', a lover of music and poetry (Wagner and Whitman were his favourite composer and author), himself a writer and convinced that he must create a style of architecture com-pletely different from that of his contempor-aries, all of whom he despised, with the exception of Richardson and Root.[15]

Sullivan's ambitions took the form, in early works like the Rothschild building of 1881, of lush decoration in cast iron and carved stone. In 1886 the firm of Adler and Sullivan was commissioned to build a complex of buildings on Wabash Avenue containing an auditorium, a hotel and offices (Figs. 239 and 241); there is a marked difference between the first designs and the final version, due probably to the influence of the Marshall Field Wholesale Store opened in 1887.

While in most of the contemporary buildings of the Chicago school – for instance the Home Insurance building by Le Baron Jenney – the stylistic veneer was extremely slight and attempts at giving façades gradation went almost unnoticed, Richardson's building was perfectly graded and finished according to classical canons; the eight internal floors were surrounded with a covering of masonry and divided into four groups by great arches, perfectly graded so as to become narrower and more numerous towards the top. Compared with the experiments of the local school this was obviously a step backwards, but the resulting architecture was spacious, simple and perfectly resolved, while the surrounding buildings had many weaknesses, faults and drawbacks.

It was just this integrity which Sullivan found so inspiring; in the auditorium he too used a traditional masonry structure with secondary elements in iron, and grouped the numerous external openings within a broader architectural framework, emphasizing the vertical gradation by using granite and rough ashlar on the three lower floors and smooth sandstone from the fourth up; there was scarcely any decoration, and the perspective effect was obtained with the judicious arrangement of masses and materials. The same procedure was followed in the Walker building, almost contemporary with it (1888–9) where reminiscences of Richardson were clearer than ever.

From 1890 onwards Sullivan tried to apply these compositional principles to the skyscraper; the main attempt, as Wright[16] attests, was the Wainwright building in St Louis (1890–1). The essential feature of a skyscraper is that of having many identical floors; in fact, apart from one or two lower floors and the top one, the intermediate ones are so numerous that they could not be differentiated without serious structural contradiction, but the possibility of resolving this problem architectonically with the means mentioned above depended on just this mastery of the recurrent rhythm; for this reason Sullivan had the idea of treating the whole intermediate zone as a single element and therefore of emphasizing the vertical partitions, which would be con-

trasted with the horizontal lowest section and the attic.

This was the origin of the verticalism so typical of Sullivan's skyscrapers. In 1896 Sullivan gave a theoretical exposition of this method of planning:

'It is my belief that it is of the very essence of every problem that it contains and suggests its own solution . . . Let us examine, then, carefully, the elements, let us search out this contained suggestion, this essence of the problem.

The practical conditions are, broadly speaking, these:

Wanted – first, a storey below ground, containing boilers, engines of various sorts etc. – in short, the plant for power, heating, lighting etc.

Second, a ground floor, so-called, devoted to stores, banks, or other establishments requiring large area, ample spacing, ample light and great freedom of access.

Third, a second storey readily accessible by stairways – this space normally in large subdivisions, with corresponding liberality in structural spacing and expanse of glass and breadth of external openings.

Fourth, above this, an indefinite number of storeys of offices piled tier on tier, one tier just like another, one office just like all other offices – the office being similar to a cell in a honeycomb, merely a compartment, nothing more.

Fifth, and last, on top of this pile is placed a space or storey that, as related to the life and usefulness of the structure, is purely physiological in its nature – namely, the attic. In this the circulatory system completes itself and makes its grand turn, ascending and descending . . . The practical horizontal and vertical division or office unit is naturally based on a room of comfortable area and height, and the size of this standard office room as naturally predetermines the standard structural

**239, 241** *(above) Chicago, The Auditorium (Adler & Sullivan, 1887)*
**240** *Buffalo, Guarantee building (Sullivan, 1895)*
**242** *Grinnell, Iowa, Merchants National Bank (Sullivan, 1914)*

unit and, approximately, the size of window openings . . . hence it follows inevitably, and in the simplest possible way, that . . . we will in the following manner design the exterior of our tall office building.

Beginning with the first storey, we give this a main entrance that attracts the eye to its location and the remainder of the storey we treat in a more or less liberal,

expansive, sumptuous way – a way based exactly on the practical necessities, but expressed with a sentiment of largeness and freedom. The second storey we treat in a similar way, but usually with milder pretensions. Above this, throughout the indefinite number of typical office tiers, we take our cue from the window-cell, which requires a window with its separating pier,

**243**   *Chicago, Carson, Pirie & Scott building (Sullivan, 1899)*

its sill and lintel and we, without more ado, make them look all alike because they are all alike. This brings us to the attic which, having no divisions into office cells, and no space requirement for lighting, gives us the power to show by means of its broad expanse of wall and its dominating weight and character, that which is the fact – namely, that the series of office tiers has come definitively to an end.

We must now heed the imperious voice of emotion. It demands of us: what is the chief character of a tall office building? And at once we answer; it is lofty. This loftiness is to the artistic nature its thrilling aspect. It is the very open organ-tone in its appeal. It must in turn be the dominant chord in his expression of it, the true excitant of his imagination. It must be tall . . . it must be every inch a proud and soaring thing, rising in sheer exultation . . .'.[17] (Fig. 240).

Sullivan clearly believed that differentiated composition of this type was a natural fact and therefore always compatible with the functional nature of the subject; he also appears to have had in mind a kind of architecture regulated by objective neces- sities, leaving to the imagination only the task of accentuating the basic characteristics of the building. Yet when he went deeper into his subject he saw that his theoretical descriptions were leading him towards a completely novel form of architectural ex- pression, while the recurrent rhythm of the typical identical storeys was not compatible with strictly defined compositions, resolved in terms of juxtaposition of basement, inter- mediate zone and attic. Thus in designing the Carson, Pirie & Scott Store – built between 1899 and 1904 – Sullivan was led to stress just this rhythm of the identical windows of the six typical floors, simply making the top floor slightly lower, with windows set back (when the building was erected three more floors were added and Sullivan, possibly

thinking that uniformity over nine floors was excessive, made seven identical and two slightly lower, to prepare the eye for the attic floor, which was set back; later Burnham and Co., designing the extension of the building along State Street, did away with the attic and treated the three upper storeys all in the same way, while recent alterations to the top part have extended the simplifi- cation to the whole building). Here the inter- nal honeycomb structure was allowed to appear on the outside as well, without any forcing of the vertical or horizontal, and since inter-relations between the masses were now less intense, elaborate ornament, as in his earlier works, distinguished the bottom section from the body of the building (Fig. 243).

As has been noted several times, Sullivan's architectural style varied a great deal from one work to another; one would not have thought, at first sight, that the author of the Wainwright building was also responsible for the Carson, Pirie & Scott building. The link, was rather to be found in Sullivan's theoretic thought; he was stimulated in his experiment by exceptional lucidity of judgment, but in the passage from theory to practice was hampered by a basic uncertainty which was, ultimately, the cause of his professional failure.

With a clear-sightedness reminiscent of Morris, he noted that architecture was conditioned by the type of technical, social and economic organization on which it was based:

'Architecture is not just an art to be exercised with a greater or lesser degree of success. It is a social manifestation. If we want to know why certain things are as they are, in our architecture, we must look to the people; for our buildings as a whole are an image of a people as a whole, although specifically they are the individual image of those to whom, as a class, the public has delegated and entrusted its power to build. Therefore, by this light, the critical study of our architecture becomes, not a study of art, . . . but in reality a study of the social conditions producing it . . .'.[18]

But Sullivan had a conventional concept of society, founded on the near personification of certain ideas of freedom, democracy and individual enterprise; this concept demanded an effort of imagination, but it did not commit Sullivan to agitating for the transformation of existing society, as Morris had done; with his customary lucidity he was aware of this limitation, and wrote: 'I do not propose to discuss social conditions; I accept them as a fact and say immediately that the project of the tall building for use as offices must be taken into consideration and faced from the first as a problem to be resolved: a vital problem, demanding a vital solution.'[19]

Starting from this intellectual and basically elusive position Sullivan criticized the contradictions of the Chicago school severely, but assumed that each of the problems touched upon could be resolved theoretically, therefore by means of individual effort; one should be able to 'invent' the solution of an intellectual problem just as the electric lamp had been 'invented' by Edison, and once it had been invented, should be ready to enter reality without any further process of adaptation. As long as society conformed to the theoretical pattern he had of it and behaved, at least in part, according to his own ideals, then the imperfect transition between theory and practice could be disguised and Sullivan's attitude worked; but when the society in which he worked changed its behaviour, beneath a weight of demands that Sullivan's ideological system could not accommodate, then he found himself suddenly isolated

After he broke off relations with Adler in 1895 and finished his work with Carson Pirie and Scott in 1903, Sullivan's career declined; he lived on for another twenty years almost forgotten, receiving a few commissions for minor buildings, particularly small banks in country towns – in Grinnell, Iowa (1914), (Fig. 242), Sydney, Ohio (1917), Columbus, Wisconsin (1919) – where he concentrated on increasingly subtle and refined decoration. Writing was another means of escape: from 1901 to 1902 he published his first piece of systematic writing, *Kindergarten Chats*, in serial form in the 'Interstate architects and builders'; from 1922 to 1923 he published his *Autobiography of an Idea*, also in parts, in the 'Journal of the American Institute of Architects', and it appeared in book form in 1924; his last book, *A system of Architectural Ornament according with a Philosophy of Man's Power*, also came out in 1924, the year of his death.

Sullivan's situation *vis-à-vis* society was in a sense similar to that of many European architects after 1890, and to describe it one might use the term *avant-garde* as it will be used in the following chapters; in America this situation appeared about a decade earlier, and in a particularly tense cultural situation. The experiment ended with a violent defeat, and Sullivan paid for it in person; a cultural drama became his personal tragedy.

## 3 Early works of Frank Lloyd Wright

Frank Lloyd Wright (1869–1959) was eighteen when he entered the studio of Adler and Sullivan in 1887, while the plan for the Chicago Auditorium was under way, and he worked with them on it until 1893; while still employed by them he began to work on his own as well and in 1893 opened his own studio on the top floor of the Garrick building in Chicago. This was the beginning of the most extraordinary career of any architect of our time; Frank Lloyd Wright died at the age of ninety, in 1959, after having designed over three hundred buildings and

**244, 245**   *Two details of the Carson, Pirie & Scott building*

made a lasting impression on three generations of architects.

Since his influence covered the whole
period of the formation and development of
the modern movement, Wright will be
discussed several times in the course of this
historical account; however, in considering
the constant characteristics of his long period
of production, one must first consider his
formation in Chicago, since his personality
is comprehensible only in relation to this
cultural experience.

Wright talks of Sullivan and Adler with
affection and gratitude, but also with a
certain detachment; from the beginning he
shared Sullivan's ambitions, to create a new
architecture, independent of traditional styles
and close to modern life; but he did not
experience either the worries or the difficulties that Sullivan had in his attempt to
interpret the specific reality of life in Chicago,

and he regarded them as weak and sentimental.[20]

From the beginning, indeed, the abstract
terms used by Sullivan to describe the
society of his time and to formulate its
architectural problems were, for Wright,
definite and indisputable realities (this difference of attitude may possibly find a partial
explanation in the fact that Sullivan spent
two years in Paris, where he acquired a
number of burdensome conventional ideas
but also the ability to doubt, whereas Wright
felt no doubts); in this way Wright was safe
from any failure, in notable contrast to
Sullivan, whose activity declined sharply
after 1893 because he had acted not in the
context of a real historical situation, but of
an imagined abstract one.[21]

He believed that, beyond specific historical
circumstances, there existed a state of
nature, a genuine kernel of life, which was

usually hidden and contaminated by the external impositions and constraints of the outside world; Wright sometimes described it in general terms, (for instance: 'Its supreme characteristic is called initiative. When individual initiative is strong and active, there life bursts forth in plenty'[22]), sometimes considered it as a characteristic of the true American spirit. By keeping close to this vital nucleus, a type of architecture might finally be produced that was free from all conformism and normative systems; the adjective 'organic' was applied to any form of organization in which the principle was taken into account, and therefore to society and architecture, which run closely parallel:

'An organic architecture means more or less organic society. Organic ideals of integral building reject rules imposed by exterior aestheticism or mere taste, and so would the people to whom such architecture would belong reject such external impositions upon life as were not in accord with the nature and the character of the man who had found his work and the place where he could be happy and useful because of it'.[23]

Just as the eighteenth-century liberals defined their political and economic systems in a primarily negative way, as liberation from the old system of rules and restrictions, so Wright talked of his architecture in mainly negative terms, as 'independence from all external imposition, wherever it may come from; independence from all classicism – old or new – and from all devotion to the "classics"; independence from the "crucifixion of life" by current commercialism or academic standards',[24] and found numerous ways of qualifying what he did not want: classicism, the major and minor axes, the fifty-seven varieties, entablature, dome, skyscraper etc. He himself may have glimpsed this aspect of his thought when he talked of 'artistic liberalism'.[25]

There is no point in discussing these theoretical assertions, with their eighteenth-century abstractness. But it is important to understand them as clarifying Wright's position as a designer; in fact by taking the precaution to protect himself in advance from any practical involvement in the problems of modern society, Wright could tackle almost any problem as an opportunity to exercise his personal fancy and provide a formally perfect solution.

In this way, like an old master, he was able to develop his ability to plan and to foresee the spatial effect of his planned forms, more perspicaciously than any other architect of our time; any discussion of Wright must be about formal matters, and it is only on these terms that his activity can be aptly characterized; as Zevi says, 'the only real point of discussion about Wright is that of his concept of space'.[26]

Wright's attitude may be seen, beyond any particular controversy, as part of the wave of formalist re-thinking which scattered the Chicago school after the Columbian Exposition; it is by no means a coincidence that Wright should have begun his career just at that moment.

Long before any school in Europe, the Chicago school had begun to reconsider certain basic problems of architecture in the light of the needs of modern industrial society; since this episode was linked to certain special circumstances, the activities of the Chicago school waned when the circumstances changed; then cultural discussion too dwindled to a mere debate on form. Burnham and most Chicago architects chose neo-classicism and proposed this style, every one of whose consequences had already been calculated, to the new governing class; but Wright and a few others (G. Elmslie and B. Griffin) chose a limitless anti-classical experimentalism and looked for opportunities to exercise it along the boundaries of the world of business and official building.

In this way a split developed between the conformist majority and the nonconformist minority, similar to that which occurred in Europe at the same time but with one important difference: the American scene was far vaster and more varied and there was plenty of room for both schools of thought. Thus the two experiments followed independent courses, with few confrontations, and were far less driven to emerge from their respective limits or go beyond the conventional terms of the controversy.

The first period of Wright's activity, up to 1910, includes numerous one-family houses, the so-called 'prairie houses' (Figs. 246–51), a few other buildings including an important office block (the Larkin building in Buffalo, 1905) and a church, the Unity Temple at Oak Park of 1906 (Fig. 255). As has been noted, the point of departure for the experiments was Richardson rather than Sullivan, or Sullivan in his early period, that of the Auditorium, because of the insistence on the differentiation of the various elements and the close association between decoration and natural materials; in the Larkin building, too, there is a feeling for sensational effects of mass and for sweeping decoration giving movement to the whole building, quite different from the minute incrustations applied on buildings of the Chicago school.

The main difference, however, did not lie in formal preferences but in the confidence and orderliness of the invention, made possible by the fusion of the various separate stylistic threads and their organization into a fluid and strongly personal style. The designs of Sullivan and his contemporaries were almost always effortful and hesitant because they were encumbered by unresolved conflicts between the various demands to be met; Wright's plans, on the other hand, were conceived instantaneously and with an absolute sureness of touch, because the needs were selected in advance and adopted as elements of a personal investigation.

Wright himself, in 1930, described as follows the main points of the architectural programme carried out in his Prairie Houses:

'First – to reduce the number of necessary

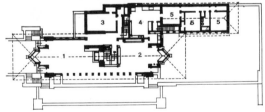

*Upper Floor*

*Lower Floor*

1 *living room*
2 *dining room*
3 *guest room*
4 *kitchen*
5 *servants' rooms*
6 *billiard room*

7 *childrens' playroom*
8 *hall*
9 *heating*
10 *laundry*
11 *garages*
12 *courtyard*

**246, 247** *Oak Park, Robie house (Frank Lloyd Wright, 1909)*

**248, 249** *Oak Park, Two views of the Moore house (Frank Lloyd Wright, 1895)*

parts of the house and the separate rooms to a minimum, and make all come together as enclosed space – so divided that light, air and vista permeated the whole with a sense of unity;

Second – to associate the building as a whole with its site by extension and emphasis of the planes parallel to the ground, but keeping the floors off the best part of the site, thus leaving that better

part for use in connection with the life of the house. Extended level planes were found useful in this connection.

Third – to eliminate the room as a box, and the house as another by making all walls enclosing screens – the ceilings and floors and enclosing screens – to flow into each other as one large enclosure of space, with minor subdivisions only. Make all house proportions more liberally human,

with less wasted space in structure and structure more appropriate to material, and as a whole more livable. *Liberal* is the best word. Extended straight lines or streamlines were useful in this.

Fourth – to get the unwholesome basement up out of the ground, entirely above it, as a low pedestal for the living portion of the home, making the foundation itself visible as a low masonry platform on which the building should stand.

Fifth – to harmonize all necessary openings to "outside" and "inside" with good human proportions and make them occur naturally – singly or in a series in the scheme of the whole building. Usually they appeared as "lightscreens" instead of walls, because all the "architecture" of the house was chiefly the way these openings came in such walls as were grouped about the rooms as enclosing screens. The *room* as such was now the essential architectural expression, and there were to be no holes cut in walls as holes are cut in a box, because this was not in keeping with the ideal of "plastic". Cutting holes was violent.

Sixth – to eliminate combinations of different materials in favour of mono-material as far as possible; to use no ornament that did not come out of the nature of materials to make the whole building clearer and more expressive as a place to live in, and give the conception of the building appropriate revealing emphasis. Geometrical or straight lines were natural to the machinery at work in the building trades then, so the interiors took on this character naturally.

Seventh – to incorporate all heating, lighting, plumbing so that these systems became constituent parts of the building itself. These service features became architecture and in this attempt the ideal of an organic architecture was at work.

Eighth – to incorporate as organic architecture – so far as possible – furnishings, making them all one with the building and designing them in simple terms for machine-work. Again straight lines and rectilinear forms.

Ninth – eliminate the decorator. He is all curves and all efflorescence, if not all "period".'[27]

Yet examining the houses built up to 1910 in the light of these remarks, one is faced with a large and disconcerting variety of types of architecture. Some are masterpieces, executed with astonishing ability (Hickox house at Kankakee, Illinois, 1900; the Willitts house in Highland Park, 1902; Coonley house at Riverside, 1908; the Robie house, Chicago, 1909 (Figs. 246, 247, 251 and 254)). Other works were immoderate and patently forced (the Moore house in Chicago, 1895 (Figs. 248 and 249); the Dana house at Springfield, 1903) where the plan seems to be out of control, or rather the control itself seems to have been reduced to a passing curiosity for ingenious experiments in combination, sometimes making use of traditional stylistic ingredients without a qualm (as in the Blossom house in Chicago, 1892, and the Husser house of 1899).

These inconsistencies may be due to Wright's enormous output and the short time that he could have devoted to each plan, but they do indicate Wright's committed attitude towards his buildings; when he used certain forms he was not concerned that the results should be consistent with the preceding ones or transferable to others, and therefore independent of the particular purpose for which they had come into being. His interest was often exhausted by a single experiment; even in his best works there was a sort of detachment, of indifference for the means used which was not always compensated for by the spontaneity and freshness of the original conception.

It was during this period that Wright wrote his first theoretical work: this was the text of a lecture given in 1903 at Hull House, Chicago, with the title *Art and Craft of the Machine*. Pevsner[28] classes this writing with those of Loos and Van de Velde, as contributing to that line of thought promoting collaboration between art and industry; in fact Wright revealed an admiration for the spirit of the machine even greater than that of the Europeans; but the terms of the European controversy had a quite different meaning for him. Industry and machines interested him mainly as means to lessen the friction between conception and realization and to make the designer's control as direct and complete as possible; for this reason he considered them in a purely instrumental way, without concerning himself with the problem of mass-production and the new cultural responsibilities that derived from it, because he was considering the machine in the abstract, as an ingredient in an ideal process that was actually realized in an individual form in his personal activities.

In 1909 the art critic F. Francke, a Harvard professor, suggested to Wright that he should go to Germany; soon afterwards, possibly at Francke's suggestion, the Berlin editor Wasmuth offered to publish a monograph on his work. In 1910 Wright went to Europe where he organized an exhibition of his plans in Berlin as well as the material for the Wasmuth publication. It was at this time that Wright first became acquainted with the old buildings of Europe and with the works of the European *avant-garde* architects; he was particularly struck with the works of the Austrians Wagner and Olbrich.[29]

Back in America, his repertoire expanded to include new elements; in 1911 he began to build his house at Taliesin, Wisconsin, and in 1914 the Midway Gardens in Chicago, where he made use of European elements, absorbing them completely into his method of design; from 1916 to 1922 he spent long periods in Japan, where he built the Imperial Hotel in Tokyo.

After his stay in Japan, Wright's production waned and his fame declined, but after 1930 he once more began to design with youthful exuberance. From then onwards his activities were constantly increasing and were followed with interest throughout the world.

This exceptional capacity for resurgence was the practical proof of the architectural ideal to which Wright adhered from the beginning. He wished his architecture to be unconnected with contingent factors, founded on men's permanent needs and therefore capable of resisting change: 'Beauty seems to have made no sense for long at any time. I believe the time has come when Beauty . . . must make sense for our time at least.'[30]

Entrenched in this position, Wright was safe from all change of circumstances and could utilize any new inspiration, taking it up as a temporary point of departure. In the architecture of the European masters he saw only a new style, the 'fifty-eighth variety'[31]; he did sometimes utilize the elements of European style, but he was right when he distinguished his work sharply from that of European architects; indeed these elements were selected irrespective of their original cultural function and were taken into Wright's style without at all disturbing its independent balance.

Wright is the object of a sort of myth contributed to equally by his admirers and enemies; he is regarded as having a message to be either accepted or attacked – organic architecture – which is seen as an alternative to the modern movement or as a very personal tendency, opposed to 'rational architecture'. Various American authors, developing a thesis put forward by Wright himself, identify 'organic' with 'American', and regard Wright as the champion of the architecture of the New World, as opposed to the European movement.

This myth is primarily of literary origin (it is interesting to note that writers and scholars of ancient art feel more at their ease with Wright than with other contemporary masters, because he is an artist in the traditional sense of the term and it is therefore easier to write of his work in literary terms) and must be firmly dispelled, because it makes both Wright and the movement incomprehensible and prevents an accurate evaluation of his contribution to the movement itself, which is not contained in an abstract message but in a series of real and specific historical contacts: the visit to Europe in 1910, his polemical reaction from 1925 onwards with regard to the spread of the 'international style', his influence on the generation which became active after the Second World War.

For his part Wright was remote from the interests of the modern movement and he was disinclined to give up the individualist and marginal position traditionally assigned to the artist; he conceived of architecture as an ideal representation of the world, in the

**250, 251**   *Oak Park, Cheney house (Wright, 1904) and a detail of the Robie house*

classical fashion, and for this reason he transferred the problems of contemporary society into the realm of the imagination, where they could be mastered as purely formal problems.

This attitude fitted well into the American picture between 1890 and 1910, where there was a middle class large enough to share both Wright's enthusiasm and his enlightened

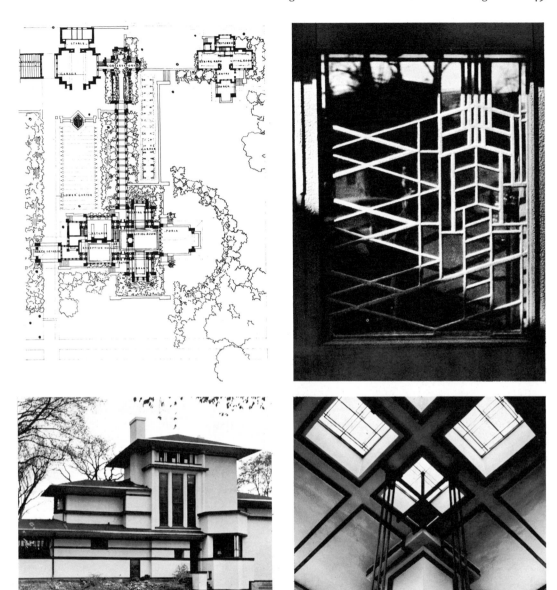

**252, 253** *(left)   Buffalo, Martin house (Wright, 1904) and Oak Park, Fricke house (Wright, 1902)*
**254, 255** *(right)   Oak Park, Detail of the Robie house and the Unity Church (Wright, 1906)*

abstract rationalism – in fact this was the most completely successful period of Wright's production – but the changes taking place in American society, particularly after 1930, made this attitude ever less apposite. Thus Wright's activities became increasingly self-absorbed, ever more a personal matter; he could remain faithful to his inspiration only by maintaining a position of detachment, by making everything at Taliesin a direct projection of his personality; during the whole of his career he never collaborated with anyone, nor took part in a competition, nor agreed to join a professional association nor to juxtapose his name, in any way, with those of the common run of mortals.

But even though he cut off all direct contact, he did increase the measure of his indirect influence enormously, and buildings designed by him were used as terms of comparison by all contemporary architects. In this way his contribution to the formation of the modern movement is decisive: having begun his activities during the last decade of the nineteenth century and having disposed in advance, even if only for his own part, of any difficulties that might hinder the formation of a new style, he attained an extraordinary freedom in formal choice long before the great European architects; this became a very vital point of reference for current trends of activity.

It so happened that his work should become known in Europe in 1910, just when Europeans most needed liberating formal contributions to help break the age-old association between classical culture and constructional practice; at this moment knowledge of Wright was certainly one of the immediate forces to move European culture towards its decisive turning point.

The protagonists of the modern movement have recognized this function of the American master. Oud wrote:

'Considering the confusion of opinions which, after the excessive certainty of previous generations, made a problem like a whiplash of every reasonable pressure it

is plain that Wright, thoroughly understood, could not fail to appear as a revelation. Free from all precious detail, blessed with a style all his own despite his exotic features and fascinating despite the simplicity of his motifs, Wright was immediately convincing. His work was so solidly constructed despite its elasticity, which made his buildings seem to have grown up with the very earth they stood on, the interplay of the plastic elements so natural, changing as on a cinema screen, the distribution of the spaces so natural and apparently so effortless, that there were no doubts about the inevitability of such a style for us as well; function and comfort were splendidly synthesized in the only style possible for our time'.[32]

And Mies van der Rohe:

'The more we are absorbed in the study of these creations, the greater becomes our admiration for his incomparable talent, the boldness of his conceptions and the independence of his thought and action. The dynamic impulse emanating from his work invigorated a whole generation. His influence was strongly felt even when it was not actually visible.

So after this first encounter we followed the development of this rare man with wakeful hearts. We watched with astonishment the exuberant unfolding of the gifts of one who had been endowed by nature with the most splendid talents. In his ever-growing power he resembles a giant tree in a nude landscape, which year after year attains a more noble crown'.[33]

# European avant-garde movements from 1890 to 1914

# Introduction

Towards 1890 traditional artistic thought was rapidly entering a phase of crisis. The effort of holding together the various architectural experiments within the framework of historicism, outworn and stretched in all directions, was on the verge of complete failure, while the grounds for a revival in architecture – of a technical nature, like advances in building technique, and of a cultural nature, like the encouragement of the Arts and Crafts movement – had grown sufficiently to have an effect on the general problem of style, and to offer a coherent alternative to subjection to historical styles.

This crisis occurred during the last decades of the nineteenth century, and had repercussions on architectural thought, for the first time in many years, as a whole, not in separate sectors. This was a period of exceptional activity, in the fields of both theory and practice; there was a rapid succession of both ideas and experiments, attenuating or eliminating from the architectural repertoire the usual stylistic references and constantly transforming the repertoire thus renewed.

I shall discuss the immediate causes of the various experiments one by one. But now I shall consider the remote and general causes, which fall under four headings.

## 1 The new theories of art

The ramifications of philosophical debate are only of indirect importance for this history, and the observations I shall make do not concern the theoretical meaning of the various discussions – which is intelligible only in relation to preceding theories – but certain common tendencies, which indicate a changed attitude towards problems of contemporary art.

Having lost their faith in the great idealistic systems, where the distinctive features of art vanished into the lofty realms of dialectic, a group of German philosophers attempted to construct a theory more relevant to the specific nature of the artistic experience, drawing partially on Herbartian formalism. Among these M. Schasler[1] made a sharp distinction between beauty in nature and beauty in art, which is necessarily related to the ugly, and E. Hartmann[2] made use of the ugly to distinguish the various categories of beauty. From the examples given it is clear that these writers associated 'beauty' with the precepts of the classical tradition, and the 'ugly' with the flouting of these precepts; they thus demonstrate that interest has moved on towards new formal combinations, differing from the traditional ones.

Positivists like Ch. G. Allen,[3] G. T.

**256**   *Van Gogh,* Cypresses in the Night Sky, *1890*

Fechner,[4] M. Guyau,[5] with their attempts at physiological, experimental and social aesthetics, drew attention to relations between art and the natural and social sciences, and revealed the inadequacy of the old artistic rules, confronting them with the novelties introduced by scientists; E. Grosse[6] proposed making a sort of natural history of art, studying the work of the various peoples and particularly of the primitive peoples, thus broadening the traditional field of artistic culture, opening the way for the revaluation of exotic and primitive art.

The most important theorist of this period was K. Fiedler who published his essay on the origin of art in 1887,[7] at a crucial moment in the controversy over modern art.

Fiedler postulated an absolute antinomy between beauty and art; the first was the pleasure that certain images afford us and might be found either in objects of nature or of art, and was limited to the practical sphere; 'to tend towards the beautiful does indeed seem something very elevated, while the fact does not rise much above man's everyday customs which have their root simply in the aim of rendering life pleasant. Basically the beautiful and the good may be reduced to the pleasant and the useful';[8] art on the other hand 'raises the sensitive intuition to consciousness, and its main effect lies in the characteristic form of knowledge that it offers',[9] a knowledge which is conceived of in a Kantian way as an active regulating function, 'one of the ways given to man to grasp the world'.[10]

The theory of beauty, or aesthetics, was therefore different from the theory of art. 'The precepts that aesthetics claims to lay down for art, with regard to harmony, rhythm, and symmetry, are concerned only with its decorative aspect, but do not touch its intrinsic being,'[11] which is cognitive in kind.

By aesthetics Fiedler plainly meant the aesthetics of classicism, as did Schasler and Hartmann, so that his theory helped to shatter the already shaken authority of the traditional rules. But he went further, and claimed that art could not have any rules of any sort, nor could it be expressed in general or collective movements: 'tendencies born of the majority and for the mass of men will always fail in their attempt to a true light'[12] while 'true art can find its own realization only in single isolated individuals'.[13]

Thus Fiedler, notwithstanding his refusal to involve himself in the trends of contemporary art,[14] foretold both the point of departure and the limitations of the imminent *avant-garde* movements.

The point of departure was the new concept of art as an active, constructive experience, 'the integratory element of the modern conception of the world'[15]; in this respect Fiedler may be regarded as a precursor not only of the *avant-garde* but also of the modern movement, as Argan has observed.[16] The source of the limitations was the restricted, aristocratic notion of art as an individual experience and as 'something exceptional, produced by exceptionally gifted men',[17] as Benedetto Croce had already claimed in 1901; for this reason Fiedler's thought did not go beyond the mental confines of the *avant-garde*.

Starting from Fiedler's ideas and using the theory of Vischer's[18] *Einfühlung*, H. Wölfflin[19] and A. Hildebrand[20] formulated the method of 'pure visibility' which con-

siderably modified criticism of figurative works of art and influenced the programmes of many *avant-garde* artists including Van de Velde.

1901 saw the first publication of Croce's *Aesthetic*, destined to have a lasting influence on Italian artistic thought; the Neapolitan philosopher – taking as his starting point De Sanctis and the Viconian tradition – vindicated the imaginative and intuitive nature of art, energetically criticizing any defilement by the rational or practical.

In the field of art history the works of Riegl[21] and Wickoff[22] on late antique art and of Gurlitt[23] and Wölfflin[24] on the Baroque, show that interest had moved from classical and golden periods to the so-called periods of decadence, which, however, were objectively valued for their intrinsic features. The various pairs of concepts introduced by art historians – from Nietzche's Apollonian-Dionysiac to Burckhardt's architectural-spatial, the plastic-pictorial of Wölfflin and the tactile-optical of Riegl – all had a certain measure of tendentiousness, since the first term corresponded to that which was ascertained by tradition, the second to that which was to be re-evaluated in the face of general custom.

Critics often noticed this link between their work and the tendencies of contemporary art. Riegl claimed that 'even the art critic could not free himself from the particular needs of his contemporaries with respect to art',[25] and Gurlitt wrote, talking of Borromini:

'Anyone considering taking part in a work of transformation of those forms of older art which seem to us in many ways unsatisfactory, so that they should be more in tune with the changing times, and anyone who does not quail at the prospect of seeking out new forms of expression for new materials and new building function, will find spiritual kinship, observing Borromini's buildings'.[26]

## 2   The general dissatisfaction with eclecticism

Eclecticism, as has been said in Chapter 4, tried to weather the attacks of its adversaries by broadening its theses and turning itself into a sort of artistic liberalism, which implicitly jeopardized its ideological foundations. This crisis was experienced as a feeling of uneasiness and dissatisfaction not only by theorists but also by designers.

From neo-classicism onwards a certain feeling of guilt was permanently observable, but between 1880 and 1890 it was far more in evidence; many architects deplored the existing confusion in style and eagerly awaited the birth of some new and original tendency.

Camillo Boito (1834–1914) wrote:

'The state of architecture today is further from the criteria of the philosophy of history, and is meaner generally, than it was at the end of the last century and during the first thirty years of this one. Then at least it was an art, connected with certain intellectual needs of its time: beauty had an ideal, an aim, a basis, and although it was often sought in vain, something at least was found – uniform, monotonous and dreary perhaps, but serious at least and not unworthy of a nation. Now architecture is, with few exceptions, a plaything of the fancy, an ingenious combination of forms, a weird whirl of pencils, compasses, rulers and set-squares. The architectural organism still exists, indeed it has even improved during these last few years; but the symbolism is mad and pointless, with the odd lucid moment. The arithmetical tyranny of the classical could not fail to produce the present disarray. And perhaps a true art may emerge from this anarchy, an art which is freedom of imagination combined with the rule of reason'.[27]

In England, George Gilbert Scott (1811–78) wrote:

'Nothing is more striking at the present day than the absence of true creative power in architectural art. I am not speaking of individual artists. We have many men who, under more favourable circumstances, might have produced great and even original works. It is even remarkable how much is produced under existing circumstances by individual men of genius. But we have produced no national style, nor do we seem likely at present to do so. We have broken the tradition which maintained the continuity of art history, and made each successive style the natural outcome of its predecessor. Everywhere we meet with reproductions of ancient styles, attempted revivals of lost traditions, nowhere with any genuine power of creating new forms of beauty united to new requirements. Indeed, it is difficult to see how, when tradition is broken up, or has exhausted itself, a new and genuine architecture is to be originated. We must look for this among the unknown possibilities of the future'.[28]

These authors have no concrete suggestions to offer for emerging from the present state of confusion and for finding a new style, but they demonstrate that the problem was in the air, so that the first activities of Horta, Van de Velde and Wagner met a common need and fell on ground prepared to receive them.

## 3   The example of the painters

The innovations of *avant-garde* architects from 1890 onwards were closely related to the work of the painters. This time it was no longer a matter of a mere similarity of formal preferences, as happens more or less plainly in all ages, but of an exchange of results, because of which the activities of certain architects presuppose the activities of certain painters, and vice versa.

As Pevsner has observed, the decisive

change as far as architecture was concerned was the breaking away from Impressionism of Cézanne, Rousseau, Gauguin, Van Gogh and Seurat. The most important aspects for our purposes are the following: *the reaction against naturalism.* If in one sense, by separating optical elements from the representation of conceptual ones, impressionism went counter to traditional naturalism, in another sense it constituted the development and conclusion of this very naturalism, because it selected and reflected all reality within the play of appearances, without excluding anything, and it retained, indeed perfected a receptive, contemplative attitude to any aspect of reality. Cézanne and the following generation wished to bypass changing appearances and to arrive at the truth hidden beyond them. Cézanne explained his method of approach as follows:

'I have my motif . . . a motif, you see, is this [he . . . draws his hands apart, fingers spread out, and brings them together again, strongly, strongly; then joins them, presses them together and contracts them, making them interlace]. There you have it; that is what one must attain. If I pass too high or too low, all is ruined. There mustn't be a single link too loose, not a crevice through which may escape the emotion, the light, the truth. I advance, you understand, all of my canvas at one time – together. I bring together, in the same spirit, all that is scattered. All that we see dispersed, vanishes; is that not so? Nature is always the same, but nothing remains of her of that which she appears to us. Our art ought to give the shimmer of its duration with all the elements, the appearance of all its change. It ought to make us taste it eternally. What is underneath? Nothing perhaps. Perhaps everything. You understand? Thus I join these straying hands. I take from right, from left, here, there, everywhere, tones, colours, shades. I fix them, I bring them together. They make

lines. They become objects, rocks, trees, without my realizing it. They take on volume. They acquire value. If these masses, these values, correspond on my canvas and in my sensibility to the outlines and spots of colour which I have set down and which are there before our eyes, very good! my canvas joins hands. It does not hesitate. It does not pass too high or too low. It is true, it is compact, it is full'.[29]

The art of the neo-Impressionists 'sacrifices the anecdote to the arabesque, nomenclature to synthesis, the ephemeral to the constant and gives to nature, weary by now of her precarious reality, an authentic one'.[30] Gauguin declared: 'When the artist wants to create something, he has no need to imitate nature, he takes the elements offered by nature and creates a new element from them.'[31]

There was a return to the subject-picture, as Pevsner has observed, but in a sense different from the traditional one, because the meaning of the content was preferably indirect, allusive and the result of the accentuation of strictly pictorial means (Cézanne: 'You may have poetry in your head perhaps but never, unless you wish to fall headlong into the literary, should you try to introduce it into your painting, because it will be there of its own accord.').[32]

*The active and constructive attitude towards what is real.* Cézanne said, 'Painting is registering and organizing sensations of colour . . . When you paint, the eyes and the brain must help each other; you must work to develop them together with the logic of organized impressions of colour.'[33] The analogy with Fiedler's thought is evident, as has frequently been noted.[34] In the case of Van Gogh, the obligation is human as well as artistic: 'My torment resolves itself into this question: what can I do? how can I be useful in some way? how can I know more and get to the bottom of this or that thing?'[35]

*The isolation of all artists.* The impressionist group was probably the last 'school' in the old sense; the painters of the following generation were isolated experimenters, each sharply critical of the others, and every one of whom ended by developing his own personal style, far more easily recognizable than had been the case in any previous age.

To some degree, every painter felt ill at ease and out of place. Cézanne: 'I will remain a mere primitive on the path that I myself have discovered . . . Perhaps I have come before my time; I was the painter of your generation [to Gasquet] rather than of my own.'[36] And Gauguin: 'As an artist, instinctively and without knowing why, I am an aristocrat.'[37]

*The tendency to theorize.* While all tending to evolve their own personal styles, they also wished to demonstrate the general validity and communicability of this style by laying down a series of formal precepts and supporting them with theoretical commentaries. This had happened before, but not to such an extent; for instance the breaking down of colours, which was an approximative tendency in Impressionism, became an exact and almost scientific technique in neo-Impressionism. The association between forms and states of mind was theorized about by the symbolists and by their spokesmen, for instance M. Denis and A. Turier. Often these theoretical formulations were the medium for influence between painting and architecture, as was the case with cloisonnism and symbolism, which were certainly among the sources of *art nouveau.*

Since innovations in the field of painting normally preceded those in the field of architecture – the same happened later with cubism and abstract painting *vis-a-vis* the modern movement – there have been several attempts (Giedion, Sartoris) to explain the second as derivations of the first and to assign to painters of this period the function of guides or forerunners.

But this reasoning was conducted in terms that did not take into account the conditions of the moment. Both architects and painters were working to change the conventions inherited from the past, but one of these conventions was precisely the existence of painting and architecture as separate activities. According to Morris's definition, architecture 'embraces the consideration of the whole external surroundings of the life of man', and the renewal of architecture included that of the figurative arts, while questioning their independence at the same time. Painters and architects, therefore, did not only influence one another, but strictly speaking even did the same work.

In painting, because of its greater immediacy, new discoveries emerged sooner but remained settled only temporarily, and were destined to be made use of to give a new form to the environment in which man lived and worked, for the design of utensils, furniture, buildings, cities. The value of the contributions of Cézanne, Gauguin, Van Gogh – like those of Braque, Mondrian, Van Doesburg – can really be estimated only in view of this utilization; it was Van de Velde who confirmed the importance of the *cloisonnistes,* just as in the post-war period it was Oud who convalidated the importance of Mondrian, Breuer who convalidated Klee and not vice versa.

## 4   Social conditions and personal involvement

The revolutionary movements in painting and architecture were comprehensible only if one bore in mind the fact that they were conducted, in the name of society as a whole, by very small groups of people.

As is well known, these experiments coincided with the long period of peace and economic prosperity known as *la belle époque.* But one cannot rightly consider prosperity as the determining cause of the cultural innovations of this period; in fact it can be shown that the main innovations were already emerging between 1890 and 1895 while the circumstances of the new economic balance – the inversion of the price curve, the introduction of the gold standard, the expansion of international trade – were felt only during the following fifteen years, and particularly in the first years of the twentieth century.

It is perhaps more accurate to say that the favourable conjuncture of economic circumstances, acting on the cultural developments already under way, procured them a much greater area for development than might otherwise have been the case. Increased profit margins encouraged the reformist tendencies of the ruling classes; thus opportunities of work for *avant-garde* artists multiplied, and so did the instruments of diffusion of a comparison between the new experiments.

But all this did nothing to lessen the gulf between culture and society. The new technical developments, while they facilitated cultural interchange, created a series of structural problems that the culture of the time was in no position either to interpret or even to recognize. Daring formulae succeeded one another in a crescendo of audacity, but their detachment from real problems only became more pronounced, creating a sense of growing unease. Meanwhile the political and economic forces that controlled technical progress did not tend to identify themselves with the aims of the new culture: they merely granted the progressive élites greater freedom of movement, leaving them entire responsibility for their experiments, while philosophers theorized about the autonomy of each new experiment as a vital condition of its intrinsic value.

For this reason *avant-garde* enterprises always began by asserting their own freedom and originality in relation to all preceding ones, and were promoted by single people or small groups who could retain their independence from the rest of society while putting forward theories supposedly valid for all.

This gave rise to a sort of contradiction, which characterized the culture of this period and which we shall discuss in some detail, using the term *avant-garde*. This was a proposal to make everyone a party to a jealously-guarded individual experiment, to speak to everyone while refusing to listen to anyone.

This contradiction emerges more clearly if one considers the relationship between single works and theoretical programmes. From the Renaissance onwards every concrete artistic problem has been thought of as a practical manifestation of an abstract problem, while the resolution of this single case meant taking a stand, at the same time, with regard to a general stylistic problem. In the nineteenth century this need became more acute, because the use of one style or another was now the object of a voluntary choice, though one which was still based on an external element: local tradition, ideas offered by the purpose of the work, the client or body which had commissioned it etc.

But now artists were trying to eliminate all of these references; formal choice became so agonizing that it absorbed all energies, and so delicate that it demanded indifference to all incidental circumstances; painters, for example, chose their subjects in the most casual way and painted for themselves, without worrying about the final destination of their works. Thus the balance between general aims and particular ones was disturbed: either the artist refused to subordinate his decisions to a general aim, or else he attributed a general validity to the decision that he was taking at that moment. In this way two contrary distortions were appearing: either the single work was regarded as an experience in itself, with no possible terms of comparison, or else it was regarded as valid as a demonstration of a universal method, to be communicated to everyone.

Personal involvement increased enormously under these conditions, and the

257 *A.H. Mackmurdo, Cretonne, 1885 (Victoria & Albert Museum)*
258 *W. Crane, Linear interpretation of a ballerina's leap (from* Line and Form, *1902)*
259 *Aubrey Beardsley, Illustration for Oscar Wilde's* Salome, *1892*
260 *E. Munch,* The Vigil, *1896*

personality of an artist became a far more vital factor than in the past. Indeed all choice was validated, in fact, only by the individual talent of the artist, and the style built up by an individual or small group was presented as an alternative to a widespread tradition, deriving from the concerted contributions of many generations. Thus the individual was placed in a much more exposed and dangerous position, and ended by involving his whole spiritual being in the pursuit of his aims as an artist.

The most impressive cases of this tyranny of artistic concerns over human ones were found in painting and literature. In the first half of the century Murger described the *vie de Bohème* and told of poets, painters and musicians drawn beyond the circle of normal life by their artistic commitments. But his descriptions were of pleasant honeyed idylls compared with the tragic lives of some of the great artists of the end of the nineteenth century, for instance Rimbaud and Van Gogh. In architecture things were rather different, for the architect is never alone before his work, but many, like Mackintosh and Loos, paid personally for their nonconformist artistic vocations.

# nine

# Art nouveau

It is difficult, in a general historical work, to treat this subject satisfactorily.

The period of which we are talking is both close to us and remote from us; less than fifty years have passed, and many of its protagonists have only recently died (e.g. Perret, Hoffmann and Van de Velde), yet the impression is of a series of events set in the distant past. It is as if the two world wars that have intervened, apart from destroying an incalculable number of *art nouveau* furnishings and ornaments, have also broken all links of intimacy between us and the people who designed them.

Studies and data available are incomplete, and reflect the theoretical prejudices rather than the realities of the period. What remains is the portrait, not of what it was, but of what it thought it was: a complicated genealogical tree of trends, in the persons of a small number of original artists, but little or no evidence about the changes taking place in current production, and of their relationship with leading movements of the time.

An attempt to unravel the muddled skein of trends, setting them precisely in their time and place and specifying the adherence of the various artists to one or the other, would take us out of our way and would obscure the true nature of the problem. A more fruitful pro-cedure, and one more compatible with the present state of studies, might be to avoid ready-made classifications and to describe some of the artists and most famous experiments.

The term *art nouveau* will be used in the broadest possible sense, to include all the European *avant-garde* movements that are referred to by a comparable term (*Jugendstil, modern style, liberty*); only two anticipatory distinctions will be made, and they are ones which really seem to require separate treatment: one for the English movement of Morris's successors, which was discussed in Chapter 6 so as not to break the continuity of the line of thought from Ruskin onwards, and the others for the experiments of the Frenchmen Perret and Garnier, which were based on a specific national tradition and will be discussed in Chapter 10.

The nature of *avant-garde* thought facilitates the separate discussion of experiments in architecture and town-planning; the latter also constitute the most suitable point of reference for evaluating the relationship between the élites and ordinary production and will be discussed at the end in an attempt to reach a general conclusion (Chapter 9).

## 1   Victor Horta

All historians agree that the European movement for the renewal of the applied arts originated in Belgium, between 1892 and 1894, and was born *ex abrupto* with Horta's Tassel house in Brussels, Van de Velde's furnishings for his house at Uccle and the first truly original furniture designed by Serrurier-Bovy. These works appear to be absolutely without precedent and the elements of the new style, which was to be called *art nouveau*, were here already perfectly and consistently elaborated.

Various hypotheses have been put forward for indirect sources. Giedion[1] has described the free, open attitude of *avant-garde* culture in Belgium. In 1881 two rich and cultured lawyers founded the review *L'Art Moderne*, gathering the best artists of the time around them. Three years later the group called 'Les XX' was formed, lasting until 1893 and including among its members the painters Knopff, A. W. Finch and J. Ensor; Maus, the secretary, organized various exhibitions of paintings from 1884, to which the most important artists of the European *avant-garde* contributed: Rodin, Whistler, Renoir, Seurat, Pissarro, Van Gogh. Seurat's famous painting *Dimanche à la grande Jatte* was exhibited for the first time in Brussels in 1887.

Schmalenbach[2] and Pevsner[3] have emphasized the contribution of the symbolist painters and the symbolist movement, which reached its peak about 1890, influencing the work of many European artists including Gauguin and his companions at Pont-Aven, the Nabis, Munch, Hodler, Ensor. The dates are highly significant: the Pont-Aven school was born in 1888 and exhibited for the first time at the Paris exhibition of 1889, the Nabis group was formed the same year, while Aurier published his summary of the aims of symbolist painting in 1891, following Moreas' 1884[4] manifesto of literary symbolism. Munch and Hodler were influenced by the symbolist programme between 1890 and 1892, and all the painters more or less affected by this trend were represented at the exhibitions of the Galerie Le Barc, held twice yearly from 1891 onwards.

In Belgium symbolism had a large following (partly because of the presence of Maeterlinck in the literary field) and had a decisive influence on the work of many of the 'XX', Ensor, Knopff, Finch and above all J. Toorop, who was certainly a source of inspiration to Horta and Van de Velde. Horta however, in a letter to Pevsner,[5] minimized the importance of these contacts and claimed not to have wanted to imitate the style of painters, but to do as the painters were doing, creating for themselves a language that was both personal and free from imitation.

England's influence is universally recognized by writers on *art nouveau*, and has been exhaustively discussed by Schmutzler.[6] Suggestions for possible precursors have included Burne-Jones, Morris, Mackmurdo, the sculptor A. Gilbert and even William Blake; one of the most important factors was certainly the brief active life of Aubrey Beardsley (who died in 1898 at the age of twenty-four).

The relations between England and Belgium were numerous and well-documented. Toorop spent some time in England and was in contact with the Pre-Raphaelites. In 1891 English Liberty furnishings appeared in Brussels for the first time, in the window of the Compagnie Japonaise in the rue Royale, and at about the same time Finch, who was of English descent, acquired some English furnishings which made a great impression on his friends.

Also in 1891 the 'XX' exhibited objects of applied art along with their paintings and sculpture, including some children's books by Walter Crane; in 1892 they created a *section d'art artisanal* with reproductions of works by S. Image and H. Horne, and books printed by Morris's Kelmscott Press; it was in this section that one of the first works by Van de Velde was exhibited, an embroidery pattern, and Van de Velde himself – who was

**261, 262, 264** *(above)    Viollet-le-Duc, Decorative ironwork (from* Compositions et dessins, *1884 and* Entretiens sur l'architecture, *1872)*
**263, 265** *(below)    E.J. Marey,* Horizontal Projection of Flying Seagull *and* Stereoscopic Trajectory of a Point at Base of Lumbar Vertebrae of a Man Walking *(about 1890; from Giedon,* Mechanization Takes Command*)*

the source of most of this information[7] – openly acknowledged the importance of English teaching: 'There is no doubt that the work and influence of John Ruskin and William Morris were the seeds that fertilized our spirit, that aroused our activity and brought about the complete renewal of ornament and the forms of decorative art'.[8]

England contributed much more than formal inspiration to the continental *avant-garde* movements: she contributed the theses elaborated by Ruskin and Morris, the conviction that architecture must affect the whole scene of the modern town and that it was part of a vaster task, that of modifying the whole complex of current forms of society. Without English teaching, it would be impossible to understand the interest shown by Van de Velde and Hoffmann – to mention only two names – in furnishings and the relative processes of production, the didactic concerns of Wagner and the moral ones of Loos.

The relationship between the Belgian movement and French culture, on the other hand, has been little investigated (Figs. 261–5). It was known that Horta spent some time in Paris after 1878; this was the period when Viollet-le-Duc, Vaudremer (1829–1914) and others of the 'Union syndicale des architectes français' tried to give up all reference to the medieval styles and to invent a new language of their own, to satisfy their rationalist theories without any compromise. None of them actually managed to emerge from the deadlock of eclecticism, but their transcription of the traditional repertoire became brief and allusive and sometimes tended to weld stylistic references into an abstract chromaticism – as in Vaudremer's Lycée Buffon – or into a free play of lines as in Viollet-le-Duc's iron ornaments, made famous by their reproduction in the *Entretiens* and *Compositions et dessins*.[9] The moralistic theories of the French master were certainly shallower and less original than those of Morris, but they had far more success at the time, marshalling artists and sometimes even public opinion against eclecticism and arousing expectation of an imminent change of direction in the arts. A last important factor was the Paris universal exhibition of 1889, where artists from all over Europe were able to meet and where French eclectic culture made a magnificent effort to invent a new

type of decoration suited to iron buildings, combining utilitarian and ornamental elements such as riveted surfaces and decorations in cast iron or cut sheet iron.

The masters of the Belgian movement were Victor Horta (1861–1947) and Paul Hankar (1857–1901) in architecture, Henry Van de Velde (1863–1957) and Gustave Serrurier-Bovy in interior decoration and applied arts. As Van de Velde said: 'the work of all four of us was lumped together by the one quality obviously common to the whole of it: its newness. This was how the term *art nouveau* originated';[10] nonetheless the aims of the various artists were markedly different among themselves.

Horta was the strongest character and at the same time the least concerned with theory. He had attended the Academy at Ghent, his native town, had then been to Paris and had finished his studies at the Brussels Academy in 1881; he had then begun work in the studio of Alphonse Balat (1818–95) and designed his first buildings – two funeral monuments and three private houses – in Ghent between 1883 and 1885; these were very simple buildings, giving no hint whatsoever of how his architecture was to develop.

Between 1885 and 1892 he designed no buildings but wrote and reflected, absorbing the numerous stimuli which were inspiring the European *avant-garde* of the time. In 1892 and 1893 he built the Tassel house in the rue de Turin in Brussels, which brought him sudden fame and gave rise to lively argument (Figs. 266–8). But it was not only a controversial stab at tradition; it was the carefully thought-out essay at creating a new architecture, free from any reference to the past yet perfectly controlled in every detail, confident and convincing; it demonstrated the possibility not only of a new vocabulary but of a new syntax, different from that of any historical style.

The Tassel house was based on a traditional style of building in Brussels: a building

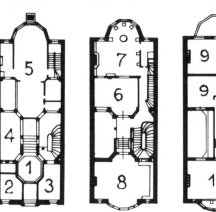

1 hall
2 cloakroom
3 study
4 small sitting room
5 living room
6 ante-room
7 bedroom
8 drawing room
9 servants' rooms
10 workroom

**266, 267, 268**  *Brussels, Details and plans of the Tassel house in rue de Turin (Horta, 1893)*

set between two others, very narrow, with only two short façades on to the street and garden. The main façade does not stand out much from those on either side, and one has to look carefully when walking along the street to distinguish Horta's work; but it can be recognized if one examines the fabric of the stonework carefully. The usual bow-

**269, 270, 271**  *Brussels, Maison du Peuple (Horta, 1897)*

window is achieved by bending the whole surface into a double S; the facing stone, the iron and woodwork round the windows, with their precise, elaborate joins, form a highly calculated and compact whole. Inside, through a door of coloured glass, is a hallway dominated by the famous staircase; the steps are in natural wood, supported by a visible

metal structure; the framework formed of the tubular supports and horizontal cross-sections is emphasized by ornamental iron-work in elegant flowing curves; similar motifs appear painted on the walls and in mosaic work on the floors.

After this Horta built many other houses, shops and storehouses, all in Brussels; the

Maison du Peuple – built in 1897 to house the offices of the Union of Socialist Workers – was regarded as his masterpiece (Figs. 269–71). Here too the organism was restricted from the start by the shape of the site, set in narrow streets and just off a small square, and the architecture fits in amid the surrounding elements with impeccable fluency. The structure is of steel within a discontinuous masonry framework, like many French buildings of the time, surrounding the large windows with the natural wood frames. The masonry, alternately of brick and grey stone, encloses the expanses of glass and links the building to the surrounding architecture, which is entirely of stone. Here there is perfect unity between structure and ornament; inside too, in the *halle des manifestations*, the ornamental design on the ceiling makes use of the supporting beams, and in the lecture hall on the upper floor the reticulated transversal girders also serve to decorate the ceiling space (Fig. 270).

Horta analysed the texture of his buildings in great depth, with a daring unequalled at this time, but he was more or less indifferent to distribution. His famous volumetric freedom was more apparent than real; variations in level in the interior of the houses in the rue de Turin and other of his private houses were a common feature of French and Belgian building at this time, and the curved façade of the Maison du Peuple may look free in a photograph, if one takes no account of the surrounding houses, but in fact it is faithfully based on the alignment of the two radial streets running into the round *place*. On the other hand his use of materials, the way of breaking up the walls, of resolving articulations, joints and details, do reveal an exceptional sureness of judgment, consistence and rigour. It is as though he were buoyed up by his own controversial proposal to create a new style as an alternative to any historical one, as though he scrutinized his designs with an unflinching severity so that they should be faultless and so that each

element should be accurately and perfectly connected to each other; for this reason he preferred natural materials and left all joins visible, resolving them in such a way that they would have a decorative value as well (Figs. 272–4).

Horta's architecture has aged well and fits effortlessly into the fabric of nineteenth-century Brussels; this personal and ambitious artist was also amazingly discreet: he did not wish to provide the inhabitants of his houses with accommodation that was too inconvenient or too committed, in order to fulfil his own artistic ideals, and he wanted to convince the spectator with the logic of his architecture, not to bowl him over with its eccentricity. But this in its turn constitutes one of Horta's limitations: he thought that the problem of architecture was simpler than it was and could really be reduced to a style, to a coherent and technically irreproachable manner of composition. He wanted to settle this problem immediately, by arriving both at an internal balance of style and at an immediate agreement with the public, with building processes, with the urban scene of his time, without leaving margins for any further development. For this reason Horta was the most exquisite of the *art nouveau* artists, but in a way he was also the most old-fashioned, the nearest to an architect of the past.

The weakness of his position became evident when he lost contact with successive developments; in his last works – the Palais des Beaux Arts of 1920 and the Brussels Central Station of 1925 – Horta fell back upon a tired neo-classicism, and became a firm adversary of the innovators of the '20s, using his vote to defeat Le Corbusier at the Geneva Competition in 1927. (Chapter 14).

There is probably no other example in the history of architecture of an artist who made so important a contribution in his youth and then declined so soon, living on for a further thirty years. His lot – and to a lesser degree that of the other masters of *art nouveau* –

**272**  *Brussels, Detail of the Solvay house (Horta, 1895)*
**273, 274**  *(below)  Brussels, Details of the Horta house (Horta, 1898)*

**275, 276**   *Two rooms furnished by Horta, exhibited at Turin in 1901 (from the publication on the Turin exhibition of 1901, by A. Koch)*

**277** *Desk and chair by Van de Velde exhibited in 1957 at the Kunstgewerbemuseum in Zurich*
**278** *Caricature by Karl Arnold on the discussion at the Congress of the Werkbund in 1914: Van de Velde is proposing the individual chair, Muthesius the standard chair and the carpenter a chair for sitting on (from Van de Velde,* Geschichte meines Lebens)

shows how phases of cultural development were becoming shorter, and how involvement in one phase was not enough to fill a human life.

## 2 Henry Van de Velde

The inspiration moving Horta – and his contemporaries Hankar and Serrurier-Bovy, within the more modest limits of their experiments – was in fact 'the desire to enjoy all the excitement and prestige of inaugurating a renascence';[11] the absence of adequate rational control may have facilitated their research and made the definition of their repertoire easier, but it soon immobilized their activities in their newly gained positions, and when the prestige of novelty had faded, it drove them to take refuge in a new, if broadened, eclecticism.

Van de Velde's case was different. From the first he aimed at clarifying the basic tenets of the movement, at formulating his experiences so that they would be communicable and would give rise to a general renewal of the methods of planning. While his contemporaries took mainly formal inspiration from England, he, for the first time on the Continent, interested himself in the moral principles of Morris's teaching, and developed them with extraordinary perception:

'Little by little I came to the conclusion that the reason why the fine arts had fallen into such a lamentable state of decay was because they were being more and more exploited by self-interest or prostituted to the satisfaction of human vanity. In the form of "easel pictures" and "salon statuary" both were now being executed as often as not without the least regard to their eventual destination like any other kind of consumer goods. It seemed clear, therefore, that the old, relatively frank and straight-forward transactions for the sale and purchase of an artist's work might soon give place to the odious modern machinery by which commercial publicity hoodwinks the public over the quality or value of whatever it is paid to advertise. Thus in the not far distant future we could expect to find genuine works of art insidiously branded with the same sort of mendacious descriptions and fictitious valuations as ordinary mass-produced merchandise for household use'.[12]

This clarification is very important. Indeed the invention of new forms might be used to overcome subjection to historical style and to give life to a new movement, but it could also be considered as an end in itself, and the invented forms, abstracted from the actual contact with the needs that gave rise to them, could be utilized for practical purposes of profit and prestige. Art could exert its regulating function in society if it took it upon itself to control methods of production and distribution of household objects, i.e. if it set itself up as an instrument of overall planning; if on the other hand it limited itself to modifying the shapes of objects, it would be the latent commercial interests of society that would plan artists' activities by the same methods, turning them into mere decorators.

For this reason Van de Velde could not adhere to the position of Horta and his contemporaries:

'My hopes of what liberation from tutelage to the past and the dawning of a new era in design might bring about were just as high as theirs, but such an illusory prospect failed to satisfy me. I knew we had to delve far deeper, that the goal to be striven for was a much more vital one than mere newness, which by its very nature can be only ephemeral. If we were to attain it we must begin by clearing away those obstructions which the centuries had accumulated in our path, stemming the inroads of ugliness and challenging every agency that corrupts natural taste . . . I firmly believed that I could achieve my ends . . . by virtue of an aesthetic founded on reason and therefore immune to caprice. And as one who was fully aware how falsehood can sully inanimate objects in precisely the same way as it degrades the character of men and women I felt confident my probity would be proof against the manifold insinuations of imposture'.[13]

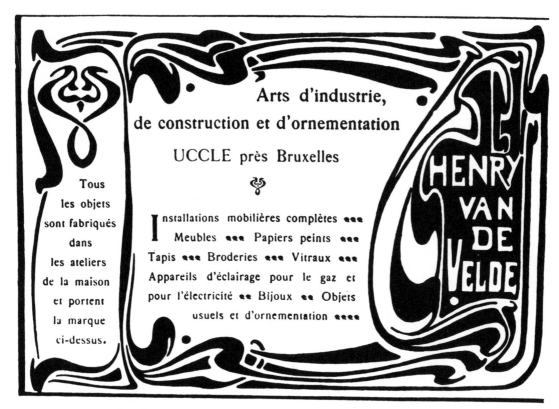

**Arts d'industrie,
de construction et d'ornementation**

**UCCLE près Bruxelles**

Tous
les objets
sont fabriqués
dans
les ateliers
de la maison
et portent
la marque
ci-dessus.

Installations mobilières complètes ●●●
Meubles ●●● Papiers peints ●●●
Tapis ●●● Broderies ●●● Vitraux ●●●
Appareils d'éclairage pour le gaz et
pour l'électricité ●● Bijoux ●● Objets
usuels et d'ornementation ●●●●

HENRY VAN DE VELDE

**279**  *Publicity for Van de Velde's 'atelier' at Uccle (1898)*

Van de Velde's first opportunity to venture into the field of interior decoration was the furnishings of his house at Uccle, near Brussels, in 1894; in accordance with his principles, he set himself to find an objective justification for every formal element, of a functional nature in so far as this was possible, or if not of a psychological nature, utilizing the contemporary theories of the Einfühlung; the shape of the lines, outlines, decorative designs etc. was seen in relation to the positions people would be forced to adopt by the demands of work and leisure, tension and relaxation. This aim drew him towards smooth and flowing forms, similar to those of Horta but simpler and more severe, particularly at the beginning. This simplification – hitherto unheard of, except in England – was probably the cause of the immediate and disputed fame of his furnishing, and of the intensity of both positive and negative reaction.

At the same time Van de Velde began his activities as theorist and propagandist;[14] he gave his first lecture at Brussels in 1894, to the group 'La Libre Esthétique' which had made up 'Les XX' the year before. While recognizing the precedence of the English movement, Van de Velde believed that the experiences of Morris and his successors were too aristocratic, too detached from society, and claimed that rebirth of the arts would emerge from the trusting acceptance of machines and mass-production.[15]

In 1897, following the refusal of the Université libre de la Belgique to approve the appointment of two foreign professors, a group of teachers resigned and founded an independent institute called the Nouvelle Université, and promptly invited Van de

**280, 281, 282**  *Van de Velde, Two buckles (1904) and a rocking-chair (1903; from the catalogue of the 1957 exhibition at the Kunstgewerbemuseum at Zurich)*

Velde to teach the decorative and industrial arts.

Meanwhile Van de Velde's fame was spreading abroad. In 1895 the art dealer S. Bing, accompanied by the art critic J. Meier-Gräfe, visited Van de Velde in his house at Uccle and commissioned him to design some interiors for him; these were exhibited in Paris in 1896 and in Dresden in 1897. While in France he received a mixed welcome,[16] in Germany Van de Velde found fertile ground already prepared by Meier-Gräfe himself and by the publication *Pan* founded by him in 1895.

In 1898, like Morris, he set up his own workshop for applied arts, the 'Arts d'industrie, de construction et d'ornamentation Van de Velde & Cie.', with his partners Bodenhausen, and D. and K. Hermann; in 1900 he moved to Hagen, where he reorganized the Folkwang museum; in 1902 he was appointed director of the 'Weimar Kunstgewerblicher Institut' – which after the war became Gropius' Bauhaus – and built a new

building for the school as well as many other houses in 1906.

From 1907 – when the Werkbund was founded – Van de Velde's activity was closely linked to those of the German masters, in the heart of the organism that may be regarded as the matrix of the modern movement. His clear intellectual vision of the architectural problem had taken him to the place where, amid difficulties of all kinds, the most complete and fruitful solution was incubating. His limitation *vis-à-vis* the initiators of the modern movement was essentially a limitation of sensibility; it was almost as though he were surprised at the rapidity of developments – in the years between 1907 and 1914 the rhythm of events was positively precipitous – and feared that the delicate balance of artistic expression might be lost in the great organizational undertakings of the Germans. It is probably in this context that one should view his quarrel with Muthesius at the meeting of the Werkbund in 1914, described by Pevsner:

**283, 284, 285** *(left)   Van de Velde, Work-room for J. Meier-Gräfe (1896) and two interiors of the Esche house at Lauterbach (1906; from K.E. Osthaus, V. de V., 1920)*
**286, 287, 288** *(right)   Van de Velde, silver tea-service and two interiors from his house at Weimar (1906; from Osthaus, op. cit.)*

'Muthesius stood up for Standardization (*Typsierung*), Van de Velde for Individualism. Muthesius said: "Architecture and the entire sphere of activity of the Werkbund tend towards standardization. It is only by standardization that they can recover that universal importance which they possessed in ages of harmonious civilization. Only by standardization . . . as a salutary concentration of forces, can a generally accepted and reliable taste be introduced." Van de Velde responded: "As long as there are artists in the Werkbund . . . they will protest against any proposed canon and any standardization. The artist is essentially and intimately a passionate individualist, a spontaneous creator. Never will he, of his own free will, submit to a discipline forcing upon him a norm, a canon".'[17]

This declaration, by a man who twenty years before had proclaimed the need to accept industrial production, cannot be regarded as a recantation, and the author himself later told Pevsner that he was no longer of this opinion. It was rather the transposition of an artistic judgment on to a theoretical plane, since no-one who had taken part in the formation of *art nouveau* in the rarefied atmosphere of *fin de siècle* Brussels could easily accept the clumsy German simplifications in the years just before the First World War.

Van de Velde was certainly the clearest thinker among the masters of his generation. The importance of his contribution should be gauged not only by considering the works he wrote or designed personally, but also his work as an organizer, his ability to inspire, the energies he was capable of arousing in others.

As well as being one of the first to set the *art nouveau* movement in motion, he was the only one to have a clear idea of the provisional character of the position in which it became fixed. For this reason he was only partly of the *avant-garde*; if as a designer he did remain wholly within its ambit, as a master he moved beyond it and entered the modern movement, supporting its successive developments whole-heartedly; during his long old-age (until his death in 1957) Van de Velde continued to support the forward-

looking experiments of the successive generations, but wisely held himself apart from them, refraining from joining in the fray in any partisan position. Between the two wars he lived in Belgium, directed the Institut supérieur des arts décoratifs de la Cambre, followed the development of European architecture in his writings[18] and designed the occasional building, to some degree taking into account the new international repertoire (some private houses, the Hanover Old People's Home in 1929, the Belgian pavilion at Paris in 1937[19] and at New York in 1939).[20] After the Second World War he settled in Switzerland, where he wrote his memoirs.[21]

The autobiographical sketch ends with these words:

'Just as evil is for ever seeking to corrupt virtue, so throughout the history of art some malignant cancer has ceaselessly struggled to taint or deform man's purest ideals of beauty. The brief interlude of *art nouveau*, that ephemeral will o' the wisp which knew no other law than its own caprice, was succeeded, as I had foretold, by the hesitant beginnings of a new, a disciplined and purposeful style, the style of our own age. Two world wars have prolonged its growing pains. But step by step it pursues its conscious advance towards maturity. And that maturity, when finally attained, will synchronize with the realization of a rationalized aesthetic, whereby beauty of form can be immunized against current infections from the noisome parasite fantasy'.[22]

### 3   Charles Rennie Mackintosh

The works of Morris, Voysey, Ashbee and Mackmurdo influenced the continental *avant-garde* movements, while the experiments of Horta, Van de Velde and the Viennese were received in England with diffidence and suspicion, and were often

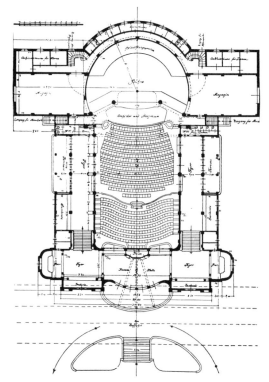

**289, 291** *(above)   Van de Velde, Bookbinding and plan of the theatre for the exhibition of the Werkbund in Cologne (1914; from G.A. Platz,* Die Baukunst der neuesten Zeit, *1927)*
**290, 292** *(below)   Hagen, Two views of the Springmann house (Van de Velde, 1913; from Osthaus,* op. cit.*)*

harshly criticized as being too precious (Walter Crane: 'the decorative illness known as *art nouveau*'.)[23]

But away from the main centre, in Glasgow, there emerged a group of artists who were in the thick of the European *avant-garde* controversy and indeed art histories do not hesitate to class them as belonging to the *art nouveau* movement (Zevi, Madsen, Pevsner etc.).

1 entrance
2 office
3 shop
4 changing rooms
5 professors' rooms
6 lesson hall
7 drawing hall
8 library

*Ground Floor*

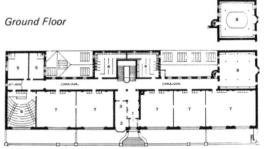

**293, 294, 295** *Glasgow, Art School (C.R. Mackintosh, 1898–1909; from T. Howarth,* Charles Rennie Mackintosh, *1952)*

They attained notoriety, first, through the activities of a group of painters known as the 'Glasgow boys' – J. Guthrie, J. Lavery, E. A. Walton – who exhibited their works in London in 1890 (here too, as in Belgium, painters' experiments preceded those of architects). A few years later, in the Glasgow art school, a group of artists with wider interests emerged – architects, painters, decorators – which included G. Walton, brother of the painter, C. R. Mackintosh,

H. Macnair, the two Macdonald sisters and I. Morris. Mackintosh, Macnair and the two Macdonalds – who afterwards became their respective wives – were also known as 'the four' and often worked together.

Charles Rennie Mackintosh (1888–1928), the most gifted, entered the firm of Honeyman and Keppie as a designer in 1890; four years later he became a partner and remained with them until 1913; meanwhile 'the four' were exhibiting in London in the Arts and

**296, 297, 298**   *Glasgow, Hill House (Mackintosh, 1902–6; from Howarth,* op. cit.*)*

Crafts Exhibition of 1896, and in 1897 Mackintosh obtained his first important commission as a freelance designer: the new art school in Glasgow (built between 1898 and 1899 and extended between 1907 and 1909) (Figs. 293–5) and the first tea-rooms for Miss Cranston.

In these works Mackintosh put forward a new and fascinating interpretation of the *art nouveau* repertoire: the linear arabesques of Beardsley-type decoration were used as means of the spatial qualification of the various sections: a new and more direct relationship was established between the stone framework – often square and solid – and the fitments in wood or metal, curved

**299**   *Furniture by Mackintosh exhibited at Turin in 1901 (from Koch* op. cit.)

with delightful and imaginative fantasy.

Soon afterwards, exhibiting his furniture at the Vienna Secession in 1900 and at the international exhibition at Turin in 1902, Mackintosh found himself suddenly famous throughout Europe. In 1901 the German editor A. Koch organized a competition for the plan of an 'art lover's house' which was

**300** *Furniture by Mackintosh exhibited in Turin in 1901 (from Koch* op. cit.)

won by Baillie Scott, but Mackintosh's designs – published with the others in 1902 – aroused the most discussion and comment.[24] Meanwhile he built two houses in Glasgow one of which, Hill House (Figs. 296–8) is the main source of information for Mackintosh's taste in domestic furnishings, since many of its contents have survived, whereas almost all his other work for interiors has been dispersed. After 1913, when he moved to London, he no longer received architectural commissions and died

**301**　*Mackintosh, water-colour, 1923–7 (from Howarth,* op. cit.)

in 1928 in poverty, partly because his habitual heavy drinking made social contact difficult.

An accurate estimate of Mackintosh's work should take into account his relationship with tradition, which in England was rather different from on the continent.

A spirit of conservatism and of reverence for national traditions was one of the constant features of English culture; furthermore reference to a determined portion of this past, the Middle Ages, was linked with the teachings of Ruskin and Morris. For this reason the Glasgow movement, unlike continental movements, did not represent a reaction against traditional or historical styles, but drew largely on the past, either from the conventional neo-Gothic or from the local Scottish baronial architecture (though English writers, also because of their attachment to tradition, tended to over-estimate this factor in the work of Mackintosh and his colleagues). In 1903 Mackintosh took part in the competition for Liverpool Cathedral with a design that. was pure Gothic, though up-dated with original ornament.

Furthermore, the general mood of retrospection made life hard for *avant-garde* artists. Anyone wishing to attempt new experiments had to fend for himself, at the price of considerable effort, and society was certain to take a very long time to accept them.

This is why English *avant-garde* production was so uneven in quality and why Mackintosh never managed entirely to fulfil his incomparable talent; even his best works have a strained quality where hard and sharp forms alternate with languid and delicate ones, sometimes brusquely juxtaposed so as to give extraordinarily exciting but tense effects. This may to some extent explain the fate of this brilliant, lonely artist, isolated and shunned in the very country where artistic culture was best prepared for him and richest in experience, and where Morris had initiated the debate on modern art over a generation earlier.

During the first decade of the twentieth century *avant-garde* excitement gradually died down in England, and Mackintosh's heritage, like that of Morris, passed to the continental movements.

The main reason for this check, even if not the only one, was certainly of a social nature. In England the differences between the classes had always been marked but was compensated for by considerable mobility in a vertical sense and by the singularly open-minded attitude of the ruling class, which had managed to settle the clash of interests into a relative balance; the cultural advances of the Victorian era were won by a fairly small élite (of which Morris was a typical representative) but inspired by fine and noble ideals.

Now however social disparities hardened into class conflicts – in 1893 the Labour Party was founded, and sent its first representatives to Parliament in 1906 – and the ruling class, closely threatened in its interests, became more rigid in its adoption of consistently conservative positions, removing its support from the progressive intellectuals that it had itself produced. Artistic traditionalism – which for Morris was a feeling of Romantic nostalgia for the past and even a spur to modify the present – suddenly became important as a covering for social traditionalism; Pevsner writes:

'So long as the new style had been a matter which in practice concerned only the wealthier classes, England could foot the bill. As soon as the problem began to embrace the people as a whole, other nations took the lead, nations that lived no longer, or never had lived, in the atmosphere of the *ancien régime*, nations that did not accept or did not know England's educational and social contrasts between the privileged classes and those in the suburbs and slums . . . A similar antipathy [to change] prevented the ruthless scrapping of traditions which was essential to the achievement of a style fitting our country. So, at the very moment when Continental architects discovered the elements of a general style for the future in English building and English crafts, England herself receded into an eclectic neo-classicism, of great dignity sometimes, but with hardly any bearing on present day problems and needs. For country-houses and town-houses neo-Gothic and neo-colonial

302 *Vienna, Underground station on the Karlsplatz (Otto Wagner, 1894–7)*

became popular; in public buildings, banks, etc., solemn rows of colossal pillars reappeared . . .'.[25]

## 4 Otto Wagner

Austrian architecture used historical styles with unbending exactitude until the end of the nineteenth century, with a constant preference for the neo-classical; the only important link with the revolutionary movements emerging in the west was the teaching of G. Semper, who had worked in England with H. Cole. This may perhaps be one of the reasons that Austrian classicism was generally clear and balanced, and relatively immune from the complications which affected academic culture elsewhere.

The sudden regeneration of architectural thought in the last decade of the nineteenth century should certainly be seen in relation to the social and political evolution of the Empire – universal suffrage was introduced for the election of part of the deputies for the first time in 1896 – and there is an equally obvious parallel between the Secession and the liberal tendencies of the minister Korber (1900–4). But the Austrian movement was led by one dominant personality, that of Otto Wagner (1841–1918) who influenced the younger generation by precept and example.

Wagner, born in 1841, was twenty years older than Horta and, until the age of fifty, worked only within the classical Viennese tradition, attaining great professional eminence. In 1894, appointed professor at the Vienna Academy of Art, his inaugural lecture affirmed the need for a radical renewal of architectural thought to bring it into line with the needs of the modern age, and he developed this theme further in

**303**  *Vienna, Underground station in the Schönbrunn park (Wagner, 1894–7)*

his book *Moderne Architecktur*, published the following year.[26] Meanwhile he was designing the underground stations in the Austrian capital (Figs. 302–3) where the basic neo-classical plan was attenuated and simplified, while a new decorative style triumphed over the usual imitative repertoire. In his later works, including the Postal Savings Bank of 1905 (Fig. 308) the Steinhof church in 1906 (Figs. 304–5) and the University Library of 1910 (Figs. 309–10) Wagner matured his style in contact with the experiments of younger architects – especially of Olbrich, who worked in his studio from 1894 to 1898 – and put forward a coherent alternative to traditional styles, free, at least superficially, from historical stylistic references.

Wagner's programme was similar to that of the Belgians or of the Glasgow school: the new architecture must free itself from all imitation and take modern technical conditions into account. The crucial point was this word 'new' which indicated the rejection of tradition and the faith in individual freedom, and appeared – itself or a synonym for it – in all programmatic formulae of the time.

But different attitudes were concealed beneath these formulae. Wagner understood the renewal of architectural style in a restricted way: he did not usually move far from normal schemes of composition, from rigid symmetrical plans, from the usual distribution of decorative elements, but preferred to restrict plastic elements to the surface: points for usual chiaroscuro were occupied by flat ornamental designs, usually light on dark, and the articulation between volumes was reduced to combinations of lines. In short, the traditional repertoire was given new life by the transpositioning of formal values from plastic to chromatic,

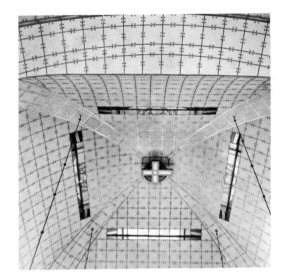

**304, 305** *(left)   Vienna, Steinhof church (Wagner, 1906)*
**306**   *Vienna, Housing block (Wagner, 1911; from J.A. Lux,* Otto Wagner, *1914)*
**307**   *Title of the book* Die Wagner-Schüle, *Leipzig, 1902*

from the three-dimensional to the flat
(Riegl would say: from tactile to optical
values).

But this was not a mere decorative change;
the whole architectural organism was animated and transformed by this treatment,
and the rigid range of traditional elements
became elastic, yielding, adaptable to new
needs.

This procedure, so rich in consequences,
became general in the following decade and
was to become one of the basic components
of European taste, even when the modern
movement had eliminated the references to
historical styles. For the moment, however,
it was closely linked to the neo-classical
repertoire, which provided the terms of
comparison for every new element.

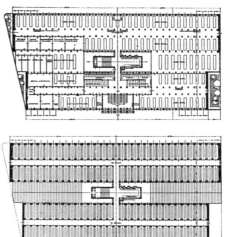

**308** *(above)* *Vienna, Postal Savings Bank (Wagner, 1905)*

**309, 310** *(below)* *Vienna, University Library (Wagner, 1910; from Lux,* op. cit.*)*

Rather than regeneration one might perhaps talk about an extension of tradition. The passage from conformist to nonconformist experiments was neither sudden nor complete; new forms made their appearance side by side with classical ones, from 1894 onwards, but Wagner continued to design buildings in the classical style, when circumstances demanded it, until he was very old, and he delighted in retaining the occasional classical element even in his most modern and daring moods – an architectural order, as on the façade of the church at Steinhof, or a fragment of an order – almost as a remnant that had not been subjected to this process of transposition. Viennese architects of the following generation often did the same (including Loos in the villa at Montreux and the house on the Michaelerplatz) and it should be remembered that all of them, however unlike in temperament and rich in imagination, tended to fall into a sort of stale neo-classicism (Olbrich's villa Feinhals in Cologne; Hoffmann's Austrian pavilion at the Werkbund exhibition in 1914; Loos' plan for the Chicago Tribune).

Even Wagner's controversial theories ran along lines of almost traditional argument. He fought academic tradition mainly in the name of individual freedom; he had noted that the stylistic discipline so admired by past ages had hardened into an inert, passive conformism, and in contrast to this he set the artist's spontaneity, which must be guided only by his temperament:

'The artist is primarily a productive creature with his own individual bent; creativity is his most important virtue. There can be no protectionism in art, because any protection of the weak tends to lower the artistic level. In art only the strong should be encouraged, because only their works act as ideal models, i.e. in an artistically stimulating way. It has already been said: "No pity for mediocrity in art . . .". Our artistic culture, and therefore the progress in art, is in the hands of original spirits'.[27]

Wagner's modernist liberalism had obvious affinities with the traditionalist liberalism of Guadet; it was no coincidence that both began to teach in the same year in the academies of Vienna and Paris respectively and offered two different interpretations of a common thought, which was the initial leaven of all current movements in the various countries of Europe.

As was the case with political liberalism in the late eighteenth century, the new mood was defined in a mainly negative way, as a liberation from traditional shackles, and all discussion was had in terms of the past, which was continually present as a term of comparison; the organizational problems which the new tendency had necessarily caused were allowed to remain vague, and the legitimacy of re-establishing the old bonds in order to tackle such unexpected problems was uncontested. One need only consider the unproductiveness of the Wagnerian method as far as town-planning was concerned, and the aristocratic and conventional nature of his plans for the extension of Vienna.

The persistent connection between the new movement and tradition – which for Wagner acted as a link between the various phases of his experiment, and which was communicated to the younger generation in his teaching – did in a way limit the Austrian experiments as compared with those of other western *avant-garde* movements, but was also the main reason for the success of the Austrian school. For Wagner's experiments and those of his followers not only proposed a consistent alternative to traditional styles, they also provided a method of attacking and transforming the whole vast repertoire of forms, and of visual and mental habits inherited from the past, and of transforming them to eliminate them definitively.

For this reason the Austrian school, while it was largely responsible for that irritating compromise between classicism and modernism – with its smooth, elongated arches, 'columns without capitals, symmetrical, simplified masses, abuse of stone facing and so on – which is known as the 'twentieth-century style' and which has influenced so much European building between the wars, did also avoid an early crystallization into a set decorative pattern and prepared the ground for the modern movement more directly

**311** *Vienna, Secession building (J.M. Olbrich, 1898)*
**312** *G. Klimt,* The Three Ages, *1908*
**313** *Vienna, Detail of the interior decor of the Stift house (Olbrich, 1900; from L. Hevesi,* Ideen von J. Olbrich*)*

than any other contemporary school.

## 5   Joseph Maria Olbrich

Of Wagner's disciples, Joseph Maria Olbrich (1869–1908) was the closest to his master and most clearly embodied his ideal of a free artist 'who has retained his natural sensibility uncorrupted'.

After studying at the academy under Hasenauer he was awarded the Prix de Rome and travelled in the Mediterranean countries; on his return to Vienna in 1894 he worked for six years in Wagner's office and designed the decoration for the building for the underground. In 1897 he joined the movement for the Secession and designed the building for their exhibitions (Fig. 311) the following year. In 1899 he was called to Darmstadt by the prince E. L. von Essen, to build the Kunstler-Kolonie on a hill near the town: this was a group of houses and exhibition halls for a group of artists patronized by the Sovereign: the young architect P. Behrens, the painter H. Christiansen, the designer P. Burck, the sculptor L. Habich, the decorator P. Huber, the jeweller R. Bosselt. Olbrich designed the buildings, the general layout, the furnishings, gardens, settings for the exhibitions, publicity and even the crockery and uniforms of the restaurant waiters (Figs. 314–21).

The complex was opened in 1901 with a collective exhibition of the group's work, was enlarged with new buildings in 1904 for a second exhibition and was completed in 1907 with a large exhibition building, which included the famous tower known as the Hochzeitturm. In 1908 Olbrich moved to Dusseldorf to supervise the building of the great Tietz stores, and died suddenly the same year.

Olbrich died before he was forty, at the beginning of the most important period for the European *avant-garde* movements, but his production had been large and remarkably consistent. He designed with extra-ordinary facility and without apparent effort, but what most surprises the present day observer is the fact that his innumerable ideas were almost always translated into reality with impeccable technical exactitude.

The tower of the exhibition building is a perfect example; the walls, of unfaced red brick, are broken up by repeated ornaments in stone and fields of blue and gold mosaic (Fig. 321); the top section is faced with glazed tiles of deep scarlet dotted with small iron balconies, and the topmost roof is of wood, covered with burnished copper; unlike Horta, Olbrich did not utilize only a limited number of materials and typical combinations, but enjoyed using a large variety which enabled him to obtain a vast range of colour effects; the result was an extraordinary variety of juxtapositions, but all so successfully applied that even after fifty years the building has scarcely deteriorated at all and its sumptuous decorative coverings are almost intact.

It seems almost incredible that Olbrich should have been in direct control of all these details, but it was just this precise attention to every technical difficulty which gave this architecture its immediate expressive lightness, similar to that found in the works of Horta. This integrity which today may seem unattainable because of the enormous increase in organizational problems, is perhaps the chief reason for Olbrich's fascination, and can be explained in only one way: by the complete understanding between the designer, suppliers and executors, which does not seem to have been at all shaken by Olbrich's innovating tendencies.

This implies that the novelty of Olbrich's architecture lay in his choice of forms, but left technical procedures and traditional organizational relationships unchanged; it was a superficial reform that extended the repertoire of eclectic culture without trying to force its conceptual boundaries.

Indeed during his last years, when he had to tackle particularly demanding subjects,

**314** *Darmstadt, Matildenhöhe, Detail of Olbrich's house (Olbrich, 1901)*

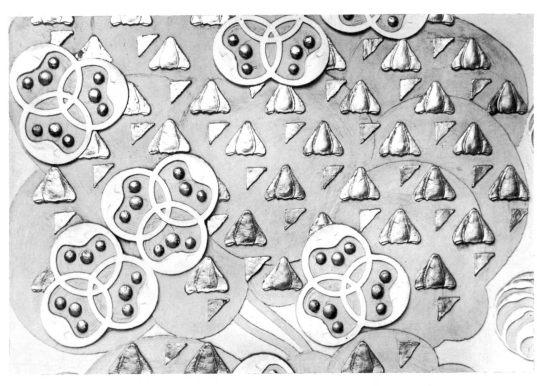

**315, 316, 317**   *Darmstadt, Matildenhöhe, Three aspects of the Ludwig house (Olbrich, 1901)*

Olbrich fell back upon neo-Gothic models in a way that seemed absolutely natural – in the Tietz stores – and neo-classical ones – in the Feinhals house – and reverted to stiff organisms reminiscent of Wagner.

## 6   Joseph Hoffmann

Joseph Hoffmann (1870–1956) one year younger than Olbrich, studied at the Academy with Wagner, joined the Secession and made his début in 1898 with the furnish-

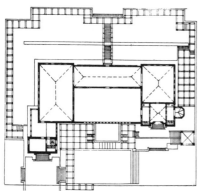

**318, 319, 320**  *Darmstadt, Matildenhöhe, Exhibition Palace (Olbrich, 1907; the lower view is from G.A. Platz, op. cit.)*

ings of a room at the first Secession exhibition, immediately giving evidence of his interest in interior decoration.

This was the time when the first products of applied art by the European *avant-garde* movements were reaching Vienna. Here in 1897 the Baron von Scala organized the first exhibition of English furniture, and Von Muthesius made known the works of Van de Velde. In 1899 Hoffmann was appointed professor at the 'Kunstgewerbeschule', and in 1903, together with Kolo Moser, he set up his own workshop, the 'Wiener Werkstatte', to which he devoted most of his energies from then onwards.

Meanwhile he was fulfilling a series of

INHALT·

TITELZEICHNVNG
WIDMVNG·
V-XII
EINFVHRVNG·VON
LVDWIG·HEVESI –
1 – 78
ILLVSTRATIONEN·
IN·ZINKÄTZVNG··
A–G
FARBIGE·FLÄCHEN
ORNAMENTE·  ·IN
LITHOGRAPHIE  ⊐
ORIGINAL LITHO=
GRAPHIE ⌣ OLBRICH

**321** *(left)   Darmstadt, Matildenhöhe, Base of the Hochzeitturm (Olbrich, 1907)*
**322, 323** *Typographic compositions (from Hevesi, op. cit.)*

architectural commissions: several nobles' houses in and around Vienna (Fig. 331), then his first public building, the sanatorium at Purkerstorf (Fig. 330). Here, encouraged by the nature of the task, Hoffmann simplified his architectural style to its very limit: the final building was a block of stonework plastered in white, topped by a simple slab-

| | | |
|---|---|---|
| 1 | entrance | 15 coal |
| 2 | cloakroom | 16 larder |
| 3 | hall | 17 refrigerator |
| 4 | music room | 18 garage |
| 5 | platform | 19 courtyard |
| 6 | sitting room | 20 bedroom |
| 7 | smoking room | 21 bathroom |
| 8 | dining room | 22 W.C. |
| 9 | terrace | 23 children's room |
| 10 | breakfast room | 24 nanny's room |
| 11 | pantry | 25 servants' bedrooms |
| 12 | kitchen | 26 dressing room |
| 13 | servants' rooms | 27 guest rooms |
| 14 | servants' dining room | 28 work-room |

*(from B. Zevi,* Storia dell'architettura moderna, *1950)*

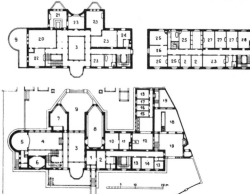

**324, 325** *Brussels, Palais Stoclet (Hoffmann, 1905–14)*

like roof and broken by a series of windows of various shapes; a band of blue-and-white check tiles runs down each right-angled corner to give the desired effect of the transposition of volume onto the plane. This building is usually regarded as an anticipation of rationalism, but in itself it can be defined exactly within the limits of the Wagnerian method and was one of the possible results of the process of chromatic transcription of traditional models; it cannot be judged without reference to this tradition. This can be seen from the rigidly geometrical plan, the carefully considered relationship between

**326**    *Brussels, Detail of the Palais Stoclet*
**327**    *J. Hoffmann, Design for a sideboard (from L. Kleiner,* J. Hoffmann, *1927)*

the parts, the care taken in differentiating the various floors by varying the shape and spacing of the windows.

In 1905 Hoffmann began work on the Palais Stoclet in Brussels, and continued to do so until 1914 (Figs. 324–6, 328–9). It is significant that Hoffmann should excel himself in an absolutely exceptional work, so

**328, 329** *Brussels, Two details of the Palais Stoclet*

large and sumptuous as to warrant the name of 'palace'. The breaking down of the volume of the building into squares, edged with dark bands, is done here with a facing of white Norwegian marble framed in bronze cornices, while the partial symmetry, recognizable in the plan and in the view on to the garden, was enlivened by a series of variants, each symmetrical in itself but freely grouped according to functional needs. As in Olbrich's Freiekunst, this was a calculated deviation from the rules of perspective, possibly based on a reference to certain less well-known aspects of past tradition – a similar method of composition was used in late Roman times and yet another in English Gothic, taken up again by the medievalist architects of the nineteenth century – or more possibly on calculation of the dynamic effects to be obtained from a limited modification of current visual habits; in any case this method of composition was dependent upon expert manipulation of past styles and had to be backed by a very alert sensibility, directly controlling every detail.

The visitor to the Stoclet Palace is immediately conscious of the numerous and delightful details that Hoffmann lavished on it; here too the strict technical propriety and excellent state of repair – facilitated by the use of valuable materials and the assiduous care taken of the building by its owners – are fundamental conditions of the architecture. Even the garden, of smooth lawns and evergreen trees and hedges cut in geometrical shapes, is more or less immune to the passage of time; all this gives the work a sort of monumental abstractness, since it preserves unaltered the forms of a past life and even inspires a certain unease, like the wax figure of a character from the past.

Both the Purkersdorf sanatorium and the Stoclet Palace were entirely furnished from the 'Wiener Werkstatte'. Hoffmann influenced his contemporaries far more through this firm than through his actual architectural works. It was through him that the Arts and Crafts tradition was freed from any trace of medievalism, so that the taste of the 'Wiener Werkstatte' was finally in a position to act as arbiter of taste to all Europe, even to France and England where it partly ousted similar local traditions (Fig. 327).

'Viennese furniture' is something one used to come across in almost every furniture shop; after the First World War it began to look a little old-fashioned, but continued to flood middle-class homes with its flowered armchairs, wardrobes with· light panelling and beds with moulded bedheads, all of which still echoed the stylistic elements of Hoffmann, albeit somewhat blunted by the lengthy process of passage through so many hands.

For similar reasons between the two wars – after Wagner's death – Hoffmann became the most sought after designer in Vienna; we shall discuss this aspect of his work later on, in Chapter 16.

## 7    Adolf Loos

The events of the life of Adolf Loos (1870–1933) and his theories distinguish him from his Viennese contemporaries. Born in Brno and educated in the provinces, he was deaf until the age of twelve, and it is possible that this physical handicap influenced his character and his destiny; he was by nature a lone wolf as an individual and as an artist, a 'modern Diogenes' as Persico has called him.[28]

Between 1893 and 1896, while the modernist controversy was beginning in Vienna, Loos was travelling in England and America; when he returned home he had difficulty finding work, did some interior decoration and designed his first building in 1904: the Villa Karma at Montreux (Fig. 333) was plainly inspired by Wagner with its partial symmetry, use of extensive surfaces and clean-cut openings, contrasting with the isolated Doric order marking the main entrance; but the white plaster, which equalized the various elements of the building, eliminated the usual interplay, and traditional determination of volume was re-established, making the building more solid, if less elegant than the Wagnerian models.

Meanwhile Loos was also becoming active as a theorist and polemicist; he wrote articles and gave lectures, and in 1903, for a short time, even published a review with the significant title 'The other – a periodical for

**330** *(above)   Purkersdorf, Sanatorium (Hoffmann, 1901)*
**331, 332** *(below)   Vienna, Primavesi house (Hoffmann, 1914) and the Austrian pavilion at the Cologne exhibition (Hoffmann, 1914; from Platz,* op. cit.*)*

the introduction of western civilization into Austria'. Loos was an implacable enemy of the Secession; he regarded the Wagnerian appeal for the freedom of the arts, and Hoffmann's decorative inspiration as a sort of cultural dissipation, basically similar to the

**333** *Montreux, Karma house (A. Loos, 1904)*
**334** *Vienna, Steiner house (Loos, 1910; from A. Sartoris,* Gli elementi dell'architettura funzionale, *1932)*
**335** *Vienna, House on the Michaelerplatz (Loos, 1910)*

traditional styles against which Wagner and his followers were battling. For this reason he set modesty and discretion against the cult of originality ('Beware of being original; designing may easily drive you towards it. You must make a great effort, while design-

ing, to ward off all original ideas. But this thought should be enough to conquer this temptation: how will the men for whom I am working live in this house or in these rooms in fifty years' time?'[29]), and the impartial assessment of propriety against the worth of novelty. ('One may do something new only if one is going to do it better. Only the new inventions – electric light, concrete etc. . . . can change tradition.'[30]) and finally arrived at a complete separation of art and utility, placing architecture in the sphere of utility alone ('Architecture is not an art . . . anything that fulfils a purpose is excluded from the sphere of art'.)[31] In 1908, in his famous article 'Ornament and Crime', Loos claimed that architecture and the applied arts should make do without any ornament, which itself should be regarded as a survival of barbaric custom.

Loos' works after 1908 are almost the practical demonstration of this thesis (Figs. 334–5). The house on the Michaelerplatz of 1910 and the Steiner house of the same year, on the outskirts of Vienna, struck contemporaries by their absolute elimination of every non-structural element: they are masses of smooth masonry with windows and other apertures cut out of them, while a tabular cornice or simple coping marks the juncture with the roof.

These buildings were regarded as the first examples of European rationalism and they certainly influenced the work of Gropius, Oud, Le Corbusier and other post-war masters. But the terms of Loos' argument were those of traditional culture; he accepted *a priori* the antithesis between beauty and utility, between decorated and undecorated objects, then came down on the side of utility and the elimination of ornament. The modern movement began to cast doubt on the meaning of these very terms, and within its ambit a theory like Loos' became an irrelevance.

The appeal to 'reason', too, had two different meanings. Loos' reason was the Wagnerian *necessitas*, i.e., a complex of general rules inherent in the very nature of building (which for this reason, according to Wagner, should agree *a priori* with the general rules governing beauty, while according to Loos they should be in conflict with

them). Gropius' reason was an active regulating principle, in which the antitheses between necessity and beauty were reconciled, since the true value of things was not to be found anywhere in nature but was a product of man's industry.

The simplicity of Loos' architecture – and of some of Hoffmann's – derived from the Wagnerian process of simplification of the traditional repertoire. One need only consider how the abandoning of certain stylistic values (incidental decoration, colour) demands to be balanced by the rigorous preservation of others (planned inter-relation of volumes); for this reason the sanatorium at Purkersdorf was more rigorously symmetrical than the Stoclet Palace, and the Steiner house more so than the villa at Montreux. In these works the theories of the Viennese school were not abandoned but only carried to their limits.

Another aspect to be taken into account was the American contribution that Loos absorbed during his travels of 1893–6. Zevi stressed this aspect, connecting it with the free use of space in the vertical sense that Loos allows himself in his buildings[32] (Figs. 336–7).

But this important critical pointer has yet to be analysed more closely, to establish the nature of this 'conception of space'. Loos was accustomed, partly because of his training as a craftsman, to regard architectural forms as capable of being directly and instinctively grasped, independently of the mediation of design. In America he found this tendency confirmed not by the ambitious programmes of the *avant-garde* – where design, on the contrary, plays so important a part – but in the sense of dimensional propriety of current domestic building, in the open-minded faithfulness to the demands of function.

In this way he was led to reconsider the artificial division of a building into superimposed storeys, which entailed attributing a fixed height to all rooms, i.e., seeing the

**336** *Vienna, Interior of Scheu house (Loos, 1912)*

relations between them in an exclusively graphic way, in terms of the plan. But Loos claimed that each room ought to have the height judged most suitable for it, individually, neither more nor less; only in this way could its character be regulated with the desired spontaneity, without its being forced to correspond to the adjacent rooms. Design should intervene only to inter-relate the various rooms within the body of the main building, offsetting the variations in levels in the most profitable way possible. This was the start of a new compositional procedure that he discussed under the name of 'Raumplan'.

Neutra, a pupil of Loos, has recounted how about 1900 the master 'unleashed a revolt against the habit of indicating dimensions in figures or measured drawings. He felt, as he often told me, that such a procedure

**337**   *Vienna, Interior of Scheu house (Loos, 1912)*

dehumanizes design. "If I want a wood panelling or wainscot to be of a certain height, I stand there, hold my hand at that certain height, and the carpenter makes his pencil mark. Then I step back and look at it from one point and from another, visualizing the finished result with all my powers. This is the only human way to decide on the height of a wainscot or on the width of a window".'[33]

Loos saw a human value as being connected with this immediate and experimental evaluation in each architectural element; hence his hatred, both technical and moral, for waste of any kind, which was probably the basic reason for his polemic against the ornate and for his theory of the Raumplan. It was in this connection, too, that Loos made his most important contribution to the modern movement, i.e. a sort of parsimony about space, in contrast to the wasteful indifference of

**338**  *Vienna, Interior of Moller house by Loos*

academic architects; in the place of the empty, unlimited field of space waiting like a kingdom to be boldly conquered, Loos saw the space where human activities took place, i.e., a limited, concrete reality, almost as a precious coin to be spent in the most circumspect way possible.

He conceived of the relationship between man and environment in a restricted way, limiting himself to considering certain corres-

pondences between the measurement of openings and human stature and movements, to be established by direct experiment; in this way he began to overemphasize the part of intuition in the architect's work and to conceive of planning as a strictly individual task. Gropius extended this reasoning, including in Loos' space all the human activities, both individual and corporate, and put forward an integrated notion of planning

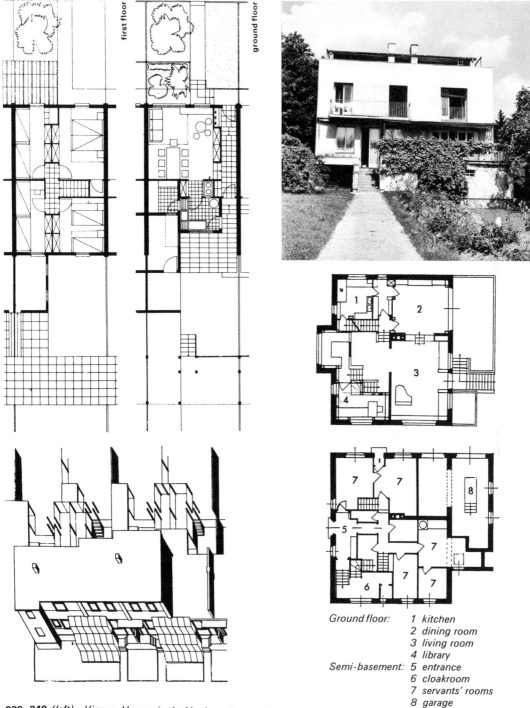

first floor

ground floor

Ground floor:  1 *kitchen*
2 *dining room*
3 *living room*
4 *library*
Semi-basement:  5 *entrance*
6 *cloakroom*
7 *servants' rooms*
8 *garage*

**339, 340** *(left)  Vienna, Houses in the Heuberg district (Loos, 1921–3)*
**341, 342** *(right)  Vienna, Moller house (Loos, 1928; plan from* Casabella*)*

in which all men's active faculties were taken into account. In this way Loos' solitary experience passed into the modern movement and became the common property of successive generations.

For his part, Loos remained faithful to his own individual attitude and remained in his lonely position even after the war, when many of his ideas had been taken up by the international movement.

Between 1920 and 1922 he had the opportunity of working on a large scale when he was appointed chief architect of the city of Vienna. This was probably the peak of his career though it has not been sufficiently studied: he designed an experimental district in Heuberg, which was only partly built, and many types of building that were never realized at all but which were the most advanced experiments in popular building at the time, not only in Austria but anywhere in Europe. But it was then, too, that Loos' personal limitations made themselves most clearly felt: his incapacity to transmit his personal experience to others, in a non-intuitive way, or to deduce an objective method from it. In 1922 he condensed his ideas on distribution in one of the most perfect of his private houses, the Rufer house in Vienna, then moved to Paris where he built a house for Tzara in 1926. During his last years he went back to his own country, where he worked remote from current controversy, and produced three more masterpieces: the Moller house in Vienna (1928), the Müller house in Prague (1930) and the Khuner house in Payerbach, of the same year where, with his use of natural materials and technological detail, he anticipated a sphere of interest which was to become widespread in the following decade.

## 8   Hendrik Petrus Berlage

In the second half of the nineteenth century P. J. H. Cuypers (1827–1921) brought to Holland an echo of the rationalism of Viollet-le-Duc and offered a mild and correct interpretation of the local Gothic tradition. Here as in other countries of northern Europe the neo-Gothic had national, progressive connotations as against the conservative and international neo-classicism, but the debate remained within the terms of eclectic culture and was of mainly local interest.

Hendrik Petrus Berlage (1856–1934) grew up in this environment, but developed a highly original set of theories from these premises and one which brought with it a possibility of bringing all medievally inspired European architectural thought up to date.

Berlage had studied at the Zurich Polytechnique from 1875 to 1878, when Semper's teaching was still very much alive; at first he worked at Frankfurt, then travelled in Italy and the German countries. After 1881 he settled in Amsterdam, opened an *atelier* with T. Sanders, and with him took part in the 1885 competition for the Stock Exchange, where they received fourth prize. In 1897 he was commissioned to build it; its construction, carried out between 1899 and 1903, marked a vital turning point in his experience and the beginning of a positive renaissance of Dutch architecture (Fig. 343).

What exactly was the importance of this work? The general tone was plainly inspired by the Flemish Romanesque and Gothic; but historical reference was used as a starting point for an original constructional analysis, and the utilitarian elements were frankly in evidence, producing absolutely novel decorative effects; downspouts for instance, embedded in a socket in the brick wall and protected by stone attachments, or the motif of the heads of the tie-bars or, in the interior, the riveted structures of the roofing, with the tie-beams and their supports rhythmically crossing the great rooms. Furthermore, obvious though the stylistic reminiscences are, the onlooker senses a new and fresh treatment of all parts of the structure, and feels with particular immediacy the consistency and grain of the traditional materials –

**343, 344** *H.P. Berlage, Amsterdam Stock Exchange (1903) and offices of De Nederlanden*

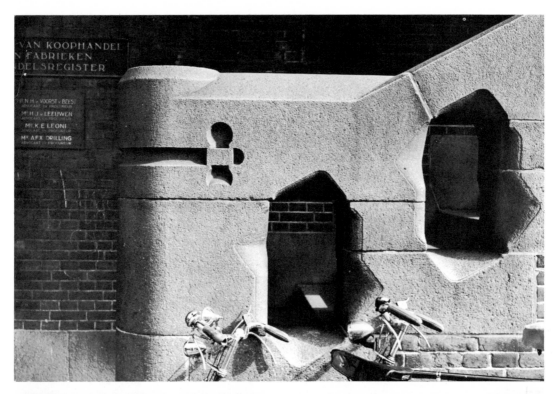

**345, 346, 347** *Amsterdam, Details of the Stock Exchange*

stone and brick – as if he were seeing them for the first time; this effect is due mainly to the original expedient of passing from one material to another with absolute smoothness, precisely where tradition would have demanded some plastic elaboration, and of setting much of the sculptural decoration flush with the wall, obtaining it by concave carving in sunk relief rather than in the reverse (Figs. 345–7).

This expedient is of the greatest importance in understanding Berlage's methods; it is used, as in Wagner, to translate plastic effects into chromatic ones, but its systematic use made it so basic that it might almost be said to break the whole traditional language in two, in that it systematically kept apart the geometrical aspect, as it would appear from a drawing of volumes only, from the physical, resulting from the distinction between the materials used. In this way a new degree of freedom was introduced into all traditional forms and combinations, and the current repertoire was utilized so that it could be set free from current uses and habits and adapted to new ones.

Berlage's programme was similar to Wagner's; both proposed a sort of up-to-date version of the stylistic heritage they had learned about and absorbed in the first period of their activity (Berlage was forty-seven when the Amsterdam Stock Exchange was started). Wagner made use of the classical style, on which an unbroken aristocratic tradition of several centuries weighed heavily, and was therefore chiefly concerned with demonstrating the possibility of a free and personal interpretation of it. Berlage worked with the medieval repertoire, treated from the first with polemical and liberating aims, which carried with them the rational motivations of Viollet-le-Duc and the moral aspirations of Ruskin, and he was led to delve deeper in order to discover the ultimate foundations of these views. Furthermore, Berlage – a far more perceptive theorist – was careful to make his attitude as impersonal as possible and to formulate an objective methodology, as widely acceptable as possible; in this way his teaching went deeper and was more productive than that of Wagner, particularly in the field of town-planning, as will be shown in Chapter 11.

The Dutch master realized, more clearly than any of his colleagues, that *avant-garde* culture was basically the product of an emergency; while 'the great architectural style of the future community'[34] was being prepared, it was in fact necessary to re-organize the instruments offered by current tradition, to subject them to rigorous analysis, to anchor subjective choices to a series of objective considerations and to set them within a rational series of steps.

But this rationalization of the legacy of tradition was as yet incomplete; between the objective and subjective components of planning, between formal method and formal choices Berlage postulated, basically, a sort of parallelism in that he associated certain of the requirements with certain figurative precepts – for instance the new treatment of organisms in ordinary stonework with the use of joints fused with the flat surface of the wall.

This dualism was revealed by his successors, since his teachings could be developed mainly in the direction of rationalism – as was the case with the group 'De Stijl', which tried to formulate a method so precise as to reduce personal judgment to a minimum – or else by freeing the element of personal choice from all rules, as was the case with the group of young people who began to be active after 1910, Van der Mey, Kramer, De Klerk.

## 9  The spread of art nouveau

The description of European *avant-garde* movements in terms of single personalities or groups might give the idea that each set of experiments was more isolated from the others than in fact was the case. At this time cultural contacts were exceptionally intense, movements and artists inspired each other in many ways and to search for the sources of each separate experiment is more or less useless, so close-knit was the play of the various influences.

To put the previous remarks into correct perspective, one must consider the chief mechanisms by which the ideas and images of *art nouveau* spread throughout Europe and elsewhere; for this reason I shall also touch upon less important experiments which were dependent on the main ones described so far.

The Belgian *avant-garde* movement, as has been said, grew up around the weekly review *L'Art Moderne*, founded in 1881, which came out until the First World War;

**348, 350** *(above)   The Hague, Gemeente Museum (Berlage, finished in 1934)*

**349, 351** (*below*)   *M. De Klerk, Design for a nautical club at Amsterdam, 1922* (*from* L'Architecture Vivante)

it was around this that the group 'Les XX' gathered in 1884, to become 'La Libre Esthétique' in 1894. The first certain relations with England were in connection with the exhibitions of 'Les XX' from 1891 onwards, where objects designed by Morris and his school were exhibited. In 1894 Van de Velde began his series of lectures, though they were not collected in a single volume until 1901.

Meanwhile in England the associations for the teaching and spread of the applied arts mentioned in Chapter 6 were being formed. In 1893 the review *The Studio* began to appear – and was soon very widely read, making English production known throughout Europe and presenting the works of the most important *avant-garde* continental artists in England – and, in 1896, the *Architectural Review*.

In Germany some years later than in Belgium, a similar group for the renewal of the decorative arts was formed, though it is impossible to prove that one was a direct derivation of the other; there were of course common pictorial sources (Toorop, already, successful in Belgium some years earlier, had already exhibited in Munich in 1893). In 1894 Herman Obrist (1863–1927) opened an embroidery workshop in Munich, and in the same year Otto Echmann (1865–1902) left painting for the applied arts, from 1895 supervising the illustrated part of the *avant-garde* review *Pan,* whose taste spread throughout all German speaking countries.

Soon afterwards, mainly through Van de Velde, the Belgian movement spread throughout Europe, ousting local schools. In 1896 the German dealer S. Bing opened his shop in Paris – under the sign *Art Nouveau* – where he presented Van de Velde's furniture to the French public, and the following year he organized an exhibition at Dresden using much of the Paris material. Both in France and in Germany Van de Velde's ideas were in the air, and many designers and craftsmen had been moving

in this same direction for some years, for instance Emile Gallé (1846–1904) in Nancy; the appearance of a logical example provided a solid methodological foundation, and gave these experiments the support needed for them to become transformed into a real movement.

But in France things went differently: both academic culture and the technical tradition – themselves interlinked, as we have said – were basically unsympathetic to new contributions and put up strong resistance to their diffusion. For this reason the new movement only affected a limited portion of French production, i.e. furnishing, traditionally regarded as quite separate from architecture, and a part of domestic architecture. In practice *art nouveau* became a decorative style – backed by the reviews *Arts et Décoration* and *L'Art décoratif* which came out in 1897, and also by the *Revue des arts décoratifs* which changed its allegiances at just this time – and was rapidly drawn into the sphere of traditional eclecticism.

In Germany on the other hand the movement met with less resistance and kept its original character of a movement of structural regeneration. In 1896 the review *Jugend* appeared, giving its name to the new style, and in 1897 *Decorative Kunst*; in Munich in the Glaspalast a big exhibition of applied arts was being held, and in Munich too August Endell (1871–1925) designed the photographic studio 'Elvira', with its controversial façade with a large abstract motif. The new tendencies were supported by the authoritative critic A. Lichtwark, director of the Hamburg Gallery.

Soon afterwards the influence of the Vienna school began to make itself felt decisively. Wagner's inaugural lecture was given in 1894 and the book *Moderne Architecktur* appeared a year later; his total commitment to the school bore fruit a few years later when a group of young artists, among whom were several of his followers, founded the Secession in 1898 and began to publish the

**352** *Amsterdam, Detail of the Stock Exchange*
**353** *Paris, house by J. Lavirotte, 1904*

periodical *Ver Sacrum.*

Among the sources of the Secession – apart from the Belgian *art nouveau* which was by now the common property of all Europe – was certainly a knowledge of English furniture, exhibited in 1897 in the Museum of art and industry. According to Pevsner, knowledge of Mackintosh, whose works had been published in *The Studio*

from 1897, may have had an influence from the very beginning; in any case it is certain that Mackintosh's influence became important from 1900, when a room completely furnished by him and his group was exhibited in the Secession building; soon afterwards F. Warndorfer, backer of the Wiener Werkstatte, furnished his Viennese house with furniture by Mackintosh.

**354, 355** *(left)  Paris, Main stairway of the large store Lafayette (1912) and one of the metro stations (H. Guimard, 1900)*
**356, 357** *(right)  Drawing by R. d'Aronco for the Turin exhibition of 1902 (from* Casabella*) and printed material by G.P. & J. Baker (H. Naper, 1905, Victoria & Albert Museum)*

**358, 359** *Furnishings by the firm Carlo Gollia & Co. of Palermo, exhibited at Turin in 1901 (from Koch, op. cit.) and the colophon of the publishing house of Koch*

The production of the various European *avant-garde* movements was exhibited side by side for the first time at the universal exhibition in Paris in 1900.

At this point *art nouveau* entered the current repertoire of French architecture, as an addition to their eclectic repertoire, and since, traditionally, the exhibitions were the field for the most advanced experiments, it made its mark on most of the buildings designed for this occasion. The results of this influence were the reverse of pleasing; the most controversial work was the gate facing the Place de la Concorde, built by J. R. Binet in the form of a huge arch surrounded by scrolls and obelisks; newspapers and periodicals made lively comments on this highly contrived piece of work, defined it as a 'crinoline', 'salamander' and lastly, since it resembled its designer, as the 'Binet gate'.[35]

But it was the contents of the pavilions that interested art connoisseurs. Belgium, France, England and Germany and many other countries exhibited objects of interior décor, *objets d'art* and furniture in the new style, and the Austrians' décor and products were unanimously regarded as the best.

A French critic wrote:

'Of all nations, Austria succeeds best in satisfying the desire for the novel, is able to give proof of the most ingenious and abundant fantasy, the most agile and most delicate. Wherever one goes, to the sections of the chemical or photographic industries, of leather or wool; linen or stationery, civil engineering or agriculture, painting or drawing, everywhere there was refinement and almost always positive results; wood took on the most diverse tones, adorned with reliefs, plated with galvano-plastics; and sometimes the natural raw material was used, very successfully. Here one should really linger, describe the furnishings one by one, praise their architects in a worthy fashion: Messrs. Baumann, Hoffmann, Otto Wagner and Deesey'.[36]

And an Englishman:

'The two rooms with furniture and décor by Niedermoser are fine examples of the latest "fashion" in furnishing. Their style is light and delicate, and above all extremely

original . . . The phrase *art nouveau* which is seen and heard throughout the Exhibition, has no greater justification than in the displays of Austrian furnishing, where the most recent decorative tendencies are applied without exaggeration and do not reach the point of absurdity. As much cannot be said for other nations making efforts in the same direction'.[37]

A second opportunity for comparison between *avant-garde* experiments was the international exhibition at Turin in 1902. During precisely these years Italian culture was giving signs of new life and making a marked effort, if not to enter the European battlefield, at least to keep up with developments beyond the Alps.

In 1892 the periodical *Arte Italiana decorativa e industriale*, edited by Boito, began to appear; then, in 1895, *Emporium*, the other review of decorative art published by the 'Istituto d'arti grafiche di Bergamo'. For the moment the two periodicals were inspired by a dignified eclecticism; Boito's thought – in 1893 Hoepli published his *Questioni Pratiche di belle arti* – did not go beyond the limits of eclecticism, but he was acutely aware of the contradictions and ferments of contemporary culture.

In this scene, poor in independent energies but intently receptive, European *avant-garde* movements found an echo soon after 1900, and were the indirect cause of a certain number of unconventional works and discussions. (The episode coincides chronologically with the series of liberal ministers, begun in 1901 with the Zanardelli – Giolitti cabinet).

In 1901 Giuseppe Sommaruga (1867–1917) built his first work inspired by *art nouveau*, the Palazzo Castiglioni in Milan. Ernesto Basile (1857–1938) made use of the same sources at the agricultural exhibition in Palermo. In 1902 Raimondo d'Aronco (1857–1923) built the pavilion for the Turin exhibition (Fig. 356), openly inspired by the

**360** *Turin, Music pavilion at the 1901 exhibition (R. d'Aronco; from Koch,* op. cit.)

Viennese Secession and by Olbrich in particular. At the same time the Humanitarian society of Milan, founded in 1893, extended its activity to applied art and committed the supervision of its workshop-schools to a pupil of Boito's, Gaetano Moretti (1850–1938) who exhibited some dignified furnishings at the Turin exhibition.

In Spain Antonio Gaudí (1852–1926) was working at the margins of *art nouveau,* but certainly along the same lines as the innovating spirit running throughout Europe. His starting point was traditional eclecticism, and he showed a particular interest in the Gothic and in structural problems – following the teaching of Viollet-le-Duc – and from his earliest work revealed a boldness, love of sensational effects, capacity for the immediate and almost physical grasp of the qualities of material – particularly the roughest, the most raw – which were unparalleled in recent tradition, though they have links with the remote tradition of Moorish and Churrigueresque architecture.

Between 1900 and 1910 he gave up all reference to period styles and built his most important works: the Guell park, the Battló and Milà houses in Barcelona, where he took up various suggestions from the *art nouveau* repertoire but elaborated them with absolute originality (Figs. 361–3). During the last part of his life Gaudí worked almost exclusively on the Church of the Sagrada Familia, begun in 1884 in the Gothic style and continued with a series of increasingly free modifications of period references.

Gaudí is a figure of the greatest importance and in other circumstances one would say much more about him, but his experiment remained isolated in a hostile or indifferent atmosphere and did not have an influence proportionate to its importance on architecture in Spain or anywhere else.

From 1900 onwards Germany became the centre of European architectural thought. That artists on the continent became further acquainted with the English movement – and

particularly with Mackintosh – was due primarily to Hermann von Muthesius (1861–1921), who was the cultural attaché at the German embassy in London from 1896 to 1903; in 1901 he published the book *Die englische Baukunst der Gegenwart*; from 1904 to 1908 the three volumes *Das englische Haus* and discussed current English production in numerous articles and lectures; after Koch's competition for the art lover's house he wrote the preface to the volume published in 1903, with the three designs by Scott, Mackintosh and Bauer. Olbrich was in Germany from 1899, first in Darmstadt and then in Düsseldorf. Van de Velde was in Weimar from 1902 and the two volumes of his collected lectures came out, also in German, in 1901 and 1903. Berlage's theoretical booklet was published in Leipzig in 1905.

The 'Deutsche Werkstätte', a firm founded in 1898 by Karl Schmidt of Dresden, was inspired initially by English models but moved towards mass production and standardization during the first decade of the twentieth century, and, in 1910, put low-priced unit furniture on the market. In 1907 the 'Deutscher Werkbund' was founded, co-ordinating all the *avant-garde* experiments in the field of applied arts and making possible a periodic comparison between the productions of the various countries through its exhibitions.

In the years immediately before the First World War Wright's taste spread throughout Europe; in 1910 the editor Wasmuth invited Wright to Berlin, organized an exhibition of his works and produced a volume of illustrations, *Ausgefuhrte Bauten und Entwurfe,* which was republished in 1911 in a shortened version with a preface by Ashbee. In the same year Berlage, travelling in America, visited Wright's works, was enthusiastic about them and preached Wright's gospel in his own country.

In 1914, on the eve of the war, the Werkbund opened its exhibition in Cologne, where all the important forces in *avart-garde*

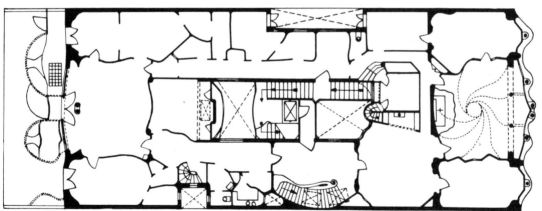

**361, 362, 363** *Barcelona, Details of the church of the Sagrada Familia and the Battlo house; plan of the Battlo house (A. Gaudí, 1905)*

culture were represented: the buildings of Van de Velde, Hoffmann, Behrens, Gropius, and Taut all revealed a great variety of different orientations but were still unstable and highly sensitive to mutual influence; it was the faithful image of the culture of the time, formed of heterogenous experiments which were nonetheless well acquainted with one another, spurred each other on and were based on an efficient organization of cultural exhibitions, associations, books, journals etc. The modern movement, which was born with the intention of mediating between these diversities, took advantage of these same instruments.

# ten

# France's contribution:
# Auguste Perret and Tony Garnier

## 1 The French cultural and technical heritage

The experiments described in the preceding chapter have various features in common: more or less direct theoretical inspiration from Morris's movement, a preference, within the sphere of tradition, for medieval models (with the partial exception of the Austrian), a strong interest in furnishing and the applied arts and certain formal preferences, among which was the tendency to transpose plastic elements into those of line and colour.

The revolt against tradition – for reasons of artistic independence, as with Wagner, or of moral rectitude, as with Van de Velde – was the most important common characteristic, though it was a purely negative one. The adjective *nouveau* (like the other terms *modern*, *jugend* etc.) had above all this polemical meaning of rejection of the particular balance between traditional stylistic repertoire and constructional technique on which European artistic culture had hitherto been based.

But it was natural that the spread of *art nouveau* should only partially affect France, which had once been the main repository and authorized interpreter of the above-mentioned tradition. As we have said, when *art nouveau* came to France it did not create a horizontal division as elsewhere, between the progressive élite and the conservative majority, but rather a vertical one by types of production, and the cultural crisis of the Académie did not much compromise either cultural habits or the prestige of the traditional models.

But at the same time as *art nouveau* two other *avant-garde* experiments of a completely different nature also appeared – those of Perret and Garnier – based precisely on the main stream of French tradition, and offered an original re-elaboration of this line; these too were isolated attempts, made possible by the progressive tendencies of a section of the ruling class, but they differed from other current attempts elsewhere in Europe by the difference in the pressure of cultural habits. This distinction is vital to explain the distribution of the energies which combined to form the modern movement, and particularly the position of Le Corbusier in relation to other contemporary masters.

French architectural culture was based on classicism and on a sophisticated technical tradition, bound by a process of mutual adaptation which had gone unchallenged over so many decades as to make them appear

**364** *Paris, Esders tailoring establishment (A. Perret, 1919)*

almost indistinguishable. But the physiognomy of this tradition was threatened with dispersal by eclecticism, which accustomed architects to combine both period styles and the materials and systems of building.

Perret and Garnier revolted against contemporary eclecticism and turned to the two complementary principles of earlier tradition: to classicism – understood in an almost philosophical sense, as the spirit of geometry and clarity – and to structural coherence; reinforced concrete lent itself marvellously to this second principle; it was just beginning to be used at this time, and, with its virtues of static continuity and adaptability, soon became the favourite building material of French architects.

Portland cement was a material discovered at the beginning of the century by the Englishman Aspdin; the patent of 21 October 1824 said:

'The mud or dust of roads paved with limestone material or, if this material is not available in sufficient quantities, calcined limestone material is mixed with a set quantity of clay, then mixed with water, manually or by machine, until it is reduced to a smooth paste; this is then dried, broken into small pieces and heated in a lime kiln, until all carbonic acid is driven off; the product is then reduced to powder with pestle and grindstone and is ready for use'.[1]

Towards 1845 it began to be produced industrially, and the first attempts were made to combine concrete with iron, to give it the resistance to tensile stress that it did not possess on its own; in 1847, F. Coignet designed the first roof in pre-moulded concrete and reinforced with iron rods for a terrace at Saint-Denis, actually built in 1852; in 1848 Lambot designed his boat, and in 1849 Joseph Monier (1832–1906) made the first flower-pots reinforced with a metallic mesh. For the moment it was used only for small objects, and it was only the curiosity of later workers in the same field, who witnessed the advances made in reinforced concrete in the last decades of the nineteenth century, that made known the names and works of these precursors.

Monier soon realized that the new building system could be put to many uses and after patenting his pots in 1855, took out a series of patents in the following years for the use of reinforced concrete in pipes (1868), panels (1869), bridges (1880). They were promptly put into effect: a reservoir at Fontainebleau in 1868, followed by another larger one and, in 1875, the first bridge, with a span of sixteen metres.

In 1879 Monier's patent was ceded to Germany and Austria, and in 1887 the Actien Gesellschaft fur Beton und Monierbau was formed, building a large number of bridges in the German-speaking countries. Between 1885 and 1890 other contributions came from America (Ward, Hyatt and Ransone); in 1880 François Hennebique (1842–1921) began his career, working on the problem of floors in concrete reinforced with iron rods, and built the first one in 1888 in Lombardtzyde, in Belgium. About 1890 François Coignet obtained various patents for building water mains with concrete pipes and in 1891 built the first floor with pre-fabricated girders made in Biarritz. After 1892 Hennebique worked more intensively: his firm opened forty-two agencies abroad and during the following decade made about

seven thousand manufactured products, among which were the floors for the Grand Palais and Petit Palais for the Paris universal exhibition in 1900. In 1904 Anatole De Baudot (1834–1915) built the church of St Jean at Montmartre in reinforced concrete (Figs. 365–6), boldly leaving the internal supporting skeleton plainly visible; De Baudot was a former pupil of Labrouste and Viollet-le-Duc and was the first to use the new material in a work of civic importance, with plainly controversial intent; as with Viollet-le-Duc, the basic skeleton was designed on Gothic models so as to make it acceptable to contemporary taste.

Meanwhile theoretical studies were being carried out with important contributions from Germans, particularly F. Emperger around 1895 – and the need arose for regulations controlling the various systems of calculation in use (Hennebique, Cottancin, Rabut etc.). In 1892 the French Commission for the study of reinforced concrete was set up, in 1897 Rabut held the first course on the subject at the École Polytechnique and in 1903 the Chambre syndicale de constructeurs en ciment armé de France was formed. Finally, in 1906, the first official regulation was issued in France, whose example was followed by other countries.

## 2   Auguste Perret

Auguste Perret, son of a builder, attended the École des Beaux Arts in the last decade of the nineteenth century, though without obtaining a diploma, while working in his father's business; about 1905 he and his brother Gustave founded the firm A. and G. Perret Architectes, and the two of them with their brother Claude established the building firm Perret Frères Entrepreneurs.

Their first important work was the house at 25a rue Franklin, in Paris, completed in 1903, where for the first time the reinforced concrete skeleton was used in such a way as to effect the outward appearance of the

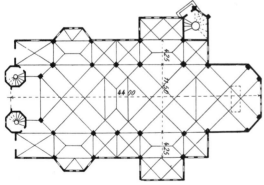

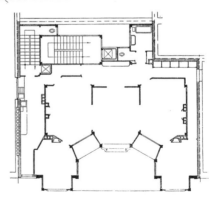

**365, 366** *(left) Paris, Church of St-Jean de Montmartre (A. De Baudot, 1904)*
**367, 368** *(right) Paris, House at 25a rue Franklin (Perret, 1903)*

building (Figs. 367–9).

The problem was to utilize a strip of ground between two other buildings, fairly wide but not very deep; the Perret brothers decided to avoid having any important windows at the back, but to have all five living rooms on each floor facing the road, opening them in a semi-circle around a central recess; they also increased the area of the two lateral rooms by having them cantilevered out over the street.

Such an arrangement would be very complicated with ordinary masonry. Similar distributional difficulties – common in Paris

**369**    *Paris, House in rue Franklin*

**370** *Paris, Garage in rue Ponthieu (Perret, 1905)*

because of the high cost of building land – had already often been solved with supporting frames in iron and, in recent years, in reinforced concrete, as in the building at Number 1, rue Danton.

But the iron and concrete were inside, hidden by a masonry façade as in Horta's Tassel house. Perret regarded this dualism almost as architectural duplicity, and believed that the organism should be treated uniformly inside and out, particularly as in this case almost all the surface was in fact taken up by the numerous windows; for this reason he presented the concrete skeleton quite clearly, by distinguishing it sharply from the screen walls, formed of the casing and panels covered in tiles with floral designs (Fig. 374).

Naturally this crusading intention was not carried out without a few compromises; the supporting structures, protected by a facing of stone, were adapted so as to be less offensive to current taste and so as to resemble the usual divisions into rectangular panels; occasionally this treatment meant falsifying structural expression, as at the base of the cantilevered parts, where the horizontal elements' function as corbel is disguised by making the strip continuous, so that the whole of the protruding body appears, paradoxically, to be without support (this intention is declared by the small *pendentifs* which allude, in the traditional manner, to the absent support). This was an opportunity for polemical satisfaction in demonstrating the resistance of the new material, as in Hennebique's house in Bourg-la-Reine; this taste was later to disappear, when reinforced concrete became a widely used material and when the eye became accustomed to the way it worked.

The garage of rue Ponthieu, of 1905, was similarly designed so that the frame of reinforced concrete, projected on to the façade,

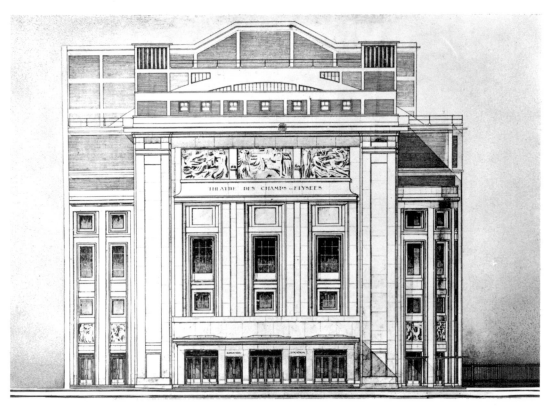

**371** *Paris, Drawing by Perret for the theatre of the Champs Élysées (1911–12; from P. Jamot,* A.-G. Perret et l'architecture du béton armé, *1927)*

should be a determining factor in its composition (Fig. 370); here there is nothing more than a complex of plaster-covered girders and pillars framing varying-sized panes of glass, and only the symmetry of the whole and the outline of the vertical pilasters allow the spectator to draw any comparison with the traditional organization of a façade.

The characteristics of Perret's architecture already appear clearly in these two works, and they remained constant in the magnificent works he did immediately after the war – the Esders clothing factory (1919), the church of Notre Dame du Raincy (1922–3) and of Montmagny (1926) (Figs. 375–6), the theatre for the exhibition of the decorative arts of 1925, the concert hall for the École Normale de Musique, the Garde-Meuble National, the administrative building for the Admiralty Research Laboratories (1930), the

house in the rue Raynouard (1932) where he set up his studio: severity, bold, formal simplification and at the same time an obstinate faithfulness to certain traditional rules of composition. The structures, and therefore the façades, are instinctively symmetrical in conception, and the constructional elements, though simplified, retain an undoubted resemblance to the elements of the traditional repertoire.

A structure in reinforced concrete of the type used by Perret consists of a skeleton of pillars and girders upon which the horizontal structures, the external non load-bearing walls and any internal divisions are supported. But classical architecture too was founded on a cagework of linear elements, the architectural orders, which were used to relate the various parts of the building to the general overall plan; this function was

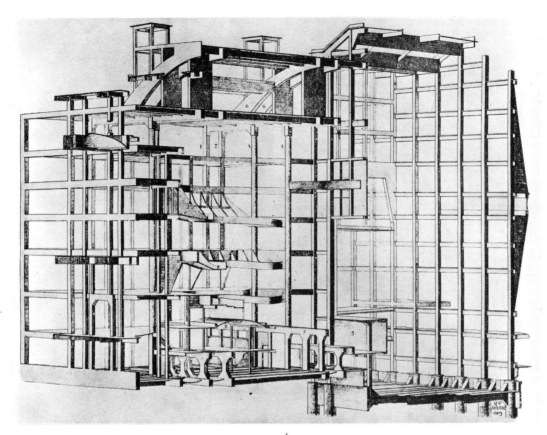

**372**  *Paris, Drawing by Perret for the theatre of the Champs Élysées (from Jamot)*

also performed even when the orders were simplified or, indeed, reduced to a framework of completely plain elements, because habit made it possible to endow these elements with the same properties of spatial reference.

The French tradition, as we have said, was based on the correspondence between classical rules and building practice, and through this correspondence they became so automatic as to pass for natural laws. Perret, steeped in this tradition, was naturally led to identify the concrete framework (which was a fact of construction) with the framework as it was to appear on the outside of the building, and to transfer to the first the needs and associations of the second. Hence the desire for symmetry and the continued suggestion of the architectural

orders, if not as formal presences, at least as terms of comparison; in fact in many more recent buildings, for instance the Museum of Public Works of 1937, Perret ended by treating the upright supports as columns and the girders as entablatures.

On this association, sometimes concealed, sometimes carried to the limits of neo-classicism, Perret based all his architecture; he expounded his conviction theoretically when he wrote:

'The conditions imposed by nature are permanent, those imposed by men are temporary. The inclemencies of the climate, statics with its laws, optics with its distortions, the individual sense of line and form, impose permanent conditions . . . the great buildings of our time consist of a

**373, 374**   *Paris, Champs Élysées theatre and a detail of the rue Franklin house*

skeleton, a structure in steel or reinforced concrete. The framework is to the building what the skeleton is to the animal; as the animal's skeleton, measured, balanced, symmetrical, contains and supports the most various and most variously situated organs, so must the structure of a building be composite, measured, balanced and also symmetrical'.[2]

This cultural limitation also applied in the

technical field and prevented Perret from following and interpreting, beyond a certain point, just those advances that were being made in connection with his own favourite material: reinforced concrete. He probably believed that he had discovered the constructional system best suited to the realization of traditional works, since the unity of its elements was real and not apparent, as in the classical orders composed of several blocks of hewn stone; but hampered by the

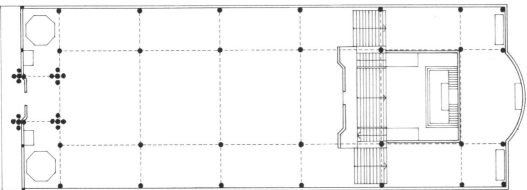

**375, 376**   *Le Raincy, Church of Notre Dame (Perret, 1923)*

idea of the skeleton of girders and supports he was prevented from allowing the particular qualities of reinforced concrete to find expression – the structural solidarity between girders, uprights and slabs – and therefore from accepting the unbroken structures used by his contemporary Maillart from 1910 onwards.

Perret's faith in the universal rules of architecture, although unfounded in our eyes, cannot be discounted as a mere personal quirk, and must be considered within its historical framework. The association between classicism and the science of building was all the more tenacious in that, after losing its ideological bases in the second

**377, 378**   *Montmagny, Church of St. Teresa (Perret, 1926)*

half of the eighteenth century, it had been limited to the practical and organizational sphere; the form of the calculations and the habits of the building site still largely reflected the old parallelism, and even the normal terminology used with regard to reinforced concrete – pillar, plinth, architrave, corbel, portal, span – was that of the classical orders.

A whole century of experiment had approved and reinforced this convention from which all advances in modern engineering were born. Perret lived in the midst of it, he was the heir of Durand, of Labrouste, Dutert, Eiffel; his particular merit was to have sensed that this glorious tradition, impoverished by eclecticism, still had a margin of unexplored possibilities to help resolve the problem of our time, and to have developed these possibilities courageously. In doing this, however, he ruined the last chances of structural classicism, and revealed definitively that that path ended in an impasse, because the initial premises were rooted in an outdated mode of thought.

With Perret the last cycle of French academic culture was concluded, with incomparable dignity, once and for all.

### 3  Tony Garnier

Tony Garnier (1869–1948), the son of a textile designer, was brought up in Lyon where the ideals of Proudhon's socialism were still very much alive; he was a pupil at the Académie de France in Rome, and here, for the Grand Prix de Rome of 1901, he presented his design for an industrial city, all in reinforced concrete, iron and glass.

It naturally enraged the jury and did not win the prize. Two years later, however, Garnier won the first prize with a complete plan for the reconstruction of the town of Tusculum, consisting of tens of thousands of Doric, Ionic and Corinthian columns. But he never gave up his favourite subject of study, the industrial town, and in 1904 completed his plans to present them in Paris in a personal exhibition (Figs. 379–81). Later the work was published in a volume where Garnier expounded as follows the criteria he had used:

'The architectural studies we are presenting here, in a long series of plates, concern the organization of a new city, the industrial City, since most cities founded from now on will be based on industrial considerations, so that we have considered the most general case. Furthermore in a city of this kind all the uses of architecture may find their rightful place, and it is possible to examine them all.

Making our city of medium size (by supposing that it has about 35,000 inhabitants) we have always aimed at the same goal, that of carrying out studies of a general nature, which would not have been justified by the study of a village or very large city. Again to this end we have imagined that the land on which the buildings would stand was partly flat and partly hilly, and crossed by a river.

The main factory is situated on the plain, at the confluence of the smaller river with the larger. A railway runs between the factory and the city, which is somewhat higher up, on a plateau. Higher up still are the hospitals, protected from cold winds, as is the city itself, and facing south, on terraces which overlook the river. Each of these elements: hospitals, town, factory, is isolated so as to permit future development in case of need; this has enabled us to carry out the study from an even more general point of view.

Seeking for arrangements which would best satisfy the material and spiritual needs of the individual, we have been led to establish regulations for each sector: building regulations, sanitary regulations and so on, and we have supposed that a certain degree of social progress has already taken place so as to make an extension of these regulations possible, while present day laws would not allow of this. We have therefore supposed that the public administration had the free use of all land, and that it was responsible for the water supply and that of bread, meat, milk and medicines, in view of the many precautions that should be taken with regard to these products'.[3]

The plates which follow show the plans of the city complete in every detail, with plans and views of all the buildings, and many views, particularly from above, in the broad and suggestive style of the French *Pensionnaires*. Some public buildings – for

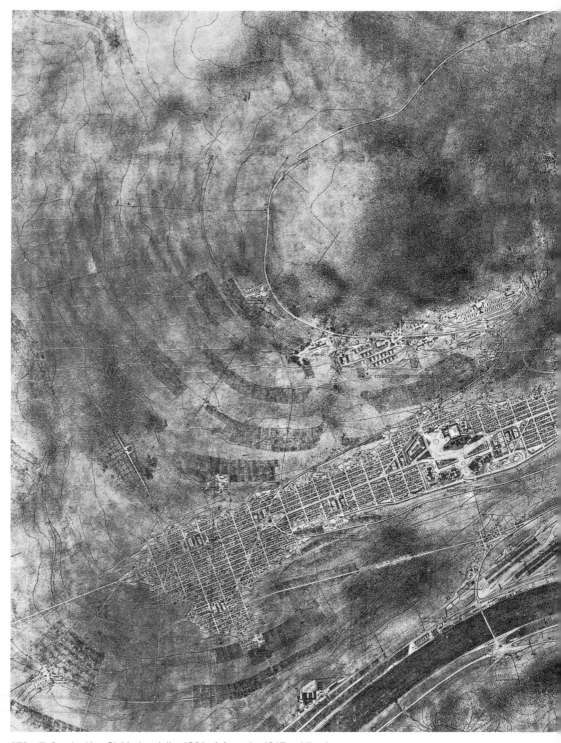

**379**   *T. Garnier,* Une Cité Industrielle, *1901–4; from the 1917 publication*

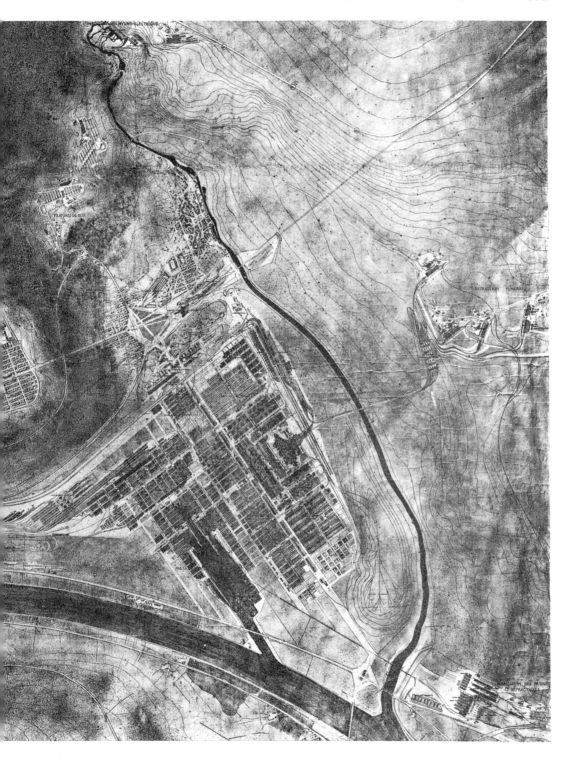

**380, 381** *Two views of the Industrial City: a residential district and the railway station*

instance the railway station (Fig. 381) and the adjacent hotel – are striking in their bold simplicity and, as Pevsner says, 'they have an absolutely post-war look about them.'[4] The residential quarters consist of small detached houses, standing along a uniform network of roads; here Garnier's idea of presenting all the plans simultaneously caused a certain stylistic monotony, but the plates are to be regarded as no more than examples, to illustrate the rules propounded in the introduction, which are very interesting:

'Many towns already have certain sanitary regulations, varying according to the geographical and climatic conditions. We have supposed that in our city the positioning and prevailing winds have led us to formulate a series of regulations which may be resumed as follows:
(i)   In the houses bedrooms must have at least one window facing south, large enough to give light to the whole room and to allow the sun's rays to enter.
(ii)   Courtyards and cloisters, i.e., all spaces enclosed by walls which are supposed to let in light and air, are forbidden. Every room, however small, must be lit and ventilated directly from the outside.
(iii)   Inside the houses the walls, floors etc. are all of smooth material, with rounded corners.

The building land in residential quarters is first divided up into blocks, of 150 metres in the east-west direction and 30 metres in the north-south; these blocks are in their turn divided into lots of $15 \times 15$ m., always with one side running along the road. Such divisions allow the land to be better utilized and to implement the building regulations mentioned above.

Each building, house or otherwise, may cover one or more lots, but the built up area must be less than half the total area, while the remainder of the lot must be used as a public garden, open to pedestrians. In other words, each building must leave a free thoroughfare, on the part of its lot that is not built up, going from the street to the building directly behind it. This ruling makes it possible to cross the city in any direction independently of the roads, and the land of the city, taken overall, is like a big park, without any fences to delimit the various sections. The space between two houses in the direction north-south is at least equal to the height of the building situated to the south. Because of this ruling, which allows only half of the land to be built on and which forbids enclosures, and bearing in mind that the land is levelled only by the down-flow of the waters, there will be no need to fear the monotony of our current rows of buildings' (Fig. 380).

Here Garnier mentions several concepts which were to become widespread at the beginning of the modern movement: the vital importance of hygienic factors (sun, air, vegetation), well-spaced buildings, independence of pedestrian routes from those for other traffic, the garden-city.

Histories of architecture usually mention Garnier only in connection with this plan of his industrial city. But if Garnier had gone no further than designing these plates in his *atelier* at the Villa Medici he would be only one of the countless Utopians that France has produced. In fact he did much more than this: he had the opportunity of applying his concepts to the great city of Lyon, and built, between 1904 and 1914, a series of exemplary public buildings and residential quarters, all within a single master plan. This experience

**382, 383**   *Lyon, Abattoirs de la Mouche (Garnier, 1909); the market hall (from the publication of the 'grands travaux') and a general view*

enabled Garnier to try out his ideas by means of contact with the actual requirements of a modern city. His buildings made valid theoretical precedents and in this result, in this bridge between theory and practice, lay his contribution to the modern movement.

This was made possible by Garnier's meeting with E. Herriot, the radical deputy elected mayor of Lyon in 1904. These two figures, almost contemporaries, drawn together by similar political and cultural convictions, soon came to an agreement, and this collaboration – not the individual gifts of either man – explains the vitality of

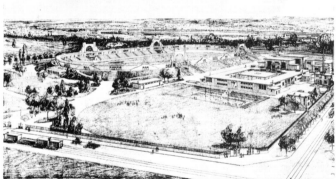

**384, 385, 386** *Lyon, Olympic stadium (Garnier, 1913): two details and a general view from the publication of the 'grands travaux'*

the works they conceived together, one as employer and the other as architect.

The first building built by Garnier for Herriot was a modest dairy with stalls in the park of the Tête d'Or, in 1904. This was followed, after a period of preparation, by his major works, and first of all by the complex for the slaughter-house and cattle market at La Mouche, built between 1909 and 1913, but used as a missile factory during the World War, resuming its original function afterwards.

This was the period when the Germans were building their monumental factories, strained expressionistic structures. There is nothing of that in this building: a modest entrance, flanked by Garnier's characteristic lantern-pillars, leads into the vast enclosure; immediately behind it is the market shed, whose tiered roof allows it to merge with the lower surrounding buildings; the magnificent hall, supported by three-hinged metal arches, with a span of 80 metres (Fig. 382) was reminiscent of the famous Paris *halle des machines* of 1889. The one dominating element is the heating plant with two chimneys in yellow brick, fluted like ancient columns, which give the general horizontal of the whole a vertical balance (Fig. 383).

In the Olympic stadium of 1913 (Figs. 384–6) the allusions to a generic Greco-Roman style are stronger than elsewhere. This can be seen in Garnier's designs reproduced in the publication of 1919, where they look like décor for a historical film, peopled by athletes in classical costume.

Nonetheless this inspiration inherited from classical studies never drew Garnier towards the massive effects which were customary in almost all stadia. The height of the outer wall, for instance, was concealed by a grassy slope which came almost to the top of the steps, so that the enormous establishment was expertly blended with its surroundings and at the same time reduced to an accessible and human scale; only the four entrances were emphasized by the great decorative arches (Fig. 385). In the original plan the stadium was to be combined with a sort of sports centre, with outdoor and indoor gymnasia, smaller playing fields, a swimming bath and a restaurant, but the building was interrupted during the First World War and was never finished.

The Grange-Blanche hospital (1915), named after Herriot after his death, is a huge garden on a slight slope, dotted with well-spaced two- or three-storey pavilions (Figs. 387–9). Here too there was no pompous organization on systems of axes; the only focal point, as in the slaughter-house, was the heating plant with its two chimneys. The buildings, which are in an excellent state of repair, show no signs of age; the relationship between the built up space and the crowd that moves within it is still absolutely clear, and the hospital appears primarily as a living instrument, so much so that one has to make a considerable effort to consider it historically.

The district known as the États Unis (Figs. 390–2) was begun in 1928, on a plan of 1920; Garnier had designed houses of three or four floors, but then two extra floors were added, so that the proportions envisaged by the architect were lost and the general effect, on first sight, is not unlike that of the usual closely built up district. Looking closer, however, one can see the subtlety of Garnier's division into blocks, based on the standard units which can be combined in many different ways and which make a varied arrangement of the buildings possible; fast-moving traffic in the central area is kept separate from slow-moving traffic in front of the shops and from the green spaces for pedestrians between the buildings, unenclosed as in the industrial city, provided with benches and punctuated with the odd concrete trellis. The buildings are related to one another within a recurrent but not symmetrical pattern; in this way this district does not appear as a clearly demarcated composition and fits easily into its urban surroundings.

In 1919 Garnier published the plans of his *Grands travaux de la ville de Lyon* with the editor Massin, of Paris, as he had done two years before with his plates for the Cité Industrielle, in which Herriot wrote:

'Tony Garnier has done me the honour of asking me to write a few lines in preface to his work on the *grands travaux* in Lyon. I comply willingly, not because I have the slightest technical competence to judge his work; but for fifteen years, being at the head of the Communal administration, I have chosen and retained Tony Garnier as one of my main collaborators. With him I settled the plan of the slaughter-house,

**387, 388, 389**  *Lyon, Edouard Herriot hospital (Garnier, 1915)*

which we hope to offer as a model for our great modern cities. With him I travelled through Germany and Denmark to put together the plan of a really scientific hospital, answering the current needs of an enlightened philanthropy and the needs of teaching. With him I conceived of the workers' city, which should provide this section of the inhabitants of our overcrowded city with hygienic and decorous accommodation.

On each occasion I have admired in him the combination of rigorous method with an artistic temperament which sought inspiration in the purest sources of Hellenism.

I am particularly grateful to Tony Garnier for having interpreted the lessons of Hellenism in their widest sense, for having struggled against those artificial conceptions which have produced so many poor efforts at imitation like the Madeleine and the Palais Bourbon. But I am particularly delighted to be able to proclaim, with his example, that architecture must be of its place and of its time. A monument to be built appears to me like a problem to be solved. First one must establish the intellectual lines of the work, define the needs it must fulfil, subordinate the appearance of the vessel to the needs of what is to be contained. We have had enough of Renaissance façades and mock Louis XIV pavilions.

Tony Garnier achieves art spontaneously because he does not seem to search for it directly. His theory – if he has a theory – is thus truly classical. It corresponds both to the classical tradition and to the French tradition. The Panthéon is admirable in its own right, but a modern copy of it would be merely ridiculous. A stock-exchange like a Greek temple is an absurdity. Versailles could be justified only by the existence of a great king. Garnier's buildings answer the needs of an age radically transformed by science.

I hope that a close study of this work will be useful for all those who are trying to work with us. When we compare the building achievement of the past with our own puny efforts we feel humiliated. Our French cities still lack all the indispensable organs for their present functions. We have at least tried to react against this sort of neglect, and I am happy to have taken part, in my attempts at town-planning, in a collaboration whose value may be estimated by consulting this collection, worthy, in my opinion, of the most illustrious French architects of the past'.

The confidence of Herriot's statement 'a monument to be built appears to me like a problem to be solved' is remarkable (all the more so if one considers that these words were written not by a technical expert but by a politician). All the factors on which the life and functioning of a building would depend were already present at the planning stage, and its insertion into the city was calculated in advance; as a result of this careful placing Garnier's buildings live on not just as architectural curios but as working organs of modern Lyon, despite their fifty years of age.

Garnier did not write or travel much, he took no part in the *avant-garde* controversies and lived in relative isolation in Lyon, far from the great centres of European culture. From the aesthetic point of view his architecture will not bear comparison with the subtleties of Horta and Van de Velde, with the severity of Loos, the daring of Wright, and may seem timid and parasitical, with its naïve claims to classical inspiration. Nonetheless in many ways Garnier's viewpoint was more advanced than that of the other masters of his time.

He had in common with Perret the limitations that were inherent in the tradition on which he based himself: the idea that there exists a sort of perennial architecture, to be adapted to the times but based on unchanging formal foundations, and therefore the allusion – tenuous but always present – to classicism; the idea of a pre-established harmony between this architectural heritage and techniques of building, and therefore the belief that one could, with these means, tackle all the problems posed by modern life and scientific and social progress. By applying these concepts to town-planning, he conceived of the city almost as a great building which could be defined and conceived of as a single whole; designing his industrial city in the Villa Medici he might be said to have applied to iron and concrete the same planning methods with which his colleagues composed their essays in the classical style. His plates, as Le Corbusier wrote, 'were the result of a hundred years of architectural evolution in France.'5

But though remaining faithful to this line of thought, Garnier went much further than Perret in the understanding of the problems that modern society posed for architecture. Perret was concerned mainly with reconciling the needs of the architect with those of the builder, but by combining the two skills in his own person he finally brought the problem within the boundaries of his own individual case, and behaved in all respects like an *avant-garde* artist, evolved his own personal style and a personal repertoire of technical solutions. With Herriot, Garnier deepened the relationship between architect and employer – indeed one should really refer to them as Herriot-Garnier rather than as either in isolation – and he did not hesitate to involve himself fully in the life of a great city, accepting all the technical, administrative, legal, economic and social difficulties deriving from this involvement and sometimes even finding practical solutions to these theoretical limitations.

He never thought of the building as an isolated object, but always bore in mind that the ultimate objective of every action taken was the good of the city itself and that the building was important only as a contribution to the life of the city. The master plan included in the publication of the *grands travaux* was not like a modern town-planning scheme, because it contained no idea of distributing the choices in various scales and various degrees, but was more reminiscent of Haussmann's plans; basically it was the link between various plans for public works. He had thus fallen prey to the theory that a dynamic reality like a city can be regulated with static measures, but in practice, through the ups and downs of planning, he was forced to experience its dynamic quality and to break through the limitations of theory. It is probable that the overall plan was constantly revised in the communal offices at Lyon, as the works proceeded, as was the case with the plan of Paris in the 'Office du

plan de Paris' set up by Haussmann, and each architectural plan gives a hint of this living link with the growing city.

The equivalent of this deeper understanding of methods of town-planning was the abandoning, from an architectural point of view, of the rules of symmetry, which could be seen particularly in the division into blocks of residential quarters. Garnier did not conceive of his buildings as accomplished facts, nor did he think of remodelling Lyon with uniform geometrical criteria; therefore instead of symmetry, he had to use other regularizing systems – for instance the indefinite repetition of basic motifs – which would adapt themselves more easily to the spatial restrictions and unforeseeable changes of plan over the years.

Since the value of Garnier's work lies in the balance actually attained between the various factors, it is particularly difficult to give an idea of it using indirect means like words, drawings and photographs. Writings count for little in the case of a personality who expressed himself almost entirely in practical work; his plans were drawn in a dull and mannered style; photographs of the actual buildings give a misleading and unflattering impression, because the uncertainties of taste are emphasized, whereas the positive qualities – technical mastery and the liveliness that comes from perfect adaptation to function – cannot be adequately represented. To estimate the true worth of these buildings one must see them in real life, walk along the avenues of the hôpital Herriot on a visiting day or go into the hall of the cattle market, crowded with men and animals: this architecture was the most advanced experiment, in the period immediately preceding the birth of the modern movement and its very limitations – the somewhat Utopian vision of the city, the frank covering of classicism – simply increase one's admiration for this man, so gifted yet so unassuming, whose contribution has still to be properly assessed by modern critics.

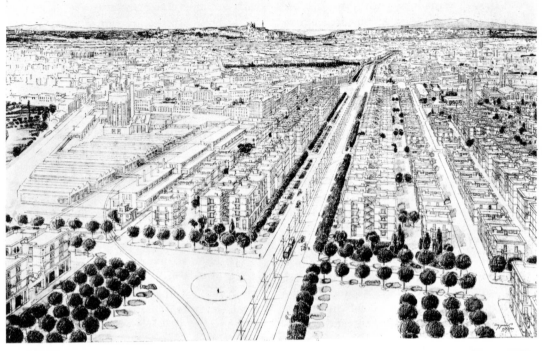

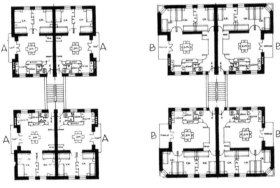

**390, 391, 392**   *Lyon, Quartier Etats Unis (Garnier,
1920–8); drawings from the publication of the
'grands travaux'*

# eleven

# Experiments in town-planning from 1890 to 1914

## 1 Progress in town-planning laws and experiments

The long period of peace after the Franco-Prussian war of 1870 favoured economic development throughout Europe; even those countries which had hitherto remained politically immobile under the *ancien régime* had now to face the consequences of the industrial revolution: sources of production were changing, the population was increasing and its distribution was changing as a result of the displacement of productive activities. The problems of town-planning control were now posed with increasing urgency and were dealt with in various ways, according to the means available and the legal, technical and cultural traditions of the various countries; sometimes situations reappeared that had been experienced several decades previously in countries like France and England where industrialization had occurred earlier, and the same mistakes were made; sometimes new answers were found for the old problems, and new laws and new planning methods were introduced. The repertoire of modern town-planning was broadened in proportion with the variety of problems to be tackled.

In England, after the basic laws passed between 1848 and 1851, the progress of the mechanisms of town-planning proceeded without pause, and the earlier regulations were gradually amended.

Despite the sanitary laws of 1866 and 1875 on regulations on popular building, crowding in English cities continued to exist and became intolerable during the last decades of the century. The philanthropic activities of private individuals were still numerous. In England in 1890 there were about forty associations working in collaboration with the administrations; these cleared areas occupied by slums, and the private individuals built new houses there. But such activities, important because of the moral attitude that inspired them and for their study of the qualitative aspects of the problem, were quantitatively insufficient and did not have any appreciable effect on the conditions of the English working classes.

At last the state decided to tackle the problem, and appointed a Royal Commission which included certain eminent names, for instance the Prince of Wales, the Earl of Shaftesbury, Chamberlain and Chadwick. In the course of the enquiry a guardian of the poor from Bristol observed: 'If the cost of putting up buildings is too high for the operation to be remunerative, then the community must bear the weight of it'; and a civil servant from London: 'It is quite impossible for private enterprise, philanthropy and charity to meet present demands. What cannot be done by individuals must be attempted by public bodies, since they have the authority and funds required.'[1]

The recommendations of the Commission led to the law of 1890, the Housing of the Working Classes Act, which consolidated the earlier laws of 1866 and 1875 and the regulations of the sanitary laws. Local authorities were given better grants, the process of compulsory acquisition of sites was made easier and the relevant compensation rates were lowered. But despite these advantages administrations made only a limited use of this law, and up to the First World War less than fifteen thousand dwellings were built in this way; only the increase in private initiative prevented overcrowding from becoming even worse.

About 1890 many other countries were preparing similar legislation on the problem of lodging; the two aspects of the problem – the clearing of old slums and the building of new districts, which in England were closely connected and interdependent – varied in importance according to the varying situations.

In France there had been the law of 1850 – allowing the Communes to supervise basic sanitary requirements in houses and to intervene with compulsory acquisition where this seemed opportune – which was applied on a large scale by Haussmann, Vaisse etc. in connection with the building of the new streets. Now a law of 1902, further elaborated in 1912, authorized the compulsory acquisition of houses and blocks, independently of work to be done on the roads, when they were agreed to be unsanitary, and it made possible large-scale slum clearance in the old parts of Paris and other towns. Since the population was more or less static, the problem of building new accommodation was rather less pressing than elsewhere and was serious only in the big cities where there was

a high rate of immigration and where the inhabitants of the recently demolished slum quarters needed rehousing. Here too private enterprises, with humanitarian aims, were founded (Société philantropique de Paris, Fondation Rothschild etc.); in 1890 the Société française des habitations à bon marché was founded, and in 1894 managed to get a law passed granting state aid to these enterprises, while in 1906 the Conseil supérieur des h. b. m. was set up, as the moving spirit behind everything related to this problem. In 1912 all previous rulings were gathered together in a single Consolidation Act.

In Belgium compulsory acquisition was regulated by the law of 1867, which had certain peculiarities: when more than half the land to be acquired belonged to a single landlord or corporate group, the latter might be permitted to carry out the work themselves; in this way a sort of collaboration was made possible between the authorities and private individuals which made it possible to effect various developments in the old towns and to build up new planned districts in the suburbs, even if the communes did not possess large stretches of public land.

State intervention in popular building was limited to certain concessions granted by the law of 1889 for workers who wished to own their homes; only in 1919 was the Société nationale des habitations et logements à bon marché founded, similar to the French society, and a regular building policy came into existence.

In Italy in 1885 a serious epidemic, which broke out in Naples, brought the problem of the sanitary control of buildings into the forefront; compulsory acquisition of land, regulated by the law of 1865 and rigorously restricted to the execution of public works, such as roads, railways etc., was extended to slum districts for reasons of health. In the field of popular housing the first law was passed in 1903 (Luzzatti's law) further elaborated and extended in the consolidation

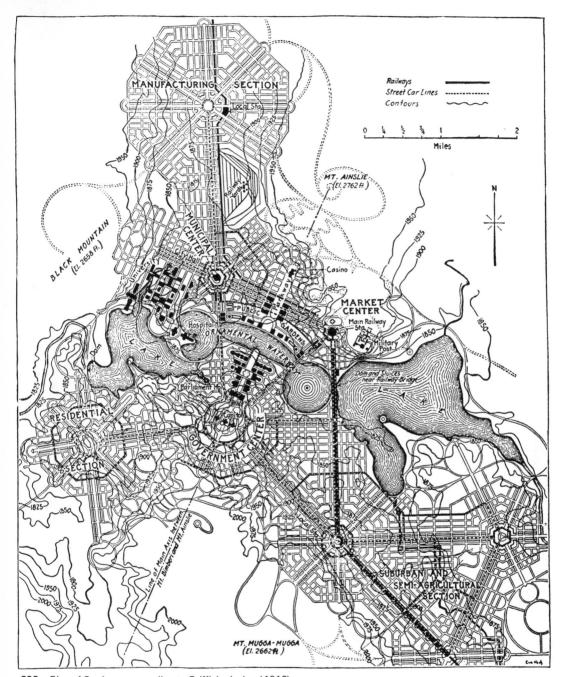

**393**   *Plan of Canberra, according to Griffin's design (1913)*

act of 1908; rather than to the normal administrative organs, the task was handed over to independent institutions for popular housing, which built workers' dwellings directly and rented them at moderate rates. This solution, basically different from those arrived at in other countries, had the virtue of working very promptly, but it did introduce into Italy a sharp division between subsidized building and private building, discouraging all intermediate forms of co-operation and partial subsidy; furthermore, by distracting the communal authorities from this task, in the end it cut subsidized building adrift from town-planning, thus laying the foundations for a dangerous dualism. These merits and defects were later to become permanent features of Italian building policy, and were confirmed after the Second World War with the setting up of INA-CASA.

In Germany legislation was not uniform because of the federal structure of the State. Popular building became a very important problem with the rapid industrialization of the country after 1870. The most widespread solution was the co-operative society, whose workings were controlled by the law of 1868; in 1889 a new measure stimulated this form of association, by acknowledging the principle of limited liability, and the state began to give financial support to these enterprises. This was the beginning of the great development of German co-operative building; the 38 building co-operatives of 1890 had already grown to over 1,400 in 1914, and about 50,000 dwellings had been built before the war.

At the end of the century Krupp of Essen built further districts of accommodation for their workers: Alfredshof (1894), Altenhof (1900) and Margarethenhöhe (1906) (Fig. 399).

German legislation was designed to discourage isolated enterprises and to encourage corporative ones, which would produce homogeneous complexes; the Prussian law of 1904, for example, prohibited building outside certain determined limits without a special colonization permit granted only to those in a position to give certain guarantees.

The sites needed for these enterprises were obtained, after a certain point, by means of compulsory acquisition. In 1901 the burgomaster of Hamburg, Adickes, succeeded in

passing a law allowing the Communes to take over whole stretches of land as the city's rate of expansion demanded and to plan their use with rational criteria, giving back to the owners a piece of land equal in value to that given over in the first place. This law, known as Adicke's law, was adopted in many of the German states.

The activities considered so far were only rarely set within a general plan. The idea of a master plan to co-ordinate the various departmental activities made little progress, despite the tradition of regulations and Baroque planning, because the old methods of planning were not adapted to the far more complex reality of the modern city.

But in almost all large cities, in the second half of the nineteenth century, the need for town-planning schemes was felt. We have talked at length about Paris, but equally important were the grandiose redevelopment of Vienna after the demolition of the walls in 1857, completed by the ruling of 1885 and the zoning measures of 1893 – the city was divided into twenty districts and stipulations were made about the type of building and number of its storeys allowed in each one – and by the green belt ruling of 1905; the series of plans for Rome as a capital, from 1883 (Viviani plan) to 1908 (St Just plan); the great American examples discussed in Chapter 8, and in particular the plans of Burnham and Bennett for San Francisco (1905) and Chicago (1909). In the first years of the twentieth century Anglo-Saxon town-planning thought was in a position to design and build two great cities which were to become the capitals of the two greatest British colonies: New Delhi in India, designed by Edwin Lutyens (1869–1944) in 1911, and Canberra in Australia (for which a competition was held, won by Walter Griffin [1876–1937] of Chicago in 1913).

All these experiments were closely connected with the particular conditions in each city, and since certain problems basically connected with the success of these plans were of a general legal order and could not be tackled locally, all the plans mentioned hitherto made possible only the partial control of the forces at work in a city. Here tradition was essentially negative, because it generated the conviction that the modern city could be regulated by the same instruments of formal control as had been applied to the pre-industrial city, by-passing legal and economic matters and highlighting problems of formal elegance.

The possibilities of progress were therefore essentially linked to the improvement of general legislation. The most important example of a comprehensive legislative text, in which all the problems of subsidized building and town-planning were dealt with in an orderly fashion, was the Dutch law of 1901. Towns with more than 10,000 inhabitants were to draw up plans for redevelopment, specifying modes of procedure for the demolition of slum quarters, for the maintenance of satisfactory ones and for the building of new ones; a distinction was made between general town-planning schemes, which were to be reviewed every ten years, and detailed schemes, and it was specified that the compulsory acquisition of sites and of any buildings could take place only after the drawing up of detailed plans. Furthermore the administrations were granted loans whose interest was to be paid by the State, and which would cover even up to 100 per cent of the cost of the sites and buildings, and they in their turn were authorized to grant sites and subsidies to the co-operatives and bodies concerned exclusively with popular housing, profiting from a well-regulated and simplified system of compulsory acquisition.

In this connection Dutch cities had the advantage of an age-old tradition; in fact, apart from the Hague, the large towns all stood on flat land reclaimed from the sea, and could be extended only after the relevant land had been suitably prepared, with hydraulic manoeuvres which naturally had to be precisely co-ordinated; for this reason,

from the earliest times, the expansion of the cities was effected by means of the compulsory acquisition of outlying areas, organization by the authorities and re-sale of building land.

The most important example was the seventeenth-century development of Amsterdam, based on the three semi-circular canals around the sixteenth-century nucleus. As the city grew in size the Administration continued to acquire a fund of building land, and in 1896 decided not to re-sell the land it acquired, but only to lease it. This was the solution later to be adopted by most Dutch cities.

The Dutch law made possible the plans for the extension of Amsterdam (1902 onwards) and of Rotterdam (1903) and encouraged an intensification of subsidized building; before the First World War about 35,000 dwellings were built, financed by the state in various ways.

After Holland, England passed the first town-planning law in 1909, based on the same intention to unite in a single law all rulings relevant to popular building and town-planning schemes.

The procedure for compulsory acquisition of sites for popular housing was subsequently perfected and linked with the drafting of plans; but, unlike what happened in Holland, the planned improvements were carried out mainly on private land, and the law attempted to equalize the treatment meted out to the various landowners, fixing improvement rates to be paid by those who benefited and compensation for those who lost; it did not function well, and until the Second World War enormous sums were paid in compensation, while rates were hardly ever paid; the failure of this system drove the English legislature to adopt a different system in 1947, when building land was nationalized.

In other countries similar general town-planning laws were passed only in the post-war years. Meanwhile a large number of enterprises and cultural institutions concerning themselves with town-planning problems had grown up; in the first decade of the twentieth century the bases of what one might call 'classical' town-planning thought had been laid and were instrumental in inspiring the relevant legislation almost everywhere; it is their shortcomings that are at the root of many current difficulties.

In this field too, German culture made conclusive contributions. The review *Städtebau* was published in Berlin from 1904, and the German treatises, from that by Baumeister of 1876 to that of Stübben of 1890, were read everywhere. In Dresden in 1903 a town-planning exhibition, possibly the first ever, was held and was followed by the Berlin exhibition of 1910, the 1913 one at Ghent, and the 1914 one in Lyon. The first School of Civic Design, on the other hand, was founded in 1909 at the university of Liverpool.

The problem of the modern city was a matter of interest to men of letters, too, and they tried to imagine the city of the future, into which they projected the desires and worries of the present: in 1899 Jules Verne's *La journée d'un journaliste américain en 2899* came out (in 1879 he had published his *Les cinq cent millions de la Bégum,* inspired by Richardson's utopia) and in 1905 *A Modern Utopia* by H. G. Wells.

The mood of this thought, confident that the problems of the modern city could be solved analytically, that solutions could be formulated with an almost scientific precision and at the same time full of enthusiasm for the 'magnificent great leap forward' of human society, can be effectively illustrated by this speech by Herriot, mayor of Lyon, given at the 1914 exhibition:

'The administration of an average sized city must cease to be empirical and become a real science. To foresee that rational development of a human centre, to arrange the necessary open spaces and fresh air, to take responsibility for its maintenance, to

defend it from the dangers of all kinds that threaten it, to provide for the transport of its inhabitants, to procure them clean water, to relieve them of their refuse, improve their dwellings, choose the best lighting system, supervise the food supply and control essential provisions such as milk, eliminate falsification and fraud, protect young infants, modernize schooling, make cleanliness general, complement national teaching with local teaching, create hygienic conditions for work, promote or perfect social institutions, organize the fight against infectious diseases, transform our hospitals, orphanages and crèches, ascertain what is the real duty of a welfare office, encourage the physical culture and the sports that are so indispensable for city-dwellers, make this city flourish in every possible way, crown this effort at being scientific with the intervention of art – is this not a programme truly worthy of consideration?'[2]

## 2   The teaching of Camillo Sitte

Camillo Sitte (1843–1903) was an Austrian architect, director of the Salzburg Staats-gewerbeschule, author of various religious buildings and development schemes for several Austrian cities and the possessor of a vast store of historical culture acquired during numerous travels in Europe and the east.

In 1889 he published a short book *Der Städtebau nach seinen künstlerischen Grund-sätzen* which was much read and brought him sudden fame; there were three German editions before 1900 and a French one in 1902. The text was simple and fluent, unlike other diffuse treatises on the subject, though without the stylistic charm of the writings of Ruskin or the erudite trappings of Viollet-le-Duc; its importance and rapid popularity were due to the novelty of the point of view and to the immediate possibility of putting his suggestions into practice.

Sitte discussed the modern city, and his discussion was limited to the so-called 'artistic' field, i.e. to outward aesthetic standards to be observed in centres of civic prestige and residential quarters, but it did not simply suggest a set of conventional solutions as did the treatise-writers, nor did it simply inveigh against these solutions as a matter of principle, as did Ruskin; he observed the townscape of the new cities as it was emerging from the building sites of the previous decades, he noted its defects – monotony, excessive regularity, symmetry at all costs, poorly utilized spaces which were not inter-related and were disproportionate to the surrounding architecture – and compared them to the virtues of the old cities, particularly the medieval ones, with their picturesque yet functional groupings of buildings, asymmetrical layout and hierarchy of spaces so perfectly related to their buildings.

Sitte too, like the Romantics of preceding generations, contrasted past with present, but instead of entirely rejecting the modern city on general theoretical grounds, provided a reasoned analysis of its single faults and managed to suggest some practical remedies, to re-establish in the modern city at least some of the values he so admired in the old ones: spaces that were inflexible or too large could be suitably subdivided to create clearly defined complexes of buildings; ill-defined forms could be replaced by more enclosed ones; symmetry could be mitigated by partial symmetry, monuments could be moved from the geometrical centres of squares to less obvious spots, and so on. In fact the book ended with a chapter suggesting that the disproportionately large expanses of the Viennese Ring should be broken up and that suitably dimensioned squares should be built round the main buildings.

Sitte's theoretical convictions were somewhat limited. For him, art and utility were mutually exclusive and he regarded the recent town-planning experiments of the nineteenth century as being concerned only with technical matters, which he considered as being

at odds with art. He was largely responsible for the concept of the 'town beautiful' which has long weighed on town-planning thought, deflecting serious thought away from really basic problems.

The following text demonstrates this aspect of his thought:

'Modern systems! – Yes indeed! To approach everything in a strictly methodical manner and not to waver a hair's breadth from preconceived patterns, until genius has been strangled to death and *joie de vivre* stifled by the system – that is the sign of our time. We have at out disposal three major methods of city-planning, and several subsidiary types. The major ones are the *gridiron system*, the *radial system* and the *triangular system*. Artistically speaking, not one of them is of any interest, all three are concerned exclusively with the arrangement of *street patterns* and hence their intention is from the start a purely technical one. A network of streets serves only the purpose of communication, never of art, since it can never be comprehended sensorily, can never be grasped as a whole except in a plan of it. In our discussions so far street networks have not been mentioned for just that reason, neither those of ancient Athens, Rome, of Nurenberg nor of Venice. They are of no concern artistically, because they are inapprehensible in their entirety. Only that which a spectator can hold in view, what can be seen is of artistic importance, for instance, the single street or the individual plaza.

It follows simply from this, that under the proper conditions an artistic effect can be achieved with whatever street network be chosen, but the pattern should never be applied with that really brutal ruthlessness which characterizes the cities of the North-West and which has, unfortunately and frequently, become the fashion with us. Artistically contrived streets and plazas might be wrested even from the gridiron system if the traffic expert would just let the artist peer over his shoulder or would set aside his compass and drawing board now and again. If only the desire were to exist, one could establish a basis for peaceful coexistence between these two. After all, the artist needs for his purpose only a few main streets and plazas; all the rest he is glad to turn over to traffic and to daily material needs. The broad mass of living quarters should be business-like, and there the city may appear in its work-clothes. However, major plazas and thoroughfares should wear their 'Sunday best' in order to be a pride and joy to the inhabitants, to awake civic pride, and forever to nurture great and noble sentiment within our growing youth'.[3]

Despite these prejudices, Sitte made two important contributions to the town-planning thought of his time.

In the first place, by reviving interest in old towns – and not just for isolated monuments – he halted the unfortunate habit of isolating them (as R. Baumeister wrote in 1876: 'Old buildings should be spared but cleaned and restored',[4]) he provided the premises for the preservation of whole complexes, if not of whole districts, and put an important psychological barrier in the way of indiscriminate demolition of the kind carried out by Haussmann.

In the second place, with his over-simplified formal suggestions, he offered architects a train of thought that would inevitably lead them to consider the basic problems of modern town-planning; Sitte tackled problems from the outside, but by attempting to give a potential concrete reality to the comparison between the old and the new town by proposing a study of instructive cases and by suggesting a method of intervention, he was helping to bridge the gap between theory and practice, and inspired a series of experiments which were to lead to

the transcending of the theory itself, by working from visible facts towards non-visible causes.

Some passages seem to anticipate these consequences, for instance that describing the difficulties that would be incurred by imitating the organic complexity of part of an old town:

'Such a purpose cannot be achieved with the ruler or with the geometrical straight street line. In order to produce the effects of the old masters, their colours as well must form part of our palette. Sundry curves, twisted streets and irregularities would have to be included artificially in the plan: an affected artlessness, a purposeful unintentionalness. But can the accidents of history over the course of centuries be invented and constructed *ex novo* in the plan? Could one, then, truly and sincerely enjoy such a fabricated ingenuousness? Certainly not. The satisfaction of a spontaneous gaiety is denied to any cultural level in which building does not proceed at apparent random from day to day, but instead constructs its plans intellectually on the drawing board . . . . Modern living as well as modern building techniques no longer permit the faithful imitation of old townscapes, a fact which we cannot overlook without falling prey to barren fancies. The exemplary creations of the old masters must remain alive in us in some other way than through slavish imitation; only if we can determine in what the essentials of these creations exist, and if we can apply these meaningfully to modern constructions will it be possible to harvest a new and flourishing crop from the apparently sterile soil'.[5]

These words are truly modern and relevant today, and might be applied to many contemporary groups of subsidized buildings, whose complexity and organic appearance are obtained artificially in the planning, without corresponding in any way to the technical and administrative functioning of the undertaking.

## 3   The garden city movement

Howard's garden city movement had two sources, themselves inter-related: on the one hand the tradition of the Utopias of the first part of the nineteenth century, particularly that of Owen, understood as a perfect and self-sufficient community, a synthesis of town and country, with the social implications traditionally connected with it; on the other hand the concept of the single family house set amid greenery, which was in a sense an adaptation of the preceding ideal elaborated by Victorian thought in the second half of the century, with the emphasis on privacy rather than social relations: an attempt at releasing family life from the crowding and disorder of the metropolis and at making the town as like the country as was reasonably possible.

This ideal was already expressed in Ruskin's writing: 'clean streets with free countryside all around; a belt of fine gardens and orchards, so that from every point in the city, with a few moments' walk, one can reach the pure air, the grass and the distant horizon'.[6] In 1871 Ruskin himself founded the St George's Guild to build a garden suburb in Oxford, but the enterprise failed. An admirer of his, Lever, a soap manufacturer, managed to realize this programme in 1887 near Liverpool, at Port Sunlight: a group of six hundred small houses in the Gothic style on an estate of 56·6 hectares, grouped in small villages and surrounded by gardens and kitchen gardens, rented out at moderate prices to employees of the firm.

A similar experiment was made in 1895 by the chocolate manufacturer Cadbury at Bournville, near Birmingham: five hundred houses in a much larger estate, about 186 hectares, in no prescribed style but with a fixed proportion between land and buildings. From 1898 onwards an increasing number

of such enterprises was realized, owing to the influence of Ebenezer Howard (1850–1928) and his movement. His particular contribution was to have formulated a consistent theory, removing these experiments from the authority of individual contractors; at the same time he concluded the Utopian line of thought by separating the abstract and impracticable side of it from the practicable and distinguishing in a rational way between these aspects of urban life which had perforce to be collectivized, and those which could safely be left to private enterprise.

Howard reasoned as follows: the private ownership of building land meant that the value of land rose increasingly from the outskirts to the centre of town, and caused the owners of urban land to exploit it intensively, crowding the buildings and causing congestion in the streets; furthermore the concentration of interests led to an unlimited growth of the city, so that congestion was continually growing and driving back the countryside. If private speculation could be eliminated, the buildings could be set as far apart as was needful and there could be open spaces everywhere; the stimulus to unlimited growth would also disappear and the size of the town could be suitably established so that the countryside was within walking distance. In this way, according to Howard, the benefits of the town – social life, public service – could be combined with the benefits of the country, quiet, greenery, healthfulness etc. Thus the idea of a garden city was born.

Howard was an employee in the London Courts and while reading a book by Bellamy on the American co-operative movement[7] – according to his own account – he had the idea of applying these principles on a smaller scale to an experimental town. He put forward his idea in a small book that came out in 1898 under the title *Tomorrow, a Peaceful Path to Real Reform*;[8] in the same year he founded a society, the Garden City and

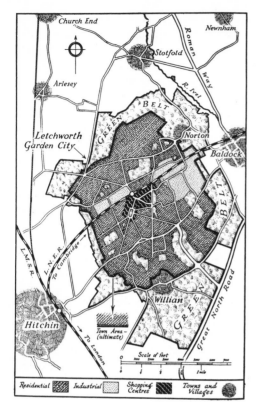

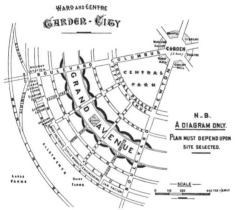

**394, 396** (*above*)   *Original plans for Letchworth* (B. Parker & R. Unwin, 1902) *and for Welwyn* (L. de Soissons, 1919)
**395**   *Diagram of a garden city* (from E. Howard, Tomorrow)
**397**   *Letchworth, Commercial centre*

**398**  *Letchworth, Aerial view*

Town-Planning Association and published
a review, in an attempt to arouse public
interest and concern.

In his book Howard described the future
city and also provided some plans for it,
though he stressed that they should be
regarded as the merest outlines, since the
project would have to be adapted to the site
selected (Fig. 395); since he was not a

technical specialist he talked mostly of the
financial details of the enterprise and insisted
on the fact that this was essentially a concrete
proposal, not an ideological concept. The
garden city was to be managed by a limited
company, which would own the land but not
the buildings, services or economic activities;
everyone would be free to run his life and
business as he thought best, though he would

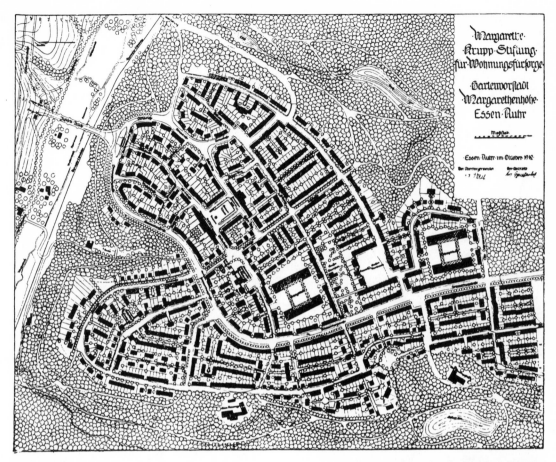

**399** (*above*)   *Plan of the Margarethenhöhe district near Essen (1906; from B. Schwan,* Stadtebau und Wohnungsweben der Welt, *1935*)
**400, 401** (*below*)   *Two views of Hampstead Garden Suburb (1907)*

obey the city's regulations and, in return, would profit from the benefits of a well-regulated community. But Howard was still hampered by the traditional idea that the new city should be self-sufficient and based on a harmonious balance between industry and agriculture, and for this reason he intended that the garden city, with its houses and industries, should occupy one sixth of the land available; the rest was to be destined for agriculture and the urban nucleus was to be surrounded by a ring of farms, all under the same central authority.

In 1902 he founded the first Company and the following year began to build the first garden city, Letchworth, about eighty kilometres from London (Figs. 394, 397 and 398): the plan was made by B. Parker and R. Unwin, the roads and basic services were built by the Company and the land leased for ninety-nine years. The ruling was extremely detailed: not only was there a prescribed regulation for the relationship between houses and gardens, for the types of fence and of trees to be planted and so on, but the Company insisted that shops should be completely separate from living quarters, that artisans wishing to work in industry should move out of their original zone, it limited the number of professional people not only within the city but within each district, so that each would have an adequate clientele, restricted the keeping of domestic animals so as not to inconvenience the neighbours, prohibited the sticking of posters except in special places, the setting up of smoky or ill-smelling industries, the hooting of sirens at the beginning and end of work in the factories and the ringing of bells in churches or schools.

The agricultural belt was reduced to less than half that suggested in Howard's plan. The city was intended to hold thirty-five thousand but was populated very slowly and even after thirty years of life did not have half the anticipated number of inhabitants; the Company's capital was never fully sub-

scribed, either, and it had to issue debentures, so that the ownership of the land was never in the hands of the inhabitants as a whole, but of outside shareholders.

In 1919, after the First World War, Howard made his second attempt, started a second Company and began to build Welwyn Garden City, about half-way between Letchworth and London (Figs. 396 and 403–6). A smaller site was chosen, the agricultural belt was reduced still further and a population of fifty thousand inhabitants anticipated. Also, the Company undertook the building of the houses, leasing them for 999 years and granting the trade monopoly to a subsidiary company.

This time success came more quickly; Welwyn had thirty-five thousand inhabitants before the Second World War, though this progress was probably due to reasons other than those foreseen by Howard: to the proximity of London and the possibility of living in the garden city while working in the capital. Thus the self-sufficiency envisaged by Howard was to prove not only unrealizable but positively detrimental to the success of the garden city. The agricultural belt became progressively smaller, lost all economic importance and became a mere green belt in both Welwyn and Letchworth, safeguarding the cities' self-imposed limits.

Thus the garden city proved to be viable, unlike earlier Utopias, but finally became a town just like any other, subject to the pull of the capital, variable in size and with a basic organization not unlike that of an ordinary town. The original conception left its mark pleasantly in the elegance of the layout of the roads, in the uniformity of the buildings and in the distribution of open spaces.

The same could be said of the inhabitants. At the beginning of the experiment, according to Purdom 'a new energetic spirit reigned among the inhabitants of the new city' including at Letchworth, 'a bookbinder, a Catholic historian, a Blake scholar, various poets and philosophers, social reformers,

**402, 403**   *Welwyn Garden City, Road and one of the building plans (from P. Wolf,* Wohnung und Siedlung, *1926)*

actors and singers, five or six painters, a builder, a few retired clergymen, an ornithologist, an anarchist, journalists, socialists, chemists, nurses, doctors etc.'⁹

They were conscious that they constituted a unique community; for example the assembly of the first inhabitants of Letchworth decided to prohibit the opening of pubs and to impose other particular restrictions. But as time passed and the population increased, the two communities became increasingly similar to the ordinary London suburbs, and today their inhabitants are mainly workers in industries that have moved out of London.

Howard's experiment had a widespread influence in Europe; after 1900 a large number of suburbs, in the main cities of Europe, took on the form of garden cities – among the most important was the Krupp's Margarethenhöhe near Essen (1906) (Fig. 399) already mentioned, Hampstead Garden Suburb near London (1907) (Figs. 400–1) and, after the war, the garden cities of the Chemin de Fer du Nord (1919–24), Floréal and Logis on the outskirts of Brussels (1921), Monte Sacro in Rome (1920) Radburn in New York (1928) and, after 1932, the American green belts. The term 'garden city' must be understood with limitations: not a city but a satellite district of a city, with a favourable ratio between buildings and green spaces and subject to certain regulations, to ensure that the character of the district was respected.

In passing a historical judgment one must make a sharp distinction between Howard's theory and its consequences. Howard, like the Utopians of the early nineteenth century, set out to resolve the problem of the city, i.e. to regulate the organization of a community that was self-sufficient both in terms of economic resources and basic services; in the pursuit of this aim he came up against a difficult and more complex problem: the organization of a sub-multiple of the city. The greatest complication lay in the fact that the problem of the city was a problem of maximum efficiency: here the problem was to give the community everything it needed to satisfy its various requirements; the problem of the district, on the other hand – if not understood in a purely quantitative sense – was a problem of gradation; it was a question of isolating a suitably-sized unit

within the city itself and of seeing what services and what activities should be provided on this scale and what others on the larger scale relevant to the whole city. From this point of view it was irrelevant whether the district was made up of one-family houses or of intensively built multi-family blocks.

It was to Howard's credit that he posed this problem even though his intentions were different. Hitherto, the city had been thought of as a compact, unarticulated body. Between the family and the inhabitants as a whole – in town-planning terms between the single apartment and the city – there existed that 'immense void' mentioned by de Tocqueville,[10] since the processes of growth of the industrial city had swept away any intermediate link just as, in the political field, liberal thought had hoped to do away with all structures standing between the citizen and the power of the state. From Howard onwards the problem was plainly how to fill up this space with an appropriate degree of flexibility to the city. In this sense Howard's thought was in advance of its time, and anticipated one of the basic problems of the modern movement.

Its drawback, on the other hand, lay in having temporarily dispersed the ideal inheritance of the Utopians and pushed the problem of the city, as the place where all human activities came together, into second place. Howard did envisage a new city, but he conceived of it in too restricted a way, with the characteristics and amenities of a single district, and the self-sufficiency he considered desirable was envisaged for these hybrid units, thus prompting the idea of breaking the traditional city up into so many separate and individual pieces.

This gave rise to a school of thought – Geddes, Mumford, Gutkind – which retained a Ruskinian dislike of the metropolis and preached the end of all great cities, which were to be replaced by settlements scattered over a large area,[11] and it produced several formulae, for instance that of the 'self-sufficient district', which have lain heavy on town-planning for a long time, concealing the real nature of the problems. Only the city, in reality, can be said to be self-sufficient in any way; for the separate district the problem has two complementary aspects, autonomy and integration, which are mutually limiting.

This failing in Howard's thought emerged in the very tone of his theorizing. His own view was very narrow compared with the generous, open-minded attitude of Owen; he put the ideal city on a realistic level, but in doing so lost something of its very essence. Owen's parallelograms were absurd fancies, but they did contain an element of revolution that the Edwardian middle class could make their own only by diminishing it to such an extent that it no longer constituted a social threat.

The formal characteristics of the garden city faithfully reproduced the merits and defects of this attitude. Howard did not concern himself with architecture and left both the pattern of the city and the style of architecture unspecified; the architects working with him, imbued with Shaw's medievalism, drew up complex flowing plans and neo-medieval buildings, though they also availed themselves of the abstract freedom of eclecticism, combining allusions to a variety of styles. In the numerous districts based on Howard's models this formula was often carried to exaggeration, the ground plans becoming labyrinthine and stylistic combination running riot; this type of district was satirically described by G. K. Chesterton in 1908, at the beginning of *The Man who was Thursday*:

'The suburb of Saffron Park lay on the sunset side of London, as red and ragged as a cloud of sunset. It was built of a bright brick throughout; its skyline was fantastic, and even its ground plan was wild. It had been the outburst of a speculative builder, faintly tinged with art,

who called its architecture sometimes Elizabethan and sometimes Queen Anne, apparently under the impression that the two sovereigns were identical'.[12]

But this misplaced Romanticism and love of the picturesque also led, on the other hand, to important results in architectural thought; they accustomed architects to considering the townscape as an organic whole, and drew their attention towards a number of minor factors – paving, trees, fencing, benches, signs – which completed the architectural scene and brought about important modifications in the fabric of the towns generally; in short, they laid the foundations for the modern theory of townscape.

But there is another way of interpreting the garden city that is simpler and possibly fairer, ignoring the theory of self-sufficiency and considering only the Ruskinian desire to live amid more pleasant and restful physical surroundings, with green spaces and the country easily available; all the rest is in a way a mere consequence of this and a way of glossing over social and economic problems to avoid their interfering with those of the countryside. The most important aspects of Howard's activities were probably those connected with restrictions on the use of the countryside: the Letchworth and Welwyn regulations on fencing, the planting of trees, maintenance of public open spaces, the types of building that were permitted or prohibited, the suppression of certain kinds of noise.

## 4  The linear city of Arturo Soria

Arturo Soria y Mata (1844–1920) was a Spanish engineer born six years before Howard; he devoted the first part of his life to politics, together with his mathematics professor Manuel Becerra, later a minister. Then he devoted himself to engineering studies and produced a number of plans

**404, 405, 406** *Welwyn Garden City Residential areas*

and inventions and to numerous industrial enterprises, often connected with his studies.

Important among his theoretical suggestions was that of the *ciudad lineal*, put forward for the first time in an article of 6 March 1882 in the Madrid newspaper *El Progreso*. Struck by the congestion of the traditional city, built in concentric rings around an

**407-410**   *Studies for the improvement of the urban areas (photomontage from P. Geddes,* City Development, *1904)*

original nucleus, Soria proposed a radical alternative: a 'ribbon' of a limited width but with one or more railways running along its axis and of an indefinite length: 'the most perfect type of city possible will be that running along a single road, with a width of 500 metres, and which will stretch, if necessary, from Cadiz to St Petersburg and from Peking to Brussels'.[13]

This type of city would be built starting from one or more of the ordinary cities but might subsequently form a network of triangulations between the cities themselves, thus producing a completely novel form of settlement.

The central road would have to be at least 40 metres wide, tree-lined and with the electric railway (*ferrocarril*) running down the middle; cross-streets would be about 200 metres long and 20 metres wide; building would cover only a fifth of the land, the smallest lot being 400 square metres, of which 80 would be occupied by the house itself and 320 by the garden. Soria had in mind an extensive area of separate small houses: 'Every family would have its own house, every house a garden and vegetable plot'.

As far as his socio-economic theories were concerned, he was basing himself on those of Henry George[14] and realized that the practical creation of his city must depend on the possession of new legal instruments for the control of building land; in this way Soria's model was reminiscent of that of Howard, i.e. it constituted an attempt at eliminating, within the capitalist economy, the inconveniences caused by the capitalist organization of landed property.

Later, in the prosperous climate of the last decade of the nineteenth century, Soria tried to put his model into practice; he planned a linear city shaped like a horseshoe around Madrid, 58 kms. long, between the village of Fuencarral and that of Pozuelo de Alarcón. A vital feature of this undertaking was the building of a railway line, which was in fact begun in 1890, starting from Alarcón.

Soria believed that the enterprise should remain private and independent of all public control or subsidy: he therefore had difficulties in acquiring the land, since he could not have recourse to compulsory acquisition, and the portion of the city he did manage to realize (about a quarter of the circle) lost the features of regularity laid down by the plan, so as to adapt itself to the possibilities of the land acquired. Furthermore, the use of the lots could not be regulated nor kept constant, so that today Soria's city, affected by the growth of the ordinary suburbs of Madrid, retains nothing of its original conception.

Soria's idea was important and productive, even though his practical specifications were over-simplified. He was the first person to sense the close connection between the new means of transport and the new city; he saw that they should act not only as expedients to facilitate the movement of traffic within a traditional fabric, but should themselves lead to a different fabric, not so much intensive as extensive. However, even he thought only in terms of traditional functions, i.e., of the place of residence and its amenities, and did not take industry into consideration, while in fact it was only concentration on the relationship between places of residence and places of work that gave value to his linear model.

Soria's idea was in fact developed by the next generation, starting precisely from this relationship which, repeated indefinitely – and for this reason only – gave the city a linear form: this happened in the theoretical studies made by Germans during the twenties, developed and partially applied during the following decade in Russia and in the *cité linéaire industrielle* of Le Corbusier.

Naturally Soria's *ferrocarril* is only the germ of the complex system of means of communication necessary to the modern city, but the idea of the street-city relationship is already clear, in the modern sense, in his initial article of 1882.

## 5  Berlage's town-planning

The masters of the European *avant-garde* usually worked in isolation from town-planning, either because of a cultural barrier connected with the very concept of *avant-garde*, as in the case of Horta and Mackintosh, or because of the impossibility of any kind of collaboration with the authorities, as was the case with Wagner.

The two important exceptions were Garnier and Berlage. Garnier's experience has been described in Chapter 9 and we have noted his internal limitations (lack of gradation between town-planning and architectural decisions) and the external ones (Lyon's *grands travaux* depending on the meeting of two equally exceptional people: Garnier and Herriot); Berlage's experience was, in many ways, the more important and more instructive for the future, because it was based on the application of a general law, the Dutch law of 1901 which clearly distinguishes between the various levels of planning: the general plan, detailed plan, architectural designs. Berlage's works in town-planning belonged to the normal administration of various Dutch cities, and found an immediate echo wherever similar administrative methods were applicable, for instance in Germany.

His first and best-known work was the extension of South Amsterdam, commissioned in 1902 and amended on various occasions until the drawing up of the definitive design in 1917.

Outside the circle of the Baroque walls, the growth of Amsterdam during the second half of the nineteenth century had continued at random, with roads following the lines of the pre-existing canals and allotments. Now, planning its new expansion according to a comprehensive plan, Berlage at first made designs for a mixed quarter, partly of intensive building with a geometrical street system and partly of sparser building with irregularly curving streets; later, forced to utilize the land more intensively – the price

of sites was high and could not be allowed to affect building enterprises beyond a certain limit – he planned a district of uniform roads formed of the intermingling of certain symmetrical motifs sufficiently complex to avoid the usual dreary division into square blocks (Figs. 411–12).

As a basic unit he decided to use a block from 100 to 200 metres long and 50 wide, four storeys high and with an enclosed garden, to be treated as an architectural whole. Given the size of the blocks, the roads were necessarily wide, some very wide, with fast-moving traffic in the centre and slower house-to-house traffic at the two sides; in this way Berlage also rejected the separation of traffic, bringing through routes into the heart of the new district (Fig. 413).

The choice of the block depended on two factors: one organizational because the construction of the buildings was usually entrusted to building co-operatives, and the number of dwellings in a block normally corresponded to the average size of a co-operative – and the other formal, the desire to exert some kind of consistent architectural control over fairly extensive areas of town. The instruments of Berlage's plan – a symmetrical street system and the use of blocks with uniform façades – belong to the academic tradition, so much so that the use he aimed to make of them has been referred to as a 'sort of town-planning *revival*'.[15] Its novelty on the other hand lay in the fact that he was largely conscious of the temporary character of these expedients, and used them as means to eliminate, rather than to resolve, certain problems.

Behind the use of the block there was the problem of the continuity of a district, which can be fully resolved only if a uniform style existed; in this way the seventeenth-century canals were bordered with the narrow façades of the merchants' houses, each with its own design but forming a unified whole because of the basic stylistic agreement between them. Since this agreement no

**411, 412**   *Amsterdam, Zuid district (Berlage's plan, 1917)*

longer existed, the only solution was to insist upon a plan made up of large enough consistent elements so as to obtain – if not the absolute and mechanical unity that could be obtained by extending such prescriptions to whole streets and squares, as was done in France – a reasonable distance between possible variations; in this way at least the tone of the architecture would not be tense

or broken, as usually happened, by too frequent changes in style, and the general impression was one of relative repose (Figs. 414–15).

Behind the problem of the street system there was the problem of the general layout of the district and of its relationship with the city as a whole: Berlage did not feel he could tackle this, and evaded the issue by laying

**413, 414, 415** *Amsterdam, Buildings in the Zuid district*

down a superficial ruling which would at least limit the planner and give him a guide line for the composition of the whole.

The insertion of the new districts into the body of the city was therefore effected along certain large-scale perspectives and since there was more than one point of juncture, there were various aspects to its symmetrical motifs, which were themselves inter-linked. (Berlage also applied a similar principle to some of his buildings, for instance to the Gemeente Museum in the Hague which, because it faces on to two main roads, was based on two orthogonal axes of symmetry.)

The realization of the plan after the war, carried out mainly by the young Michael De

Klerk, (1884–1923), P. L. Kramer (b. 1881) and H. T. Vijdeveld (b. 1885) (the so-called Amsterdam school), was faithful to Berlage's intentions. The use of the block, the unity of materials and the discretion of the Dutch architects produced a comfortable, civilized and orderly district with a continuity rarely found in so extensive a complex. Though it includes plenty of green spaces, the general effect is not countrified; quite the reverse. Yet the density never becomes crowding, and the peaceful succession of blocks, apart from the occasional eccentric façade, has that quality Berlage prized above all others: 'the quality that distinguishes old monuments from the buildings of today – quiet'.[16]

Berlage was town-planning adviser to various Dutch cities: the Hague, Rotterdam, Utrecht. The plans studied for these cities were generally speaking less successful than the one for Amsterdam; sometimes Berlage's taste for symmetrical plans led him to solutions that were contrived and artificial, for instance the plan for a district of the Hague that was a sort of Renaissance city shaped like a hexagonal star (this tendency was later to influence the earlier districts designed by Oud).

The limitations of Berlage's method, which in architecture led to consequences more easily controllable, came to the surface more clearly in town-planning; his theoretical teaching therefore remained without adequate formal illustration, and left unsolved the rift between form and function.

The German town-planning experiments of the early twentieth century were partly linked with the teaching of Berlage. Some, for instance the plan for the south part of Berlin, Schönenberg, by B. Mohring, was also formally inspired by Berlage, with strongly marked axes of symmetry. Usually, however, the new German districts were more haphazard, often with curved, asymmetrical roads, both because of Berlage's influence and because the ground, unlike that of Holland, was hilly.

The example of Berlage as town-planner clearly revealed the merits and defects of *avant-garde* culture when faced with a concrete problem such as the development of a city.

Berlage worked in the most favourable circumstances, upon a basis of precise laws, collaborating with enlightened Civil Servants and in the presence of one of the most solid and well-rooted local traditions, which acted as a stabilizer against the wilder flights of experiment. He himself had a reliable sense of what was feasible and planned with effective possibilities of interpretation in mind, so that its execution did not represent, as so often happened, a watering down of the original, but even a positive enrichment, as with the extension of Amsterdam. For this reason the south part of Amsterdam appears to us as a perfectly finished reality, and arouses the same amazement as we feel when faced with the perfection of Olbrich's *Freiekunst*, of Hoffmann's Palais Stoclet and Berlage's Bourse, where the original architectural invention appears so perfectly at one with executive processes, with the functioning and life of the building, where the architect worked out the detail with unfailing taste and technical propriety, where the conflict of an intricate historical situation was temporarily resolved in the harmony of the design.

But the solution could not be developed any further, and to tackle the new and urgent problems, the particular balance that had been established, precariously, in a moment of transition between the old and new cultures, would have to be abandoned.

The fascination that these details exercise on architects of today is connected with the fact that they have a technical and formal perfection unattainable today. They were the last products of a happy age in which the problems of architecture were much more simple, and being relatively close to us in time – their authors were living among us until very recently – they give us the feeling

**MUZIEK·PARADIJS·HELD**
**XYLOGRAAPH·QUADRAAT**
**SCHELP·BANKET·SCHRIFT**
**BETOOVERING·WONDER**
**YACHTCLUB·MOED·ECHT**
**GOD·ZEE**

H. P. BERLAGE—

AMSTERDAM.

**416**  *Typographical characters designed by Berlage (from A. Koch's publication on the 1901 Turin exhibition)*

that this perfection must still be within our reach.

But things have changed, and any attempt at evoking any moment of the past by imitating its formal results is quite pointless; we should understand the lesson of the masters of the European *avant-garde* by trying, as they did, to keep ahead of the problems and demands of our time, even knowing that the results will not be as brilliant, because our difficulties are much greater.

The right way of looking at the experiments of this period is, even today, the one suggested by Persico who in 1935 – while the modern movement, after its first flowering, was going through a period of severe trial – wrote the following about Hoffmann's Palais Stoclet:

'Thirty years after the Palais Stoclet, architecture needs to consider the path it has travelled so as not to break away from its tradition, i.e. from its intimate *raison d'être*. In the face of German nationalism, the birth in Russia of an 'academic' taste, the growth in Italy of the most discredited forms, one must look to the past to discover the reason. The end of modern architecture will not come, as the less convincing polemicists claim, from the coherence of European rationalism, nor does its salvation consist in the return to the 'classical' or 'national' forms; but in being faithful to a real tradition, in comparison with which the other tradition of the orators, professors and newspapers appears grotesque and paradoxical. We are not discussing the Palais Stoclet with the intention of holding it up as a model for contemporary architects; we are putting it in perspective, and hope to draw some useful conclusions from this. First of all, faithfulness to its own time, understood not in the arbitrary or obsequious sense that every artist in search of work has in common with all reactionaries, but as a particular historicity of the imagination, in the contact between style and the most lively ideas of the time. Viewed in this way, the Stoclet Palace is a supreme example. It is the product not only of the teachings of Wagner and the aspirations of Olbrich, but also of the most vital ideals of the European middle classes, who were responsible for the rejection of neo-classical forms and the victory of the early rationalism, with the universal exhibitions, use of new techniques and the principles of 'art for all'. Will the architects of today manage to instil as much life into art? To renounce the temptations of rhetoric, to follow the tradition of European architecture unswervingly? These questions, hanging threateningly over the fate of modern architecture, make one look at the Palais Stoclet as at a monument from a golden age of art'.[17]

# Notes

## Preface

1 'The Prospects of Architecture in Civilization', lecture given at the London Institution, 10 March 1881, in *On Art and Socialism*, London, 1947, p. 245.
2 'The Art of the People', lecture given at the Birmingham Society of Arts and School of Design, 19 February 1879, in *On Art and Socialism*, pp. 47–8.
3 G. C. Argan, *Walter Gropius e la Bauhaus*, Turin, 1951, p. 27.

## Introduction

1 Facts and quotations referring to this episode are taken from G. M. Jaffé, *Le mouvement ouvrier à Paris pendant la Révolution française* and are quoted in Chapter XI of C. Barbagallo's book *Le origini della grande industria contemporanea*, Florence, 1951.
2 Barbagallo, *op. cit.*, pp. 30–1.
3 Barbagallo, *op. cit.*, p. 33.
4 Barbagallo, *op. cit.*, p. 35.
5 Barbagallo, *op. cit.*, p. 40.
6 Barbagallo, *op. cit.*, p. 41.
7 Barbagallo, *op. cit.*, p. 38.
8 T. S. Ashton, *The Industrial Revolution*, O.U.P., 1948, p. 4.
9 Dr. Johnson, quoted in T. S. Ashton, *op. cit.*, p. 11.
10 Quoted in C. A. de Tocqueville, *L'Ancien Régime*, Blackwell, 1933, p. 20.
11 Charles Dickens, *A Tale of Two Cities*, 1859.
12 G. M. Trevelyan, *British History in the Nineteenth Century*, London, 1922.
13 De Tocqueville, *op. cit.*, p. 149.
14 'Dell'arte del disegno de' Greci e della bellezza (1767) written by Winckelmann in Italian, from *Il bello nell'arte*, Turin, 1943, p. 125.
15 'Dissertazione sulla capacità del sentimento del bello nell'arte e sull'insegnamento della capacità stessa' (1763) from: *Il bello nell'arte*, *op. cit.*, pp. 77–8.

16 J. J. Rousseau, *The Social Contract*, (1762) Book II, Chap. III.
17 L. Salvatorelli, *Storia del Novecento*, Milan, 1947, p. 855.
18 De Tocqueville, *op. cit.*, p. 73.

## Chapter 1

1 T. S. Ashton, *The Industrial Revolution*, O.U.P., 1948.
2 G. Galilei, 'Dialogo sui massimi sistemi' (1638), *Il Dialogo*, day III.
3 G. Rondelet, *Traité théorique et pratique de l'art de bâtir*, introduction.
4 P. L. Nervi, 'Tecnica costruttiva e architettura' in *Architettura d'oggi* Florence 1955, p. 8.
5 G. Monge, *Géometrie descriptive*, editions from 1799 onwards.
6 Le Corbusier, *Oeuvre complète, 1938–46*, Zurich 1955, p. 170.
7 G. M. Trevelyan, *British History in the Nineteenth Century*, 1922.
8 T. S. Ashton, *The Industrial Revolution*, *op. cit.*, p. 20.
9 G. Albenga, 'Le strade ed i ponti', in *Storia della tecnica dal Medioevo ai nostri giorni* by A. Uccelli, Milan 1945, p. 665.
10 Rondelet's Treatise, Bk. V and Plates 102–4.
11 Quoted in G. Albenga, *op. cit.*, p. 692.
12 Rondelet's Treatise, *cit.* Vol. I., p. 227.
13 J. R. Perronet, *Descriptions des projets et de la construction des ponts de Neuilly, de Nantes, d'Orléans, de Louis XVI* etc., Paris, 1788.
14 Rondelet's Treatise, *cit.*, Plate 151.
15 Rondelet's Treatise, *cit.*, Bk. VII, Section 3 and Plates 147–71.
16 S. Giedion, *Space, Time and Architecture*, O.U.P., 1962, p. 189.
17 M. Chevalier, *Lettres sur l'Amérique du Nord*, Brussels, 1837, Vol. I, p. 354.

18 J. Gloag and D. Bridgewater, *A History of Cast Iron in Architecture* London, 1948, pp. 152–5.

19 Rondelet's Treatise, *cit.*, Plates 160 and 164.

20 Rondelet's Treatise, *cit.*, Plate 162 and appendix (from Plate 'P' onwards).

21 P. Lavedan, *Histoire de l'urbanisme, époque contemporaine*, Paris, 1952, p. 74.

22 M. Henrivaux, *Le verre et le cristal* Paris, 1883, p. 228.

23 Rondelet's Treatise, *cit.*, Vol. II, p. 105.

24 L. Hautecoeur, *Histoire de l'Architecture classique en France*, Paris, 1953, Vol. V, p. 330.

25 L. Hautecoeur, *op. cit.*, Vol. V, pp. 108–9.

26 De Tocqueville, *L'Ancien Régime, ed. cit.*, p. 186.

27 Giedion, *op. cit.*, p. 209.

28 L. Hautecoeur, *op. cit.*, Vol. VIII, p. 461.

29 Quoted in M. Besset, *Gustave Eiffel*, Italian translation, Milan 1957, p. 17.

30 J. L. N. Durand, *Précis des leçons données a l'école royale polytechnique*, Paris 1823, Vol. I, p. 6.

31 Durand, *op. cit.*, Vol. I, p. 16.

32 Durand, *op. cit.*, Vol. I, p. 53.

33 Durand, *op. cit.*, Vol. I, pp. 53–4.

34 Durand, *op. cit.*, p. 71.

## Chapter 2

1 Only in 1888 did rural districts get a democratic government like those of the towns, with the setting up of the County Councils.

2 Hilaire Belloc, *Shorter History of England*, Harrap 1934, 'The Reorganisation', p. 565.

3 H. M. Croome and R. J. Hammond, *Economic History of Britain*, London, 1947, p. 207.

4 Croome and Hammond, *op. cit.*, p. 220.

5 V. H. Bernoulli *La Città ed il suolo urbano* (1946). Ital. translation, Milan 1951, p. 54.

6 Quoted in J. H. Clapham, *An Economic History of Modern Britain, the Early Railway Age*, Cambridge 1950, p. 39.

7 Clapham, *op. cit.*, p. 40.

8 Clapham, *op. cit.*, p. 41.

9 Clapham, *op. cit.*, p. 539; from F. Engels, *Die Lage der arbeitenden Klassen in England*, Leipzig 1845.

10 Quoted in P. Lavedan, *Histoire de l'urbanisme, époque contemporaine*, Paris, 1952.

11 Clapham, *op. cit.*, p. 539, from *Report on the State of Large Towns and Populous Districts*, 1844, p. 338.

12 Clapham, *op. cit.*, p. 540, from *Report on the Sanitary Conditions of the Labouring Population*, 1842, p. 381.

13 Clapham, *op. cit.*, p. 542.

14 Clapham, *op. cit.*, pp. 537–8, from *Report on the Sanitary Conditions of the Labouring Population*, 1842, p. 212.

15 Clapham, *op. cit.*, pp. 544–5, from *Report on the State of Large Towns and Populous Districts*, 1844, p. 68.

16 *Census of 1851*, quoted in Clapham, *op. cit.*, p. 537.

17 A. Blanqui, quoted in Lavedan, *op. cit.*, p. 68.

18 Quoted in Lavedan, *op. cit.*, p. 89.

19 Quoted in E. Tedeschi, *L'architettura in Inghilterra*, Florence, s.d., p. 141.

20 Quoted in L. Hautecoeur, *Histoire de l'architecture*

*classique en France*, Vol. VI, Paris 1955, p. 288.

21 *Annales archéologiques* 1852, XII, p. 164; see Hautecoeur *op. cit.*, Vol. VI, p. 328.

22 A. W. Pugin, *The True Principles of Pointed or Christian Architecture*, London, 1841, p. 23.

23 F. Hoffstadt, *Principi dello stile gotico cavati dai monumenti del Medioevo ad uso degli artisti ed operai, ed ora dal francese in cui vennero tradotti dall'alemanno volgarizzati dal cavaliere Francesco Lazzari*, Venice, 1858, Preface.

24 Hautecoeur, *op. cit.*, Vol. VI, pp. 336–7.

25 J. Ruskin, Preface to second edition of *The Seven Lamps of Architecture* 1855.

## Chapter 3

1 Persigny, *Mémoires*, p. 251, quoted by Lavedan, L'arrivée au pouvoir, in *La vie urbaine*, nouvelle serie, nos. 3–4 (1953), pp. 181–2.

2 G. E. Haussmann, *Mémoires*, Paris 1890, Vol. II, pp. 9–10.

3 Haussmann, *op. cit.*, Vol. II, Chap. XX, pp. 507–34.

4 The complete budget of Haussmann's works is to be found on pp. 337–40 of Vol. II of the *Mémoires*; the following is a summary of it:

*Outgoing expenses:*

| | |
|---|---|
| main thoroughfares | 1,430,340,385.5 |
| architecture and fine arts | 282,791,696.5 |
| street equipment and parks | 178,370,624.8 |
| water mains and sewers | 153,601,970.2 |
| various | 70,476,924.8 |
| | 2,115,781,601.8 |
| other expenses (concessions redeemed in communes annexed in 1859, expenses connected with the communal debt and loans incurred by Haussmann etc.) | 437,886,822.3 |
| Total: | 2,553,668,424.1 |

*Income:*

| | |
|---|---|
| resources within the city budget (minus ordinary expenditure) | 1,171,243,444.5 |
| state subsidies | 95,130,760.7 |
| sale of land acquired and demolition material: | 269,697,683.5 |
| loans obtained in various forms | 1,171,596,535.4 |
| Total: | 2,553,668,424.1 |

5 Haussmann, *op. cit.*, Vol. II, p. 53.

6 Haussmann, *op. cit.*, Vol. II, pp. 311–12.

7 Haussmann, *op. cit.*, Vol. I, p. 10.

8 *Coningsby* 1844, and *Sybil*, 1845.

9 M. A. Delannoy, *Études artistiques sur la régence d'Alger*, Paris 1835–7.

10 P. Coste, *Architecture arabe, ou monuments du Caire*, Paris, 1839.

11 P. Coste, *Voyage en Persie*, Paris, 1843.

12 O. Jones, *Plans, Elevations, Sections and Details of the Alhambra*, London, 1842–5.

13 J. Gailhabaud, *Monuments anciens et modernes des différents peuples à toutes les époques*, Paris, 1839; English translation, London 1844.

14 *Vorlesungen über Aesthetik*, Leipzig, 1829.

15 T. Gauthier, *Les jeunes-France*, Paris, 1832, XIII.

16 R. Kerr, *The Gentleman's House, or How to plan an*

*English Residence from the Parsonage to the Palace,*
London 1864, quoted in *Architectural Review,* Vol.
110 (1951), p. 205.
17 L. Avray, quoted in J. Wilhelm, *La vie à Paris,*
Paris, 1947.
18 Haussmann, *op. cit.,* Vol. I, p. 32.
19 Haussmann, *op. cit.,* Vol. III, p. 482.

## Chapter 4

1 Tallis's *History and Description of the Crystal Palace,*
1851, p. 11.
2 Issue of 12 June 1852, quoted in J. Ruskin, *The
Opening of the Crystal Palace considered in some of its
Relations to the Prospects of Art,* London 1852.
3 L. Bucher, *Kulturhistorisches Skizzen aus der
Industrieausstellung aller Völker,* Frankfurt 1851,
quoted in S. Giedion *op. cit.,* p. 251.
4 Giedion, *op. cit.,* p. 251.
5 Giedion, *op. cit.,* p. 259.
6 In: *Paris-Guide par les principaux écrivains et artistes
de la France,* Paris 1867, p. 2007.
7 *L'Esposizione di Parigi del 1878 illustrata,* Milan
1878, p. 3.
8 *L'Esposizione di Parigi del 1889 illustrata,* Milan,
1889, p. 83.
9 Folchetto, *Parigi e l'Esposizione universale del 1889,*
Milan, 1889, p. 22.
10 H. de Parville, in *Parigi e l'Esposizione universale del
1889,* p. 62.
11 *L'Esposizione di Parigi del 1889 illustrata,* p. 31.
12 R. Marx, *L'Architecture* 1890, p. 382, quoted in
L. Hautecoeur, *Histoire de l'architecture classique en
France,* Vol. VII, Paris 1957, pp. 402–3.
13 Quoted in L. Hautecoeur, *op. cit.,* Vol. VII, p. 405.
14 Quoted in M. Besset, *Gustave Eiffel, op. cit.,* pp. 17–
18.
15 *Le Temps,* 14 February 1887.
16 Folchetto, in *Parigi e l'Esposizione universale del 1889,
cit.,* p. 7.
17 *L'Esposizione di Parigi del 1889 illustrata,* p. 18.
18 *Journal* VIII, 25, 1889.
19 Quoted in Hautecoeur, *op. cit.,* Vol. VII. pp. 294–5.
20 *Revue générale d'architecture,* 1866, p. 8, quoted in
Hautecoeur, *op. cit.,* Vol. VII, p. 411.
21 *L'Architecture* 1889, p. 433, quoted in Hautecoeur,
*op. cit.,* Vol. VII, pp. 298–9.
22 F. Jourdain in *L'Architecture* 1889, p. 350, quoted in
Hautecoeur, *op. cit.,* Vol. VII, p. 299.
23 J. Guadet, *Eléments et théorie de l'architecture,* Paris,
1894, Vol. I, pp. 2–3.
24 Guadet, *op. cit.,* vol. I, pp. 80–1.
25 Guadet, *op. cit.,* vol. I, p. 82.
26 Guadet, *op. cit.,* vol. I, p. 83.
27 Guadet, *op. cit.,* Vol. I, p. 85.
28 Guadet, *op. cit.,* Vol. I, p. 90.

## Section 2  Chapter 5

1 Charles Dickens, *Hard Times,* Everyman's Library
(Dent) 1954, p. 19.
2 Dickens, *op. cit.,* p. 46.
3 Dickens, *op. cit.,* p. 99.

4 C. Baudelaire, *Les fleurs du mal,* Le Cygne, I, nn. 7
& 8.
5 Quoted in J. W. R. Adams, *Modern Town and
Country Planning,* London, 1952.
6 H. Heine, *English Fragments,* English translation,
Edinburgh 1880, p. 8.
7 Quoted in J. H. Clapham, *An Economic History of
Modern Britain, the Early Railway Age.* Cambridge,
1939, p. 545.
8 B. Russell, *Freedom and Organisation, 1814–1914,*
London, Allen & Unwin, 1934, p. 133.
9 M. de Riancey, quoted in Lavedan, *Histoire de
l'urbanisme, époque contemporaine,* Paris, 1952, p. 89.
10 J. Stuart Mill, *On Liberty,* Everyman's Library (Dent)
1954, p. 165.
11 P. J. Proudhon, *La capacité politique,* quoted in
E. Dolléans, *Histoire du mouvement ouvrier,* I, (1939).
12 L. Veuillot, *Les Odeurs de Paris,* quoted in J.
Wilhelm, *La vie à Paris,* Paris, 1947, pp. 20–2.
13 V. Sardou, *Maison Neuve* (Vaudeville, 4–12–1866)
Act I, Scene XII.
14 G. E. Haussmann, *Memoires,* Vol. II, pp. 310–11.
15 J. Ferry, *Comptes fantastiques d'Haussmann,* Paris,
1868, p. 23.
16 F. Engels, *The Housing Question,* London, 1942,
Marxist-Leninist Library, Vol. VII, p. 48.
17 Engels, *op. cit.,* p. 50.
18 Engels, *op. cit.,* p. 73.
19 F. Engels, *Die Lage der arbeitenden Klassen in
England,* Leipzig, 1845, 1.
20 W. Morris, *The Earthly Paradise,* London, 1868,
Prologue.
21 S. Butler, *Alps and Sanctuaries,* 1881, quoted in
J. Gloag, *Industrial Art Explained,* London, 1946,
p. 80.
22 G. B. Shaw, *Cashel Byron's Profession,* The Modern
Press, London, 1886, p. 56.
23 E. Manet, *Préface au catalogue de l'exposition de ses
oeuvres,* Paris, 1867, quoted in J. Wilhelm, *op. cit.,*
p. 83.

## Chapter 6

1 C. N. Ledoux, *L'architecture considérée sous le rapport
de l'art, des moeurs et de la législation,* Paris, 1804.
2 William Morris, *News from Nowhere,* London, 1891.
3 Robert Owen, *Report to the county of Lanark* (1820),
in *A New View of Society and Other Writings,*
London, 1927, p. 266.
4 R. Owen, *Report to the Committee for the Relief of the
Manufacturing Poor,* 13 March 1817.
5 *London Newspaper,* 30 July 1817, 15 August 1817,
22 August 1817, 10 September 1817.
6 Owen, *Report to the County of Lanark,* p. 264.
7 Owen, *op. cit.,* pp. 267–8.
8 Owen, *op. cit.,* p. 276.
9 Owen, *op. cit.,* p. 285.
10 F. Podmore, *Robert Owen, a Biography,* (1906)
quoted in B. Russell, *Freedom and Organisation,
1814–1914,* (1934), p. 190.
11 C. Fourier, *Traité de l'association domestique-
agricole* (1832), in E. Poisson, *Fourier,* Paris 1932,
pp. 141–3.

12 See J. B. Godin, *Solutions sociales*, Paris, 1870.

13 C. Duveyrier, in *Le Globe* 1931, quoted in E. Persico, *Profezia dell'architettura*, in *Scritti critici e polemici*, Milan, 1947, p. 196.

14 M. Chevalier in *Le Globe*, 1932, quoted in P. Lavedan, *Histoire de l'Urbanisme, époque contemporaine*, Paris, 1952, p. 76.

15 See P. Lavedan, *op. cit.*, pp. 84–8.

16 A. Massaulard, *Six mois en Icarie*, quoted in A. Prodhommeaux, *Histoire de la communauté icarienne*, Nimes, 1907, p. 292.

17 K. Marx & F. Engels, *The Communist Manifesto*, London, 1948, p. 44.

18 W. Sombart, *Le socialisme et le mouvement social au XIX siècle*, Paris, 1898, pp. 24–7.

19 W. Sombart, *op. cit.*, pp. 25–30 and p. 31.

20 See Giedion, *Mechanization Takes Command*, New York, 1948, p. 346.

21 Quoted in H. Read, *Art and Industry*, London, 1934, p. 15.

22 A. W. Pugin, *Contrasts*, London, 1836.

23 A. W. Pugin, *The True Principles of Pointed or Christian Architecture*, London, 1841, p. 23–5, quoted in J. Gloag, *Industrial Art Explained*, London, 1946, p. 63.

24 *Journal of Design*, Vol. V, 1851, p. 158, quoted in S. Giedion, *op. cit.*, pp. 351–2. On the discussions aroused by the 1851 exhibition, see W. Whewell, *Lectures on the Result of the Exhibition*, London, 1851.

25 On H. Cole see the volumes edited by A. S. & H. L. Cole, *Fifty Years of Public Work of Sir Henry Cole*, London, 1884.

26 *Plans, Elevations, Sections and Details of the Alhambra*, 1842–5; *Designs for Mosaic and Tessellated Pavements*, 1842; *The Illuminated Book of the Middle Ages* (in collaboration with H. N. Humphrey) 1844; *The Polychromatic Ornament of Italy*, 1846.

27 *An Attempt to Define the Principles which Should Regulate the Employment of Colour in the Decorative Arts*, London, 1852.

28 Quoted in Giedion, *op. cit.*, p. 354.

29 *One Thousand and One Initial Letters Designed and Illuminated by O. J.*, 1864; *Seven Hundred and Two Monograms*, 1864; *Examples of Chinese Ornament*, 1867.

30 G. R. Redgrave, *Manual of Design Completed from the Writings and Addresses of R. R.*, London, 1876.

31 S. Image, in the Introduction to the edition by J. M. Dent & Sons, 1907, of *The Seven Lamps of Architecture*.

32 'The Lamp of Truth', VI, pp. 34–5 of the edition mentioned.

33 'The Lamp of Truth', IX, pp. 39–40.

34 'The Lamp of Truth', XIX, p. 53.

35 I. Ware, *The Complete Body of Architecture*, London, 1756, quoted in J. Gloag, and D. Bridgwater, *A History of Cast Iron in Architecture*, London, 1948, p. 116.

36 'The Lamp of Truth', XIX, p. 54 of edition mentioned.

37 J. Laver, *Life of Whistler*, London, 1930, p. 175.

38 *Oxford and Cambridge Magazine*, 1857.

39 'The Lamp of Sacrifice', I, p. 7 of edition mentioned.

40 'The Prospects of Architecture in Civilization', lecture given at London Institution, 10 March 1881, in *On Art and Socialism, cit.*, pp. 245–6.

41 'Art under Plutocracy', lecture given at University College, Oxford, 14 November 1888 in *On Art and Socialism, cit.*, p. 139.

42 *On Art and Socialism, cit.*, p. 7.

43 *Art and its producers*, lecture given at *National Association for the Advancement of Art* at Liverpool in 1888: in *On Art and Socialism, cit.*, p. 216.

44 *William Morris*, Victoria and Albert Museum, H.M.S.O., 1958.

45 Quoted in *Thieme Becker K. L.*, Vol. 25.

46 *On Art and Socialism, cit.*, p. 7.

47 H. Jackson, introduction to *On Art and Socialism, cit.*, p. 11.

48 Quoted in N. Pevsner, *Pioneers of the Modern Movement*, 1936, p. 25.

49 Pevsner, *op. cit.*, p. 34.

50 Richard Norman Shaw, *Architectural Sketches from the Continent, Views and Details from France, Italy and Germany*, London, 1872.

51 *Should We Stop Teaching Art?* London, 1911, p. 4, quoted in N. Pevsner, *op. cit.*, p. 11.

52 In *Whistler Stories*, collected by D. C. Seitz, Harper and Bros., New York and London, 1913.

## Section 3    Chapter 7

1 J. M. Fitch, *American Building*, Boston, 1948, p. 37.

2 Quoted in Fitch, *op. cit.*, p. 40.

3 *Notes on the State of Virginia* (1782) quoted in Fitch, *op. cit.*, p. 35.

4 Quoted in F. R. Hiorns, *Town Building in History*, London, 1956, p. 346.

5 *Objects for Attention for an American* (3 June 1878) quoted in Fitch, *op. cit.*, p. 36.

6 Fitch, *op. cit.*, p. 58.

7 C. Hood, *Warming Buildings*.

8 D. B. Reid, *Theory and Practice of Moving Air*.

9 Quoted in Giedion, *Space, Time and Architecture*, p. 214.

10 R. W. Emerson, *Complete Works*, Boston 1888, Vol. V, p. 10.

11 Quoted in P. Lavedan, *Histoire de l'urbanisme, époque contemporaine*, Paris, 1952, p. 236.

12 Quoted in Giedion, *A Decade of New Architecture*, Zurich, 1951, p. 5.

13 C. Sitte, 'City Planning According to Artistic Principles', *Columbia University Studies in Art history and Architecture No. 2*, Phaidon Press, 1965, p. 125.

14 Le Corbusier, 'La Catastrophe féerique', in *L'Architecture d'Aujourdhui*, 1938, n. I, p. 12.

15 G. H. Gray, *Housing and Citizenship*, New York, 1946, p. 8.

16 Quoted in J. Ford, *Slum and Housing*, Cambridge 1936, Appendix, Table 1A.

## Chapter 8

1 Giedion, *Space, Time and Architecture, cit.*, pp. 350–2.

2 In the pamphlet entitled *The Art of Preparing Foundations for all Kinds of Buildings with Particular Illustrations of the Method of Isolated Piers as followed in Chicago*, quoted in F. A. Randall, *History of the Development of Building Constructions in Chicago*, Chicago, 1949, p. 18.

3 See Randall, *op. cit.*, p. 14.

4 In *Engineering News*, 1895, quoted in Randall, *op. cit.*, p. 11.

5 F. Lloyd Wright, 'The Tyranny of the Skyscraper', lectures held at the University of Princeton in 1930, in *The Future of Architecture*, Horizon Press, N.Y., 1953, p. 153.

6 E. Cecchi, *America Amara*, Florence 1946, p. 13.

7 In the *Engineering Record* 25 July 1896, quoted in Randall, *op. cit.*, p. 106.

8 H. Monroe, *J. W. Root*, New York, 1896, p. 141, quoted in Giedion, *op. cit.*, p. 372.

9 F. Lloyd Wright, *The Future of Architecture*, cit., p. 151.

10 Monroe, *op. cit.*, p. 107; Giedion *op. cit.*, p. 380.

11 Monroe, *op. cit.*, p. 147.

12 See P. Lavedan, *Histoire de l'urbanisme, époque contemporaine*, Paris, 1952, p. 250.

13 Several examples from between 1832 and 1856 appear in Giedion, *op. cit.*, pp. 356 ff.; a more thorough examination of the same subject is given by H. R. Hitchcock in the recent *Guide to Boston Architecture 1637–1954*, New York 1954.

14 F. Lloyd Wright, *Io e l'architettura*, Vol. I, pp. 151 and 167.

15 F. Lloyd Wright, *op. cit.*, Vol. I, pp. 142 and 161.

16 F. Lloyd Wright, *The Future of Architecture*, cit., p. 151.

17 L. Sullivan, 'The Tall Office Building Artistically Considered', in *Kindergarten Chats*, New York, 1947, p. 203.

18 L. Sullivan, *Kindergarten Chats*, Lawrence, 1934, p. 8.

19 L. Sullivan, *op. cit.*, p. 202.

20 F. Lloyd Wright, *Io e l'architettura*, Vol. 1, p. 162.

21 Even the United States, which Wright regards as the home of organic architecture, is an idealized place, which he likes to call 'Usonia', a name taken from S. Butler; see Wright, *The Future of Architecture, Organic Architecture*, p. 262.

22 *Io e l'architettura*, cit., Vol. III, p. 849.

23 Quoted in B. Zevi, *Towards an Organic Architecture*, Faber, 1950, p. 89.

24 Quoted in Zevi, *op. cit.*, p. 89.

25 F. Lloyd Wright, *Architettura e democrazia*, cit., p. 36.

26 Zevi, *Frank Lloyd Wright*, Milan, 1947, p. 12.

27 F. Lloyd Wright, *The Future of Architecture*, cit., 'The Cardboard House', p. 141.

28 Pevsner, *Pioneers of the Modern Movement from William Morris to Walter Gropius*, 1936, p. 33.

29 F. Lloyd Wright, *Architettura e democrazia*, cit., p. 43.

30 Quoted in Zevi, *Towards an Organic Architecture*, cit., p. 90.

31 F. Lloyd Wright, 'Organic Architecture', in *The Future of Architecture, cit.*, p. 228.

32 J. J. P. Oud, *Hollandische Architektur*, Munich, 1926, quoted in B. Zevi, *Storia dell'architettura moderna*, Turin, 1955, pp. 465–6.

33 Quoted in P. Johnson, *Mies van der Rohe*, New York, 1947, p. 196.

## Section 4   Introduction

1 M. Schasler, *Aesthetik*, Leipzig, 1886.

2 E. Hartmann, *Philosophie des Schönen*, Leipzig, 1890.

3 C. G. Allen, *Physiological aesthetics*, London, 1877.

4 G. T. Fechner, *Vorschule der Aesthetik*, 1876.

5 M. Guyau, *L'art au point de vue sociologique*, Paris, 1889.

6 E. Grosse, *Die Anfänge der Kunst*, Freib. i. B., 1894.

7 K. Fiedler, *Der Ursprung der künsterischen Tätigkeit*, Leipzig, 1887.

8 Fiedler, *Aforismi sull'arte* (1914), Italian translation, Milan 1945, n. 8, p. 77.

9 Fiedler, *op. cit.*, n. 12, p. 80.

10 Fiedler, *op. cit.*, n. 41, p. 104.

11 Fiedler, *op. cit.*, n. 17, pp. 83–4.

12 Fiedler, *op. cit.*, n. 197, p. 200.

13 Fiedler, *op. cit.*, n. 195, p. 196.

14 'There is one idea that might easily gain ground that is to be rejected out of hand, and that is the idea according to which the development of a new conception of the essence of art would necessarily introduce a new norm for artistic production. This would constitute a return to the old aesthetic way of thinking. In no case can the new vision of reality produce new artistic canons. Art, in reality, must be considered free of all theoretical reflection on its own essence and this reflection, in its turn, can refer only to what art has so far produced, and can under no circumstances concern itself with what should be produced. It finds the guarantee of its own worth not in the practical consequences of a new turn of artistic realization, but in the new light it has been able to shed on already known fields of art throughout the centuries. Fiedler, *op. cit.*, n. 225, pp. 215–16.

15 Fiedler, *op. cit.*, n. 40, p. 104.

16 G. C. Argan, *Walter Gropius e la Bauhaus*, Turin, 1951, pp. 33–5.

17 B. Croce, *Aesthetic as Science of Expression and General Linguistics*, ('Vision Press', P. Owen, 1962), p. 416.

18 R. Vischer, *Uber das optische Formgefühl*, Leipzig, 1873.

19 H. Wölfflin, *Prolegomena zu einer Psychologie der Architektur*, Munich, 1886.

20 A. Hildebrand, *Das Problem der Form in der bildenden Kunst*, Strasbourg, 1893.

21 A. Riegl, *Stilfragen*, Berlin 1893; *Spatromische Kunstindustrie*, Vienna, 1901.

22 F. Wickoff, *Wiener Genesis*, Vienna, 1893.

23 C. Gurlitt, *Geschichte des Barockstils in Italien*, Stuttgart, 1886. *Geschichte des Barockstils, des Rococo und des Klassizismus in Belgien, Holland, Frankreich, England*, Stuttgart, 1888. *Geschichte des Barockstils, und des Rococo in Deutschland*, Stuttgart,

1889.

24 H. Wölfflin, *Renaissance und Barock,* Munich, 1888.
25 A. Riegl, in the Introduction to *Spatromische Kunstindustrie cit.*
26 C. Gurlitt, *op. cit.,* pp. 365–6.
27 C. Boito, 'Lo stile futuro dell'architettura italiana', in *Architettura del Medioevo in Italia,* Milan 1880; see *Casabella* n. 208 (1955), p. 73.
28 G. G. Scott, *An Essay on the History of English Church Architecture* (1881), p. 1.
29 J. Gasquet talking to Cézanne, Eng. tr. in *The Leaflet,* 3 October 1931. Quoted in W. Hess, *I problemi della pittura moderna,* Italian translation, Milan 1958, p. 29.
30 P. Signac, *D'Eugène Delacroix au néoimpressionisme,* Paris 1921.
31 P. Gauguin, *Avant et après,* Paris 1903. Hess, *op cit.,* p. 44.
32 J. Gasquet, in Hess, *op. cit.,* p. 20.
33 J. Gasquet, in Hess, *op. cit.,* p. 22.
34 A. Banfi, preface to *Aforismi sull'arte,* K. Fiedler, *cit.,* p. 66.
35 Vincent Van Gogh, *Letters to his Brother,* n. 133; Hess, *op. cit.,* p. 30.
36 Hess, *op. cit.,* p. 27.
37 J. de Rotonchamp, *P. Gauguin,* Paris 1906; Hess, *op. cit.,* p. 45.

## Chapter 9

1 Giedion, *Space, Time and Architecture, cit.,* p. 293.
2 F. Schmalenbach, *Jugendstil,* Würzburg, 1935.
3 Pevsner, *op. cit.,* p. 77.
4 *Mercure de France,* March 1891.
5 Pevsner, *op. cit.,* p. 100.
6 R. Schmutzler, 'The English Origin of Art Nouveau', in *Architectural Review,* February 1955, p. 108; 'Blake and Art Nouveau', August 1955, p. 90.
7 Van de Velde, *Die Renaissance im modernen Kunstgewerbe,* Leipzig, 1903, pp. 61 and foll.; 'Extracts from his Memoirs, 1891–1901', in *Architectural Review,* September 1952, pp. 145 *et seq.*
8 Van de Velde, *Die Renaissance, cit.,* p. 23.
9 Viollet-le-Duc, *Entretiens sur l'architecture,* Paris, 1872; *Compositions et dessins,* Paris 1884, Plates 6–12.
10 Van de Velde, *Extracts, cit.,* p. 148.
11 Van de Velde, *op. cit.,* p. 148.
12 Van de Velde, *op. cit.,* p. 146.
13 Van de Velde, *op. cit.,* p. 148.
14 Van de Velde's lectures are collected in two volumes: *Kunstgewerbliche Laienpredigten,* Berlin 1901, and *Die Renaissance im modernen Kunstgewerbe,* Berlin, 1901, and Leipzig, 1903.
15 Pevsner, *op. cit.,* p. 31.
16 In favour were the critics T. Nathanson, C. Mauclair; against, A. Alexandre, O. Mirbeau and A. Rodin, who said: 'V. de V. is a barbarian'. See *Extracts, cit.,* p. 152.
17 Pevsner, *op. cit.,* p. 40.
18 Post-war writings by Van de Velde, 'Formules d'une esthétique moderne', Brussels, 1923; 'L'Orientation du goût en architecture' in *Europe,* 1923; *Vers une construction collective,* fifth manifesto of the 'De Stijl'

group, Paris, 1923; 'Devant l'architecture', in *Europe,* 1924; *Der neue Stil in Frankreich,* Berlin, 1925.
19 In collaboration with Eggerick and Verwilghem.
20 In collaboration with Stynen and Bourgeois.
21 The autobiography was published by H. Curjel, under the title *Geschichte meines Lebens,* Munich, 1962.
22 Van de Velde, *op. cit.,* p. 155.
23 Quoted in Pevsner, *op. cit.,* p. 114.
24 *Haus eines Kunstfreundes,* with preface by H. von Muthesius, Darmstadt, 1902.
25 Pevsner, *op. cit.,* p. 29.
26 Reprinted in 1914 with the title *Die Baukunst unserer Zeit.*
27 The quotations are taken from the summary in Chapter IV of the biography by J. A. Lux, *Otto Wagner,* Munich, 1914.
28 E. Persico in *Casabella,* 1933; see *Scritti critici e polemici,* Milan, 1947, p. 145.
29 Quoted in L. Munz, *Adolf Loos,* Milan, 1956, p. 11.
30 Munz, *op. cit.,* p. 13.
31 Munz, *op. cit.,* p. 27.
32 B. Zevi, *Storia dell'architettura moderna,* Turin, 1955, pp. 110–11.
33 R. Neutra, *Survival through Design,* O.U.P., 1954, p. 300.
34 Quoted in J. P. Mieras, *Hollandische Architektur des 20. Jahrhunderts,* Berlin, 1926, p. viii.
35 See A. Quantin, *L'Exposition du siècle,* Paris, 1900.
36 R. Marx, *La décoration et les industries d'art à l'Exposition Universelle,* Paris, 1900, pp. 39–40.
37 Special number of *Art Journal* edited by D. Croal Thomson, London, 1901, p. 112.

## Chapter 10

1 M. Foerster, O. Graf, M. Thullie, A. Kleinlogel, E. Richter, A. Berrer, J. Melan, *Entwicklungsgeschichte, Versuche und Theorie des Eisenbetons, I, Die Grundzüge der geschichtlichen Entwicklung des Eisenbetonbaues,* Berlin, 1921, p. 1.
2 A. Perret, *Contribution à une théorie de l'architecture,* Paris, 1952.
3 T. Garnier, *Une cité industrielle, étude pour la construction des villes,* Paris, 1917.
4 Pevsner, *op. cit.,* p. 176.
5 Le Corbusier, introduction to the first edition of his *Oeuvre complète, 1910–1929,* Zurich, 1930.

## Chapter 11

1 Under entry 'Housing' in *Encyclopaedia Britannica.*
2 Quoted in D. Bellet and W. Darvillé, *Ce que doit-être la cité moderne,* Paris s.d., p. 22.
3 C. Sitte, *op. cit.,* p. 91.
4 R. Baumeister, *Stadterweiterungen in technischer, baupolizeilicher und wirtschaftlicher Beziehung,* Berlin, 1876, quoted in Sitte, p. 31.
5 Sitte, *op. cit.,* p. 111
6 Ruskin, *Sesame and Lilies* (1865).
7 E. Bellamy, *Looking Backwards, 2000–1887,* Boston, 1888.

8 Reprinted in 1902 with the title *Garden Cities of Tomorrow.*

9 C. B. Purdom, *Building of Satellite Towns*, London, 1925.

10 De Tocqueville, *op. cit.*, p. 73.

11 P. Geddes, *City Development*, Edinburgh, 1904. L. Mumford, *The Culture of Cities*, New York, 1938. E. A. Gutkind, *The Expanding Environment*, London, 1953.

12 G. K. Chesterton, *The Man who was Thursday*, 1908, p. 9.

13 The quotations are taken from a text by C. Flores which accompanies the Spanish edition of this *History of Modern Architecture.*

14 H. George, *Our Land Policy*, 1871, further developed in 1879 with the title *Progress and Poverty.*

15 G. Canella, 'L'epopea borghese della scuola di Amsterdam', in *Casabella*, n. 215 (1957).

16 Quoted in Giedion, *Space, Time and Architecture*, p. 311.

17 E. Persico, 'Trent'anni dopo il palazzo Stoclet', in *Casabella*, July, 1935, reprinted in *Scritti critici e polemici*, Milan, 1947, pp. 183–4.